THE POLITICAL THEORY OF THE HUGUENOTS OF THE DISPERSION

Pierre Jurieu

THE POLITICAL THEORY OF THE HUGUENOTS OF THE DISPERSION

WITH SPECIAL REFERENCE TO THE THOUGHT AND INFLUENCE OF PIERRE JURIEU

BY

Guy Howard Dodge

With a new preface by the author

"Rebellion to tyrants is obedience to God"

OCTAGON BOOKS

A DIVISION OF FARRAR, STRAUS AND GIROUX

New York   1972

Reprinted 1972
by special arrangement with Columbia University Press

OCTAGON BOOKS
A DIVISION OF FARRAR, STRAUS & GIROUX, INC.
19 Union Square West
New York, N. Y. 10003

320.1
D644p
1972

LIBRARY OF CONGRESS CATALOG CARD NUMBER: 79-159178

ISBN 0-374-92213-6

Printed in U.S.A. by
NOBLE OFFSET PRINTERS, INC.
New York, N.Y. 10003

To
My Mother
and Father

PREFACE TO THE OCTAGON EDITION

The reprint of this analysis of Pierre Jurieu and Huguenot Political Theory at the time of the Dispersion includes a new prefatory word, briefly surveying the literature relevant to this subject, which has appeared since the first publication of this volume in 1947.

About a decade ago two general books were published dealing with theology and politics among the Huguenots in Exile, mainly in Holland. One was written by W.J. Stankiewicz, entitled *Politics and Religion in Seventeenth-Century France* Berkeley, 1960. Since this is *A Study of Political Ideas from the Monarchomachs to Bayle, as Reflected in the Toleration Controversy,* only the last chapter is devoted to the "consequences of the Revocation." The rest of the work treats the political implications of the massacre of St. Bartholomew, the Edict of Nantes, and Richelieu's and Mazarin's policy toward the Huguenots.

The author of the other volume is the late Erich Haase, who has left a monumental *Einführung in die Literatur des Refuge* Berlin, 1959, with particular reference to *Der Beitrag der französischen Protestanten zur Entwicklung analytischer Denkformen am Ende des 17 Jahrhunderts.* Grounded in an exhaustive bibliography of almost fifty pages, including manuscripts and printed sources, both primary and secondary, this study ranges over the theology, philosophy, political theory, literature, and intellectual history of the period. Although special attention is paid to the major thinkers—Pierre Bayle, Pierre Jurieu, and Jean Le Clerc—the minor writers are by no means neglected. One of the most important chapters—*In der Gelehrtenrepublik*—shows in great detail how as translators and journalists, the refugees of two generations both before and after 1700, played the role of mediators between French thought and learning outside France, thereby contributing greatly to the transition from the Age of Belief to the Age of Reason.

Interest in Pierre Bayle has continued unabated on both sides of the Atlantic in the last two decades and there is a thesis at the University of Leyden on Pierre Jurieu by F.R.J. Knetsch entitled *Pierre*

Jurieu, Theoloog en Politikus der Refuge, Kampen, 1967. Also of special relevance to this author's book are the specific studies dealing with Bayle's relation to Jurieu. In chronological order mention should be made first of Bruna Talluri, "La polemica fra Bayle e Jurieu dal 1690 al 1692" in *Atti e Memorie dell' Accademia Toscana di Scienze e Lettere "La Colombaria, "* XXIII, 1958-1959, pp. 223-254; second of Erich Haase, "Un Epilogue à la controverse Jurieu-Bayle," in Paul Dibon, *Pierre Bayle. Le Philosophe de Rotterdam* Paris, 1959, pp. 196-215; third of Karl C. Sandberg, "Bayle and Jurieu" in his *At the Cross-road of Faith and Reason. An Essay on Pierre Bayle* Tuscon, 1966, pp. 81-98; and fourth of Elizabeth Labrousse "Le Refuge Hollandais: Bayle et Jurieu" in *XVIIᵉ Siècle. Revue publié par la Societé d'Etude du XVIIᵉ Siècle* 1967 Nos. 76-77, pp. 75-93.

Haase's contribution is especially interesting, since he shows that, although Bayle never answered Jurieu's last attack upon him in 1706— *Le Philosophe de Rotterdam, accusé, atteint el convaincu*—he was defended by Jacques Du Rondel (1630-1715), a professor, first at Sedan and then at Maestricht, in a poem entitled—*La Memoire du Philosophe de Rotterdam. Vangée de la Calomnie,* which is now published for the first time in its entirety.

The most important recent general studies of Bayle, many of which include references to Jurieu, are by the following: William H. Barber, "Pierre Bayle: Faith and Reason" in Will Moore, *The French Mind: Studies in Honor of Gustave Rudler* Oxford, 1952, pp. 109-125; Bruna Talluri, *Pierre Bayle. Vita e opere. Appunti* Palermo, 1953; Antoine Adam, "Pierre Bayle" in his *Histoire de la Littérature Française au XVIIᵉ Siècle* Paris, 1956, pp. 229-250; H.T. Mason, *Pierre Bayle and Voltaire* Oxford, 1963; Elszabeth Labrousse, *Pierre Bayle: Du Pays de Foix à la Cité d'Erasme* La Haye, 1963; and by the same author *Heterodoxie et Rigorisme* La Haye, 1964; Walter Rex, *Essays on Pierre Bayle and Religious Controversy* The Hague, 1965; Craig B. Brush, *Montaigne and Bayle. Variations on the Theme of Skepticism* The Hague, 1966; and Ira O. Wade, "Pierre Bayle and the History of Ideas" in his *The Intellectual Origins of the French Enlightenment* Princeton, 1971, pp. 542-624.

The definitive biography of Bayle and the most thorough syn-

thesis and systematic exposition of his thought is to be found in Labrousse's two volumes, which are based on more than a decade of research. Paul Dibon in his book *Pierre Bayle. Le Philosophe de Rotterdam* has collected several important *Etudes et Documents,* among the
most significant of which for our subject, are his own "Redecouverte
de Bayle" pp. VII-XVII and Richard H. Popkin's "Pierre Bayle's
Place in 17th Century Skepticism" pp. 1-19.

What emerges from these recent studies is the interpretation that,
although the great influence of Bayle on the *philosophes*—Voltaire and
Montesquieu—is still accepted, scepticism is no longer seen as the key
to Bayle's writings. The English historian, William H. Barber, for
example, has stressed Bayle's fideism, which is related to Elizabeth
Labrousse's conclusion that Bayle owes a great deal to the liberal Calvinist tradition of the French Reformed Academy of Saumur.

It is Walter Rex, however, who contends the most cogently that
Bayle of the Seventeenth Century is not yet Voltaire of the Eighteenth.
In his book he examines the "sources of the *Commentaire Philosophique,*" such as Calvinist Rationalism in France from the time of the
Synod of Dordrecht in 1618 to the Revocation in 1685. (French Protestantism has also been investigated in this period by Emile G. Leon-
ard in *Histoire Générale du Protestantisme,* Paris, 1961, Volume II,
Chapter VII, pp. 312-389 entitled "Etablissement et désétablissement
du protestantisme francais," and by Brian G. Armstrong, in *Calvinism
and the Amyraut Heresy. Protestant Scholasticism and Humanism in
Seventeenth-Century France* Madison, 1969.) In addition, Rex treats
"the theological and political crisis of the Huguenots in Exile," with
special reference to Bayle's Article on David in the *Dictionnaire historique et critique.* He shows that, to Voltaire, Bayle's attack on David
illustrated the barbarism of the Christian faith, while, to Bayle, it was
intended to be an assault on Jurieu with David standing for William
of Orange and was so understood by contemporaries.

The other dispute, after the Revocation, besides the one between
Jurieu and Bayle, was between Jurieu and Bossuet, to which an article
by C.G. Christofides, entitled "The Controversy between Bossuet and
Jurieu" in *Symposium* XIV (1960), pp. 121-128 is devoted. There is
also a section in Thérèse Goyet's *L'Humanisme de Bossuet* Paris, 1965,

Volume II, pp. 441-451 on Bossuet's *Cinquième Avertissement aux Protestants sur les lettres du ministre Jurieu contre l'Histoire des Variations*. The great work on this subject, however, is still Alfred Rebelliau's *Bossuet, historien du protestantisme: Etude sur l'histoire des Variations et sur la controverse entre les protestants et les catholiques au dix-septième siècle* Paris, 1909.

The influence of Huguenot political theory in England at the time of the Puritan Revolution, the Exclusion Crisis (The Jansenist, Antoine Arnauld and the Huguenot, Pierre Jurieu, argued over the Popish Plot, for example), and the Revolution of 1688 has been traced by J.H.M. Salmon in *The French Religious Wars in English Political Thought* Oxford, 1959. There he relates how the United Provinces sheltered both Whigs, like John Locke and Gilbert Burnet, and Huguenots, like Pierre Jurieu and Jacques Abbadie. He believes that "Abbadie and Locke expressed similar views" and "so did Jurieu and Burnet."

As a result of the author's study of *Benjamin Constant as a Political Theorist* (forthcoming), he has discovered how Jurieu's theory of popular sovereignty was cited and repudiated after the French Revolution by both Conservatives and Liberals. Louis de Bonald in *Essai Analytique sur les Lois naturelles de l'Ordre Social ou du Pouvoir, du Ministre et du Sujet dans la Société* (Paris, 1800); Jean Claude Clausel de Coussergues in *Considérations sur l'Origine, la rédaction, la promulgation`et l'exécution de la Charte* (Paris, 1830); and Prosper de Barant in *Questions Constitutionelles* (Paris, 1849)—all rejected Jurieu's contention that "there needs to be in a society a certain authority which does not need to be right to validate ist acts and this authority is only in the people." This principle, according to Clausel de Coussergues, was sustained by both Jurieu and Rousseau. But to Robert Derathé in *Jean-Jacques Rousseau et la Science Politique de Son Temps* Paris, 1950, pp. 120-123 it was used by Jurieu only in the limited way of justifying "the change of dynasty in England." Furthermore, Derathé and this author, who is still at Brown University, are in agreement that Jurieu's theory of popular sovereignty is not the same as Rousseau's. (On varying interpretations of Rousseau's theory see Guy H. Dodge, *Jean-Jacques Rousseau: Authoritarian Libertarian?*

Lexington, Mass., 1971), since Jurieu never assumed, like Rousseau, its inalienability. Nor did Jurieu ever conceive of the social contract in the revolutionary sense of Rousseau but was content to rely instead on the governmental compact between the ruler and his subjects in the conservative tradition of Barbeyrac, Grotius, and Pufendorf.

Guy Howard Dodge

Brown University
Providence, Rhode Island
April, 1972

Preface

THE present study examines another link in the long history of the principles and struggles of Church and State. It is the first attempt in either English or French to deal extensively with the political theory of the Huguenots of the Dispersion as a whole. This body of Huguenot thought which was elaborated after the Revocation of the Edict of Nantes in France and the Revolution of 1688 in England has an importance second only to the political ideas of the French Monarchomachs of the sixteenth century. It involves the original impetus of the Glorious Revolution on the Continent as well as a significant but neglected stage in the historical development of the principle of religious tolerance.

The two main problems which are treated are popular sovereignty and tolerance. In the discussion of these concepts the emphasis has been placed upon Pierre Jurieu, the Theodore Beza of his age, since as a political thinker he towers above all the other French Calvinists in the late seventeenth century, such as Jacques Abbadie, Antoine Coulan, Isaac de Larrey, Tronchin du Breuil, Elie Benoit, La Combe de Vrigny, and even the great Pierre Bayle. As the leader of the orthodox and intolerant party which alone advocated resistance, he was also the center of the controversy over the doctrine of religious tolerance. This struggle involved figures like Elie Saurin, Isaac Papin, Gédéon Huet, Henri Basnage de Beauval, Noël Aubert de Versé, Jean Le Clerc, Isaac Jaquelot, De La Conseillère, and, of course, Bayle. Any analysis, however, of Huguenot theories of religious liberty per se has been excluded, except in so far as they are related to Jurieu in whose political system theocracy and revolution are reconciled.

Never before has Jurieu's political thought been considered on the basis of all his writings that are still in existence. In fact, until very recently he has been mainly studied, either indirectly through Bossuet's answer to his celebrated *Lettres Pastorales* or with direct reference only to the *Pastoral Letters* and *Les Soupirs de la France esclave,* with no attention at all paid to his other numerous works, which are concerned with politics.

With a Sheldon Travelling Fellowship from Harvard University the author was very fortunate in being able to complete the research for this book in Europe during 1938–1939, just a year before the war that made such a large part of the source materials unavailable. This situation justifies in part the rather extensive use of quotations in this exposition in both the text and the notes. The French is given in its seventeenth century form but the selections in the text have been translated, of course, into English. It is essential to adopt this method in the study of political theory, in order to convey the true import of the sources. Moreover, the mere citation of pages would be quite meaningless when such a large number of the documents are inaccessible.

The anonymous character of many of the important sources, especially in the case of Pierre Jurieu, has made this study particularly complicated in that the problem of authorship and the interpretation of the works in question were so closely interrelated. With reference to so important a writing as the famous *Les Soupirs de la France esclave,* the outline of the new external and internal evidence for the authorship of Jurieu, whose political theories from the core of this book, was of sufficient significance to be incorporated in the main part of the exposition rather than in an appendix. This was necessary, since such information was so intimately connected with the general background of contemporary controversy.

In acknowledging the assistance rendered to the author in the preparation of this book, deep indebtedness and gratitude go first and foremost to Professor Charles H. McIlwain, now Emeritus, of Harvard University, whose inspiration, valuable counsel, and guidance have made this study possible. All those who have had the rare privilege and honor of working with him will understand how meaningful is any association with this great teacher, scholar, and man. I have profited greatly from the many fruitful suggestions on the problems involved in the political implications of Calvinism offered by Professors Roland H. Bainton of Yale University, Joachim Wach of the University of Chicago, Carl J. Friedrich of Harvard University, William F. Church of the University of Kentucky, and Mr. Walter D. Brown Jr. Special thanks are due to Professors John H. Randall, Jr., and Herbert W. Schneider of Columbia University. I also greatly appreciate the encouragement of President Henry M. Wriston and my colleagues in Political Science at Brown University—Professors Matthew C. Mitchell and Leland M. Goodrich. My wife has aided me in more ways than I can tell in all stages of the preparation of the manuscript and in reading proof. Finally, I recall with pleasure the kind consideration extended to me by the staffs of various European and American libraries, particularly the French Protestant Library in Paris and the Walloon library in Leyden.

It is appropriate that a book dealing with Christianity and politics be completed in the American home of the great English philosopher, George Berkeley, Bishop of Cloyne and Dean of Derry. In 1712 he opposed the Lockian brand of political theory with *Passive Obedience; or, The Christian Doctrine of Not Resisting the Supreme Power, Proved and Vindicated upon the Principles of the Law of Nature.* Of Newport in Rhode Island he wrote in a letter of 1729: "Here are four sorts of Anabaptists, besides Presbyterians, Quakers, Independents, and many of no profession at all. Notwithstanding so many differences here are fewer quarrels about religion than elsewhere, the people living peaceably with their neighbors of whatsoever persuasion."

Guy Howard Dodge

Whitehall
Middletown, Rhode Island
September, 1946

Contents

THE POLITICAL
THEORY OF THE
HUGUENOTS OF
THE DISPERSION

Chapter One

INTRODUCTION

ACCORDING to Figgis, "whether the motive was opportunism or conviction, the fact remains that to religious bodies the most potent expression of political principles has been due." [1] In order to demonstrate the essential truth of this generalization with regard to French Calvinism in the sixteenth century, it is only necessary to recall such writings of the Protestant Monarchomachs as the *Franco-Gallia* (1573) of Francis Hotman, the *De jure magistratuum in subditos* (1574) of Theodore Beza, and the famous *Vindiciae contra tyrannos* (1579) of Hubert Languet or Philippe Duplessis-Mornay, which were published after the terrible events of August, 1572—the massacre of Saint Bartholomew. It will be the purpose of this study to attempt to show that the Huguenots of the Dispersion, after the Revocation of the Edict of Nantes in France and after the Glorious Revolution in England, once more advanced a body of political speculation in the works of men like Pierre Jurieu and Jacques Abbadie, which, although much less celebrated, will nevertheless substantiate by and large the above judgment concerning the contribution of religious groups to the general theory of the state. In fact, in this period religion was still a powerful motivating force underlying political speculation, as it had been for centuries in the Middle Ages. With some qualification occasioned by the rapid expansion of secularism, "it is right to treat the growth of political ideas as a branch of ecclesiastical history" [2] in this age as well as in the whole of the preceding one. But before turning to a consideration of the political thought of the Dispersion, it will be necessary first to become acquainted with the general position of the Huguenots during the period between the epoch-making French Calvinist books of the sixteenth century and the equally remarkable literature of the late seventeenth century.

[1] John N. Figgis, *Studies of Political Thought from Gerson to Grotius, 1414–1625,* p. 5.
[2] *Ibid.*, pp. 23–24.

With the French religious wars in mind, it has been held that there never existed anything which could be called the political theory of the Huguenots, unless it was the desire to see the establishment of the Calvinistic doctrine and discipline by the ruler.[3] But even this view must be qualified, since the French Protestants ended by accepting mere toleration. As a party the Huguenots were only partially religious, since dissatisfied magnates of the realm made common cause with the pastors for purely secular reasons, and their attitude always varied with the rapidly changing circumstances. Upon the death of the Duke of Anjou in 1584 and especially after 1585, when Pope Sixtus-Quintus under the influence of the Catholic League had declared the King of Navarre to be a heretic and deprived of his rights to the crown, even Francis Hotman abandoned his former republicanism in favor of the hereditary right of Henry IV to the succession according to the Salic Law.[4] With the granting of the Edict of Toleration at Nantes in April, 1598, by the now Catholic sovereign, the expressions of Huguenot loyalty far exceeded the earlier protestations of respect for the king (while denouncing his advisers) which had preceded the massacre of Saint Bartholomew. In fact, a strange alliance developed between the Calvinists and the Gallican *Parlements* and was directed against the Jesuits with their theory of the indirect power of the Pope over princes, as sustained by Cardinal Bellarmine and Franciscus Suarez.[5]

An excellent illustration of this alliance between the Huguenots and the Gallicans is to be found early in the next reign upon the occasion of the meeting of the Estates General in 1614, which was assembled at the time of Louis XIII's majority. Supported by the Protestant representatives of the nobility, the Gallican Third Estate proposed in its *cahiers* to

---

[3] J. W. Allen, *A History of Political Thought in the Sixteenth Century*, pp. 302–304.
[4] See Hotman's *Brutum fulmen papae Sixti V adversus Hernicum sereniss.* He recast the *Franco-Gallia* as *De jure regni galliae libri tres* (1585), and three years later published *De jure successionis regiae in regno Francorum.* Cf. also the defense of hereditary right by Philippe Duplessis-Mornay (Mémoire contre la Maison de Lorraine) in *Mémoires et correspondance de Mornay*, II, 403–418. Such a complete volte-face led Pierre Bayle, when treating Hotman in his *Dictionnaire historique et critique*, to characterize Huguenot doctrines as "ambulatoires . . . vrais oiseaux de passage qui vont en un pays pendant l'été, en un autre pendant l'hiver. . . ."
[5] See Jean Bedé de la Gourmandière, *Le Droit des roys contre le Cardinal Bellarmin et autres jésuites*, and Duplessis-Mornay, *Le Mystère d'iniquité.* The doctrine of the Gallican *Parlements* took the form, "Le roi ne tient que de Dieu et de son épée."

introduce into the oath of allegiance and to establish as a fundamental law of the realm that since the king holds his crown from God alone with no mediatory power intervening, there is no authority on earth, either spiritual or temporal, which has the right to deprive him of it or to dispense any of his subjects from allegiance to him. This article was denounced and defeated by Cardinal du Perron, who represented the clergy and the Catholic nobility, as having been presented by "enemies of religion and the state in order to introduce Calvin and his doctrine." [6]

Although the acts of the Calvinists during this troubled period from the death of Henry IV in 1610 to the Peace of Alais in June, 1629, were not always compatible with their protestations of fidelity to the king, still with very rare exceptions the Huguenots no longer relied upon republican theories in order to legitimize rebellion. Instead they remained wedded to the absolute power of the sovereign.[7] But after their political power had been forever broken by Richelieu, who deprived them of their political assemblies and places of surety, the Huguenots found it definitely to their interest to avoid completely all political agitation and to attach themselves even more closely to the monarchy upon whose word alone depended their religious toleration.

In this halcyon period of French Protestantism from 1630 to 1660, when the Catholic Church was in the throes of the Jansenist controversy, the Huguenots sang a veritable chorus of praise for royalism.[8] They took no part in the disturbances of the *Fronde* during the minority of the king. This loyalty was sufficiently appreciated by the sovereign for him to reaffirm the Edict of Nantes in a declaration of May, 1652, which expressed his satisfaction over having such faithful subjects. In these three decades it can be readily seen that there is little to substantiate Emile Faguet's dictum that the Protestants are the oldest French republicans. However, these extreme monarchical theories of the Huguenots were precipitated not by the current of republican ideas of Frondeurs like Claude Joly but rather by the civil war in England, which

[6] Jacques Davy, Cardinal du Perron, *Harangue faicte de la part de la chambre ecclésiastique*, pp. 11 ff.
[7] For a more detailed account of this period see Charles Mercier, "Les Théories politiques des Calvinistes en France au cours des guerres de religion," *Bulletin de la Société de l'Histoire du Protestantisme français*, July–September, 1934, pp. 393–397.
[8] See A. Galland, *Les Pasteurs français*.

had finally led to the execution of Charles I. The events across the Channel brought about a recrudescence of the fatal stigma of rebellion and sedition upon the French Calvinists, for it could not be denied that their co-religionists in England were fighting against their legitimate ruler, who was not only the uncle of Louis XIV but also God's anointed. Realizing only too well that such actions in England greatly weakened the status of Calvinists in France, the Huguenots quickly adopted the only logical course in the situation, that of advocating the most extreme and uncompromising theories of royal absolutism.[9] These doctrines in some respects even surpassed the position of such lawyers as Le Bret in his *Traité de la souveraineté du roy,* which was published in 1632. One pastor, Jean Daillé, went as far as to declare: "Our property, our bodies, our lives belong to the king, and reserving only our consciences, which concern only God, everything remaining is entirely devoted to his service." [10] In general, however, it can be said that such views are typical of Huguenot political thought in the middle of the century.

But in spite of all these demonstrations of fidelity, the early years of the decade of the sixties were grievous for the French Calvinists, since both the clergy and the king started on the road leading to the Revoca-

[9] See Moise Amyraut, *Discours de la souveraineté des roys;* Samuel Bochart, *Lettre de M. Bochart à Mr. Morley.* There is a thesis on this work by A. Galland entitled *Quid Samuel Bochartus de jure regum, anno 1650, disseruerit* (1897). Note also Pierre Dumoulin (the younger), *Regii sanguinis clamor ad coelum adversus parricidas anglicanos* (1652); Claude Saumaise, *Defensio regia pro Carolo Primo* (1649). See the latter's famous controversy with John Milton, who, in his first *Defensio pro populo anglicano* (1651), which was a direct answer to Saumaise, included such Huguenots as Bochart in the same school of thought as Hobbes and Bossuet. *Ad Joann. Miltonem responsio,* Saumaise's reply to Milton, was published posthumously in 1660. It is important to note that Saumaise's earlier book was later reissued by an anonymous author, minus the parts pertaining to Charles I, as a *Traité de l'autorité royale,* dedicated to Louis XIV in 1691, in answer to the various republican theories which had been generated by the English Revolution of 1688.

[10] This same passage was later placed in contrast to the theories of resistance advocated by the extreme party of the Dispersion, headed by Jurieu. See the anonymous *Réponse des fidèles captifs en Babylone à la Lettre pastorale de M. Jurieu qui est dattée du 1 Novembre 1694 & qui a pour titre la XXII de la III année, 1695.* Probably written by Henri Basnage de Beauval, it cites as the source of Daillé's statement his *Innocence de notre religion;* but this item is not listed in Eugène et Emile Haag, *La France protestante,* Paris, 1846–59, as among his writings. But see his *Réplique aux deux livres de MM Adam & Cottiby,* 1662. Without citing its author, Jurieu himself attacks this declaration in his *Avis à tous les alliez . . . sur le secours qu'on doit donner aux soulevés des Cevennes,* 1705.

tion. They marked the beginning of the personal rule of Louis XIV, the prohibition of future national synods after 1659, and the signing of the Peace of the Pyrenees, which ended the war of thirty years duration with Spain. With this development the king was now free to turn to domestic concerns. In 1665 the General Assembly of the French Clergy proposed a further abridgment of the Huguenot liberties according to the narrowest possible interpretation of the Edict of Nantes, and in the following year the actual era of persecution began. The attacks did not become systematic or constant, however, until after the Peace of Nimwegen in 1678 and the conversion of the king several months later under the influence of Madame de Maintenon. In 1681 the dreaded Dragonnades commenced; they were but the climax of a long series of hostile acts against the Protestants upon the part of the government.

These developments resulted in what has been very well described as an attitude of "desperate royalism" [11] on the part of some Huguenots. Once more the loyalty and fidelity of the Protestants is contrasted with the seditious doctrines of the Jesuits.[12] But the most extreme example of royalist doctrine was presented on the very eve of the Revocation in 1685 by Elie Merlat, who, as a refugee pastor at Lausanne, had himself previously felt the iron hand of persecution in a French prison. In August, about two months before the Revocation, he published without change a *Traité pouvoir sur les absolus des souverains* which he had written four years earlier. This little treatise, which has not received the attention it deserves, exhibits the faith that if the king could be once again persuaded of the supreme loyalty and devotion of his Huguenot subjects, he would protect rather than destroy their church, which ever since the Reformation had been such a strong bulwark against Papal pretensions.

Merlat begins his brief treatise with a consideration of the origin of government, declaring that all men are equal by nature and that there is no dependence or domination among human beings except that which is occasioned by the difference between fathers and children and the

---

[11] Galland, *Les Pasteurs français*, p. 54.

[12] "Où est-ce qu'on enseigne communément que les rois ne dépendent que de Dieu même et qu'ils ont un pouvoir divin, que nulle personne ecclésiastique, nulle communauté de peuples ne peut leur ôter? N'est-ce pas dans la religion protestante? Où est-ce qu'il est au moins permis de croire que la royauté n'est qu'une autorité humaine qui demeure toujours soumise aux peuples qui l'ont donnée ou à l'église qui la peut ravir? N'est-ce pas dans l'Eglise romaine?" Paul Fétizon, *Apologie pour les réformés*, p. 174.

diversity of natural gifts. If this state of innocence could have endured without the introduction of sin, there would have been no need for rulers and subjects, since every individual would have resorted to reason for the law and to his will for the magistrate. But the advent of sin brought disorder and confusion in its wake; force regulated the actions of man, while the only limit to his desires was the lack of power. In order to restrain this sinful license, God created sovereign powers and the same reason which brought about their establishment in general is the determining factor in the various degrees of ruling authority in the world. History and experience reveal that absolute and unlimited power was only erected gradually, and it is only to be considered as the extreme remedy which God uses against the increasing corruption of men.

Merlat admits, of course, that the consciences of men belong only to God, but the secular authorities are recognized as having external administrative authority over the church, which consists in taking care that everything in that realm is well ordered and that there are no scandals. But even when the civil power encroaches upon the rights of God, subjects should never call it to account, much less resist its commands. Instead they should suffer in silence with patience, tears, and prayers to God, or at the very most seek safety in flight according to the Scriptural admonition.[13]

In matters directly involving the conscience, however, Merlat recognizes the duty of disobedience, following the maxim of Scripture concerning obedience to God rather than to man,[14] but it is to take only the passive form, and whatever punishment is meted out by the ruler as a result must be endured patiently.[15] In all concerns of this temporal existence such as life, honor, property, and reputation, the prince has unlimited power. These matters make up the material of power, which consists of two degrees or manners—tempered when princes rule by the laws and justice, and absolute when "their sole will is the principle of their actions." [16] Only anarchy results when subjects attempt to con-

---

[13] Matthew, 10.23.   [14] The Acts 5.29.

[15] On this point the Catholic theory of Bossuet was exactly the same. See his *La Politique tirée des propres paroles de l'Ecriture sainte*, Book VI, Art. ii, 5th and 6th propositions.

[16] *Traité du pouvoir absolu*, pp. 23–59. Absolute power of kings is described as "cette éminence & cette immense dignité qui les elève à tel point au dessus de leurs sujets qu'il n'y a nulle proportion des uns aux autres, ni aucune loi commune qui puisse permettre

trol their rulers, whose authority occupies the same place in civil society as the infallibility of the word of God in the church.[17] Sovereigns, therefore, "have no law which binds them with respect to their subjects" and, following Hobbes, the force of the law "is not strictly in its justice but in the authority of the legislator." [18] It is difficult to imagine a more extreme justification of absolutism, even though Merlat declares that kings must answer to God for their wickedness; God, however, often sends an arbitrary government as a punishment upon His sinful people. Therefore, absolute power is no less than a right of impunity belonging to kings with regard to their subjects, very similar in nature to the power of life and death of fathers over children and of masters over slaves. Even Bossuet never went so far as this, since he always placed great emphasis upon the heavy duties of the prince.[19]

Merlat's authorities in support of such rulership are the usual Scriptural passages stressing obedience to the powers that be and condemning resistance.[20] In addition he quotes at length from Hobbes [21] (by whom, like Bossuet, he was strongly influenced), to show that the fear of anarchy is also a reason for the institution of absolute power. But Merlat denies that man is not a sociable animal by nature and that he loves only himself, yet he concedes that the malice of most men destroys society and that most people have only their own interest in view. He concludes that

que les peuples ayent droit de régler la volonté & les actions de leurs Princes: de sorte que cette volonté alléguée ferme la bouche aux sujets & les oblige à l'obéissance sans qu'il leur soit loisible de se faire raison à eux-mêmes des torts que cette volonté exécutée peut leur faire ressentir dans toutes les choses qui appartiennent à la vie corporelle."

[17] *Ibid.*, pp. 166–167. "Comme dans la religion, la force de la foi procède uniquement de la vérité incontestable de Dieu qui y parle: aussi dans les états du monde, la force du gouvernement procède uniquement de l'autorité inviolable des princes qui dominent. . . . Et comme l'erreur, une fois soupçonnée dans le fondement de la créance, renverse la religion: aussi le droit d'examen, une fois concédé aux peuples sur leurs princes dans la société civile détruit la puissance et fait l'anarchie."

[18] *Ibid.*, pp. 23–59. Cf. Hobbes statement: "It is not wisdom but authority that makes a law." *Dialogue between a Philosopher and a Student of the Common Laws of England*, in *Works*, VI, 5.

[19] See Book VII of his *La Politique tirée des propres paroles de l'Ecriture sainte*, 1709.

[20] Proverbs 16.14; 20.2; 24.21; Romans 13.1–6; I Peter, 13.14, 17; Ecclesiastes, 8.2, 3, 4; I Samuel, 24.6.

[21] On the influence of Hobbes in France see G. La Cour-Gayet, *L'Education politique de Louis XIV*, Paris, 1898, *passim*, and André Morize, "Thomas Hobbes et Samuel Sorbière: Notes sur l'introduction de Hobbes en France," *Revue germanique*, IV (1908), 195–204. See also La Cour-Gayet, "Les Traductions françaises de Hobbes sous le règne de Louis XIV," *Archiv für Geschichte der Philosophie*, XII (1889), 202–207.

Hobbes regarded as reasonable and natural an arbitrary power that a Calvinist thinks should be suffered only by conscience as a punishment of God and as an extreme remedy for sinful men.[22] From this extended analysis Merlat returns to his original premise that, no matter how great the evils resulting from the abuse of absolute and arbitrary power, they are always less than those which accompany the policy of resistance by subjects to their rulers.

But in spite of the testimony of Pierre Bayle [23] to the contrary, such an extreme view as that of Merlat cannot be regarded as typical of Huguenot political thought in those last five critical years before the Revocation. Instead, in this period it is in the more moderate writings of ministers like the temperate Jean Claude and even the fiery Pierre Jurieu that the development of French Calvinistic political ideas can best be traced. The first named of these famous pastors had been very active in the defense of the Huguenots against Jansenists such as Antoine Arnauld [24] and Pierre Nicole [25] and had even crossed swords with the great Bossuet.[26] Unfortunately he died as a refugee in Holland only two years after the Revocation, leaving behind as his last important book the celebrated *Les Plaintes des protestants cruellement opprimés dans le royaume de France* (1686). It was Pierre Jurieu (1637–1713), therefore, who became the chief actor in the great drama of religious and political struggle of the age of Louis XIV.[27] Around this commanding figure—a

[22] "Ainsi selon le fait & quant aux événémens le péché des hommes autorise les principes d'Hobbes," *Traité du pouvoir absolu*, pp. 23–59.

[23] See his review of Merlat's treatise in his *Nouvelles de la République des lettres* (August, 1685), in *Oeuvres diverses*, 1737, I, 354. "Mais quoi qu'il en soit, le parti le plus glorieux & le plus honnête pour une religion & par conséquent le plus utile . . . est celui que l'auteur [Merlat] soutient. Sa doctrine est fort commune parmi les Protestants comme il paroit par un nombre infini de livres qu'ils ont composez contre les prétentions de la Cour de Rome. On ne laisse pas de les accuser d'un esprit démocratique & de les rendre responsables de ce qu'ont écrit Buchanan, Milton & quelques autres plumes vénales pendant la tirannie de Cromwel."

[24] Jean Claude, *Réponse au livre de M. Arnaud* (1670).

[25] Against Nicole, Claude wrote *La Défense de la réformation contre le livre intitulé Préjugez légitimes contre les Calvinistes* (1673), which the powerful Jansenist had published in 1671.

[26] Claude, *Réponse au livre de Monsieur l'Evêque de Meaux.*

[27] As Jurieu himself said many years later, "J'étois demeuré seul défenseur de nos véritez, Monsieur Claude étant mort peu après qu'il fut arrivé en ce pais." Letter to Gisbert Cuper, 1714, in *Supplément à L'Histoire critique des dogmes et des cultes* (1705). Cf. Bossuet's description of Jurieu as "le seul défenseur de la religion protestante," in *Oeuvres complètes*, VIII, 1447.

theologian of international reputation, whose works were translated into English, German, Dutch, Hungarian, and Italian—the controversy raged. This "Goliath of the Protestants," this "French Burnet," [28] may be regarded as the last great Calvinistic thinker in France [29] if not in all Europe. He was not only the most prolific polemical writer of his time but he remained the center of all political speculation in the Dispersion, whether on the question of popular sovereignty or the issue of tolerance —the two most important problems in French Protestantism of the late seventeenth century. It is certainly no exaggeration to say that his career is practically inseparable [30] from the history of French Calvinism in that transitional period of European history from 1680 to 1715, which has been so well described as "the crisis of the European conscience." [31] But, as with Marsiglio of Padua long before, it has been the lot of Pierre Jurieu "to be forgotten, while his thoughts survive." [32]

[28] "Après la mort de Monsieur Claude on doit considérer Monsieur Jurieu comme le tenant universel & comme celui à qui le droit de défendre la cause générale est tout entier dévolu. C'est sur luy que roule tout le soin de la protection du parti & qui s'en acquitter fort dignement. Mr. Jurieu est l'oracle qui répondre à tout sans se fatiguer, tant ses inspirations coulent de source . . . je le considère comme un homme qui seroit sans pair si la grande Bretagne n'avoit porté Mr. Burnet qui est le Jurieu d'Angleterre, de même que Mr. Jurieu est le Burnet Français." This estimate of Jurieu is to be found in a book by the Catholic Pierre Paulian, *Critique des Lettres pastorales de M. Jurieu* (1689), p. 16.

[29] A Huguenot such as Jean-Paul Rabaut Saint Etienne (1743–1793) was too much influenced by eighteenth century rationalism to be classed as a strictly Calvinistic political thinker.

[30] Elie Benoit in his famous *Histoire de l'Edit de Nantes,* V, 730, wrote of the great Calvinist: "Jurieu paraissait incapable de se lasser ni de s'épuiser et principalement pendant ces trois facheuses années 1683, 1684 et 1685 il mit tant de livres au jour, qu'on aurait dit qu'il lui fallait moins de temps pour les composer qu'il en fallait aux Réformés pour les lire. Ses écrits avec quelques peines qu'on les fit passer en France étaient recherchés avec soin, lus avec profit, redoutés des convertisseurs, qui les trouvaient toujours à leur passage et qui ne pouvaient refuser leur estime ni leurs éloges même à la force de ces ouvrages."

[31] See Paul Hazard, *La Crise de la conscience européenne.*

[32] C. W. Previté-Orton, "Marsilius of Padua," *Proceedings of the British Academy,* XXI (1935), 169.

Chapter Two

JURIEU AND CALVINISM
BEFORE THE REVOCATION

J URIEU published his first [1] political work in 1671. His second [2] appeared in 1677, when he was a professor of Hebrew and theology at the Protestant Academy of Sedan. It was not until January, 1681, however, that he presented his views on the state of his co-religionists in France, who were then suffering the cruel Dragonnades. To prevent, if possible, the complete recall of Huguenot liberties is the purpose of his *La Politique du clergé de France; ou, entretien curieux de deux catholiques romains, l'un parisien et l'autre provincial sur les moyens dont on se sert aujourd'huy pour destruire la religion protestante dans ce royaume*. It was the last book Jurieu ever wrote in his native land. Like so many of his writings it was published anonymously, but the disguise in the form of a dialogue between two Catholics was transparent enough. An old Huguenot gentleman is frequently mentioned by the Provincial of the title, and an old Protestant jurisconcult is also introduced, both of whom serve as the mouthpiece of the Calvinists and give the book its distinctly Protestant character. The governmental authorities lost no time in attributing this work to Jurieu, who was seriously enough compromised by it to accept the call of the Walloon Church in Rotterdam, Holland. There he spent the rest of his life as a pastor and professor of theology in the famous Ecole Illustre of that city, the Academy of Sedan having been suppressed by order of the king in July, 1681.

In the preface of this interesting polemic Jurieu deplored the effects of the persecution of the Huguenots, a group which the nation should have the greatest desire to conserve if the true interests of the king and the realm are correctly envisaged and understood. According to Jurieu, it was only after the Peace of the Pyrenees in 1659, when Spain was

[1] *Examen du livre de la Réunion du christianisme*, 1671.
[2] *Traité de la puissance de l'église* (1677).

forced to come to terms with France, that the plan to destroy the Huguenots took shape. From his preoccupation with war and external affairs the king became increasingly concerned with the reformation of the state and religion. As a good Catholic, the eldest son of the church and the very Christian king, he desired to see the return of the Huguenots to the fold of the church,—a feat that would not only be a suitable climax to his many triumphs and conquests abroad but also a great contribution toward the unity of Christianity.[3] But royal prudence would prevent the execution of this plan, if only the king were not continually being influenced by the Catholic clergy.

Jurieu points out that the increase in persecution resulted from the state of peace in the realm and also from the controversy of the king with the Pope over the affair of the *Régale,* which had been raging ever since 1673 and which was to reach a climax in the Four Gallican Articles of 1682. These articles, it should be noted, were no more than the adoption by the French Catholic clergy of the ideas set forth in the *cahiers* of the Third Estate in 1614. As Mezeray had remarked in his life of Henry II, the quarrels of the king of France with the Papacy had always forced the prince to mete out severe treatment to the Huguenots, since every time a ruler attempted to defend himself against the pretensions of the Holy See he was open to the charge that he was encouraging heresy.[4] Thus, the Huguenots were suppressed for what amounted to political reasons, since in religious matters Louis XIV's absolutism took

[3] To show the extent of the victory of the secular state in the late seventeenth century Harold J. Laski points out in his *The Rise of European Liberalism,* London, 1936, p. 51, that the aim of Louis in the Revocation was political unity rather than religious truth. Cf., however, Lord Acton's "The Protestant Theory of Persecution," *The History of Freedom and Other Essays,* pp. 169–70.

[4] See *Examen des méthodes proposées par Messieurs de l'Assemblée du Clergé de France en 1682.* This was probably written by Jacques Basnage upon the authority of Pierre Desmaizeaux (*La Vie de M. Bayle,* 1732), but certainly not by Jurieu as has been held by A. E. Kaeppler in his "Bibliographie chronologique des Oeuvres de Pierre Jurieu," in *Bulletin . . . du protestantisme français,* July–September, 1935, pp. 391–440. This is evident from the fact that Jurieu composed an approbation of this book which is contained in the Preface. "La dernière Assemblée du Clergé n'ayant pu terminer les différens qui sont entre le Roy & le Pape a cherché les moyens de faire rentrer dans sa communion tous les Protestants de France afin que si d'un coté elle étoit de grands privilèges au Pape elle put le consoler de l'autre part l'espérance de remettre un si grand peuple sous son Empire, & que si on la voyoit divisée du chef de l'Eglise pour sacrifier toutes choses à l'intérêt d'un Prince temporel, on ne peut pourtant pas luy reprocher qu'elle n'avoit ni piété ni Religion" (pp. 1–2).

the form of an increasing and more extensive Gallicanism,[5] until 1693 when this policy was completely reversed in favor of ultramontanism.

When speaking of this persecution of his brethren, Jurieu is especially bitter over the fact that the Huguenots were forbidden to hang the *fleur de lys* in their churches "as if they were not good Frenchmen." [6] At this point, he recalls the history of the Catholic League, the entry of the Duke of Parma into France, and the designs of "bad Frenchmen" to receive a king from Spain in the place of Henry of Navarre. It was the Huguenot party alone which acted as the "support of the state," refusing to submit to Spanish domination; and ever since Henry IV, Jurieu continues, they have served as the protectors of the House of Bourbon, especially during the *Fronde* at the time of the king's minority.

The opposition contended that the persecution of Huguenots was no worse than that of Catholics in Protestant states. To this argument Jurieu replies that Protestant rulers cannot have the same toleration for their Catholic subjects as is granted Protestants in Catholic countries. Sovereigns can never be assured of the undivided allegiance of subjects who have sworn first loyalty to another prince, namely, the Pope, whose power is particularly magnified by the Jesuits with their teachings of disobedience, revolt, and even assassination against a ruler declared to be a heretic through excommunication.[7] It was not only the Jesuits but the whole clergy which was suspect in this regard, according to Jurieu. Here he seems to realize that he is on shaky ground, since such a sweeping condemnation of the French Catholic clergy would not be applicable to the Gallican portion of it.[8] His only method of attack, therefore, is to

[5] It should be remembered that Gallicanism took two forms—royal and ecclesiastical. The real question at issue with regard to opposition to papal control was whether authority over the French national church lay in the hands of the king or the clergy.

[6] Jurieu, *La Politique du clergé*, pp. 52–53.

[7] The Jansenist book *La Morale pratique des jésuites* (1669) by Antoine Arnauld is cited, since therein the doctrines of Jesuits like Mariana are especially condemned. Jurieu also recalls the attemps made on the life of Queen Elizabeth, the assassination of William the Silent, Henry III, and Henry IV and the Gunpowder Plot in England.

[8] The tendency of the Huguenots and the Gallicans to reach a common position *in re* the Pope is well phrased years later, even after the triumph of the Jesuits, by the *Lettres à Messieurs les Prélats de l'Eglise gallicane* (1700): ". . . sur ce fatal article de l'autorité de l'Evêque de Rome, au nom près d'Antichrist, nous parlons, nous pensons comme vous. . . . Vous convenez avec nous que les Papes se vantent à faux titres d'être infaillibles dans leur décisions & dans leurs Décrêts. . . . Vous convenez que le pouvoir

cast suspicion upon the loyal relations which existed between the king and the Gallican Church.

Jurieu begins his assault on the clergy by warning the king against the Spanish and Italian party, which are one and the same and which operate beyond Spain and Italy in all other countries of Europe through the medium of the clergy and the monks whose orders are directly under the Pope rather than under the royal bishops. If one asks whether it is not true that the Papacy has a much stronger *liaison* with Spain and Austria than with France, since these states possess no such institution as the Gallican Church, Jurieu retorts that Rome is only neutral with respect to France and Spain when it fears French power.

It is then admitted by Jurieu that the "liberties of the Gallican Church" [9] are a part of the theology sustained by the *Parlements,* which burned the bulls of excommunication against Henry III and Henry IV. He claims that he is not concerned with the theology of the *Parlements* but with that of the clergy.[10] He repeats once again that he is not convinced that the fidelity of the Catholic ecclesiastics to the king is without exception. One of his proofs is the famous incident at the last meeting of the Estates General in 1614, which has already been cited.[11] But the Huguenots are loyal to the last drop of their blood. The Catholic

---

que les Papes s'attribuent sur les couronnes des Rois & sur le temporel des états est injuste & contraire aux loix divines & humaines." Lettre V, July 10, 1698, pp. 33 ff. These letters were written by Isaac Jaquelot rather than by Jurieu, to whom Kaeppler, *op. cit.,* attributes them. For proof see *Lettres sur les avis sincères aux prélats de France* (1698), p. 3: "À M. Jaquelot sur les avis qui ont été publiés contre ses Lettres aux prélats de France."

[9] These famous "liberties" included: first, the principle that the French rulers cannot be excommunicated by the Pope nor their realm placed under an interdict nor assigned to others, and, second, the doctrine that the Pope has no power over the temporal of kings and possesses neither infallibility nor occupies a position above the General Council of the church.

[10] The favorable attitude of the Sorbonne, which was the depository of French theology, toward the Catholic League and its hostility to Henry IV are cited as examples of the true position of the clergy.

[11] Cardinal du Perron in the name of the Catholic Clergy had objected to the attempt of the Third Estate, which recalled the assassination of the two previous French kings, to establish as a fundamental law of the state: "Que nos Rois ne dépendent pour le temporel de qui que ce soit que de Dieu; que pour aucune cause il n'est point permis d'assassiner les Rois; que même pour cause d'hérésie & de schisme, les rois ne peuvent être déposez ni leurs sujets absous du serment de fidélité ni sous quelque autre prétexte que ce soit." Jurieu, *La Politique du clergé,* pp. 214 ff.

clergy, however, although recognizing the independence of the ruler
with regard to temporal matters and opposing assassination, still would
not agree to the doctrine that for no cause whatsoever can a ruler be deposed by the Pope. In the last analysis there is no difference between the
French clergy and Italian theologians so far as their attitude toward the
royal authority is concerned.[12] At the very best the French clergy, whenever the king is embroiled with Rome, suppresses its displeasure only so
long as the king appears to have the upper hand, but as soon as matters take an antithetical turn the opposition of the ecclesiastics becomes
open.

Four years later, even after the Gallican Articles of 1682, Jurieu expresses still greater suspicion of the clergy in his *Entretien sur les conférences que Messieurs du clergé de France proposent aux Réformés de
France* (1685). At this time the French clergy was intent upon various
projects of reunion of the Calvinist and Gallican Church in the realm.
Bossuet had already shown keen interest in this matter as early as 1668
when he began his *Exposition de la foy catholique,* which appeared in
1671. In that book, written for Marshall Turenne, who was converted to
Catholicism at this time, the Bishop of Meaux attempted to reduce the
points of controversy between Catholics and Protestants to the narrowest
possible extent. But Jurieu had attacked the plan in his *Préservatif contre
le changement de religion ou idée juste et véritable de la religion catholique romaine opposée aux portraits flatteurs que l'on en fait et particulièrement à celui de M. de Condom* (1680) [13] as simply a trick which

---

[12] Cf. *La Politique des jésuites,* written in 1689, which, from the preface, must be considered to be by Jurieu. "La Politique des Jésuites doit être jointe à la Politiqué du
Clergé de France afin qu'on connoisse de bout en bout & l'esprit qui anime tout le corps
de l'Eglise Romaine & toutes les sources des guerres qui ont troublé les États & des persécutions que les Protestants ont soufertes & qu'ils soufrent au'jourd'huy." The Jesuits
act with reference to the time, place, and persons involved. ". . . ils étoient hier Espag-
nols, aujourd'huy ils sont Français, autrefois ils étoient tout entier au Pape contre la
France, aujourd'huy ils sont tout pour la France contre le Pape tout prêts à se recon-
cilier avec le Pape & Faire à la France le pis qu'ils pourront quand ils en seront requis
par leur intérêt," pp. 163–164. See also *Prévarications du Père Lachaise,* which is probably from the pen of Jurieu.

[13] Cf. Jurieu's *Suite de Préservatif contre le changement de religion,* (1683). The book
of Brueys (who had been converted by Bossuet in 1682), which Jurieu refuted, was an
Examen des raisons qui ont donné lieu à la séparation des protestants (1683). See also
Jurieu's *Le Janséniste convaincu* (1683).

Bossuet was employing to secure the return of the Protestants to the fold of the church.[14]

Jurieu commented further on the question of reunion in another little book entitled *Lettre de quelques Protestants pacifiques au sujet de la réunion des religions, à l'assemblée du clergé de France qui se doit tenir à Saint-Germain-en-Laye le . . . du mois de Mai, 1685.*[15] In this pamphlet the sinister intentions and bad faith of the clergy are stressed, even though Jurieu acknowledges that "the Gallican church is to-day the purest part of the Roman church." [16] But Jurieu insists that even if an agreement could be reached between the two churches, it would not be free from interference on the part of Rome. He concedes, however, that "the clergy no longer speaks in 1685 under the authority of Louis the great as it spoke in 1618 under the minority of Louis XIII." [17] In spite of the prevalent Gallicanism, however, Jurieu warns again of a time when the clergy, because of a change of interest, will revert to its former position.

In contrast to this very questionable loyalty and fidelity of the Catholic subjects of the king, Jurieu emphasizes that the Calvinists by birth, in-

[14] See Jurieu's discussion of another plan of reunion by the unorthodox Protestant, Isaac d'Huisseau (*La Réunion du christianisme*, 1670) in "Avis aux protestants de l'Europe" in his *Préjugez légitimes contre le papisme* (1685). For a full exposition of the problem of reunion see Chapter VI of this study.

[15] A comparison of this anonymous tract with either the *Préservatif* or the *Avis aux protestants de l'Europe* establishes the authorship of Jurieu, although Paulian in his *Critique des Lettres pastorales de M. Jurieu* (p. 522) attributes it to Jean Claude; this is contradicted, however, by Bayle in his *Dictionnaire*, article "Claude," Remarque H.

[16] *Lettre de quelques protestants*, pp. 5–14. The support which Jurieu gave to Gallicanism in many of his writings led Bayle to declare several years later at the height of his quarrel with him that if Louis XIV would only act toward the Pope as Henry VIII of England had done, Jurieu would eulogize his sovereign rather than oppose him. See Bayle's *La Cabale chimérique*, p. 245. In his dispute with Nicole, however, over the nature of the church Jurieu declared in his *Traité de l'unité de l'Eglise* (1688), p. 334: ". . . il n'y a que deux idées de l'unité qui soyent compatibles avêc la raison: la nôtre qui pose Jesus Christ pour centre unique & qui définit le schisme & les Schismatiques par rapport à ce centre. Et celle de la cour de Rome & ses adhérens qui pose le Pape pour centre de l'unité. *Le sentiment de l'Eglise gallicane tient un milieu incompatible*." (Italics mine.)

[17] *Entretien sur les conférences*, pp. 67–69. Cf. the opinion of another Protestant book, which appeared several years later and which has been attributed wrongly to Jurieu— the *Présages de la décadence des empires* (1688), pp. 243–244. "Il est vrai qu'il semble que depuis peu le Clergé a réparé cette ancienne faute par la décision des quatres articles, mais il ne faut pas compter sur ses démarches présentes."

clination, interest, and religious principle are faithful to their ruler. Like
his predecessors at the middle of the century, he reiterated the same
propositions in defense of princes and governmental authority [18] which
have already been noted.

In his *Suite de la politique du clergé ou les derniers efforts de l'innocence affligée,* which was one of the first writings that appeared after
his arrival in Holland, Jurieu confronts the very common contemporary
accusation that the Huguenots are the instigators of rebellion and that
they wish to alter the state as they have reformed the church.[19] In his
answer to this charge he declares that revolt has two objects, either the
alteration of the form of government of a state, as during the English
civil wars under Cromwell, or the introduction of foreign aid and the
passage of the state under another domination. Can anyone in his senses
believe, asks Jurieu, that the Huguenots wish to substitute a "popular
state for a monarchy"? They certainly would have nothing to gain nor
could they be better protected by exposing themselves to the "authority
and madness of a beast as fierce and unreasonable as the people." [20] Like

[18] In an impassioned passage Jurieu summarized the attitude of the Huguenots: "Sommes nous Turcs, sommes nous Infidels? Nous croyons en Jesus Christ. . . . Nous respectons
les Rois, Nous sommes bons sujets, bons citoyens: fidèles dans le commerce. . . . Nous
sommes Français autant que nous sommes Chrétiens réformez. Nous verserons jusqu'à
la dernière goute du sang de nos veines pour servir nôtre Roy & pour conserver nôtre
Religion jusqu'à la mort. . . . *Craindre Dieu & honorer le Roy* [from St. Peter] sont
les deux Principes d'où dépendent toute la vray Piété & toute la bonne morale." *Politique
du clergé,* pp. 113–114, 198. Cf. similar statements in his *Les Derniers Efforts de l'innocence affligée* or *Suite de la Politique du clergé* (1682), pp. 145 and 15. "Il n'y a
point de protestant dans le royaume qui ne venère et je puis dire qui n'adore Votre
Majesté comme la plus brillante image que Dieu ait posée de lui-même sur la terre."
[19] See the statement of Richard Simon after he had read *La Politique du clergé* in a
letter to the Huguenot Frémont d'Ablancourt: "Les livres composés par les vôtres tendent
à diminuer l'autorité absolue des monarchies et à établir des Républiques. Vos ministres
pour la plupart, ne sont point nés pour des monarchies telle qu'est la France et prennent
certaines libertés qui ne se peuvent souffrir que dans des républiques ou dans des états
où le roi n'est pas le maitre absolu." *Lettres choisies de M. Simon,* I, 30. See also a
passage in Simon's *Lettre de quelques nouveaux convertis de France.* "Leti dans son
Teatro Britannico, parto 4, lib 3, p. 53, dit nettement que les Protestants de France &
de Genève ont tous dans le coeur une espèce de gouvernement populaire qu'ils croyent
s'accommoder mieux avec l'état de l'église que le Gouvernement monarchique." Cf. also
the exclamation of King James I: "If you aime at a Scottish Presbytery, it agreeth as well
with Monarchy as God and the Devill." Quoted in Charles H. McIlwain, *The Political
Works of James I,* p. xc.
[20] *Les Derniers Efforts,* p. 25. Jurieu also shows his contempt for the people in his
Le Tableau du socinianisme (1690), p. 491, where he speaks of them as "ce monstre

all Calvinists Jurieu reveals here his dislike for the masses. This should
be kept in mind in connection with his theory of popular sovereignty at
the time of the English Revolution of 1688. Certainly the conclusion of
most French writers that he is one of the direct precursors of the French
Revolution is quite unwarranted.[21]

But if the Huguenots condemned "a popular state," they were even
more opposed, argued Jurieu, to being under the domination of Protestant England and Holland or Catholic Spain as the Catholic League had
so fervently desired. Although Jurieu admits in one place in the dialogue
that Christian morality does not extend so far as to prohibit a legitimate
defense against an unjust attack, he seems in general in this tract to pro-
scribe the protection of religion by force of arms.[22] With regard to the
civil wars of the sixteenth century, with which the Calvinists were being constantly reproached, Jurieu maintained that religion was only ac-
cidentally involved. Those struggles were political, between two factions
—Montmorency and Guise—during a period when the realm was under
a minority. In the beginning it was not against the king but against the
Guises that the Huguenots took up arms. This was lawful, since subjects
do not owe to those who have usurped the royal authority the same
obedience as is due to legitimate rulers like Francis I and Henry II. Even
if it is true, concludes Jurieu, that the Huguenots in the sixteenth century did take up arms to preserve their lives, such actions can be over-
looked in an epoch of terror.

But what of the status of the Edicts of Pacification, which guaranteed
the privileged position of the Huguenots in the state? Obviously their
nature has a very close connection with the right of resistance. In the
Politique du clergé de France Jurieu considers the edicts as perpetual

---

à cent têtes." Cf. the *Vindiciae contra tyrannos* (1610), Secunda Quaestio, p. 43: "An
vero universam multitudinem belluam, inquam, illiam innumerorum capitum, tumultuari
& concurrere in eam rem quasi agmine facto oportebit? Quis vero in ea turba ordo esse
queat? quae consilii quae rerum gerendarum species?"

21 Frank Puaux, *Les Défenseurs de la souveraineté du peuple sous le règne de Louis
XIV*, pp. 91–92. See also P. Pic, *Les Idées politiques de Jurieu et les grands principes
de 89.*

22 "Ces emportez & ces impatient en prenant les armes agiroient contre les principes
de la Religion & contre ceux de leur Religion en particulier, je l'avoue." *Suite de la
Politiqué du clergé*, pp. 26–90. Cf. Jurieu's ninth *Lettre pastorale* of the third year,
dated January 1, 1689: "Examen de la question s'il est permis de défendre sa Religion
par les armes," to which an affirmative answer is given.

laws, verified in all the *Parlements* and confirmed by repeated royal declarations, until they can be said to possess the status of irrevocable rules which lie at the very foundation of the peace of the state. They are as fundamental as the acts of Parliament in England which determined the status of religion under Edward VI and Elizabeth and which could only be quashed by the Parliament conjointly with the king.[23] At any rate these edicts are to be distinguished from mere laws or administrative orders affecting civil and criminal procedure, which the sovereign can revoke. They are, in fact, treaties between the ruler and his subjects, solemn pledges upon God whereby certain liberties were conserved and no power to secure their repeal is provided. Furthermore, even though in his mind the Catholic clergy was most instrumental in propagating the contrary view, Jurieu insisted that the obligation to keep a promise is as binding upon states as upon individuals, for good faith is the very basis of civil society.

But it is in an "Avis aux protestants de l'Europe tant de la Confession d'Augsbourg que de celle des Suisses," which was printed with his *Préjugez légitimes contre le Papisme* (1685), that Jurieu sets forth his most elaborate outline of the nature of these irrevocable edicts.[24] He there asserts that they can be considered under five heads—as treaties, simple edicts, royal concessions, privileges, and donations, but whatever their character they are to be regarded as beyond the power of recall by the sovereign. Now, first, if they are treaties they must be observed "according to universal law and the law of nations common to all peoples." Otherwise the ruler and his subjects would be continually in opposition to each other, since there would be no assurance that the king would keep his word.[25] Secondly, the very fact that at the head of the Edict of

---

[23] Jurieu asserted later in *Les Soupirs de la France esclave,* Mémoire III, p. 33, and in *Le Tableau du socinianisme,* pp. 491–492, that a decision to change the religion of a state should be taken by the king and the Estates conjointly. It was in itself a courageous act to point out at this time, while he was still in France, that "les peuples d'Angleterre ont de grands privilèges" and that "les rois ne sont pas en droit de faire absolument tout ce qui leur plait." *Politique du clergé,* pp. 146–149.

[24] Cf. C. Ancillon, *L'Irrévocabilité de l'Edit de Nantes prouvé.*

[25] Cf. Jurieu in his *Réflexions sur la cruelle persécution,* pp. 7–8. "C'est rendre la domination des Rois odieuse que de dire qu'on ne se peut fier à leurs paroles, . . . c'est exposer un peuple aux fureurs & aux caprices d'un tyran . . . c'est rompre le frein des loix . . ."

Nantes stand the words "perpetual and irrevocable" [26] is an unmistakable indication that certain edicts depend upon the mere will of the king, while others can only be changed with the consent of both the interested parties in concert or by one alone (that is, the king), in case of the disappearance of the people to whom the edict was granted. Thirdly, as there are certain concessions which are irrevocable, such as the grant to a society of merchants of permission to form a commercial company in the Indies, certainly then the permission which the Protestants obtained to set up a church government is not to be recalled. But it is held that the Calvinists are merely tolerated in Catholic states and therefore a ruler has the right to suppress such a group. To Jurieu such reasoning is simply the confusion of a "lawful religion" with a "tolerated religion." For example, the Catholic religion is a "tolerated religion" in Holland without legal guarantees and not "a lawful religion," which includes express authorization by edicts, laws, or declarations. Fourthly, as privileges, the Edicts of Pacification are also irrevocable, since "the term privilege comprises by nature irrevocability." In fact, every privilege is perpetual unless the time limit is expressly stated. Furthermore, there is no state so despotic that its chief cities do not possess privileges, exemptions, or rights, the revocation of which would be attended by disorders and confusion, unless the inhabitants deserved such action. Finally, even as donations, the edicts cannot be rescinded, since there are irrevocable donations "according to all the intentions of civil and canon law." [27]

When it became more than ever apparent that the irrevocability of the Edict of Nantes would not be recognized by the king once he could, by forced conversions, employ the fiction that there were no longer any Protestants in the realm, Jurieu began to adopt a firmer attitude with regard to the monarchy and its persecution of his coreligionists. The dedication of his *Réflexions sur la cruelle persécution que souffre l'Eglise réformée de France,* which he published in 1685, is in itself most signifi-

---

[26] See Jurieu's *Relation de tout ce qui s'est fait dans les affaires de la religion réformée* (1698), in which he held that the king in suppressing Protestantism in France "violoit toutes les loix de son Royaume, des loix fondamentales, des loix appellées perpétuelles & irrévocables; des loix vérifiées dans tous les Parlements de France, recues & consenties par tous les Ordres de l'Etat; des loix renouvellées par tous les Prédecesseurs & Ancestres de Prince à présent régnante & enfin des loix confirmées par eux-mêmes" (pp. 12–13).
[27] The pages to the *Avis aux protestants* are unnumbered.

cant and daring. Most books of the time were dedicated to Louis XIV; but it is to "the king of kings" that Jurieu pays his homage—to God as his only ruler. His book is no less than a violent protest against the virtual worship of the monarch by his subjects which then prevailed.[28] Princes act, in fact, as though they were endowed with all the rights of God, since they even attempt to extend their domain over conscience, which belongs to Him alone. He concludes that only from God can the Huguenots expect deliverance. Gone forever are the days when the princes of the blood can be relied upon to defend their liberties, since they have been reduced by the king to the position of mere courtiers at Versailles. Moreover, even the Protestant nobles are too worldly and sinful to be impressed by the destruction of Jerusalem.

The continuation of the policy of persecution will sow the seeds of civil war and provide a constant temptation toward revolt,[29] warns Jurieu. Especially during a time when France is engaged in foreign wars, will the Huguenots attempt to break their chains. If, as formerly, one of "the magnates" were to take action, he would have the support of all the discontented elements, who would have a right to aid him, since "in all divine and human laws there is no provision which gives power to kings to violate consciences." But even in that fatal year of 1685 Jurieu seemed to cling still to the position that, wrongful as it is for kings to possess an unlimited power, nevertheless the only sanction was to wait for that day "when God will hold them to account for their rule." [30]

Now in any consideration of this general problem of the right of resistance or the responsibility of the king for his government in the seventeenth century, it must be remembered that the principal method of approach and attack employed by Catholic contemporaries was the historical. There had been a great increase in historical consciousness and in the idea of historical relativity, with the result that in the last terrific ecclesiastical offensive in France from 1669 to 1685, the question of the religious wars of the preceding century was hotly debated in nearly every

[28] Jurieu cries out to God: "Vous souffrez qu'on appelle quelques hommes Roys, comme vous-mêmes les appeles Dieux, quoy qu'ils ne participent pas davantage à votre majesté royale qu'à votre majesté divine. . . . Avez-vous donc cessé d'être notre Roy, n'avez-vous retenu que la divinité, avez-vous renoncé à la Royauté?"

[29] Cf. *Les Derniers Efforts*, pp. 178–179.

[30] Jurieu, *Réflexions sur la persécution*, pp. 44–46. Cf. *La Politique du clergé*, p. 250.

polemical performance by both Catholics and Protestants. The principal accusation by the former was that the civil wars of the sixteenth century were caused by Calvinism, which, therefore, had no right to exist in a realm where complete obedience and religious unity are indispensable politically in order to insure the absolute authority of the sovereign.

The leading Catholic authors in this historical method of attack upon Calvinism were Antoine Varillas,[31] Pierre Soulier,[32] and Louis Maimbourg. It was the latter's *Histoire du calvinisme,* published in 1682 and dedicated to the king, which was the most violent and the most able diatribe against the Protestants at the time. This volume, written by a Jesuit in the pay of the king after he had been expelled from the order for his strong Gallicanism, is a long condemnation of Calvinism from beginning to end. In great detail Maimbourg traces its history in France with special emphasis on the incidents of foreign intervention and rebellion.[33]

Although there were several answers [34] to this vehement critique, Jurieu's *Histoire du calvinisme et celle du papisme mises en parallèle; ou, Apologie pour les réformateurs, pour la réformation et pour les réformés, divisée en quatre parties contre le libelle intitulé L'Histoire du calvinisme par M. Maimbourg* (1683) can be considered the official orthodox reply.[35] In his preface Jurieu maintained that the accusations of rebellion against the Protestants are to be regarded as more than a menace to their security in the state. They are an attack on the very truth of their faith, since Scriptural passages such as those to be found in Saint Paul, the Acts of the Apostles, and all the histories of the martyrs, stress

---

[31] *Histoire de Charles IX, Histoire de Francois I.*

[32] *Histoire des Édits de Pacification* (1686).

[33] Protestantism is characterized as "une espèce de République établie dans la Monarchie." See the Epitre, and Book I, p. 2, and Book VI, p. 502, of *Histoire du calvinisme,* Paris, 1682.

[34] See the following: Jean Rou, *Remarques sur l'histoire du Calvinisme de M. Maimbourg* (1682); Jean-Baptiste de Rocoles, *L'Histoire véritable du Calvinisme* (1683). This last book bears such a close similarity to at least the first two parts of Jurieu's reply to Maimbourg that it could very well be taken for a resumé prepared by the Rotterdam theologian himself. See Paul Fétizon, *Apologie pour les réformés* (1683); and Pierre Bayle, *Critique générale de L'Histoire du Calvinisme par M. Maimbourg* (1682).

[35] Jurieu's book was refuted by a new convert by the name of Gauthereau in *La France toute catholique sous le règne de Louis le grand* (1684). See also Louis Ferrand's *Réponse à L'Apologie pour la réformation* (1685) which Jurieu answered, in his *Le Vray Système de l'église* (1686), in the form of *Réflexions sur l'Escrit de M. Ferrand.*

the principle of passive obedience. Even if Calvinism is scheduled to be destroyed, Jurieu believes that it should perish innocent. It is this dogmatic certainty of possessing absolute truth which distinguishes so completely Jurieu's answer to Maimbourg from that of Bayle.

With the object of painting Calvinism all white and his enemies all black, Jurieu proceeds at once to a justification of the religious or civil wars of the preceding century. He begins by announcing that there are two methods of approaching this problem—the first to argue that these wars were just and the second to show that Calvinism was not responsible for them. He will attempt the latter tactic. It is the innocence of Calvinism that Jurieu wishes to establish even if Calvinists are guilty: "Calvinism is not obliged to answer for all the actions of Calvinists." Furthermore, the examination of the civil wars is to be based "on the maxims and rules of worldly morality," [36] since, according to a strict interpretation of the principles of Scripture, even foreign wars are illegitimate, except perhaps wars of self-defense, in which force is opposed to force.

In response to Maimbourg's accusation Jurieu concedes that a religion cannot be established by fire and the sword and still remain a true religion, but he refuses to go so far as to hold that every war which contains "some principle of religion and some design of defending religion" is illegitimate and unjust. He then poses the question [37] whether a prince who sees his own religion under persecution in a neighboring state and whose intercessions have been disregarded, has the right to bring aid in the form of armed forces. He is certain that the stronger party in the adjacent state would reply in the negative, since the ruler can control "the external part of religion as well as the civil laws," while the oppressed party would contend that the cause of justice and truth is the cause of all. Jurieu refuses to commit himself as to which group has reasoned the better. He does hold, however, that as a matter of practice, should the Turks condemn all Christians in their states to death, then Christian princes, if their interventions were scorned, would be obliged to unite in forcing by arms the Mohammedan kings to spare

[36] *Histoire du calvinisme et celle du papisme* (2d ed., 1823), Part II, p. 489.
[37] Cf. the *Vindiciae contra tyrannos,* Quarto Quaestio, p. 200: "an iure possint aut debeant vicini Principes auxilium ferre aliorum Principum subditis, religionis purae causa afflictis aut manifesta tyrannide oppressis?"

these subjects of Christ. Moreover, no one would regard such action as an attack upon the authority of neighboring sovereigns, but instead as a duty and a merit. Jurieu concludes from this that those who made war on France in favor of the Huguenots, such as the English and the Protestant princes of Germany, are not to be blamed, for "the laws of nature and Christianity oblige us to aid poor innocent people," who are being massacred. But he admits that if the Huguenots had merely experienced harsh treatment, they should and would have endured it patiently.[38]

With regard to the action of the French Protestants, Jurieu asks if there is ever a case in which armed resistance would be permitted to those who abuse the royal authority. For example, during the reigns of Francis II or Charles IX, if upon some other pretext than religion the best parts of the state had been massacred, would the French people have been obliged to suffer such action? If the nobles and the estates had joined with the people in opposing the tyrants who had possession of the king, would such a procedure have been rebellion? Jurieu's reply is an emphatic negative. Furthermore, Jurieu finds several examples of such conduct approved by God in the Old Testament. In addition, he proclaims that the doctrine that kings are to be obeyed even when they act contrary to "justice and truth" is a "monstrous theology," which supports only tyranny. Since it was conceded that resistance is permitted by the nobles, the estates, the people, and the princes against an evil administration of the realm, then is it unreasonable and unjust to forbid such action simply because the princes of the blood and the people are of a different religion from the sovereign? Besides, does Christianity "despoil men of the use of the law of nations and the right inseparable from human nature"?[39] Thus, Jurieu concludes that not every war in which religion is intermingled is illegitimate.

After these preliminary reflections he turns to a more detailed consideration of the civil wars; he refused to call them religious conflicts, since religion was not the cause but only the pretext or occasion for them.[40] They were primarily wars of state, faction, and interest like all

[38] *Histoire du calvinisme et celle du papisme*, Part II, pp. 507–510.
[39] *Ibid.*, pp. 510–512.
[40] See Jurieu, *Lettres Pastorales aux fidèles de France*, XVIII, May 15, 1687, First Year, pp. 435–436. Cf. Merlat, *Traité du pouvoir absolu*, p. 255.

other civil wars, although Jurieu is forced to grant that Calvinism was one source of the disturbances. He cites various contemporary authorities like Michel de Castelnau, Mezeray, D'Aubigné, and the Cardinal d'Ossat to substantiate this view in addition to his own detailed analysis of the origins of the seven civil struggles. He especially defends the action of the princes of the blood, the King of Navarre, and the Prince of Condé in repelling violence by force.[41] The Huguenots, furthermore, only used the German and English troops as auxiliaries. They were never introduced to rule in France, but the Catholic party would have delivered the country into the hands of Spain.

With regard to the fourth civil war, which began with the massacre of Saint Bartholomew, Jurieu admits that the Huguenots could no longer claim to be fighting for the rights of a prince of the blood. In this case "defense against oppression as cruel as that suffered by the Protestants is a natural right inseparable from all men in whatever condition they are." Charles IX lost not only royal dignity but also all humanity by his tyrannical act. Obedience is due only to a true king—never to a tyrant. Even though the first Christians were martyred without defending themselves, Jurieu refuses to denounce the resistance of the Huguenots who loved life enough to defend it against unjust violence.[42]

But aside from the particular circumstances in France during the religious wars, Jurieu poses the general question whether it is always a crime to take control of the court in order to prevent bad government. On the contrary it is a duty of the magnates of the realm to remove evil councilors from the king during his minority in the interest of the state.[43] In this manner Jurieu tentatively presented a secular theory of resistance which is quite divorced from religion.

Having justified and defended Calvinism, Jurieu next turns to the method of counterattack upon Catholicism, in the last two parts of the reply to Maimbourg. In his third recrimination against "Papism" he examines a question of right rather than of fact, namely, whether Catholicism or Protestantism is the more conducive toward inciting sub-

[41] "Un prince du sang et les principaux officiers de la couronne avoient d'assez grands caractères pour se faire donner liberté de conscience dans la minorité d'un roi, qui ne faisoit rien par lui-même." *Histoire du calvinisme et celle du papisme,* Part II, pp. 539–542.

[42] *Ibid.,* pp. 561–562.   [43] *Ibid.,* p. 549.

jects to revolt against sovereign authority. Although he is answering Maimbourg, at the same time Jurieu also replies to Antoine Arnauld's *Apologie pour les catholiques contre les faussetés et les calomnies d'un livre intitulé La Politique du clergé de France.* The substance of the great Jansenist's attack on Jurieu in that book is contained in the title to the third chapter—"That the most wicked books against the sovereignty of kings and the most capable of instigating revolt on the part of subjects against them have been written by the pretended reformers and refuted by Catholics." Special mention is made of George Buchanan, David Pareus,[44] Junius Brutus, and the author of the *De jure magistratuum in subditos et officio subditorum erga magistratus.*

Jurieu disposes of the last two with the curt statement that since they are anonymous, they are without authority and require no reasoned refutation. As for Buchanan and Pareus, he declares first that their maxims [45] are not those of the Huguenots, who have disavowed them

---

[44] The objectionable book of Pareus in question was his *In divinam ad Romanos S. Pauli . . . Epistolam Commentarius,* Genevae, 1613. In this treatise he adopted the same line of argument as Beza and Junius Brutus: ". . . subditi non privati sed in magistratu inferiori constituti; adversus superiorem magistratum se, rempublicam & Ecclesiam seu veram religionem etiam armis defendere jure possunt: his positis conditionibus 1) cum superior magistratus degenerat in tyrannum 2) aut ad manifestem idolatriam atque blasphemias ipsos vel subditos alios suae fidei commissos vult cogere 3) cum ipsis atrox infertur injuria 4) si aliter incolumes fortunis vita & conscientia esse non possint 5) ne praetextu religionis aut justitiae, sua quaerant 6) servata semper & moderamine inculpata tutela juxta legis." Quoted in Antoine Arnaud, *Apologie pour les catholiques,* I, 54–56. James I had this book condemned by the University of Oxford and refuted by the English theologian, David Owen. Later Philip Pareus, the son of David, attempted to defend his father by asserting that by "sovereign magistrate" in the condemned book is meant rulers who are not absolute.

[45] ". . . voici quelles sont leurs maximes selon les extraits de l'apologiste [Arnaud]. I Que le roi est sujet à la loi, mais que le peuple est audessus des loix. II Que le peuple qui a donné l'empire à un prince est en droit de lui préscrire de quelle manière il doit gouverner. III Qu'il n'y a pas de rois légitimes que ceux qui sont soumis aux loix. IV Que chaque particulier d'entre le peuple est inférieur au roi, mais que tout le peuple pris ensemble lui est supérieur. V Que les peuples sont en droit d'obliger le prince à se contenir dans les loix s'il veut sortir et de s'opposer à sa tyrannie s'il veut devenir tyran. VI Et enfin qu'on peut défendre par les armes la religion et les loix du pays sous ces conditions 1) Que le prince soit devenu tyran. 2) Qu'il veuille contraindre ses sujets à une manifeste idolatrie. 3) Qu'il fasse à ses sujets des injures atroces, c'est à dire qu'il exerce sa cruauté sur leurs personnes et son avarice sur leurs biens sans garder aucune mesure. 4) Qu'il n'y ait point d'autre voye de sauver sa vie et sa conscience, parce qu'on ne doit prendre les armes qu'à la dernière extrémité. 5) Que ceux qui prennent les armes contre le prince ne le fassent point sous un faux prétexte de piété ou de justice. 6) Et enfin que l'on se conduise dans cette guerre défensive contre le prince de manière qu'on ne viole point les loix de la modération et de la douceur; mais

many times and in whose authentic writings such doctrines find no place. Certainly this is not only a weak but scarcely truthful defense. Second, he holds that Buchanan did not go so far as to maintain that kings could be assassinated·when they are not obedient to the church and when they become heretics, but that this position had been advocated by many Catholics. Instead, in the view of the famous Scot, so long as a ruler does not violate the consciences, persons, and property of his subjects, his crown and life are immune from attack, even though he has become a heretic. Furthermore, both Pareus and Buchanan were attempting to restrain kings within the limits of the laws and were not like the Catholics teaching that a tyrant can be removed without waiting for his possible renunciation of tyranny. Jurieu concludes that their maxims "are undoubtedly false in the generality [46] in which these authors propose them." [47]

In the same way the doctrine of Arnauld in the *Apologie pour les catholiques* that all kings are above the laws is no less false, since each realm is governed according to usage. Jurieu proceeds then to make various distinctions. Certain kingdoms have absolute rulers, while others have sovereigns who are limited by the privileges and rights of subjects. Moreover, crowns may be either elective or successive. Of the latter type, some originate in conquest and others in the consent of the people, but the monarchies founded on conquest are the only kind in which the king is above all the laws, since the people have no voice in the erection of the government. Even here, however, the power of the ruler is not without limits. For example, if a king who rules by conquest (like a Turkish emperor) should attempt to massacre all his subjects, then they have the right to defend themselves and kill the tyrant, since "the right of self-preservation is inseparable from men and nothing can deprive them of it."

In those states where the king is established by the consent of the peo-

---

qu'on s'en tienne précisement à ce que la raison et l'équité permettent pour obliger un prince à faire son devoir." *Histoire du calvinisme et celle du papisme*, Part IV, pp. 202–203. Cf. with Jurieu's later views after the Revolution of 1688.

[46] The implication is, then, that there are particular cases where resistance is permissible, argued l'Abbé Novi de Caveirac in his *Apologie de Louis XIV et de son conseil sur la révocation de l'Edit de Nantes*, pp. 172–173.

[47] *Histoire du calvinisme et celle du papisme*, Part IV, p. 205. ". . . ils prétendent que c'est là le droit général des peuples et des rois, ce qui n'est pas vrai."

ple, the authority of the ruler is limited "by the laws which shelter the lives, honor, and property of individuals from tyranny." [48] Here the people can take action against the unjust undertakings of the sovereign. On such a basis was the French monarchy formerly governed, with the king and the estates ruling jointly as in England and Scotland. But in the France of Louis XIV the monarchs are absolutely sovereign. Thus, both the maxims of Buchanan and Pareus and Arnauld are true in certain places and false in others, since, unlike paternal authority, the form of government is not regulated by the law of nature. Instead, "royal authority depends upon usage and institution and its rights also. It is from the law of nations and the law of nature that men live under some kind of government, where there are some people who command and others who obey, because anarchy is monstrous and opposed to human and rational nature. . . . Royal and monarchical authority is then purely from positive law." [49]

Arnauld referred also to Article 40 of the Confession of faith of the French Calvinists, which stated that monarchs are to be obeyed, even though infidel, "on condition that the sovereign empire of God remains in its entirety." To the Jansenist author this meant that the Huguenots can be excused from fidelity to the ruler when he violates their religion. But Jurieu explains that disobedience is only permitted when the commands of the prince are contrary to religion and conscience; in other matters,[50] even when something is demanded which is in conflict with duty to God, obedience must follow. "Our rule is, it is better to obey God than men and this is the meaning of that clause of our article, 'on condition that the empire of God remains in its entirety.'" If the king commands participation in the Catholic mass, refusal to obey is in order, but when tributes or military service are asked submission must take place. But in Catholic doctrine, concludes Jurieu, once a prince has been judged a heretic, then obedience by subjects is no longer due in any respect.[51]

[48] *Ibid.*, pp. 206–207.　　　　　　　　[49] *Ibid.*, p. 208.
[50] Cf., however, the view of Jurieu in his last political writing: "Les rois n'ont aucun pouvoir sur nos biens & nos vies, lorsqu'ils veulent empiéter sur les droits de la conscience qui seule appartient à Dieu. Nos biens & nos vies sont attachez à nos consciences. Nous ne devons donc les abandonner que pour servir aux droits de Dieu & de la conscience: c'est à dire pour conserver le vrai culte de Dieu." *Avis à tous le alliez,* (1705), pp. 18–23.
[51] *Histoire du calvinisme et celle du papisme,* Part IV, p. 211.

Arnauld had accused the Huguenots of not condemning the doctrines of Junius Brutus and George Buchanan in their synods. To this charge Jurieu retorted that French Calvinists are not concerned with the struggles in Scotland. Furthermore, as stated above, the theory of Buchanan is applicable in certain countries but false in others. Therefore, it would have to be determined whether Scotland is one of these realms where the theory is true; this Jurieu refuses to do. Besides, Jesuits like Franciscus Suarez were denounced by a national synod in 1614. It is they, rather than Junius Brutus, whose influence led to the assassination of Henry III and Henry IV and to the Gunpowder Plot. To the accusation that Calvinism was responsible for the execution of Charles I, Jurieu retorts that, on the contrary, this detestable crime was perpetrated by fanatics and English Jesuits. In fact, in this connection he remarked that whenever the "Papists" ascribe to the Reformation as a whole the action of every fanatical Protestant sect, in so doing they abandon their customary attack on Protestantism for its numerous divisions, on these occasions holding that there is unity among all Protestants. But Jurieu had no qualms here about defending the rebellion of the Reformed group in Hungary against the House of Austria.

Enough of defense. In the last part of the work Jurieu is concerned with the history of Catholicism, which he tries to show is a source of rebellion against constituted authority. He contends that the Jansenists have proved that if the infallibility of the Pope is once admitted, then it follows that the Supreme Pontiff can depose kings, since the two propositions are inseparable. At this point, Jurieu continues, as in his earlier writings, to cast the shadow of doubt on the theology of the Gallican Church. In addition to the usual examples, such as the action of the Sorbonne against Henry III and the *Harangue* of Cardinal du Perron, cited in his *Politique du clergé de France,* Jurieu now refers to the *Sermons de la simulée conversion . . . de Henri de Bourbon (1594)* of Jean Boucher. Published by order of the Sorbonne and the French clergy, the sermons advocated the deposition of Henry of Navarre. Jurieu also recalls Boucher's *De justa Henrici Tertii abdicatione e Francorum regno* [52] (1589) and another work entitled *De justa reipublicae Christianae in*

---

[52] Grotius in the appendix to the *De antichristo,* Amsterdam, 1641, p. 59, claimed that this book was inspired not by Mariana and the Jesuits but by Junius Brutus.

reges impios et haereticos auctoritate, justissimaque catholicorum ad Henricum Navarraeum et quemcumque hereticum ex regno Galliae repellendum confoederatione (1590) by one Rossaeus or William Reynolds. Both books contain maxims of an extreme republican, if not even a democratic, character. As he had concluded in his *Préjugez légitimes contre le papisme,* after citing numerous examples in the history of Europe, "Catholicism is an inexhaustible source of seditions and revolts." [53]

In his reply to Maimbourg, in addition to his defense of Calvinism against the attacks of Antoine Arnauld's *Apologie pour les catholiques,* Jurieu set about answering the great Jansenist directly in a violent personal diatribe entitled *L'Esprit de M. Arnaud tiré de sa conduite et des écrits tant de lui que de ses disciples, particulièrement de l'Apologie pour les Catholiques* (1684).[54] Like many other Catholic writers Arnauld pretended that there was no persecution in France and that the Edict of Nantes was being respected. This gave Jurieu the opportunity of seeking the source of the cruel policy toward the Huguenots. He exonerates the king's ministers and even Bossuet, who was at this time the tutor of the Dauphin, from all responsibility. The king alone is to blame for the plight of the Calvinists, although, to be sure, he had been influenced by the clergy.[55]

The persecutors are asked to reflect upon three contemporary events of importance—the war in Germany and the entrance of the Turks into Austria, the plot in England to exclude James II from the throne, and the uprisings in the Cevennes in France. With regard to the first—the House of Austria's enslavement of the free realm of Hungary and persecution of the Protestants of that kingdom, Jurieu defended the Hungarians for turning to the Turks for protection. No one can regard such action as criminal, "because each person by the laws of nature must work

---

[53] *Préjugez légitimes contre le papisme,* Part II, p. 327. In this book Jurieu's purpose was to answer Pierre Nicole's *Préjugez légitimes contre les Calvinistes:* "préjugez pour préjugez." Nicole's book is one of the principal examples of the doctrinal as distinguished from the historical attack on Protestantism. The question put to the Calvinists was, What is the authority which is at the basis of their church and faith?

[54] Bayle later said that he would have preferred to be guilty of the authorship of a hundred books like the famous *Avis aux réfugiés* than to have written this infamous satire. See his *La Chimère de la cabale de Rotterdam* in his *Oeuvres diverses,* 1727–, II, 739. According to the anonymous *Défense de Sr. Samuel Chappuzeau contre une satire intitulé L'Esprit de M. Arnaud,* the work was called "la satire du genre humain."

[55] Jurieu, *L'Esprit de M. Arnaud,* II, 274.

for his own preservation. Kings are created for the nations and not the nations for kings. There were peoples before there were monarchs. It is the nations who have established sovereigns in order to be governed and conserved by them and not in order to be destroyed." [56] All these ideas have a very familiar ring to anyone who is at all acquainted with the literature of the Monarchomachs of the preceding century.

In his discussion of the conspiracy to exclude the Catholic Duke of York in England from the crown, Jurieu attempts to show that not only was the Protestant religion in danger but also the privileges and liberties of the realm. With regard to the disturbances in Dauphiné, Languedoc, and the Cevennes, where the Huguenots insisted upon preaching in forbidden places (*Les Églises du désert*) and upon protecting themselves if prevented from such action, Jurieu agrees that their policy was impatient and imprudent. [57] In fact, "one must only come to extreme remedies as a last resort. One of these is to resolve to repel force with force, [58] although there is nothing so natural and so just as self-defense." In self-defense many things are done contrary to the spirit of Scripture. But when it is forbidden to serve God even in secret assemblies in the woods, it is time to "rely on the maxim—'it is better to obey God than men.' " In addition to the command of God, however, the Huguenots have a privilege, granted by edicts, of preaching the truth in France. Furthermore, "nature tells each one that he has the right . . . to secure a possession so legitimately acquired," for "there is nothing in that of rebellion." If the Catholics were prevented anywhere from saying the mass, they would not be blamed for acting as the Huguenots, who, by dying, fulfill all the duties of Christianity. Besides, "if impatience seizes those who are being massacred for having worshiped God without de-

---

[56] *Ibid.*, pp. 293–294.

[57] Cf. the criticism of Bayle in his *Avis aux réfugiés,* Amsterdam, 1690, pp. 105–107: "Il n'y a donc tout au plus dans les révoltes que de la témérité et qu'un mauvais choix de circonstances." Success, then, is Jurieu's standard of judging whether an action is right or wrong. The same strand of pragmatism is also to be noted in his discussion of toleration, where he advocates the suppression of "des sectes naissantes," but not of the more numerous groups which have become more securely established. It was a doctrine of expediency which differed, however, from that of the *Politiques,* as we shall note later.

[58] Cf. John Locke's *Second Treatise on Civil Gouvernment* (1690), Everyman Ed., Chap. XIII, p. 196: "In all states and conditions the true remedy of force without authority is to oppose force to it."

fending themselves, and they begin to repel force with force, they do not act according to the laws of Christianity, which do not enjoin that, but they act according to the laws of nature. But I doubt that Christianity has come to abolish nature [59] and I am not persuaded that a man risks his salvation by guarding his life against a violent aggressor." [60] This obvious influence of natural law upon Jurieu will require careful attention later as we come to even more pronounced examples in his thinking.

Such theoretical justifications of resistance by Jurieu at this time were not without practical foundation. According to Elie Benoit,[61] even as early as 1684 there were groups of Huguenots in exile who attempted to interest the Protestant states of Europe in the conservation of the Calvinist churches in France. In the whole negotiation none was more active than Pierre Jurieu, who in 1685 in the *Avis aux protestants de l'Europe tant de la confession d'Augsbourg que de celle des suisses*,[62] argued that only by the reunion of the Protestants could the progress of Catholicism be checked. If the Calvinists were subjected, the Lutherans could not possibly hold out alone against the Catholic offensive. Certain princes like the Elector of Brandenburg, to whom he dedicated his *Préjugez légitimes contre le papisme,* were responsive toward such overtures, which extended not only to conserving the remainder of Protestantism but also even to recouping some of its losses. An entente between the Stadtholder, William of Orange, and the Elector was signed August 23, 1685, before the Revocation. But when it was discovered that England could not be relied upon for definite and certain aid in the enterprise, the whole undertaking was suspended as unsuitable for that time.

[59] In the *Déclaration de Mr. Bayle touchant un petit écrit qui vient de paraitre sous le titre de Courte Revue des maximes de morale* etc., in *Oeuvres*, 1737, II, 669–670, it is argued that this opinion simply destroys the possibility that Christian morality surpasses the Pagan.

[60] *L'Esprit de M. Arnaud*, II, 365–369.

[61] Elie Benoit, *Histoire de l'Édit de Nantes*, III, Part III, pp. 729–730.

[62] This tract was translated into English and published in London in 1689 as *Seasonable Advice to All Protestants in Europe of what Persuasion Soever for Uniting and Defending Themselves against Popish Tyranny*. Cf. also Jurieu's later treatises: *Jugement sur les méthodes rigides et relaschées d'expliquer la providence et la grâce . . . pour trouver un moyen de reconciliation entre les protestants qui suivent la confession d'Augsbourg et les réformés*, Rotterdam, 1686, and the *De pace inter protestantes ineunda consultatio sive disquisitio circa quaestiones de gratia quae remorantur unionem protestantium utriusque confessionis Augustanae et reformatae*, 1688.

Chapter Three

JURIEU AND THE
GLORIOUS REVOLUTION

NEVER since the Reformation had Protestantism been in such
danger as in the year 1685. James II, who had long since em-
braced Catholicism, now became king of England. The Elector of the Palatinate, who died without heirs, was succeeded by the
Catholic House of Neuburg. In October, Louis XIV revoked the Edict
of Nantes and in December the Duke of Savoy ceased to tolerate the
Vaudois Protestants. The work of the Counter Reformation seemed
to have been completed with the exception of the Netherlands, which
remained as the last stronghold of Protestantism in Europe.

This final and complete deprivation of their liberties had been fore-
seen by the Huguenots for several years. Their first reaction was negative: a strong protest but nothing more. It was Jean Claude who first
phrased the outraged feelings of the majority of his coreligionists in his
famous *Les Plaintes des protestants cruellement opprimés dans le royaume de France,* which he published in the year after the Revocation.[1]

Jurieu himself uttered no definite remonstrance but within the year
following the Revocation he began on September 1, 1686, his celebrated
bimonthly *Lettres pastorales aux fidèles de France qui gémissent sous la
captivité de Babylone.* He continued them for three years at the same
regular intervals until July 1, 1689, during which time he exercised the
function, as Bossuet said, of pastor among a "dispersed flock." [2] By this
means he tried to bring a measure of consolation to the Huguenots remaining in France. His general temper of submission at this time is also

[1] "Nous protestons contre l'édit du 18 octobre 1685, contenant la révocation de celuy
de Nantes, comme contre une manifeste surprise qui a été faite à la justice de sa Majesté
et un visible abus de l'autorité et de la puissance royale, l'édit de Nantes étant de sa
nature inviolable et irrévocable, hors de l'atteinte de toute puissance humaine, fait pour
être un traité perpétuel entre les catholiques romains et nous, une foy publique et une
loy fondamentale de l'Etat que nulle autorité ne peut enfreindre." Claude, *Les Plaintes
des protestants,* ed. Frank Puaux (Paris, 1885), p. 86.

[2] Bossuet, *Avertissements aux Protestants,* III, 2–3.

revealed in sermons like *La Balance du sanctuaire où sont pesées les afflictions présentes de l'Eglise avec les avantages qui lui en reviennent pour la consolation de tant de personnes qui sont pénétrées de douleur par la persécution présente que souffre l'Eglise* (1686),[3] which was dedicated to the Princess of Orange. But even in the midst of this hopeless state of Calvinism in France, Jurieu predicted the ultimate victory of his coreligionists over their persecutors. His *L'Accomplissement des prophéties; ou, La Délivrance prochaine de l'église* (1686) sets forth the probable course of this early Protestant triumph.

Jurieu's eschatology needs at least brief consideration, since it does have a definite bearing on the interpretation of both his political theory and practice. He tells us that the persecution of Calvinists in France led him to seek comfort in such Biblical passages as the eleventh chapter of the Apocalypse (*Rev.* 11. 3), where the early destruction of the empire of 1260 years (days) of anti-Christ is predicted, together with the coming of the reign of Christ. He believes that the period of the reign of anti-Christ or Catholicism [4] is to be reckoned from the year 450 or 455 A.D., which would place the end of its rule in the year 1710 or 1715. He looks for it to be destroyed not "by means of violence but by means of persuasion." [5] Furthermore, its destruction can be divided into two parts,[6] the first of which is the Reformation of the sixteenth century and the second the reformation of the seventeenth, when the remaining states will accept Protestantism. This last event will take place after the complete suppression of the external profession of the truth for three and a half years (days; *Rev.* 11.8, 9), which Jurieu rather haltingly holds could possibly be counted from October 22, 1685, when the Edict of Nantes was revoked.

Jurieu sees three possibilities of the restoration of Protestantism in

---

[3] See also his *Deux traités de morale* (1687).

[4] Jurieu had already labeled the Papacy as anti-Christ in his *Préjugez légitimes contre le papisme* (1685). This book is essentially abridged in the *Suite de l'Accomplissement des prophéties* (1687). For an answer see Jacques Gousset, *Examen des endroits de l'Accomplissement des prophéties de M.J.*

[5] *L'Accomplissement des prophéties*, II, 167–172. Cf. *La Décadence de l'empire papal* (1689). Since this is the last part with a separate title of *La Politique des jésuites*, it is probably by Jurieu.

[6] The anonymous author of *Le Cinquième Empire* refers to this view of two falls of Babylon, but disagrees with such an interpretation. For this reason this work has been wrongly attributed to Jurieu by Kaeppler in his *Bibliographie des oeuvres de Jurieu*.

France: first, by the preaching of the word as in the Reformation; second, by a secret operation of grace; and third, "by means of authority, by the royal power."[7] In fact, France would soon destroy Catholicism by a break with Rome before the end of the century, since difficulties with the Pope had already arisen over the famous Four Gallican Articles of 1682.[8] In the Fifteenth *Lettre pastorale* of the second year (1687), however, in flat contradiction to this, Jurieu warns the Calvinists not to expect that the rupture of France with Rome would be the cause of their reestablishment. Instead the restoration of their faith would be the occasion for the fall of Catholicism and "the means of the separation of the Gallican Church from the Roman."[9] But when the king of France does leave the communion of Rome, the people will have no right to revolt against him, since "the authority of the kings of France will outweigh the dominant religion." This hardly squares with the past experience of the accession of Henry IV. But Jurieu was writing in 1686 under the spell of the events in England of the previous year, that is, the succession of a Catholic ruler, James II, which he regarded as preparation for a similar course in France, namely, a Protestant king upon the French throne.[10]

These calculations and predictions of Jurieu had a tremendous influence upon the hopes of the Huguenots refugees and upon the "new converts" in France. In fact, it was said that *L'Accomplissement des prophéties* had a wider circulation than the annual almanacs. But far

---

[7] *L'Accomplissement des prophéties*, II, 188–192; see also the statement (in I, 152), "Les Princes de la terre n'ont qu'à dire non & la tyrannie de l'Antichrist tombera sans effusion du sang, fer & feu."

[8] In *La Chimère de la cabale de Rotterdam*, in *Oeuvres*, 1727, II, 725–726, Bayle held that when Jurieu was expecting the reestablishment of Protestantism without violence, he was counting heavily upon the education of the Dauphin and upon Montausier, his mentor, and on the obstinacy of Pope Innocent XI. Bayle delighted in showing that instead of a break with the Pope between 1690 and 1701 as Jurieu had predicted, France became even more "papist," for in 1693 Innocent XII quashed the Gallican Articles. According to Jurieu himself the bull of the Pope against Fénelon in 1699 completely ruined the liberties of the Gallican Church. See his *Traité historique* (1699), pp. 304–306, 316. See, for all this, Bayle's *Dictionnaire*, article "Braunbom."

[9] *Lettres pastorales*, XV (1687), pp. 346–352.

[10] *L'Accomplissement des prophéties*, II, 192, 208. Cf. the opinion of Bayle with respect to the crowning of James II that "les Protestants n'ont jamais eu une plus belle occasion de prouver qu'ils ne se vantent pas à tort d'être fidèles à leur souverain, quelque religion qu'il suive." *Nouvelles de la république des lettres*, May, 1685, Article XII, which is a review of a *Lettre sur l'état présent d'Angleterre & l'indépendance des rois* (1685), in *Oeuvres*, 1737, I, 293–294.

beyond a general moral stimulus, the book had a tendency, probably intentional, to cloak with the apocalyptic guise the diplomatic manoeuvres of the Protestant states at the time. In July of 1686 the Congress of Augsburg set about the preparation of a League which would unite not only Brandenburg, Holland, and Sweden but also even the Empire and Spain against Louis XIV. Jurieu had made a definite allusion to these negotiations in the preface to his book of prophecies and in the same place there is a hint of foreign intervention in order to reestablish Protestantism in France. But this intimation becomes a threat [11] in the foreword to his *Le Vray Système de l'église et la veritable analyse de la foi,* which was published in that same year.

In 1688 another French Protestant author [12] makes unmistakable references to the approaching downfall of France in the *Présages de la décadence des empires où sont melées plusieurs observations curieuses touchant la religion & les affaires du temps.* This prediction [13] was soon to be fulfilled in so far as the participation of European states in helping to bring about a change in the position of France was concerned, since the War of the League of Augsburg (1688–1697) against Louis XIV and the expedition of William of Orange to England began in that very same year.

According to Bayle and Desmaizeaux these developments caused Jurieu to modify his prophecy in such a way as to see the triumph of Protestantism in France no longer through a break with Rome but by a temporal calamity upon that kingdom in the form of foreign armed intervention. This is not a completely fair judgment, since the possibility of intervention by "neighboring peoples" had been envisaged as early as 1686. At any rate the tone of the *Lettres pastorales* became more belligerent in November and December at the time of William's expedition to

[11] "Nous irons bientôt porter la vérité jusques sur le trône du mensonge & le relèvement de ce qu'on vient d'abbatre se fera d'une manière si glorieuse que ce sera l'étonnement de toute la terre." Denis de Sainte Marthe, in his *Réponse aux plaintes des protestants,* p. 7, declared that this prophecy definitely was based on the League of Protestant states against France. The boldness of the language especially shocked the moderate group of refugees. See the Preface to Noël Aubert de Versé, *La Véritable Clef de l'apocalypse.*

[12] This book is attributed to Jurieu by Kaeppler, *Bibliographie des Oeuvres de Jurieu,* but on the basis of its favorable attitude toward toleration it could not have come from his pen. See the anonymous *Présages de la décadence des empires,* p. 113.

[13] *Présages de la décadence,* pp. 251–252.

England. The Prince of Orange was now pictured as the instrument through which God was effecting the fulfillment of his plans "for humbling and humiliating our persecutors of France." [14]

This conclusion is even more clearly apparent from a letter of Jurieu to William.[15] It is evident from this epistle that the Prince of Orange is regarded as the Joshua of Protestantism chosen by Providence to reestablish Jerusalem. Thus, the successes of the Allies in the War of the League of Augsburg are linked by Jurieu with the fulfillment of Scriptural pronouncements and in that way the war of 1688 took on the aspect of a religious war.[16]

But with the coming of the spring of 1689 the time for the expiration of one part of Jurieu's prophecy had arrived, and yet on April 22 there was nothing to indicate the immediate ruin of Catholicism in France and the reestablishment of Protestantism. As a result ridicule was heaped upon him by his enemies to such an extent that he inserted in the twenty-first *Lettre pastorale* of July 1, 1689 some "reflections on Chapter XI of the Apocalypse in relation to present events." Here he attempted to vindicate his predictions by showing that they had really come to pass in that year just as he had promised.

In the first place he emphatically denied that he had predicted the reestablishment of the Edict of Nantes by April 22, 1689, which was the view taken by many of his contemporaries. To foes like the newly converted Catholic, Brueys, in his *Histoire du fanatisme de notre temps et*

[14] *Lettres pastorales*, XXI, Third Year, p. 518. Cf. No. VIII (December 15, 1688), pp. 187–192, where Jurieu exclaims: "Qui sais si Dieu . . . ne donnera pas au monde un Constantin qui ruinera ce monstre du Papisme qui est un véritable Paganisme ressuscité."
[15] "Si cette nation (Angleterre) regarde votre Majesté comme son Libérateur nous vous regardons, Sire, aussi comme celui qui doit rompre nos fers & faire cesser notre captivité. Vous vous souviendrez, Sire, que Dieu ne vous a point élevé où vous êtes par un si grand nombre de merveilles pour renfermer les effects de votre piété magnanime dans les bornes d'une seule nation. Je suis persuadé que Votre Majesté répondra aux intentions de la Providence qui est de le mettre pour signe & pour miracle en Israel." J. Chaufepié, *Nouveau dictionnaire historique et critique*, III, 71, article "Jurieu." William's reply to Jurieu is also quoted here.
[16] See E. Lavisse and A. Rambaud, *Histoire générale du IVe siècle à nos jours*, VI, 130. But cf. Jurieu's *Lettre de B.D.C.S. à M.D.* (1689), where, in the guise of a Catholic, he denies that the question of religion enters the war: "Ne nous piquons pas d'être plus catholique que le pape; laissons nous conduire par le chef de l'Eglise et ne soyons pas plus sages que l'Empereur et le Roy d'Espagne." Louis XIV, of course, insisted on the religious character of the struggle and demanded the restoration of James II in the interest of Catholicism.

*le dessein que l'on avait en France de soulever les mécontents des cal-
vinistes* (1692), this prophecy was regarded solely as a means of encouraging the Calvinists in France to revolt. The basis Brueys took for such a
conclusion is a strong one. In an "Addition à l'Avis à tous les chrétiens"
in the second edition of his *L'Accomplissement des prophéties* Jurieu
had boldly asserted that "often prophets, alleged or true, have inspired
in those for whom they have been created the design of attempting the
things which were promised to them." [17]

In the *Pastoral Letter* of July 1, 1689, Jurieu insisted that a period of
several years must intervene between the resurrection of the church "by
means of zeal" and its full victory "by means of authority," when Catholicism would be destroyed in France by a full Reformation of the
realm. A semideliverance might possibly come, however, through the
reestablishment of the Edict of Nantes, but a complete triumph can only
be realized when Calvinism becomes the dominant religion.[18]

Having attempted to explain the prophecies with reference to the reestablishment of Protestantism in France, Jurieu had still to account for
the English Revolution, which he certainly did not foresee in 1686. He
endeavored to do this by arguing that France and England must be considered jointly in the fulfillment of the prophecies. By this means he
connects the crowning of James II on May 25, 1685, with the Dragonnades in France of June, 1685, as to time, and observes that the reign of
the English king was of three and a half years in duration. Furthermore,
the Prince of Orange [19] was crowned on April 21, 1689, three and a half
years practically to the day after the Revocation.

If Jurieu related the events in England and France in his prophecies,
it was another Huguenot pastor, Jacques Abbadie, who asserted boldly
that the cause of the English Protestants and that of the Huguenots was
the same.[20] At the time of the Revocation itself the French Calvinists

[17] Jurieu concludes with a violent outburst: "Voici le temps encore que les peuples
doivent manger la chair de la Bête (Papisme) & la bruler au feu, dépouiller la Paillarde
& réduire Babylone en poudre & en cendre." This vehemence profoundly shocked the
moderate refugees such as Henri Basnage de Beauval, whose comment is found in his
Réponse de l'auteur de l'histoire des ouvrages des savants.

[18] *Lettres pastorales,* XXI, Third Year, pp. 493–500; 503–510.

[19] It was also three and a half years from the crowning of James II on May 25, 1685,
to the end of November, 1688, when William arrived in England.

[20] Abbadie also included the plight of the Vaudois Protestants. See his *Défense de la
nation britannique,* p. 81.

were not certain as to just what their attitude should be toward the royal authority. It was the success of the Whigs in England which determined their final position. No longer did they need to rely completely upon the examples of revolution in the past centuries, for here was a successful model right before their eyes. Certainly no one can deny that the Revocation and the English Revolution are closely connected,[21] for it was Louis XIV's policy toward his Protestant subjects that had a great deal to do with arousing England against Catholicism.[22] Certainly it made James II's indulgence quite impossible.[23]

Louis XIV's action in revoking the Edict of Nantes also had extensive repercussions in the Netherlands, since it was a blow to the republican party there. Ever since the time of Witt, this group had favored an alliance with France as well as a defense of the Estates General in the constitutional struggle within the state. With the new turn of events, the party of William of Orange, the Stadtholder, who wanted an alliance with England, saw its stock rise to such a point that the Orangists became practically the internal masters of the state.

It is very important to understand this effect of the Revocation upon the Netherlands, which "were to the seventeenth century what the England of the Revolution was to the eighteenth and early nineteenth centuries, a working model of free institutions and the center of light for the rest of Europe." [24] This little country was without doubt the nucleus of the Huguenot dispersion, especially with regard to the production of political ideas. It was unavoidable that the French Protestants, who for

---

[21] See the following pamphlets, which appeared in 1688: *Lettre du R. P. Peters, jésuite, . . . au R. P. La Chaise; Réponse du R. P. La Chaise . . . à la lettre de R. P. Peters; Le Jésuite Démasqué.* Cf. also R. Durand "Louis XIV et Jacques II à la veille de la Révolution de 1688," *Revue d'Histoire moderne et contemporaine,* X (1908), pp. 28–44, 111–126, 162–204.

[22] In his *Lettres pastorales,* VI (of the Third Year dated November 15, 1688), pp. 141–142, Jurieu wrote: "La persécution de France a ouvert les yeux aux Anglois et leur a fait voir où le Papisme les conduisoient et ce qu'ils en devoient attendre. Cette multitude incroyable de misérables français fuyant la persécution, dont ils se sont vus accablés, les a fait penser à leur salut." Cf. Maimbourg's expression of hope in 1682 that England would return to Catholicism. See his *Histoire du calvinisme,* pp. 505–506.

[23] See the translation from the English by an unknown Huguenot of *Le Triomphe de la liberté* and *A Letter of Several French Ministers.* Bayle in his *Réponse d'un nouveau converti* in *Oeuvres,* 1727, II, 571, even accuses the Protestants of dethroning James II in order to preserve such measures of persecution of nonconformists and Catholics as the Test Act.

[24] Figgis, *Studies of Political Thought from Gerson to Grotius,* p. 218.

the most part entered the Walloon churches in Holland, should be affected by the internal political situation in the Dutch state where they sought refuge. Particularly was this true after the English Revolution, since that event divided the Huguenot party in two groups—the moderates and the zealots or extremists. The former, of whom Pierre Bayle, Jacques Basnage, Henri Basnage de Beauval, Gédéon Huet, and Isaac Jaquelot are the most notable, remained loyal to Louis XIV from whose authority alone they expected their return to France. As a result they were hostile to William of Orange and the cause of the Allies in the war of the League of Augsburg. Therefore, in William's mind they were associated with the republican opposition to his authority in the Netherlands, and among their extreme Huguenot brethren they were regarded as traitors to the Protestant cause. These religious zealots in the radical group, headed by Jurieu along with Elie Benoit and La Combe De-Vrigny, had lined up at once with William, the Stadtholder and king, in the grand coalition against France, which was regarded as no less than the embodiment of an attempt at universal monarchy and universal Catholicism.

Whether the War of the League of Augsburg was religious or not, it can be easily shown that the English Revolution of 1688 was not merely political in its implications, but also undertaken for the sake of religion. It was not simply the triumph of the English Parliament and the rights of the people but also a victory of Protestantism. In fact, such an extreme emphasis has been placed by some students upon the religious aspect of the "happy and Glorious Revolution of England" that its most famous defender, John Locke, has been pictured as almost wholly under the influence of Calvinism in his theory of the state.[25] If this is an overstatement with regard to the English supporter of William of Orange, it applies with reservations to the Huguenot pastor, Pierre Jurieu, who, as the friend of William, quite as much as Locke "deserves to be called the theorist of the Revolution of 1688." [26]

Before turning to an examination of Jurieu's defense of the English

[25] See Herbert D. Foster, "International Calvinism through Locke and the Revolution of 1688," *The American Historical Review*, XXXII (1926–27), 475–499, and Paul Hazard, *La Crise de la conscience européenne*, I, 120–21. But cf. for the contrary view, which is much more convincing, Ernst Troeltsch, *The Social Teachings of the Christian Churches*, II, 636–639.

[26] Georges La Cour-Gayet, *L'Éducation politique de Louis XIV*, p. 307.

Revolution, it is necessary to take note first of the torrent of vitupera-
tion,[27] which had been unleashed upon the Protestants after William's
expedition to England. But of all these numerous and varied attacks
none was quite so penetrating or devastating as the anonymous *Réponse
d'un nouveau converti à la lettre d'un réfugié* (1689). Although Jurieu
insisted that there was no "new convert" who could write so forcibly, he
never seems to have suspected that it was Pierre Bayle [28] who probably
was the author of this tract. Instead he dismisses the question of authorship by ascribing the work to an old pupil of the Jesuits, who has well
profited by their teachings.[29]

Although Bayle devoted most of his attention in the *Réponse d'un
nouveau converti* to the cruel attack upon the spirit of intolerance of the
Protestants, he concluded the pamphlet with some "reflections on the
civil wars of the Protestants and the present invasion of England." With
the background of the religious wars in France in mind, Bayle claims
first that so far as the question of the taking up of arms by subjects is
concerned, there is really only one course open to the Protestants, namely
that of linking their thought to "those authors beyond the mountains."
Logically they are forced to adopt the ultramontane principle that no
sovereign can be legitimate unless he is orthodox. He maliciously reminds the Protestants, however, that even though it now suits their purpose with regard to the Catholic James II, they have opposed this concept in particular when it was employed by the writers of the Catholic
League against the Protestant King of Navarre and in general whenever
they fulminate against Rome. Secondly, Bayle argues that the more the

[27] See Denis de Sainte Marthe, *Entretiens touchant l'entreprise du Prince d'Orange sur
l'Angleterre;* Antoine Arnauld, *Le Vrai Portrait de Guillaume-Henri de Nassau.* Jurieu
answered this libel directly with his *Apologie pour leurs S.S. Majestés britaniques* (1689).
Jurieu notes in the Fifteenth *Lettre pastorale* of the Third Year, pp. 347–348, the
gazetteers like Jean Donneau de Vizé, the author of *Le Mercure galant,* who composed
three tomes of satires under the title of *Affaires du temps.* Cf. also the anonymous sarcastic pamphlets, probably by Eustache Le Noble, such as *Le Couronnement de Guillemet et de Guillemette* and *le Festin de Guillemot, quatrième dialogue.*
[28] Pierre Desmaizeaux in his *La Vie de M. Bayle,* I, 246, shows the great similarity
between this tract and the famous *Avis aux réfugiés,* which is without doubt by Bayle.
In fact, it can be said that the former is simply a prelude to the latter. But, like the *Avis,*
it was also attributed to Paul Pellisson.
[29] See *Lettres pastorales,* XV, Third Year, p. 345. He also remarks that the author is
of the same religion as Clément, Ravaillac, and Jean Châtel.

Protestants defend their uprisings, the more they are actually placing themselves in the position of self-refutation. If subjects have the right to take up arms against their ruler when they think it expedient in the interest of their religion, then the prince also has a right to arm himself against them when it becomes necessary for his own sake. In the third place, Bayle warns that the Protestant arguments can be used as an apology for Catholics who might themselves take the opportunity to revolt in countries where they are persecuted. Fourthly, he held it no less than ridiculous that Protestants who have sanctioned the eradication of Catholics by Protestant rulers should claim that Catholic princes had no right to exterminate Protestants. Of course, the Catholics were charged with maintaining that the Pope can release subjects from their oath of allegiance. But how do the Protestants dare show such effrontery, asks Bayle, when they believe that the people, "that beast with a thousand heads" has "an inalienable right" to free itself from the oath of fidelity? In the fifth place if the Edicts of Pacification were secured by extortion as Soulier had held,[30] then there was proof that France had shown a greater moderation for the Protestants than any Protestant state had for the Catholics. If, on the other hand, these concessions were obtained by force of arms, then the Protestants had committed a greater crime against their Catholic rulers than Catholic subjects had in the reverse situation. Finally, he asks if the Huguenots are not making a false assumption when they seem to consider the French Calvinists as making up the whole Protestant religion, as if the Edict of Nantes included all the Reformed Church. It would certainly be ridiculous to assert that the entire Catholic Church is ravaged because of the oppression of Catholics in England. Furthermore, would the Protestants ever dare include the whole realm of France in their party?

These are some of the arguments the Philosopher of Rotterdam used to sustain his principal thesis that the spirit of the Reformation had been one of rebellion, sedition, and satire in the sixteenth century and that now, once again, it is at the basis of the invasion of England by William of Orange. Such revolutionary actions were the reason for the expulsion of the Protestants from France and their persecution from 1685 to the

[30] Cf. Pierre Soulier, *Histoire des édits de pacification*.

present (1688). Any apologies of the Revolution in England can only serve to justify the conduct of Louis XIV toward the Huguenots, concluded Bayle.

In the face of such accusations Jurieu declared in his Fifteenth *Lettre pastorale,* dated April 1, 1689, that he had reached the end of his patience. He found it necessary to outline an appropriate answer [31] to such charges against the Protestants, which would include a discussion of the power of sovereigns [32] in general and a consideration of the fundamental reasons in particular for the revolution of such recent occurrence in England. It was to this task that Jurieu turned in the Sixteenth, Seventeenth, and Eighteenth [33] *Lettres pastorales* of April 15, May 1, and May 15, 1689, respectively, in which we shall find the same mixture of Biblical arguments, historical precedents, and philosophic reasoning based on natural law as in the famous *Vindiciae contra tyrannos* of the preceding century.

Of this trilogy the first two letters treat of "the power of sovereigns, of its origin, of its limits," and of "the rights of the peoples." Jurieu admits that he must deal with a delicate matter. Nevertheless, he feels that in order to conserve the inviolable fidelity of subjects to the king, it is not necessary to adopt the extreme monarchical position of a writer like Merlat in his *Traité sur les pouvoirs absolus des souverains.* Jurieu contends that such arguments are of no value, since tyrants have no need of them to justify their acts and good rulers would make no use of them. In addition, certainly the Huguenots, of all people, do not require such maxims to oblige them to be faithful to their king, for they have always been the most willing of subjects to submit completely to the ruler even when he has seen fit to heap disgrace upon them. Experience, therefore, proves that without the aid of such doctrines, which can only lead to tyranny, one can be a good and obedient subject.

After this preliminary statement Jurieu proceeds to present his theory

---

[31] For another reply to this tract see Gédéon Huet, *Lettre écrite de Suisse en Hollande pour répondre à la seconde partie de l'ouvrage du prétendu nouveau converti.*

[32] In the Ninth *Lettre pastorale* of January 1, 1689, Jurieu had said that he did not wish to discuss the rights of sovereigns, since it was in vain to reason on this question.

[33] Extracts from the Sixteenth and Seventeenth of these important letters have been reprinted by Frank Puaux in his *Les Défenseurs de la souveraineté du peuple sous le règne de Louis XIV,* pp. 95–124.

in a more systematic fashion than in almost any of his other writings. He is concerned first with explaining the origin of political authority, which leads him to open with that familiar idea of a state of nature. It is described very briefly, however, as compared to the extended treatment at the hands of his famous contemporary, John Locke.

In the beginning men were naturally free and independent of each other with the exception of that natural dependence which God has ordained between members of the same family. Property was also naturally undivided, all worldly goods being held in common. But unfortunately such a state did not long endure, since with the coming of sin the division of goods and the establishment of government was made necessary. "It is, morally speaking, impossible that societies subsist without sovereignty and dominion." But although temporal rule is not derived "from natural divine law," nevertheless it is according to the intention and purpose of God. Nor does secular administration originate "from positive divine law"; which is to say that God, since the Fall, has not established by a general law the power of masters over slaves and that of sovereigns over subjects. It is not opposed to nature or to the positive laws of God, therefore, to be today without the division of property or without a governor. As a result, sovereign power does not spring from a necessity based upon any natural law. For example, the republic of Israel under the Judges, although goods were divided, lived without any earthly ruler. But since the Fall such a state could not last long because human passions brought disorder.[34] Hence, by a compulsion which arises from prudence and not from conscience, property must be divided and governors established. The people, being naturally free and independent, have the power then to create a sovereign or not, as they choose, but once they have established their ruler they are no longer free to obey or not to obey.[35] It is imperative, "by conscience" and "by neces-

[34] In his *Examen d'un libelle contre la religion* (1691), pp. 92–94, Jurieu declared that "la seule necessité de la conservation de la Paix" caused the formation of government and the division of property.

[35] Cf. Jurieu's statement in his *Traité de la puissance de l'Eglise* (1677), pp. 65–70: "Quand une fois les loix sont faites, quand le gouvernement est établi, le Peuple n'est plus libre, il s'est lié les mains & à toute sa Postérité." See a similar tendency in Locke, *Civil Government*, pp. 183–184: "This Legislative is not only the supreme power of the Commonwealth but sacred and unalterable in the hands where the community have once placed it."

sity" to obey the authorities that have been selected. To Jurieu these truths are self-evident.

But Jurieu insisted that the people, being naturally unhampered and independent in establishing their government, were free to choose whatever type they desired—monarchy, aristocracy, or democracy. Of these he considered the first to be the ideal type, as would almost any Frenchman during "le grand siècle." There are two kinds of monarchy, according to Jurieu, absolute as in France, where all the sovereign authority is concentrated in the ruler, and tempered as in England, where the prince divides with the people the legislative and executive powers. But none of these forms of government originates from divine law.

At this point Jurieu sets forth the distinction between two propositions, namely, "that the origin of sovereigns is from divine law" and that "one is bound to obey sovereigns from divine law." Although he acknowledges his denial of the source of sovereignty from divine law, he maintains that subjects are obliged "by all the laws of God, natural and positive, to obey sovereign powers." [36] This obligation before God holds, first, because one should in conscience keep his promises and, second, because, according to natural law, one must render to each his due. Furthermore, once the supreme authority has been conferred, it belongs to the sovereign "as his estate," and a gift creates "a very just title." Therefore, following Grotius, sovereigns can use, "according to their prudence," the authority which has been granted to them.

Nor is it to be assumed that the supreme power displays only human characteristics because of its derivation from man. On the contrary, "kings are the lieutenants of God, they are his vicars, his living images," and as such they are to be honored, respected, and obeyed "in all things which are just, honorable, needful and even in those which are harsh and vexatious, and which appear unjust, if, on the other hand, they are necessary for the welfare of the state." The inclusion of the qualification "for the welfare of the state" is followed immediately by the declaration that it is for the ruler himself to judge what is necessary (which reminds one of the opinion of the English judges in the famous Ship Money Case that the disputed taxes could only be taken in an emergency but

[36] St. Paul's Epistle to the Romans 13.5, is cited as usual to show that men must be subject to princes not only "for wrath" but also for conscience's sake.

that the king was the sole judge of whether such an emergency existed). Hence, there is little place here for the limitation of the sovereign. Just as men do not cease to be images of God because they have been begotten by other men, so kings are the images of the Divine, even though they owe their immediate origin to the people. In the erection of the supreme authority the people follow the orders of Providence and supply the operation of secondary causation over the primary.

But this very origin of the supreme power of government explains its limits. Jurieu attempts to prove this premise by the following reasoning. First, since the people create kings and give them their authority, then the cause should be in some manner greater than the effect. "Kings certainly are above nations but also peoples in certain respects are above kings." [37] Jurieu argues that this is exactly the position of the Gallicans toward the Papacy. The Pope is above the whole church as its chief, but also the entire church is above him. Second, although the people create their rulers, they cannot give them any rights which the *populus* does not possess itself. Among those rights which the people do not have "is that of making war on God, of trampling the laws under foot, of committing injustices, of destroying the true religion, of persecuting those who follow it." With regard to religion, which was after all the primary stimulus of Jurieu's thought, he argues that since the people are the defenders of the true faith, they can confer upon the sovereign the power to protect and extend it by legitimate means. Tyranny over conscience and the exercise of constraint for the purpose of forcing the belief in one religion rather than in another are not, however, to be included among the lawful methods of spreading the true religion. Since the people do not have this right of empire over consciences, its exercise being in the possession of God alone, they cannot grant it to the ruler. It follows then that one need not obey a ruler who commands injustice and violates consciences, for he cannot obtain this right either from God or from men. Third, since the people does not possess the right to destroy itself, it cannot confer a power upon kings which would work the destruction of the *populus*. Not men, but God alone, is the master of human life. Later on in his discussion Jurieu contends that since men are also not the masters of

[37] Cf. the principle of the *Vindiciae contra tyrannos,* where Junius Brutus asserts: "Princeps major singulis, universis minor." Quaestio, Secunda.

the lives or liberties of their wives and children, they cannot grant to the sovereign an unlimited power over their property, life, or liberty.

Our theologian of Rotterdam concludes that the people grant the supreme power to their rulers not for the personal pleasure or glory of the king, but for the conservation of "the community." When, therefore, its ruin is sought by a king, he is acting in a manner contrary to the ends for which he was created and his commands should consequently be disregarded. At this point Jurieu cites the famous principle of Roman law, which Cicero refers to in his *De legibus* (III, iii, 8), namely, "Salus populi suprema lex esto," a maxim which can brook no exception.[38] Since the rulers are the protectors of the people, it follows that "one cannot be bound to obey a prince who commands against the fundamental laws of the state, who orders the slaughter and massacre of the innocent, or the ruin of the community by any means whatever." [39] In Jurieu's mind these fundamental laws are such perpetual edicts as that of Nantes rather than those propositions, such as the Salic Law and the inalienability of the royal domain, which the French lawyers had in mind.

It would seem from this analysis that the limitations upon the sovereign arise from three sources, although Jurieu refuses to mark them precisely. The first is the fact that the people cannot confer upon the ruler rights which they themselves do not possess. The purely secular matters cited in this connection are, as mentioned above, the destruction of the laws and the doing of injustice. The second source of restrictions is derived from the maxim: "The safety and the preservation of the people are the sovereign law." The third source originates in the idea of contract, reserved rights, conditions, or privileges, of which more will be

---

[38] Jurieu's contemporary Locke did not fail to rely upon this precept, but it did not begin to play as large a part in his theory of the state as it did with the Huguenot pastor. " 'Salus populi suprema lex' is certainly so just and fundamental a rule that he who sincerely follows it cannot dangerously err." (*Of Civil Government,* Chap. XIII, p. 197).

[39] Cf. also the following: "Quand un prince désole un peuple par des massacres et par des action violentes, quand il s'est élevé au-dessus de toutes les lois de la raison et de l'équité, quand il veut attenter sur les droits de Dieu et violenter la conscience il est plus que certain qu'on ne peut être obligé de lui obéir, ni même de souffrir ce qu'il lui plait de faire, d'où la ruine de la société s'ensuit." *Lettres pastorales,* XVI of the Third Year.

said later. But from whatever origin, once the restraints are disregarded, disobedience is justified.

But Jurieu refused at this point to recognize the distinction between active and passive obedience. That is to say, although one need not obey kings when they act directly contrary to God, the laws, or the conservation of society, on the other hand, recalcitrance may be punished to the utmost extent, since it is appropriate to die for the sake of religion, the laws, or society. But Jurieu contends that, if a sovereign has the right to punish in any degree, at will, those who refuse to break the laws and to ruin society and religion, then he has also the right to destroy the community itself. For example, if a ruler should order one half of a city to massacre the other half upon the pretext of disobedience to an unjust command, the one half is not bound to kill the other, for there are limits to active obedience. If this ruler should have the right after that to massacre the whole city without its having the liberty to resist, then the sovereign would have the privilege of crushing the whole society, according to our theologian.

Now not only does the popular origin of government indicate its limits, but also it follows that there is a mutual pact between the people and the sovereign. It is apparent that Jurieu has in mind the governmental rather than a social compact. It is contrary to reason to conceive the absolute submission of a people to a ruler "without agreement and without condition," that is to say, "without placing its life, its property and the public in safety by some laws." One commentator [40] seems to think that by "some laws" Jurieu intends to include natural law as well as the fundamental laws of the realm. But the judgment of another [41] that Jurieu is careless with his terminology and confuses "compact and laws" seems to be the more satisfactory explanation of the ambiguity on this point. Jurieu goes so far as to say that if a people should ever be foolish enough to submit without reserve [42] and without a pact, such a treaty

[40] Charles Mercier, "Les théories politiques des calvinistes en France au cours des guerres de religion," *Bulletin . . . du protestantisme français*, July–September, 1934, p. 406.
[41] André Lemaire, *Les lois fondamentales de la monarchie française*, pp. 229–230. Cf. a passage from Jurieu's *Le Janséniste convaincu* (1683), p. 310: "Il faut qu'ils obéissent aux rois & aux magistrats qu'ils se sont faits avec telles & telles loix."
[42] Cf., however, the contradictory assertion in the *Examen d'un libelle*, p. 143: "Mais nous avouons qu'il est aussi au pouvoir d'un peuple de se dépouiller de tous des droits et de

would be void because it would be contrary to the rights of nature. This is to claim that since men are not absolute masters of their lives nor of those of their wives and children, they cannot grant an unlimited power over them to their rulers.

There is, therefore, no relation in the world which is not based upon a mutual pact, which may be either express or tacit.[43] Consequently, when one of the parties to the pact violates it, the other is released from his obligation.[44] Even a father can go so far in the abuse of his rights (which are natural and not created as those of government), that when he seeks to take away the property, honor, and life of his son, the son has not only the right to disobey but also to resist the father. The same procedure applies to a wife when her husband perverts his power. Certainly the purely instituted rights of sovereigns do not extend further than the natural right of fathers and husbands. There is then a reciprocal and mutual relationship between sovereign and subject, which is dissolved when the ruler abuses his right. Therefore, as we noted above, the contract serves as another source of limitation upon the king.[45]

Furthermore, since the sovereign is established for the conservation of society, when he exiles a subject, thereby depriving him of all the advantage of the community, then it is evident that he loses him and has no longer any rights over him. Now if, by the bad use of their authority, sovereigns can be deprived of their rights over individuals then they certainly can forfeit them over the entire society "when they abuse their power, when they become tyrants, when they wish to destroy the whole

---

se faire des souverains d'une puissance absolue et sans réserve." Here Jurieu seems to adopt Grotius's doctrine of a complete alienation. But how can the people conserve its rights when they have relinquished them all to the sovereign? In such a case Jurieu should logically, like Hobbes, have refused a right of revolution.

[43] "Il est donc certain qu'il n'y a aucune relation de maître, de serviteur, de père, d'enfant, de mari, de femme, qui ne soit établi sur un pact mutuel et sur des obligations mutuelles." Cf. Locke's *Civil Government*, pp. 155 ff.: "Conjugal society is made by a voluntary compact between man and woman." Jurieu excepts slavery, which he strongly condemns as a tyrannical usurpation contrary to all the rights of nature. As a result those who attribute such an absolute right to sovereigns outrage the rulers even more than the people themselves.

[44] As with the Monarchomachs, however, Jurieu stressed only a unilateral rupture of the contract and that on the part of the king.

[45] Cf. "Mais aussi il est en leur (le peuple) pouvoir de l'(leur liberté)engager jusques à tel degré, avec telles et telles conditions . . . c'en est assez pour faire comprendre jusqu'où vont où peuvent aller les bornes de l'autorité souveraine." *Lettres pastorales*, XVI of the Third Year.

community." In addition, "a public property" is never conferred without the reservation of the right to resist the disorders which an administrator causes by a bad administration. Therefore, the people cannot grant the control of public affairs without reserving either expressly or tacitly the right to remedy the confusion which the government can bring upon society by misrule.

If a contract between the governor and the governed is the logical conclusion from the principle of popular sovereignty, so also does this doctrine give the key to the origin of the different degrees of power in sovereigns. If the people can give authority to their kings, then they can grant more or less power.[46] Jurieu cites Poland and Germany as examples of states where the people have reserved the right to choose a successor to the crown. But the people could, on the other hand, give up this right and grant the crown to one particular family to be hereditary instead of elective. But the royal house in which the crown is inheritable does not possess it completely as an individual owns his house or field. Whenever the particular person or the family fails, then the people resume their rights, since there had been only "an assignation of sovereignty." Furthermore, since the people only gives up its sovereignty for "the preservation of the community and the safety of the nation," it follows that this surrender cannot be made to a ruler incapable of conserving society. For this reason an insane person cannot inherit a crown. Either a regent is provided or the crown is transmitted to the next heir in line for the succession. Thus, there are often attached to the succession of crowns certain conditions which must be fulfilled before the inheritance is valid. For example, the Salic Law indicates that masculinity was specified by the people as a condition imposed upon the succession to the French throne. But in addition to this type of provision, there are certain conditions "naturally attached," such as those which are "of an absolute necessity for the preservation of the people, of its laws, of its life, and of its religion." Furthermore, in granting the supreme authority to the ruler the people can reserve a part of it for themselves. For instance, the English people retain for their parliament the legislative power and that of consenting to grants.

[46] "La seule chose litigieuse en cette question, c'est de savoir jusqu'où et à quel degré un peuple se peut livrer à ses souverains." *Ibid.*

But when the people relinquish the whole of the supreme power, there is created "absolute power and arbitrary government." But according to Jurieu's enemies, his principles resulted in the condemnation of this form of government as being not only against nature and the laws of God, but also as being the target for resistance with impunity. Jurieu strenuously denied this, asserting that the people can confer absolute power on their ruler without reserving either the legislative or executive powers. Whenever they do this, the sovereign is the master of the laws, having the power to change or annul them, for he is above them. Not only can he levy taxes as he likes, and make peace and war, but he can take any measures which he thinks appropriate for the good of the state. But in spite of his admission that absolute power is legitimate,[47] Jurieu has qualms about it. He speaks of the imprudence on the part of the people when they grant such an arbitrary power, which it is always a temptation to abuse.

In this connection Jurieu makes a few remarks in passing on the question whether absolute power, which is secured by conquest or by a gradual usurpation without the consent of the people, is legitimate. He says he does not see why conquest, which is the application of pure violence, destroys the right of the people to recover their liberty, if the opportunity arises, no matter how extended the duration of the conquest. For example, when Christians enlisted under a Christian prince who sought to free them from the yoke of the Turk, they did not act wrongly, since the rights of the peoples are imprescriptible. As for the case of gradual usurpation, the tolerance of the people who permitted it without resisting serves as a tacit consent to it. In such instances it is more conducive to the public welfare to submit than to offer opposition, which would only trouble the repose of the people.

But there are those, continued Jurieu, who confuse this absolute power with unlimited power, claiming that these are identical.[48] Although the

---

[47] Cf. the opposite view of Locke: "And hence it is evident that absolute monarchy which by some men is counted for the only government in the world is indeed inconsistent with civil society and so can be no form of civil government at all. . . . For being supposed to have all, both legislative and executive power in himself alone, there is no judge to be found, no appeal lies open to any one who may fairly and indifferently and with authority decide, and from whence relief and redress may be expected of any injury or inconveniency that may be suffered from him or by his order." *Civil Government*, Chap. VII, pp. 160–161.

[48] Even Bossuet had distinguished absolute from arbitrary government. "C'est autre

former is regarded as legitimate, "power without limits" is contrary to both divine, natural, and human laws, and the law of nations. There is no supreme power which is not limited. The people cannot confer unlimited power, since they do not have such a power over themselves.[49] Since such authority implies "infinite elevation" of one subject over another, it would be sacrilegious and idolatrous to ascribe it to mere man, when God [50] alone can be the seat of this power. This conception is perhaps one of the most characteristic of Calvinism. To be sure, God has given this unlimited power to men to be exercised over animals, but it is outrageous to place subjects the same distance from their sovereigns that men are from beasts. God has this unlimited dominion over his creatures, even to make them eternally miserable, provided such action contributes to His glory, which is His unique end. Yet even He wishes to rule "according to the law and tempered power." He enters into a sort of compact with men from which it can be concluded that if God should destroy innocent societies without reason or should in any way cease to be just, He would lose the right He has over them "according to the covenants which He has negotiated." Moreover, men would no longer

chose qu'il soit arbitraire. Il est absolu par rapport à la contrainte: n'y ayant aucune puissance qui soit capable de forcer le souverain, qui en ce sens est indépendant de toute autorité humaine. Mais il ne s'ensuit pas que le gouvernement soit arbitraire; parce que, outre que tout est soumis au jugement de Dieu, ce qui convient aussi au gouvernement qu'on vient de nommer arbitraire, c'est qu'il y a des lois dans les empires, contre lesquelles tout ce qui se fait est nul de droit." In an arbitrary government, however, there are no such fundamental laws and all the subjects are slaves. See *La Politique tirée de l'Ecriture sainte,* Bk. VIII, Art. II. Cf. also Locke's view that "even absolute power, where it is necessary, is not arbitrary by being absolute." Chapter XI of his *Civil Government,* p. 188.

[49] ". . . nous ne sommes point les maîtres absolus de notre vie ni de celle de nos femmes et de nos enfants, ni même de leur liberté. On ne peut donner ce que l'on n'a pas. Et par conséquent un peuple ne peut donner à son souverain un pouvoir sans bornes, sur la vie et sur la liberté de ces enfants." *Lettres pastorales,* XVI, Third Year. Cf. Locke's statement of the same principle: "For nobody can transfer to another more power than he has in himself and nobody has an absolute arbitrary power over himself or over any other to destroy his own life or take away the life or property of another. A man . . . cannot subject himself to the arbitrary power of another; and having in the state of nature no arbitrary power over the life, liberty and possessions of another, but only so much as the law of nature gave him for the preservation of himself and the rest of mankind, this is all he doth or can give up to the commonwealth . . ." *Civil Government,* Chap. XI, p. 185.

[50] As with the author of the *Réveille Matin* in the preceding century, Jurieu believed that no people would be so foolish as to grant unlimited authority to any ruler. Therefore, the same confusion is repeated, since to all Calvinists such a thing could not be done anyway.

be bound to any obligation by these contracts. From this Jurieu believed that it would be strange to attribute to kings a power which God Himself has abdicated.

Jurieu continues by saying that he will not suggest the inconveniences attached to unlimited power, since, with Grotius, his opponents would reply that so it is with every government, limited or unlimited. But Jurieu insists that the inconveniences of a power limited by the laws of God and nature are fewer than those attending power without bounds. In the first place only tyrants need fear the power of the people, and even if popular revolt results in civil wars, there is hardly more blood spilled than when, without resisting, the people die of poverty or in prison or in foreign wars waged by a despot solely to satisfy his own ambition.

In the Seventeenth *Lettre pastorale* Jurieu continues his general discussion of the power of sovereigns and the rights of the nations, showing that even Grotius, who did not limit the power of the ruler, nevertheless made two reservations—the alienation of the state and the right of conservation. According to Grotius, resistance is justified when the ruler alienates any part of the state or when he ruins society. Even the laws of God recognize, at least tacitly, the exception of extreme necessity. He went further and cited Barclay and the examples of David and the Maccabees to demonstrate the right of even a small group to self-defense against intolerable cruelty. Jurieu was forced to concede that Grotius denied the right of resistance to Christians, even though he may have justified it in the Jews.

This gave Jurieu another opportunity to denounce those maxims "of excessive morality" and to insist once again that Christians are not to be deprived of humanity. In fact, in a later writing he goes so far as to say: "There are certain principles which have their roots in right reason, that cannot be removed by these exaggerated and misunderstood severities of morality." [51] In that case the right of conservation, which is founded in the nature of man as man and which is inalienable, cannot cease to operate simply because men have espoused Christianity. Even Grotius [52]

---

[51] *Relation de tout ce qui s'est fait* (1698), p. 53. Cf. Grotius's definition of natural law as "the dictate of right reason, indicating that any act, from its agreement or disagreement with the rational nature, has in it moral turpitude or moral necessity." *De jure belli ac pacis libri tres,* Bk. I, Chap. I ("Classics of International Law," ed. J. B. Scott).

[52] *De jure belli ac pacis,* Bk. I, Chaps. III, IV.

held that the strongest passages in the Bible,[53] which admonish Christians to show complete obedience, do not establish the necessity for unlimited patience. The other example most frequently cited was the case of the early Christians. Jurieu hedges here by saying that we do not know the reason why the first Christians perished without resisting, because we do not exactly understand the circumstances in which they were placed. Besides, whenever resistance cannot stop violence, but instead leads only to the spilling of more blood, it is best not to seek self-defense. This is enough to explain the action of the early Christians. But in general there is a right of self-defense, even if some believe that Christians should submit to massacre without rebelling. God had His reasons, and it is to honor Him that this harsh morality was permitted to exist in the Christian Church. But Jurieu insisted that these maxims did not bind the Huguenots nor were they at all essential to Christian ethics.[54]

In order to establish further his principle of popular sovereignty,[55] Grotius was cited at length once again as an authority who would bear great weight, since the famous Arminian jurist had granted an almost unlimited power to the ruler. In his *De jure belli ac pacis* he holds that "on the extinction of the reigning house the right of government reverts to each people separately" who "can select the form of government which it wished," for "in the first instance men joined themselves together to form a civil society not by the command of God, but of their own free will, being influenced by their experience of the weakness of

---

[53] Saint Luke 6.29: "And unto him that smiteth thee on the one cheek offer also the other"; see also Matthew 26.52: "For all they that take the sword shall perish with the sword."

[54] This conclusion was especially attacked by the *Réponse des fidèles captifs* from the pen of Henri Basnage de Beauval.

[55] "Le peuple fait les souverains et donne la souveraineté. Donc le peuple possède la souveraineté et la possède dans un degré plus éminent. Car celui qui communique doit posséder ce qu'il communique d'une manière plus parfaite. Et quoi qu'un peuple qui a fait un souverain ne puisse plus exercer la souveraineté par lui-même, c'est pourtant la souveraineté du peuple qui est exercée par le souverain. Il est le bras et la tête et le peuple est le corps. Et l'exercice de la souveraineté qui dépend d'un seul n'empêche pas que la souveraineté ne soit dans le peuple comme dans sa source et même comme dans son premier sujet, c'est pourquoi le souverain venant à mourir et à finir le peuple rentre dans l'exercice de la souveraineté." *Lettres pastorales*, XVII, Third Year. This is really an attempt to provide a theoretic base for absolute monarchy in popular sovereignty. It is interesting to compare a statement of Locke in this connection. "And thus the community may be said in this respect to be always the supreme power but not as considered under any form of government because this power of the people can never take place till the government be dissolved." *Of Civil Government*, Chap. XIII, p. 193.

isolated households against attack. From this origin the civil power is derived and so Peter calls this an ordinance of man (I Peter 2.13). Elsewhere, however, it is also called a divine ordinance, because God approved of an institution which was beneficial to mankind. God is to be thought of as approving a human law, however, only as human and imposed after the manner of men." Moreover, "this law, which we are discussing—the law of nonresistance—seems to draw its validity from the will of those who associate themselves together in the first place to form civil society; from the same source, furthermore, derives the right which passes into the hands of those who govern." [56]

In addition to Grotius, Jurieu cites experience and history to support the right of the peoples. Like a true Calvinist he can see no more certain guide than the examples of Biblical history. He turns to the accounts of the establishment of various Hebrew kings as related in the historical books of the Old Testament. He cites the case of the Jews who, having overthrown the yoke of the Assyrian king, bestowed the crown on the Maccabees instead of on the family of David. From profane history Jurieu mentions the transmission by the French of the crown from the first race of kings to the second and from the second to the third, in spite of the fact that there were still males in line for the succession in both races.

After presenting these various authorities to substantiate the prerogative of the peoples, Jurieu turns to an examination of the arguments used to defend unlimited power. Here again the patience enjoined by the Scriptures upon Christians is employed. But, our theologian argues, to use it to show that upon no occasion is it permitted to impede the powers which ruin society and religion logically leads to the position that the laws of Christianity forbid resistance to violence in any case whatsoever. In that event a person cannot protect his property, and frontiers should be opened to the enemy. In such a manner Jurieu felt he had easily exposed the weakness of this proof in the armory of his opponents.

Jurieu turns next to a more detailed examination of the Scriptural references which are used to support the unlimited power of kings. For example, certain authors have sought to equate the passage in I Samuel 8.11–17, in which the prophet predicted the evil a monarch would bring

[56] Grotius, *De jure belli ac pacis,* Chaps. III, pp. 103–104, and IV, pp. 149–150.

to the people, with the right of sovereigns as expressed in I Samuel 10.25. In the latter passage Jurieu maintains that what Samuel proposed to the people is called "the right of the kingdom," while in the first passage the reference is to "the treatment" which the king would give them. Samuel did not indicate that the king would have the *right* to rule tyrannically over them. Then others who favor an unlimited power, to which men can oppose only prayers and tears, point to the following selection from I Samuel 8.18 for justification: "And ye shall cry out in that day because of your king which ye shall have chosen you; and the Lord will not hear you in that day." To this Jurieu answers that by the same method it would be impossible to resist an enemy who came to take away our property, liberty, or lives, simply because God has often said through His prophets that He would not hear us. In addition, even if the authority of the Eighth Chapter of Samuel is valid, it can only prove that the power of kings is without limit with regard to property,[57] but not with regard to religion and life. Nowhere in the book of Samuel is it said that the king would abolish the true religion or destroy society itself.

The defenders of unlimited power also rely upon the example of David, who though unjustly persecuted by Saul, did not kill him but fled into the desert instead. Jurieu replies that this example is inapplicable against the Huguenots, since none of them ever claimed that it was permissible to assassinate kings,[58] no matter how wicked. The Catholics are then reproached for such assassins as Clément, Jean Châtel, and Ravaillac.

But, maintains Jurieu, the example of David does show what is legitimate in the way of resistance apart from an attack on the person of the king. Why did David assemble about him four or five hundred armed men if not for self-defense against his king, who wanted to kill him? He respected the unction of God in monarchs, but he did not believe that it was always illegitimate to resist them. However, Jurieu admitted that,

[57] Cf. the reference in the *Lettres pastorales,* XVIII, Third Year, pp. 412–414: "Parceque les biens sont infiniment moins chers que la liberté, la vie, & la religion quand il n'y va que de la perte des biens, il ne faut point résister lors qu'il y a péril que le repos public & le salut des particuliers pourroyent souffrir."

[58] In the *Lettres pastorales,* XV, Third Year, pp. 357–358, Jurieu reports that a certain Benedictine monk by the name of Jean Dariol was arrested at Rotterdam for having offered to assassinate the king of France and that there was as much rejoicing among the refugees over his capture as in Paris itself.

as a single individual, the right of revolt was not extended to David.

Thus, there is nothing in the historical books of the Old Testament to support a power without limits. Nor does Jurieu consider the many other references [59] in Scripture to the necessity of obedience to kings, even wicked ones, as substantiating the unlimited rule of princes. He recalls that there are the same admonitions for submission on the part of servants to masters, children to fathers, and wives to husbands; yet it does not follow that the power of masters, fathers, and husbands is without bounds. Even the Ten Commandments are phrased in general terms which brook exceptions touching justice, law, and necessity. For example, it is forbidden to kill, but in war and in legitimate defense killing takes place without offending God.

After divine authority the supporters of unlimited power find a weapon in the Roman legal maxim, *princeps legibus solutus est.* Jurieu answers first that another maxim, *salus populi suprema lex esto,* is more famous. Second, in the first maxim the term "prince" includes every sovereign. Therefore, it follows that unlimited obedience must be given in republics to the rulers, which would not be pleasing to the republicans. Third, by "prince" is understood either the single or plural entities which hold the whole undivided sovereignty. They are above the laws, since it is they who make them. For example, neither the king nor the English parliament possesses the entire supreme authority; together they are above the laws, but not separately. The laws above which the sovereign is placed and by which he is not bound are not the laws of God, nature, or those of the nations, but the laws which the sovereign himself has made; that is, the civil laws. With regard to the laws of God and nature, which concern religion and the conservation of society, the sovereign is not the master, concludes Jurieu in the Seventeenth *Lettre pastorale.*[60]

In the first part of the Eighteenth *Lettre pastorale,* which Jurieu intended for a justification of William of Orange and the English nation,

---

[59] Cf. the words of Solomon in Ecclesiastes 8.4: "He [the king] doeth whatsoever pleaseth him; where the word of a king is, there is power and who may say unto him, what doest thou?"

[60] These Bodinian statements are difficult to reconcile with the unlimited authority which our theologian grants, as we shall see, to the people in their representative assemblies. Like Althusius, he is silent on the question of what would happen if the organized community through its representatives should act contrary to the law of God.

he continues the discussion of general principles with regard to the power of princes and the rights of nations. In destroying unlimited power Jurieu feels that with the same blow he has abolished unlimited passive obedience, since the one is the concomitant of the other. As there is no sovereign power without restraints, it follows that there is a certain point at which resistance is sanctioned. Paradoxically enough, continues Jurieu, the English theologians who detest even "absolute power," which is far less in scope than "power without limits," have attempted to establish unlimited passive obedience. Although they wish the people to have their privileges and the king to rule only according to the laws, still they shrink from the right of the people to withstand by force any attack upon the laws. Jurieu thinks that the execution of Charles I was the cause of this contradiction. In order to prevent future outrages like the murder of God's anointed, they thought the only remedy was to place the ruler above the laws and to carry passive submission to the extreme. They were influenced in addition by the only plausible argument in the armory of the supporters of unlimited power—the inconveniences, such as civil wars and anarchy, which would follow if it were absent. Even if "power without limits" is attended by disastrous results, these results affect only some individuals, the whole body of the people being better protected against them.

In order to answer this contention Jurieu appealed to experience. He asks if Poland, Germany, and England, as limited monarchies, are not more flourishing than those states which are governed by absolute or unrestricted rulers. With the exception of the execution of Charles I, the history of England has shown fewer civil wars than that of France, which has been more frequently desolated by civil strife and assassinations than any other nation. The boundless power of the Turkish rulers has only resulted in poverty and misery in contrast to riches of countries under circumscribed authority. Thus Jurieu concludes that the inconveniences of an unlimited rule are far greater than those of a limited one.

With regard to the execution of Charles I, Jurieu once again feels it is not just to attribute this crime to Calvinist theology. Fanatics, Independents, and "Papists" are responsible. Even the most extreme and severe theological teachings with regard to the absolute power of kings cannot prevent mutinous groups from seizing and decapitating a prince.[61] Cromwell made use of such fanatics to vacate a throne upon which he himself wished to sit. In this case, also, Jurieu strongly condemned a bodily assault upon the king, the factor that had made the English regicide so terrible.[62]

There is, however, a right of self-defense that can be exercised legitimately. For this, Jurieu lays down six regulations. First, a private individual should never be committed to the sword. "The safety of the people is the sovereign law." A private individual is not a whole people. Even though a ruler may be regarded as a tyrant with respect to a certain private person, to others, however, he may be seen as the "father of the country." Therefore, it would be unjust for the public to lose its protector in order to satisfy the interest of a few individuals. (It can be readily seen that this entire argument is typically Calvinistic.) Second, even a whole nation cannot rightfully call a ruler to account for the wrong he has done to certain individuals. The people is not a tribunal, to which individuals damaged by royal attacks against liberty and life can bring their grievances. Such action would result in more loss than gain, because of the resulting disturbances.[63] Third, in all cases of iniquitous action on the part of the sovereign the rule that the safety of the people is the sovereign law must be kept in mind. If resistance to the unjust command of the sovereign might result in a greater evil to the community because of the possibility of civil wars, it would be better to submit. Fourth, when the wrongdoing of the sovereign is of such moderate character that it does not extend so far as to include "the total subversion of the laws and the loss of life and religion," then again submission is required, since, as above, resistance would be attended by greater evils than the minor wrongful acts committed by the sovereign.[64] Fifth,

---

[61] Jurieu felt that the position of the Anglican Church in condemning resistance of any sort was incompatible with "right reason" and the liberties of England, since it wanted to preserve all the gains of the Civil War period but refused to permit revolt, should the king overstep the newly drawn boundaries of his authority.

[62] "Nous ne disons pas qu'il soit permis de résister aux rois jusqu'à leur couper la tête. Il y a bien de la différence entre attaquer & se défendre. La défense est légitime contre tous ceux qui violent le droit des gens & les loix des Nations; mais il n'est pas permis d'attaquer des Rois & des Rois innocents, pour leur faire souffrir un honteux supplice."

[63] "Le peuple n'a droit de conserver que ce qui fait la seureté & le salut du peuple même, c'est à dire de la société." *Lettres pastorales*, XVIII, Third Year.

[64] Cf. Locke, *Civil Government*, p. 231: "such revolutions happen not upon every little mismanagement in public affairs."

when it is only a question of the loss of property, it is not necessary to rebel when there is danger that the "public peace" and "the welfare of individuals" will suffer. In the last analysis "property is infinitely less dear than liberty, life, and religion," an assertion which should be compared with Locke's position. Finally, open revolt against sovereign authority is to be resorted to only after the examination of all milder measures to mollify the prince. By such precautions Jurieu felt that he had answered those who demanded complete submission to political authority on the ground of the inconveniences which would result from a policy of rebellion.

With these restrictions then, Jurieu sanctioned the right of revolution, but he still felt the need for reliance upon some suitable authority. Again he employs Grotius,[65] a writer who, at least apparently, defended the unlimited power of sovereigns but who made certain exceptions to his general position against resistance by the people to the supreme power. "First then, if rulers responsible to the people—whether such power was conferred at the beginning or under a later arrangement . . . —transgress against the laws and the state, they [may] be resisted by force." It is to be noted that Jurieu did not adopt Grotius in full on this point, since Grotius included even the death penalty, in case of necessity. "In the second place if a king, or any other person, has renounced his governmental authority, or manifestly has abandoned it, after that time proceedings of every kind are permissible against him as against a private person." Jurieu thinks that the sixth exception of Grotius has special bearing on the contemporary English situation. "Sixthly in case the sovereign power is held in part by the king, in part by the people or senate, force can lawfully be used against the king if he attempts to usurp that part of the sovereign power which does not belong to him, for the reason that this authority does not extend so far. . . . In my opinion," continues Grotius, "this principle holds, even though it has already been said that the power to make war should be reserved to the king. For this, it must be understood, refers to external war. For the rest, whoever pos-

[65] Cf. "The Proceedings of the present Parliament justified by the Opinion of the Most Judicious and Learned Hugo Grotius," in *A Collection of State Tracts Published on Occasion of the Late Revolution in 1688 and during the Reign of King William III,* London, 1705, I, p. 178. Even though Grotius did deny to Christians the right to defend their religion against sovereigns by force of arms, Jurieu maintained in his *Examen d'un libelle,* p. 184, that "ce système de Grotius nous suffit pour la justification de la conduite de nos Pères & de la nôtre."

sesses a part of the sovereign power must possess also the right to defend
his part, in case such a defense is resorted to, the king may even lose
his part of the sovereign power by right of war." This last exception of
Grotius deals with a situation where "if in the conferring of authority
it has been stated that in a particular case the king can be resisted, even
though such an agreement does not involve the retention of a part of
the authority, some natural freedom of action, at any rate, has been reserved and exempted from the exercise of royal power. For he who
alienates his own right can by agreement limit the right transferred." [66]
At the conclusion of these citations Jurieu maintains that fundamentally
the opinion of Grotius is identical with his own view.

At this point Jurieu proceeded, as he had promised, to apply his general principles to the justification of William III and the English nation.
In the first place, since the people can attach the crown to one person or
to a family and since they can even transmit it from one family to another or in the same family from one subject to another,[67] certainly the
English had the right to transfer the crown from a father to the daughter
and son-in-law, overlooking the son of James II. In the same way in
France there were legitimate heirs descended from Charles Martel, to
whom the crown had been transported from the Merovingians, when
the French granted the crown to Hugues Capet.[68]

In the second place, there is always a natural mutual pact between the
king and the people even when none is expressed; and especially is there
one between the ruler and the people when the supreme authority is divided and when the people have conserved certain privileges. The English nation has not only such a natural pact with its sovereign, but also
"a positive compact from certain rights which the people has reserved."
The only question to be determined now, argues Jurieu, is whether
James II violated this pact. It is generally conceded that the king disre-

[66] Grotius, *De jure belli ac pacis,* II, 156–159.

[67] The people of Israel for example transferred the crown from the family of Saul to
the person and family of David; from the person of David to that of Absalom, his son;
and a second time from the house of Absalom to the person of David; from Roboam,
son of Solomon to Jeroboam, son of Nebab; and from the family of David to that of the
Maccabees.

[68] The crown, for example, belonged to Adonia the Elder rather than to Solomon, but
the people transferred it from Adonia to Solomon by order of God. But this command
was not important, "car où il n'y pas d'ordre de Dieu le peuple demeure en possession
de ses droits & les peut exercer."

garded all the laws of the realm in his desire to establish the Catholic religion by measures such as the repeal of the Test Act. The mutual pact included the conservation of the laws; therefore, this breach of the laws annuls the contract and legitimizes the establishment of a new king under a new compact.

Thirdly, nations give the supreme authority to their rulers only for "the preservation of their property, lives, liberty, and religion." [69] These things Jurieu tended to regard as gifts of God, which cannot be ravaged without making war on the Lord Himself. But, as has just been pointed out, with Jurieu, the rights which are to be guaranteed are the rights of the people or the nation, and not yet strictly the rights of individuals, as in Locke.[70] If the ruler acts contrary to these prerogatives of the people, he is in danger of being overthrown. James II attacked religion, the laws, the lives, and liberty of his subjects, which he had sworn to conserve. Consequently, according to Jurieu, he deserved his fate.

In general, Jurieu refused to mark precisely the bounds of the sovereign authority, but he did venture the following suggestion. "It seems to me, however, that without risking much, it can be said that these limits are to be found precisely where the safety and the preservation of the people, which is the supreme law, end." But it must be noted that this is the same argument which Hobbes used when he declared that "all the duties of rulers are contained in this one sentence, the safety of the people is the supreme law." [71] Furthermore, there is a conflict between the

---

[69] See also the converse statement: "Jamais peuple ne peut avoir intention de donner à un Souverain le pouvoir d'opprimer ses lois, sa liberté, sa religion, sa vie." Here it is to be noted, there is a conspicuous addition—the protection of the laws. It is interesting to compare Locke's judgment that men have only established political authority "for the mutual preservation of their lives, liberties, and estates which I call by the general name—property." *Civil Government*, Chap. IX, p. 180.

[70] Henri Sée, *Les Idées politiques en France au XVIIe siècle*, pp. 207–208. It is significant that Jurieu in speaking of the *populus* more frequently refers to "les peuples" than to "le peuple." Although it is impossible to maintain that Jurieu was an individualist advocating the rights of men, as has been advanced by P. Pic in his *Les Idées politiques de Jurieu et les grands principes de 89*, one of his contemporaries, Elie Benoit, who was also a member of the violent party, did talk of individual rights in a "Mémoire sur le sujet de rétablissement des Églises de France" where he wrote: "Il faut la [liberté de conscience] présupposer appartenant à l'homme, de droit naturel et divin." Quoted in Frank Puaux, "Essai sur les Négociations des Réfugiés," *Bulletin . . . du protestantisme Français*, June 15, 1867, p. 263.

[71] Thomas Hobbes, *De cive*, Chap. XIII, in *English Works*, II, 166. Cf. Bossuet's comment on this point in his *Cinquième avertissement aux protestants*, Art. XLVIII, p. 316: "Lorsqu'on allègue cette Loi fameuse: que la Loi suprême est le salut du Peuple: je

construction of the doctrine of inalienable rights as limits to the power of the king on the one side and, on the other, their effect as such only according to the measure of the *salus publica*.[72] Resistance is permitted not on account of the destruction of individual rights in themselves, but only because of the ruination of the welfare of the whole—"the community." This safety of the people rather than natural rights is the unifying content of the contract between the people and the government, the violation of which by one of the parties is the one legal ground for the right of resistance.[73] Thus, Jurieu is much less of an individualist than his great contemporary John Locke.

There is a further difference, moreover, between Jurieu and that more famous defender of the English Revolution on this theory of individual natural rights. While the former attempted to exclude the unlimited power of the king alone with this principle, Locke manifested a spirit of individualism which effects a limitation upon all government with reference to the rights of private persons. Did not Locke conclude that "the law of nature stands as an eternal rule to all men, legislators as well as others"? [74] Furthermore, even though it has been said that "Jurieu

l'avoue: mais ce Peuple a mis son salut à réunir toute sa Puissance dans un seul: par conséquent à ne rien pouvoir contre ce seul à qui il transportoit tout." Gabriel Naudé justified Charles IX and the massacre of Saint Bartholomew by this principle in his *Science des princes; ou, Considérations politiques sur les coups d'état*, II, 335: "Cette loi soi commune, et qui devrait être la principale règle de toutes les actions des princes, *salus populi suprema lex esto*, les about de beaucoup de petites circonstances et formalités auxquelles la justice les oblige." See also Rousseau in his famous *Lettre à M. Le Marquis de Mirabeau* in 1767: ". . . que deviendront vos droits sacrés de propriété dans de grands dangers, dans les calamités extraordinaires, quand vos valeurs disponibles ne suffiront plus, et que le *salus populi suprema lex esto* sera prononcé par le despote." C. E. Vaughan, *The Political Writings of Jean Jacques Rousseau*, II, 159–160. In reply to Helvetius who wrote: "Tout devient légitime, et même vertueux, pour le salut public," Rousseau commented: "Le salut public n'est rien, si tous les particuliers ne sont en sûreté." *Oeuvres de J. J. Rousseau*, XII, 59. As John Selden said in *Table Talk*, p. 93: "There is not anything in the world more abused than this sentence, 'salus populi suprema lex esto,' for we apply it, as if we ought to forsake the known law when it may be most for the advantage of the people, when it means no such thing: for, first, 'tis not salus populi suprema lex *est* but *esto*."

[72] See Kurt Wolzendorff, *Staatsrecht und Naturrecht*, p. 306.

[73] *Ibid.*, p. 299. It should be noted that in Locke the people have the "supreme power to remove or alter the legislative when they find the legislative act contrary to the trust reposed in them," which means that the people can take action, not upon the rare occasion of a breach of contract but upon the more frequent event of the nonexecution of a trust. See *Civil Government*, Chap. XIII, p. 192.

[74] *Ibid.*, Chap. XI, p. 183.

shows a foreign influence of a purely individualistic rationalism of freedom and equality which is quite remote from Calvinistic thought," [75] it
was Locke who almost completely broke from Calvinism by removing
the idea of the glory of God as the end of the state, substituting in its
place a purely utilitarian conception which was closely tied to such an
individualistic rationalism.[76] This greater secularism of Locke's theory
no doubt accounts for the fact that it was through his writings rather
than through Jurieu's that the principles of the English Revolution were
spread in France in the eighteenth century, which is said to begin with
the Glorious Revolution.

But both Jurieu and Locke were only reflecting the current of the
times in which they lived. The seventeenth century was a critical period
of transition [77] not only in ecclesiastical history [78] but also in political
theory. The immense progress in the mathematical and physical sciences
at the time of Newton was having a profound effect upon all branches
of thought and action. Political theory was gradually being detached
from its long association with theology. Already at the beginning of
the century, in Althusius and especially in Grotius, the great Arminian
jurist, the process of the gradual secularization of natural law had occurred, and had inevitably transformed Calvinism both in its theological
and political aspects. Certainly Jurieu,[79] who relied so heavily upon Grotius, did not escape the effects of this change. In addition, it is possible
that there were reciprocal influences between the English refugees in

[75] Ernst Troeltsch, *The Social Teachings of the Christian Churches*, II, 711.

[76] *Ibid.*, pp. 636–639. Cf., however, the opposite view that Locke's political thought is
principally Calvinistic as stated on page 41 of this study. See the judgment of Max
Weber that "utilitarianism is the secular form of Calvinism"; note his *The Protestant
Ethic and the Sprit of Capitalism*, pp. 259–260.

[77] Paul Hazard goes as far as to maintain: ". . . à peu près toutes les idées qui ont paru
révolutionnaires vers 1760 ou même 1789 s'étaient exprimées déjà vers 1680. Alors une
crise s'est operée dans la conscience européenne; entre la Renaissance dont elle procède
directement et la révolution française qu'elle prèpare il n'y en a pas de plus importante
dans l'histoire des idées." See his *La Crise de la conscience*, I, 294.

[78] The new epoch in church history after the conclusion of the religious wars takes
on a character which, as Friedrich Loofs says in his *Grundlinien der Kirchengeschichte*,
p. 203, "stands in no less marked contrast with the previous period of the Reformation and Counter-Reformation than that former period with the Middle Ages and the
Middle Ages with the period of the ancient church."

[79] See Hilde Daum, *Pierre Jurieu und seine Auseinandersetzung*, especially the section
headed "Jurieu, 'Théologien-Réformé' in der Wende vom orthodox-konfessionellen zum
aufgeklärten Zeitalter," pp. 35–46.

Holland, like Locke and Burnet, and the Huguenot exiles, like Jurieu
and Abbadie. It must be remembered, however, that although both
Locke and Jurieu were in the favor and confidence of William of Orange, the former (during his five-year sojourn in Holland from 1684
until the English Revolution) frequented the liberal Protestant or Arminian circles in Amsterdam, which included Limborch and Le Clerc,
who were no less than anathema to the orthodox Jurieu. But certainly
Locke, who had lived in France and knew French, must have known
about Jurieu's *Lettres pastorales;* yet the fact that Jurieu's defense of the
English Revolution appeared one year before Locke's does not necessarily prove a reciprocal influence, but indicates just as plausibly a parallel development of ideas.[80]

To return, from this long digression, to Jurieu's application of his
general principles to the justification of William and the English nation,
it only remained for him to show that James II had abandoned the
crown in order to justify resistance according to the doctrines of Grotius.
Then he went on to prove that James had attempted to encroach upon
that part of the supreme power which did not belong to him—the legislative authority of Parliament. Consequently, following Grotius again,
he could be deposed "by the laws of war"; furthermore, resistance by
force is permissible when the king encroaches upon any of the natural
liberties or privileges which the people have reserved from the sovereign
authority. Since James II was guilty of attacks upon the liberties set
apart by the English people, the action taken against him was perfectly
legitimate.

In the remainder of the Eighteenth *Lettre pastorale* Jurieu demonstrates how it was a fundamental law of the state that the English king
should be of the Protestant faith. He also devotes some space to a refutation of the pamphlet *La Lettre d'un Mylord absent de la Convention
à l'un de ses amis,* in which the legality of the Convention Parliament
that had declared for William of Orange was attacked. In demonstrat-
ing its lawful character [81] Jurieu maintained that there are "some forms

[80] Charles Bastide, *John Locke: ses Théories politiques,* pp. 295–296. According to H. R.
Fox Bourne in his *Life of Locke,* II, 165–167, the first of the *Two Treatises* seems to
have been written between 1680 and 1685 and the second during the last year of his
exile in Holland before he returned to England.
[81] For another attempt to justify the circulation of power from the Convention to

and procedures, which in order to be legitimate need not be established by laws and by the terms of the law; absolute necessity alone renders them rightful." Besides, declares our minister of Rotterdam in one of the most remarkable statements in all his writing on politics, "it is not a question even of knowing if the nation was right at bottom in all this. For even if it were wrong, it is necessary that there be a certain authority in communities, which is not obliged to be right in order to make its acts valid. But this authority is only in the nations (peoples)." [82] It might be asked at this point why, if this is true, Jurieu took so much pains to justify the English Revolution at all by such elaborate arguments.

It was this defense of absolutism in the *populus*, which aroused the opposition of Jurieu's enemies on every side. Its dangerous consequences were especially attacked in a libel [83] appearing in the form of a letter. But Jurieu replied to his opponents in the Twenty-first *Lettre pastorale*: "This maxim can only have bad results in supposing that one means that everything a people does through sedition [84] must be worth something; but that is to misunderstand the terms. Whoever says 'an act' signifies a juridical act, a decision taken in an assembly of the whole people, like the *Parlements* and the Estates. But it is certain that if the nations (peoples) are the first seat of sovereignty, they do not need to be right in order to make their acts valid, that is to render them executory. Because, once again, decisions, whether of the sovereign courts,[85]

William of Orange as king and from him back to the Convention as parliament, see Tronchin du Breuil, *Lettres sur les matières du temps*, Lettre X of May 15, 1690, pp. 152–160.

[82] Cf. with a pronouncement of Thomas Paine—"That which a nation chooses to do it has a right to do." *The Rights of Man*, in *The Writings of Thomas Paine* (ed. Conway), II, 278. See also the pronouncement of Joseph de Maistre in his *Etude sur la souveraineté* in his *Oeuvres complètes*, I, 417: "Toute espèce de souveraineté est absolue de sa nature . . . il y aura toujours en dernière analyse, un pouvoir absolu qui pourra faire le mal impunément, qui sera despotique sous ce point de vue, dans toute la force du terme."

[83] Probably the *Lettre d'un ministre aux Catholiques* by Henri Basnage de Beauval.

[84] Jurieu had admitted in the Eighteenth *Lettre pastorale* that "Tout de même que les rois deviennent tyrans en abusant du pouvoir qu'ils ont véritablement; ainsi les peuples ne laissent pas d'être rebelles quand ils font un mauvais usage de leur véritables droits."

[85] In his discussion of the attack by Basnage de Beauval on his principle, Jurieu sarcastically had noted: "Quand ce grand jurisconsulte [Basnage was a jurist] aura été condamné par les cours Souveraines, il en appellera au tribunal de la raison pour empêcher la validité des actes pris contre lui." *Lettres Pastorales*, XXI, Third Year, July 1, 1689, pp. 500–502.

of sovereigns, or of sovereign assemblies, are executory, however unjust they may be." [86]

Like Basnage de Beauval, Bossuet is especially critical of this portion of Jurieu's theory. In his famous *Cinquième Avertissement aux Protestants sur les lettres du Ministre Jurieu contre l'histoire des variations,*[87] in which he accuses Jurieu in general of overturning the very basis of government with his theory of popular sovereignty, the Bishop of Meaux maintained that in the system of the great pastor of Rotterdam it is left to the people to decide whether or not they are abusing their power. What else can be signified by the principle that the people need not be right in order to validate its acts, that is, render them executory? [88] If an assembly of the estates in executing the sovereignty of the people has the right to make laws, just and unjust, then what is to prevent it from acts of oppression which might affect even religion? This was the most telling criticism possible of Jurieu's doctrine of popular sovereignty, which could only lead to the very consequences he was so anxious to avoid. It is not the source of, but the restraints on, power which prevent it from being despotic. Even Alexander Hamilton who argued that "a

[86] Cf. the following passage from Jurieu's *Examen d'un libelle* (1691), p. 154, which helps to clarify the meaning of this statement: "Il est vray que les Souverains ne sauroyent contraindre les sujets à croire que leurs ordonnances sont justes & équitables, mais pour l'ordre ils peuvent les obliger à y obéir quoy qu'ils les croyent injustes." Jurieu insisted on the same despotic authority in the people in his *Les Soupirs de la France esclave* (1689); see *ibid.,* Mémoire, II, 102–104: "il faut qu'une Puissance soit sans bornes quand elle va à pouvoir déposer celuy qui est le principal Dépositaire de la souveraineté. Et il est aysé de comprendre que ceux qui pouvoient tant sur la personne & sur la dignité Royale devoient avoir la même puissance par tout & en toutes choses." Such statements should be compared with Jurieu's other pronouncements on the people as a great beast. Cf. Hobbes' statement: "It is not wisdom but authority that makes a law." *Dialogue of the Common Laws* in *Works,* VI, 5.

[87] This is but an elaboration of the tenth book of Bossuet's famous *Histoire des variations des églises protestantes,* 1688. Jurieu was long known only through this *Cinquième avertissement aux protestants.* In 1791 the Abbé Emery, in order to oppose the then prevalent doctrines of popular sovereignty and social contract, reprinted this reply of Bossuet to Jurieu in part, together with selections from the *Essai sur le gouvernement civil* of Fénelon, under the title of *Principes de Messieurs Bossuet et Fénelon sur la souveraineté.*

[88] "Veut-il dire que tous les arrêts, justes ou injustes, des Souverains & des Assemblées souverains sont exécutés en effet? Bien certainement cela n'est pas. Veut-il dire qu'ils le doivent être & enfin qu'ils le sont en droit? Voilà donc, selon lui-même, un droit de mal faire, un droit contre la justice, qui est précisément comme on a vu ce qu'il a voulu éviter & néanmoins par necessité il y retombe." *Avertissement aux protestants,* V, Tome II, p. 340.

dependence on the People is, no doubt, the primary control on Government" thought that "experience has taught mankind the necessity of auxiliary precautions." [89]

Modern critics have noted the apparent similarity between Jurieu and Rousseau on this point of popular absolutism.[90] With Jurieu the people can do no wrong, while to the great Genevese "there neither is nor can be any kind of fundamental law binding on the body of the people— not even the social contract itself." Furthermore, "the general will is always right and tends to the public advantage." [91] It is only because of this infallibility, however, that Rousseau sanctions an unlimited authority in the people, since it is definitely implied that if the general will were corruptible he would not have approved of an unrestrained power. But since Jurieu holds that the people need not be right in order to validate its acts, he seems to be even more absolutist than Rousseau. At any rate Jurieu here contradicts those limitations which he had placed on the people in the form of an enumeration of the rights they do not possess; namely, those of "making war on God, trampling the laws under foot, committing injustice, destroying true religion, and persecuting those who follow it." [92] But it must be remembered that when Jurieu puts limits upon power of the people, he is thinking only of the resulting restrictions upon the king's authority; for since the people establish kings, they cannot give them rights which they do not themselves possess. But what if the people should not delegate its authority to a ruler, but should exercise its rights directly in an assembly? In that event the power of the people is unlimited according to the implications of Jurieu's theory and the natural individual rights of life, liberty, property, and religion disappear. The net result is the condemnation of monarchical

[89] *The Federalist*, No. 51.

[90] There are some earlier anticipations of Rousseau's position in George Buchanan's *De jure regni apud scotos*, p. 86, where the *populus* is said to be "rege praestantior"; note also the statement "cum lex sit rege, populus lege potentior."

[91] *The Social Contract* (Everyman Ed.) Book I, Chap. VII, and Book II, Chap. III. See Paul Léon, "L'Idée de la volonté générale chez J. J. Rousseau et ses antécédents historiques," *Archives de Philosophie de Droit et de Sociologie juridique*, 1936. Cf. Rousseau in his *Economie politique* (1755) in C. E. Vaughan, *The Political Writings of Jean Jacques Rousseau*, I, 243, where he stated that the "most general will is also the most just and that the voice of the people is the voice of God."

[92] *Lettres pastorales*, XVI, Third Year, p. 368. Cf. *ibid.*, p. 370: "Les peuples n'ont pas le droit de tuer les innocents, de violer les lois de Dieu, de les anéantir, de perdre la Société sans qu'on leur résiste, donc ils ne peuvent donner ce droit aux souverains."

absolutism by a theorist who sets up a popular despotism himself.[93] But in all fairness to Jurieu it should be noted that he never adopted the idea of inalienability of popular sovereignty, which is characteristic of Rousseau's theory. Furthermore, he did not abandon the idea of a contractual relation between the people and the ruler, which was done by both Hobbes and Rousseau. So long as the theory of the governmental in contrast to the social contract was adopted by Jurieu, it was impossible for him to make the people all-powerful, since according to the terms of the compact the ruler had rights as well as the *populus*.

Although Jurieu believed that private individuals had no vocation in government, he was not saved from making the fatal mistake of identifying a representative assembly [94] with the *populus* and concluding that, since the people cannot be limited, neither can the assembly. As with Calvin and the Protestant Monarchomachs, the people in Jurieu's theory is never understood as a mass of separate individuals, but as a corporate body in the medieval sense. Therefore, seditious popular action is condemned in favor of legal action by the constituted natural or elected representatives of the people, such as the *Parlements* and the Estates of the realm. This device, however, in no way avoids the dangerous identification of an assembly with the people. Moreover, as Bossuet easily demonstrated, if a parliament is the people itself, then there is a negation of popular sovereignty, since the supreme authority is located not in the people but in an organ of government. It must be said, at least, in Rousseau's favor that he avoided the despotic implications

[93] Roger Lureau, *Les Doctrines politiques de Jurieu*, p. 77. See Charles Louandre, *Oeuvres politiques de Benjamin Constant*, pp. 3–4: "L'erreur de ceux qui de bonne foi dans leur amour de la liberté, ont accordé à la souveraineté du peuple un pouvoir sans bornes, vient de la manière dont se sont formées leurs idées en politique. Ils ont vu dans l'histoire un petit nombre d'hommes, ou même un seul, en possession d'un pouvoir immense, qui faisait beaucoup de mal; mais leur courroux s'est dirigé contre les possesseurs du pouvoir et non contre le pouvoir même. Au lieu de le détruire, ils n'ont songé qu'à le déplacer."

[94] Cf. Jurieu's definite statement in *La Janséniste convaincu* (1682), p. 310: "ce que l'on appelle les Etats d'un Royaume, le peuple en un mot. . . ." See also the same proposition in his *Traité de l'unité de l'Eglise* (1688), p. 486: "alors le peuple, c'est à dire, les Etats du Royaume. . . ." Cf. Alexander Hamilon in *The Federalist*, No. 84: "It is evident, therefore, that according to their primitive signification they [bills of rights] have no application to constitutions professedly founded upon the power of the people and executed by their immediate representatives and servants. Here, in strictness, the people surrender nothing and as they retain everything, they have no need of particular reservations."

of an identification of a representative assembly with the people by denying that the general will could ever be represented at all. In both Jurieu
and Rousseau, however, as with all theories of popular sovereignty, the
despotic and arbitrary character of the principle remains.[95]

But returning to the contemporary reaction to the *Lettres pastorales,*
Bossuet's other criticisms of Jurieu's political principles are equally co-
gent. He takes special exception to the contention that the right of conservation is inalienable. Would not this mean that every minority or
province, and logically each individual, has a right to oppose the ruler,
which would result in anarchy? As we shall see, Bayle was to make the
very same objection and it is interesting to note that in his answer
Jurieu contended that he never gave sovereignty to the people at all.[96]
Only the all pervading purpose of defending religious truth can explain
away such a contradiction with the numerous instances where sovereignty is definitely ascribed to the people in Jurieu's theory.[97]

Bossuet warns further that Jurieu's principles are detrimental not only
to kings but to all kinds of governmental authority, whether senates,
magistrates, parliaments or Estates, whenever laws are enacted which
are believed to be contrary to religion or the safety of the subjects. In addition, the whole concept of popular sovereignty as outlined by Jurieu
is absurd, for, according to Bossuet, before the establishment of government men are in a state of anarchy or continual war of all against
all, as Hobbes, who greatly influenced the Bishop of Meaux, had asserted. Furthermore, the idea that the sovereignty of the people origi-

[95] "The tyranny of a multitude is a multiplied tyranny," Edmund Burke in a Letter to
Captain Mercer, February 26, 1790, in *Correspondence,* III, 147. Cf. also B. Constant's
analysis in his *De l'esprit de conquête,* p. 110. "Or voici pourquoi son autorité (celle du
dépositaire du pouvoir) ne fut pas arbitraire: Ce n'était plus un homme, c'était un peuple.
Merveilleuse garantie que ce changement de mot." See his critique of L'Abbé de Mably
as well as Rousseau. Note also the views of John Stuart Mill on this subject in his *On
Liberty,* Everyman Edition, pp. 66–68.

[96] "Nous avons déjà comparé la puissance ecclésiastique à la puissance civile. Nous
faisons le peuple source de la puissance ecclésiastique: à cause de cela faisons-nous le
peuple Prêtre, Ministre et en droit d'administrer les choses sacrées? Il y a bien de la
différence entre avoir le pouvoir et l'autorité en main et conserver le droit de se pouvoir
contre l'abus de l'autorité." See also the following: "Chaque particulier et toutes les
parties qui composent un public se sont confédérées sous un chef qui s'appelle souverain,
par une rénonciation absolue à toute sorte de droits de souveraineté." *Examen d'un
libelle* (1691), pp. 84, 141.

[97] Mercier, "Théories politiques des calvinistes," *Bulletin . . . du protestantisme français,* July–September, 1934, pp. 407–408.

nates in a contract between the people and the ruler is impossible in Bossuet's mind, since it presupposes that the people without government have sovereignty, which instead is only an attribute of an organized body politic.[98] Jurieu had confused the independence of each man in the state of anarchy with sovereignty, concluded the great Bishop.

Although Jurieu never responded to these criticisms of Bossuet, he had answered the Bishop's condemnation of the use of arms in the name of religion. Bossuet had reopened the issue of the wars of religion of the sixteenth century in France, in the tenth book of his famous *Histoire des variations des églises protestantes,*[99] which appeared in 1688. This book has been regarded [100] as so powerful a performance that it was one of the factors along with the English Revolution in altering the thought of Jurieu and other prominent Protestants on the question of the legitimacy of resistance in the name of true religion. But since, as we shall note later, even the Revolution of 1688 was not the completely determining factor in Jurieu's political theory, this view presents a much too ambitious claim for the impact of the *Histoire des variations,* great though it was, especially on the particular subject of the book itself—the problem of the variability of the Christian faith.

In the Ninth [101] *Lettre pastorale* of the Third Year, dated January 1, 1689, entitled "Examination of the question whether it is permitted to defend religion by arms," Jurieu explained that the events in England as well as Bossuet's book made it imperative for him to attempt to satisfy those of tender conscience who have been taught that the Scriptures speak only of spiritual resistance, a principle which the early Christians followed to the letter.

[98] "S'imaginer maintenant avec M. Jurieu dans le peuple considéré en cet état une souveraineté qui est déjà une espèce de gouvernement, c'est mettre un gouvernement avant tout gouvernement & se contredire soimême. Loin que ce peuple en cet état soit souverain, il n'y a pas même de peuple en cet état. Il peut bien y avoir des familles & encore mal gouvernées & mal assurées: il peut bien y avoir une troupe, un amas de monde; une multitude confuse; mais il ne peut y avoir de peuple, parce qu'un peuple suppose déjà quelque chose qui réunisse quelque conduite réglée & quelque droit établi: ce qui n'arrive qu'à ceux qui ont déjà commencé à sortir de cet état malheureux, c'est à dire de l'anarchie." *Cinquième avertissement aux protestants,* Tome III, p. 322.

[99] The Abbé of Cordemoy defended Bossuet's treatise against Jurieu. See Louis Géraud de Cordemoy, *Lettres des nouveaux catholiques.*

[100] See Alfred Rébelliau, *Bossuet historien du protestantisme,* p. 551. For mention of other refutations of Bossuet's treatise, *ibid.,* pp. 312–323.

[101] This letter was translated into English as *Monsieur Jurieu's Judgment upon the Question of Defending Our Religion by Armes,* London, 1689.

Jurieu begins by repeating once again that the religious wars present questions of fact and the issue of right. To the former he would refer to his answer to Maimbourg's *Histoire du calvinisme*. With regard to the right to take up arms in favor of religion, Jurieu's first tactic is, as usual, to accuse the Catholics of bathing Europe in blood in order to establish and maintain their faith. He points out that even the Moslems who extended their empire and religion by force of arms did not compel the conquered to abjure Christianity in order to embrace Mohammedanism. The Christian religion only perished under Moslem domination because of the poverty, misery, and ignorance to which the Mohammedans reduced the Christians. He cites the "holy wars," the dethroning of kings and emperors by the Papacy, the suppression of the Waldensians and the Albigensians, the Inquisition, the assassinations, and the Dragonnades. But Jurieu realized that this review of the excesses of Catholicism was not a sufficient justification of the action of the Protestants when they took up arms in order to defend their faith.

In order to clear the Huguenots of illegitimate action, Jurieu felt that it was necessary to distinguish between establishing a religion and defending it. Christian morality absolutely forbids the foundation of religion by force of arms.[102] Since the Catholics have employed this method of extending their faith, "Papism" is to be regarded as the true anti-Christianity. But the defense of religion is another matter. It is generally agreed that "defense is legitimate and permitted according to the laws of nature, which the positive laws of God have not touched." Therefore, it is lawful to defend life, honor, wife, children, country, and even property. But is religion to be exposed to any outrage without a right of defense? Jurieu thinks this doctrine has been shown to be so false that a contrary maxim, *Usque ad Aras,* has been generally accepted to demonstrate that patience may be unlimited except with respect to the faith. If the principle that it is never permissible to protect religion by arms is without exception, than it ought to apply in every possible case. For

[102] See *Lettres pastorales,* XVI, where Jurieu speaks of the extension of the true religion by "des moyens légitimes" which do not include "la tyrannie sur les consciences et la contrainte à croire et à professer une religion plutôt qu'une autre. Cf. also: "Le prince est le maître de l'extérieur de la religion; s'il ne veut pas en permettre d'autre que la sienne, si l'on ne peut obéir, on peut mourir sans se défendre parce que la véritable religion ne se doit point servir de la voie des armes pour régner et pour s'établir." Here the right of resistance is condemned by Jurieu in his *Les Derniers Efforts de l'innocence affligée,* (1682), pp. 73–74.

example, if an army of Turks should invade a Christian country not to attack property, liberty, or life, but for the sole purpose of establishing their religion, would any one venture to say that the people should lay down their arms and accept Mohammedanism? How could anyone, argued Jurieu, hold that religion—for the conservation of which the sacrifice of one's children, property, and country may be necessary—should not be defended by the same methods with which temporal interests are protected?

Therefore, the principle of nonresistance by force of arms when religion is endangered is not without exception. However, when the faith is attacked by a legitimate sovereign there is no right of revolt, according to Jurieu's opponents. To this contention Jurieu replies by asking whether the Catholics would submit with tears and prayers to a sovereign in a Catholic state should he attempt to establish Lutheranism or Calvinism by violence? Since kings are not even the masters of the lives of their subjects, certainly they are not the dispensers of their religion. If a sovereign should for some temporal interest, as the refusal of tribute, massacre a whole nation or a great part of it, certainly the subjects would have the right to defend themselves by opposing force to such violence. It is generally conceded that "the right of conservation itself is an inalienable right." But if a ruler should massacre his subjects for the sake of religion, does this cause of religion destroy the laws of nature and remove from the subjects the inalienable right of conservation? Once again Jurieu draws the conclusion that if temporal concerns can be defended by force, so much the more, then, can the interests of God. Besides, "the rights of God, the rights of the people, and the right of kings are inseparable." Consequently a ruler "who annihilates the right of God and of the peoples by that act destroys his own rights. Nothing is owed to him who renders nothing to anyone, neither to God nor men." [103]

[103] This idea is repeated in identical form in Jacques Abbadie, *Défense de la nation britannique.* It is interesting to compare Jurieu's theory of the inseparability of the rights of God, the people, and the king with that first covenant in the *Vindiciae* between God, the king, and the people to the effect that the people might be the people of God. It is to be noted that nothing is ever said conversely about the people who destroy the rights of God and those of the ruler—whether it thereby destroys its own rights. As with the idea of contract, this conception is unilateral, although Jurieu does admit in the Seventeenth *Lettre pastorale* that the people become rebels by abusing their rights, and in the Sixteenth that they do not have the right to attack the true religion and the laws or to do injustice. Furthermore, in his *Apologie pour leurs majestés,* Jurieu asserts that

Furthermore, Jurieu asks, if it is never permitted to sustain the true religion by arms, then why is the memory of the Maccabees, who took up arms against the king of Syria "not only for the spiritual but also for the temporal" so revered in the church? In the same manner, the United Provinces in the sixteenth century took up arms for their religion first, but later overthrew the dominion of Spain over even their temporal interests by setting up a separate state. Essentially there is no difference between the two cases in the mind of the pastor of Rotterdam.

As to the perpetual accusation that the Huguenots were not following the example of the early Christians who suffered martyrdom rather than resist, Jurieu refers to the fact that since the Christians were such a small minority of the total population of the Roman Empire, their action was motivated not only by piety but also by prudence. They let themselves be killed because of weakness and impotence [104] rather than religious scruples. In addition, since there were among the first Christians those who did not believe in the use of the sword, either in war or even in the punishment of criminals, their patience really resulted from error and "a mistaken morality." Finally, there is a difference between *esse* and *bene* [*melius*] *esse*. Even if the early Christians did "better" in not taking up arms to protect themselves from persecution, it does not follow that those who act otherwise do not do "well" and even "better," perhaps, in certain circumstances.[105]

But more potent than the example of the early Christians in the armory of the opposition were the words of Christ: "But I say unto you, That ye resist not evil: but whosoever shall smite thee on thy right cheek turn to him the other also. And if any man will sue thee at the law, and take away thy coat, let him have thy cloak also." [106] But Jurieu objects first that in the intention of Christ it is a question here of individuals and not of societies or states. Individuals should act, according to this command of Christ, "for the good of the public peace," and for the very same reason the governors of states should act otherwise. Since the church is "a corporation and a society," it can conserve its assemblies and

the king would have the right to resist a parliament that attempted to violate the laws and revoke the privileges of the people.

[104] According to Bossuet, Jurieu received inspiration for this idea from Buchanan's *De jure regni apus Scotos*. See his *Avertissement aux protestants*, V, 224–226.

[105] The Biblical text cited in this connection is from *I Corinthians* 8.38.

[106] Matthew 5.38–39.

subjects "by all the means permitted by the law of nations and nature."
Secondly, this Scriptural passage refers to temporal and not religious
interests. Christ commanded the abandonment of a coat and cloak and
not of religion. Furthermore, the Lord did not intend to establish such
a severe morality as to make a crime of all just defense against an aggressor upon private property. Therefore, if, in spite of this command, it
is permissible according to the laws of Scripture to put up a defense
against an aggressor who seeks to seize our possessions, then this admonition certainly is not to be understood as preventing the protection
of religion by arms. On the contrary, argues Jurieu, this command of
Jesus really outlaws "this exaggerated morality," since in the Scriptural
passage the Lord sets forth the limits of our patience with respect to
mediocre injuries such as the loss of our coat and some temporal goods,
for the conservation of which it is not important enough to jeopardize
the peace. Christ does not say that one should not defend himself when
his life is endangered. But if it is legitimate to save one's life, which a
tyrant seeks for temporal reasons, then, according to Jurieu, defense is
certainly lawful when life is endangered "for cause of religion," which
is far dearer than life itself.

Another proof of that strict morality which forbids the preservation
of religion by force of arms was taken from Christ's words of rebuke
to his disciples, James and John, concerning the Samaritans who did not
receive Him. In response to the advice of His followers that He call
down the fire of heaven upon them as did Elijah, the Lord said, "You
do not know by what spirit you are driven, the son of man has not come
to destroy you." [107] But to Jurieu this meant only that the Christian religion is not to be established by force. Besides, if the Samaritans had attempted to evict Christ or His disciples from one of their houses, there
is no evidence that Jesus would have ordered His followers to yield to
this application of force. In fact, "the Gospel has not deprived anyone
of the right of self-defense against violent aggressors."

This is what Christ meant when, while walking in the garden where
He knew the Jews would come to take Him by force, He commanded
that he among His disciples who had a sword should take it. When one
of them said, "Here are two swords," He answered, "It is enough." [108]

[107] Luke 9.54–56.   [108] Luke 22.38, 51.

Of course, argued Jurieu, it was not sufficient for two men to be armed against the weapons of Judas, but His purpose was simply to show that His disciples have, in such a case, the right to resort to the use of arms. But Jurieu had to grant that Christ commanded Peter to put his sword back into the sheath and that He healed the ear of Malchus. This was interpreted to mean, however, that although Christ recognized the right to oppose force with force, He did not wish His followers to employ such methods at that time, since it was necessary for Him to accomplish the commands of His Father. The warning that "all they that take the sword shall perish with the sword," [109] does not signify at all that the use of the sword is illegitimate in all cases and especially when it is a question of religion. First, there are a hundred occasions when the use of the sword is permissible. Second, Christ would not contradict Himself, for He had just said that he who had a sword should take it, and after He was assured of two He thought that to be sufficient. Thus only he who takes the sword unjustly shall perish by it. But the sword is taken wrongfully only in two cases, either when one does not have the right, or when the privilege is exercised on occasions when God does not wish it. Saint Peter had employed the sword unjustly, not because he did not have the right, but because it was not a suitable time, since God wished Christ to die. In the last analysis, concluded Jurieu, Christ commands the use of arms "in order to establish the right which the church has of self-defense against unjust oppressors." Peter was forbidden to use the sword "in order to teach the church submission when God let it be known that His will is that it suffer."

At this point Jurieu seems to feel that he may have gone too far, for he insists that he did not intend to inspire any feeling of vengeance in the Huguenots against their persecutors in France. He is, in fact, thankful to God that there have been no actions of violence, for he admits that the destruction of their enemies would probably be accomplished at the cost of their own downfall. Furthermore, Jurieu was also quick to add that he did not intend to have his *apologia* for resistance by arms serve as a defense for all religious wars, even when "the good religion" was at stake. Since the resort to arms is always attended by sad consequences, it is better to suffer moderate oppression than to rely upon extreme reme-

[109] Matthew 16.52.

dies. But in spite of that realization, Jurieu insists that there are "extremes where Christian morality does not enjoin patience," such as a massacre like that at Vassy in the first religious war of the preceding century, which was the signal for the Protestants to resort to the inalienable right of conservation. However, when it is only a question of the protection or destruction of a few individuals, as in the reigns of Francis I and Henry II, patience is required. "But when the life of a whole people is in danger and in an extreme peril, one can have recourse to extreme remedies." [110] But, added Jurieu, there are cases where the people need not wait so long. For example, when a ruler like James II is attempting to overthrow the dominant religion, it is necessary to stop the process from the beginning, since once the king has become "master of the laws and religion," it is too late for any relief.[111]

In addition to defending the English Revolution in his reply to Bossuet's *Histoire des variations* in his *Lettres pastorales,* Jurieu also directed his attention to the momentous changes across the Channel in his *Apologie pour leurs sérénissimes majestés britanniques* (1689),[112] which was intended to serve as an answer to Antoine Arnauld's libel, *Le Vrai Portrait de Guillaume Henri de Nassau, nouvel Abçalon, nouvel Hérode, nouveau Cromwell, nouveau Néron.*

He begins this tract by informing the Jansenist doctor that public affairs and property are not governed on the same principle as private matters, for the materials of the ruler are reasonable men, while those in the hands of a private individual are animals and things. As a result, laws preventing the dissipation of private properties are never as strict as those established to prohibit the ruin of states and the destruction of societies, since animals and things are not rational beings.[113] The logical person to prevent the demolition of the state is the heir to the throne, for even

---

[110] Cf. *Lettres pastorales,* XVI of the Third Year: "Mais quand par la résistance on peut sauver sa vie, et sa religion et celle de ses frères, on peut et on doit s'en servir."

[111] For a contrary view see the Eighteenth *Lettre pastorale,* of the First Year, dated May 15, 1687, pp. 435–436.

[112] This little book was translated into English in *A Collection of State Tracts,* I, pp. 285–308.

[113] "Ainsi de ce que les particuliers ont un plein droit de faire de leurs biens ce qu'il leur plait & de les gouverner à leur fantaisie, il ne s'ensuit pas que les personnes publiques puissent gouverner les états & les sociétés selon leur caprice sans qu'on ait droit de s'y opposer & d'empêcher la dissipation qu'ils en feroient." *Apologie pour leur majestés,* pp. 16–24.

the heirs of a private estate have not been denied all right of protest except humble remonstrance.

But there is another difference between public and private properties. Birth and the law determine possession of the latter, "but it is God and the nations who determine public possessions and sovereignties . . . God as the sovereign master, the people as the masters of their property under God; God as master of all the crowns, in general; each people as master of its crown in particular." The Biblical examples of David and Saul and the abandonment by the Jews of the family of David for the Maccabees are cited again to show that God and the people are not always bound by the law of succession. In the same way the French have transferred the crown from the Merovingian line to the Carolingian and to the Capetian. But in addition to usage and example, "good sense and right reason" show that "societies, creating kings for their preservation,[114] have the right to grant the power of government to him who is judged the most capable of conserving the community and the public welfare."

In addition to the principles that kings are not the masters of reasonable men as private persons are masters of their fields and domestic animals, and that God and the people have the right to grant the crown to whomever it is pleasing, there results a third maxim that peoples as well as the church are always minors or wards and the kings their guardians. Therefore, just as the heirs of the property of a ward can prevent its dissipation, so the heirs of a crown have the right to conserve the state against ruin by the possessor of the sovereign power. Since the legitimate heir can take such preventive action even when only his own interest is involved, there is even more reason for him to take steps in the interest of religion and the state. No question of relationship to the ruler, whether son-in-law or son, should stand in the way, "because it is necessary to love God and the public welfare more than father and mother." Besides, the welfare of the ruler is not paramount, if he is permitted to go to perdition through his tyrannical actions without opposition. "On the contrary, a prince—heir to the crown—is bound to join the estates of the realm in order to disarm the tyrant and prevent him

[114] That is, "avec cette réserve que le bien & le salut de l'état & du peuple est la souveraine fin des gouvernements & la loy suprème." *Ibid.*

from reducing the kingdom to a frightful wilderness." Jurieu then proceeds to give a transparent description of the tyranny of Louis XIV, both inside and outside France.[115]

In such a situation and with the Dauphin of France in mind, Jurieu declares that the heir apparent should have a share in the government when he is no longer a minor, for in addition to the safeguarding of his inheritance, there is an even greater interest at stake—that of the republic itself.[116] Besides, the interest of the prince and the public separately there is the joint interest of them both, which obliges the heir to the crown to limit the violations of his father.

Such general considerations of the rights of the peoples and successors provided the basis for not only the plots around the Dauphin of France against Louis XIV, but also for an apology of the action of William of Orange toward his father-in-law, James II. But in addition it must be remembered that in England the legislative authority is divided between the king and the parliament, and according to Jurieu, the people had privileges which even the king and parliament cannot remove without risking resistance on the part of the *populus* as of right.[117]

The maxim *Princeps legibus solutus est* has no application here, since by "prince" is understood "the sovereign and the absolute magistrate without reservation." But the king of England must rule according to the laws. Only the king and the parliament together are above the laws. Although the Protestants take an oath of fidelity without reserve to their princes, it is done only where the laws do not stand in the way and where princes are the possessors of the whole sovereignty. But where the limits of the ruler are indicated by the laws, an oath without condition is not demanded. Therefore, the English do not violate their oath of obedience [118] when they regard themselves as no longer bound to a

---

[115] *Ibid.*, pp. 24–34.

[116] "On doit à Dieu, on doit au public préférablement à tous les devoirs du sang, de l'alliance & de la parenté." *Ibid.*

[117] "Car il est certain que dans toutes les relations de père & de fils, de femme & de mari, de maître & de serviteur, de sujet & de Roy où il y a un traité formée & certaines conditions posées; quand l'une des parties vient à rompre le traité & à manquer aux conditions l'autre n'est plus obligée." *Ibid.*, pp. 41–42. This is but a repetition of the same idea of contract, which Jurieu had stated in the Sixteenth *Lettre pastorale* of the Third Year.

[118] Cf. Jurieu's discussion of the Non-Jurors in his *Avis à tous les alliés*, pp. 23–24. He considered it a violation of the fundamental laws of the realm to take an oath to the Catholic James, since the king of England was by law the head of the Anglican Church.

king, who infringes upon the fundamental laws of the state. It was never intended by Saint Peter or Saint Paul to make the power of kings, who are limited by such laws, arbitrary.

But what about the necessity for the royal consent to laws made in Parliament? Jurieu's answer is that "the sovereign law [the safety and the conservation of the people]" always determines "the meaning of all the other laws and makes exceptions to them." [119] Just as when the king violates the laws and revokes the privileges of the people, Parliament can resist him, so it follows that if the Parliament should act in a similar manner the king would also have the right to oppose it in the interests of the nation. Thus, in the *Apologie pour leurs majestés* Jurieu attempted to prove that the heir to the kingdom is obliged by his own interest, by that of the people, and by that of God, to resist a ruler who has become the enemy of the state, the laws, and the Lord.

Since under the influence of the English Revolution of 1688–1689 Jurieu enunciated the theory of popular sovereignty which we have been considering, it has been the custom of modern authors to contrast his royalism before the Revocation with his republicanism afterward.[120] This was also done many times by his contemporary enemies,[121] such as Pierre Bayle and Henri Basnage de Beauval, but is it an accurate portrayal of Jurieu's political theory? Were there not elements in his thought as early as 1677 which form the basis of his later position? The evolutionary character of his ideas on the right of resistance to tyranny has already been suggested on the basis of his writings in defense of Calvinism.[122] The contribution of the more strictly theological sources of his theory of popular sovereignty has received scarcely any attention at all beyond mere hints, however.[123] In two different disputes over the nature of the church, which occurred before the Revocation and the

---

[119] *Apologie pour leurs majestés*, pp. 136–141.

[120] Roger Lureau, *Les Doctrines politiques de Jurieu*, pp. 120–121.

[121] The views of Jurieu in his *Politique du clergé de France* (1681) were contrasted with the *Lettres pastorales* of 1688–89. See the *Avis aux réfugiés* (1690) by Bayle; the *Réponse de l'auteur de l'histoire des ouvrages des savants* (1690) by Basnage de Beauval and the anonymous *Réponse des Fidèles captifs en Babylone* (1695), probably from the same pen.

[122] E. Kappler, "Le droit de résistance à la tyrannie d'après Jurieu," *Revue d'Histoire et de Philosophie religieuses*, Strasbourg, May–June, 1937.

[123] *Ibid.*, p. 214, and Frank Puaux, *Les Défenseurs de la souveraineté du peuple sous le règne de Louis XIV*, p. 82.

Glorious Revolution, Jurieu set forth political doctrines of the greatest importance for the understanding of his subsequent ideas upon the state and government, and yet these writings have never been examined.

Now the dependence of political ideas upon religious conceptions has been very succinctly phrased by Jurieu's first opponent, who argued that a critical attitude in the affairs of the state is contingent upon the practice of free examination in the conduct of the church.[124] Does this same conclusion apply to Jurieu's approach to political problems? [125] In order to essay an answer to this question it will be necessary to turn to a brief consideration of one of Jurieu's early writings—his *Traité de la puissance de l'Eglise* which appeared in 1677.

The immediate occasion for Jurieu's analysis of the power of the church was the publication in the previous year of the *Fasciculus epistolarum,* which was an attack upon the ecclesiastical jurisdiction by his maternal uncle, Louis Dumoulin,[126] who was the son of Pierre Dumoulin and the brother of Charles Dumoulin, chaplain of the King of England and canon of the Cathedral Church of Canterbury. In dealing with the nature and origin of the power of the church in answer to Dumoulin, Jurieu, it has been held,[127] was confronting on the ecclesiastical plane à la Rousseau the eternal problem of reconciling the conflict between liberty and authority. According to this argument, it was the same issue which was at stake in the celebrated controversy between Bossuet and Claude [128] over the nature and constitution of the church and in the famous struggle in England between the Congregationalists and Presbyterians. Jurieu's solution, then, of this antinomy between the principle

---

[124] D'Huisseau, *De la réunion du christianisme,* p. 178.

[125] Both Puaux and Kappler are in the affirmative on this point.

[126] In 1648 the Parliament had given Louis Dumoulin a professorship of History at Oxford, of which he was deprived in 1660 at the time of the Restoration, since he had taken the part of the Independents. It is interesting to note that he spoke of Jurieu as "mon neveu l'injurieux," which pun is quite an accurate indication of the character of the theologian of Rotterdam. An anonymous answer to Jurieu's book appeared in London in 1678: *La Tyrannie des préjugés.*

[127] Mercier, "Théories politiques des Calvinistes," *Bulletin . . . du Protestantisme,* p. 402.

[128] In 1678 Bossuet and Claude staged the rather theatrical debate for the soul of the niece of Turenne, Mme. Duras, who, hesitating between Protestantism and Catholicism, had demanded this discussion. Cf. Bossuet's *Conférence avec M. Claude touchant l'infaillibilité de l'Eglise,* 1682, and Claude's *Réponse au livre de M. l'Evêque de Meaux, intitulé Conférence avec M. Claude,* 1683.

of individual inspiration and the necessity for authority was to place authority in the church in the hands of the people. Such a theory formed a logical basis for the republican ideas of Jurieu, whether in the ecclesiastical or political sphere, according to this same interpretation.[129] But is this conclusion warranted from a study of the controversy over the true nature of the power of the church? Before reaching any definite conclusion, let us turn to an examination of Jurieu's answer to Dumoulin's assault upon the ecclesiastical jurisdiction.

Dumoulin had taken an Erastian line, which Jurieu himself followed later, arguing that all jurisdiction is civil and that the officers of the church can act only upon the orders of the magistrate. Ecclesiastical laws and canons have no force, then, except as authorized by the government. In other words, sacerdotal power is a branch of the civil jurisdiction. Dumoulin had also held that the destruction of the clerical power entailed the fall of the excessive papal authority. To Jurieu, however, this reasoning was as fallacious as to contend that in order to destroy heresy the Christian religion would itself have to be abolished, or in order to do away with tyranny, monarchy and even all government must be eliminated. The abuse of a power does not destroy its efficacy. Dumoulin had likewise claimed that with the destruction of ecclesiastical jurisdiction other controversies like the divine or human character of the Episcopate and the good or bad character of the Presbyterian church government would be resolved.

To Jurieu, ecclesiastical jurisdiction was particularly necessary when the magistrate was not Christian or a heretic, but in cases where the ruler is a member of the true church this jurisdiction is at least not harmful. Of course, Jurieu would admit that, rightfully conceived, the clerical administration should be submitted to the authority of the magistrate in certain things, such as the choice of days for certain ceremonies and for public holidays. He insists that no more than Dumoulin does he want the church to bear the character of "sovereign visible monarch or infallible tribunal," which can bind the conscience. A legislator or new laws are not to be desired either, but only "advisers, leaders, directors, and regulations." [130] He reminds Dumoulin that the argument over the

[129] Mercier, "Théories politiques des calvinistes," *Bulletin . . . du Protestantisme*, p. 402.
[130] *Traité de la puissance de l'Eglise*, 1677, p. 64.

presence or absence of true jurisdiction in the church is one of the points
of contention with the Roman Catholic Church. Furthermore, it should
be noted at this point that Jurieu's uncle had particularly favored the
form of church government of the Independents in England, maintaining that it was not only the government of the Apostolic church but also
the only reasonable polity, since it eliminates all power from the church.
But since Jurieu disapproved of the anarchistic claims of the Independents as much as of the extreme pretensions of the Catholics, he was forced
to steer a middle course between the various Protestant groups on the
one hand and the Catholic church on the other.[131] The Independents
were especially to be condemned, since they were schismatics, having
separated from other Protestant churches because of a difference over
discipline. The confederation of several churches under a bishop with
his clergy or under a synod are the only conceivable forms of church
government for Jurieu. To him, even if in discipline the Independents
were closer to the Apostolic church than the followers of the Calvinist

[131] It is important to note the contradictions of Jurieu as to ecclesiastical government,
which Bayle delights in presenting in his *Réponse aux questions d'un provincial* in
Oeuvres diverses, 1737, III, 1045: "Quelle est sa doctrine touchant le gouvernement de
l'Eglise lorsqu'il en parle dans le *Préservatif* (p. 334): 'Que le Seigneur Jésus Christ a
voulu que le gouvernement de son Église fut Aristocratique & qu'il l'a remis entre les mains
de gens qu'il a appelés des Évêques & des Prêtres, lesquels il a revêtus d'une égale puissance. Que cette espèce de gouvernement est de droit divin & par conséquent qu'il ne doit
être permis à personne de le changer sous quelque prétexte que ce soit.' Mais quelle est
sa doctrine sur le même point dans d'autres écrits? Que (*Janséniste convaincu,* p. 242)
terme d'aristocratique peut convenir au Gouvernement Presbytérien comme au Gouvernement Épiscopal. Mais beaucoup mieux pourtant à celuy-ci qu'à celuy-là, car le Gouvernement
Presbytérien est proprement le gouvernement démocratique, c'est le peuple qui gouverne
par ses Députés auxquelles on donne le nom d'anciens. Et le gouvernement Épiscopal est
proprement le gouvernement aristocratique parcequ'il est entre les mains de plusieurs sans
pourtant que le peuple y ait aucune part." But compare this, argues Bayle, with Jurieu's
statement in the *Janséniste convaincu,* pp. 241–243: " 'Mon sentiment est que selon l'intention de Jésus Christ, le gouvernement monarchique est exclus de l'Eglise de droit divin,
mais qu'excepté cela il n'y a point de forme de gouvernement qui soit de droit divin &
qu'il est au pouvoir de chaque Prince Chrétien d'établir en ses États tel gouvernement qu'il
lui plait pourvu qu'il ne soit ni tyrannique ni opposé à la libterté chrétienne.' Qu'excepté
le gouvernement monarchique il n'y a point de forme de gouvernement que chaque Prince
ne puisse établir en ses Etats. Quelles contradictions! Quoi si le gouvernement aristocratique
& immuable établi par Jésus Christ consiste en ce que la puissance de ceux que l'on nomme
prêtres, le gouvernement épiscopal d'Angleterre où les Prêtres sont sous la jurisdiction des
Evêques sera proprement le gouvernement aristocratique tandis que le gouvernement
presbytérien où les Evêques & les Prêtres ont une égale puissance ne sera aristocratique
qu'improprement; & il sera permis à chaque Prince Chrétien d'ôter aux Prêtres la puissance
égale à celle des Evêques dont J.C. les a revêtus & de donner aux Evêques la supériorité sur
les Prêtres. Quel sens y-a-t'il à tout cela?"

or the Anglican form of ecclesiastical polity were, they should still be regarded as criminals. This is obvious, since "there is no government which is from divine law; but possession is worth much, and provided a government is not contrary to the spirit of Christianity it must be supported when it is established and one must submit to it." [132]

The question of church government aside, what is the source of the power of the church? Jurieu begins his analysis by declaring that the ecclesiastical power may have its origin in three subjects, the Pope, the bishops or pastors, and the people. But the authority of the church may only be attributed to the whole church, that is, to the people rather than to the ministers, since the people is the largest part of the spiritual community. Thus, the church as a society resembles all other societies of the world, the government of which resides originally in the multitude.[133] The people are free in their choice of the type of authority which they desire—monarchy, aristocracy, or democracy—but with one very important restriction: "when once the laws are made, when the government is established, the people is no longer free, it has tied its hands and those of all posterity." There is, however, a qualification to the restriction. Since even by this submission to constituted authority the people does not lose "its primary right," then if a royal line should be extinguished, it could provide for its security by the election of a new king.[134]

[132] *Traité de la puissance de l'Eglise,* pp. 52–54. Cf. a statement from Jurieu's *Traité de l'unité de l'Eglise* (1688), pp. 133–135: "Mais cependant ce qui pouvoit suffire pour l'Eglise dans l'enfance (les églises apostoliques ne vivoyent point en une confédération de dépendance mutuelle) ne suffit plus aujourd'huy & il est certain que l'Eglise auroit peine à se conserver sans confédération . . . par consentement mutuel à des Synodes ou à des Evêques."

[133] Let us imagine "une société informe, c'est à dire, une multitude d'hommes, qui se soient hazardeusement rencontrés dans un même lieu & qui prennent la résolution d'y demeurer; ils sont naturellement tous libres & indépendans les uns des autres; mais ils ne sauroient faire un société bien formée s'ils demeurent dans cette indépendance; il faut nécessairement qu'ils établissent un autorité entr'eux, qu'ils choisissent un Législateur, qu'ils se soumettent à ses loix, qu'il luy donnent le pouvoir de chatier ceux qui violeront ces loix. Avant que cette autorité soit établie & qu'elle ait été conferée ou à un seul ou à plusieurs elle est dans toute la multitude. Mais parce que ce peuple ne peut pas exercer par luy-même cette autorité, il faut nécessairement qu'il choisisse quelque personne de son corps, par laquelle il fasse exercer cette puissance qu'il ne peut exercer par luy-même." *Traité de la puissance de l'Eglise,* pp. 65–70.

[134] *Ibid.* Cf. a passage from p. 310 of *Le Janséniste convaincu* . . . , which Jurieu wrote in 1683: "Il en est de l'Eglise comme des peuples, tous les peuples du monde ont reçu de Dieu & de la nature le droit de se former un gouvernement ou Monarchique ou Aristocratique ou tel qu'il leur plait. Quand ce gouvernement est établi tel que bon leur a semblé, il n'est plus en leur pouvoir de ne pas obéir. Il faut qu'ils obéissent aux Rois & aux Magistrats qu'ils se sont faits avec telles & telles loix. Mais si ce gouvernement vient à se

In his later dispute with Pierre Nicole [135] over the true nature of the church, Jurieu once again defended this proposition that every society by natural right can establish its leaders. He begins once more with a consideration of the view that if man could have remained in the state of innocence, he would have lived free and independent without the rule of some over others. Jurieu admits, however, that evils such as slavery are a consequence of sin. But he distinguished servitude from subjection and domination from tyranny, and holds that it is almost impossible to imagine a society without government even in a state of innocence, where the directors of society would have commanded according to the will of God and the good of private persons and the public would have been completely compatible.[136]

Another right, which is from nature and inalienable, is that of conservation. Therefore, it belongs to men in a state of sin as well as in a state of innocence. But there are certain natural rights, which although inseparable from man, are not exercisable in a condition of purity. Jurieu cites for example the natural right of defense against an unjust aggressor, which could not come into play until man had enemies to combat. Another natural right is that of redemanding one's own, but in a state of blamelessness, where all is held in common, this right does not apply; however, as soon as property was divided among men because of sin, it became applicable. The right of establishing government was also only employed after the Fall. But this privilege can be alienated in its exercise. The people can, for example, confer the kingship upon a certain family, which thereby inherits the dignity. But should the line fail, the people—that is, the estates of the realm—have the right either to elect a new king or even to make the crown henceforth elective.

---

corrompre entièrement ou que les Rois viennent à manquer & leur race à faillir; ce qu'on appelle les Etats d'un Royaume le peuple en un mot est en droit de rétablir un nouveau gouvernement conforme à celuy qui étoit avant la décadence & la chute de l'ancien. Car il y a deux droits qui sont inséparables des hommes, le premier est celuy de la conservation que nous nous devons à nous-mêmes avant tout autre après Dieu; le second celuy de se faire un maître quand on n'en a pas de tout fait."

[135] See his *Traité de l'unité de l'Eglise* (1688) which was a refutation of the great Jansenist's book, *De l'unité de l'Eglise* (1687).

[136] "Il doit donc demeurer constant que c'est un droit inséparable des hommes en quelque état qu'on le concoive de se faire des chefs. Il n'est pas nécessaire qu'ils ayent acquis ce droit de domination par le pêché, il suffit qu'ils ne l'ayent pu perdre." *Ibid.,* Traité Cinquième, Chap. IV, pp. 449–460.

From the proposition that every society by natural right can establish its rulers, Jurieu deduces a second principle: that the church as a society has also the right to elect its directors. This was the answer to Nicole's argument that since the Calvinists did not have true pastors,[137] because of the method of their selection, therefore, they did not have a true church. But, according to Nicole, if the church can establish its directors and its laws, then it is encroaching upon the rights of God. In reply Jurieu admits that God could detract from this natural right of societies to choose a ruler, yet He has not done it.[138]

In civil society, continues Jurieu, natural rights are exercised in accordance with human ends, while in a supernatural society they are exercised in accordance with spiritual objectives. But they are limited in their exercise "by reason, propriety, decency, the insight of good sense and more than all that by divine laws, both natural and positive." [139] For example, self-defense is a natural right but is it permissible for a son to defend himself against a father [140] or for a private individual to take up arms against his sovereign? In the same way the natural right to elect a ruler is limited. It is not legitimate, for example, to place the kingdom in the hands of a blackguard or to establish a Mohammedan prince over a Christian people. Furthermore, by natural law men are not to be ruled by women. Therefore, if a woman inherits the throne, the laws of succession are a derogation of natural law. But this is possible, however, because each person can give up as much of his natural right as he desires.

From these considerations, then, Jurieu concludes that the ecclesiastical authority has the same popular origin as civil government, although in its infancy God was directly concerned with the conduct of the church.

---

[137] See J. L. Ainslie, *The Doctrines of Ministerial Order in the Reformed Churches,* and J. T. McNeill, *"The Doctrine of the Ministry in Reformed Theology,"* Church History, XII (1943), where the ideas of Jean Claude on this point are discussed.

[138] "Il est vrai que les hommes dans les sociétés civiles ont ce droit de s'ériger un gouvernement absolument nouveau: mais c'est que ces sociétés sont purement naturelles & les hommes y jouissent de tous leurs droits naturels. Mais l'Eglise étant une société toute de pure grâce les hommes n'y conservent leurs droits naturels qu'autant que Dieu le leur permet par sa grâce." *Traité de l'unité de l'Eglise,* Chap. V, pp. 460–470.

[139] *Ibid.*

[140] Cf., however, a contradictory passage in the Sixteenth *Lettre pastorale* of the Third Year: "Il est permis par toutes les lois chrétiennes à un fils, non seulement de désobéir, mais de résister à un père qui lui veut ôter les biens, l'honneur et la vie."

The whole church has the power of the keys, therefore, but cannot exercise it alone. For this purpose it chooses pastors and ministers, to whom it gives the right of preaching, administering the sacraments, and maintaining discipline, even by excommunication, if necessary.

But what about the problem of the confederation of churches? The universal church is divided into parts—individual churches and confederated churches. These individual churches exist before the confederated churches, both in order of time and in order of nature. In fact, the confederation is not of the essence of the church at all. Although the existence of separate and different churches is subject to great inconveniences, still they have not lost the fundamental element of the church, provided they have maintained the pure word of God and a suitable discipline. It is not nature, but accident, events, and the circumstances of the diverse states which causes this union of churches. Union, however, does exist for the perfection of the church of God.

Though the power of the keys has been given by God to the universal church, it is not to be exercised by all the parts jointly, whether individual or confederated, but by "individual flocks" separately. Since they are unable to exercise it by themselves, they choose either a bishop and his clergy, or pastors and members of the laity according to the Presbyterian form of government, to employ the power of the keys, such as preaching and disciplining in their name. All these powers are to be exercised, then, over the members of an individual congregation and not with regard to confederated churches.

But God in giving to the church the power of the keys did not specify the form of ecclesiastical government, leaving it, instead, to each congregation to determine for itself whether it prefers a bishop and his priests or pastors, elders, and a consistory. There are two extremes to be avoided, however, tyranny and anarchy. The Anglican form of church government results more often in the former and the Presbyterian in the latter. In addition, the form of church government varies according to times and places, being often obliged to accommodate itself to the form of the state. But Jurieu again maintains that if the principle of the popular origin of civil society [141] were followed in the church, then controversies

[141] "Dieu a crée les hommes pour former des sociétés, il leur a donné une inclination à cela qui leur tient de loy générale, mais il ne leur a donné ni commandement, ni exemple

over the divine or human character of the Episcopate or the Presbytery would be resolved in a manner contrary to Dumoulin, who would abolish the ecclesiastical jurisdiction entirely in an attempt to terminate these disputes. In Jurieu's system the evangelical ministry in general is divine in character, but the particular types of church polity are of human institution and ordained by positive ecclesiastical law.

As against the Independents Jurieu maintained that ecclesiastical synods have the authority to censure those who disregard their commands but only because such a power is derived from the people and not from God immediately.[142] On the civil or secular side, individuals assemble and establish cities, which choose magistrates who convene to select either a king or a council to govern them. By such means authority rises from the people to the sovereign magistrate, who makes it descend upon minor magistrates and from them to the people. In the same way the authority of the synods "is precisely as great as that of the people and the particular churches." The synod has the same authority over each church that each church has over itself before the formation of the confederation, whereby it granted its power to the synod. Therefore, even though the synods have only a power delegated from the people and are not directly of divine institution nor of the essence of the church, they must be obeyed according to divine law. This conclusion is evident "by that perpetual parallel which we make between civil and religious

---

qui les détermine à une espèce de gouvernement. En général, les loix de la nature enseignent aux hommes à fuir l'anarchie & le crime & à s'établir une autorité, sous laquelle les méchans puissent être réprimez afin que les honnêtes gens vivent en seureté. Au reste que cette autorité soit dans la main d'un seul ou de plusieurs, que ce gouvernement soit monarchique ou démocratique ou aristocratique il n'importe, ils sont tous de l'intention de Dieu & de l'ordre de sa Providence." *Traité de la puissance de l'Eglise,* pp. 83–87. Cf. "Mais il y a des choses qui ont été établies par les hommes sur un fondement divin, c'est à dire sur les loix de Dieu & de la nature; de ce genre sont les puissances souveraines, elles sont établies par les hommes mais elles sont de l'intention de Dieu & leur établissement est fondé sur la loy de la Nature qui oblige les sociétés à travailler à leur conservation, c'est pourquoy l'on est obligé par conscience de se soumettre à ces puissances." But, cautions Jurieu: "les fidèles ne sont pas maîtres de leur liberté jusques à la pouvoir engager absolument jusques à se pouvoir rendre esclaves des hommes par une obéissance aveugle." *Ibid.,* pp. 103–104 and 106–107.
142 "C'est une autorité qui monte & dont le mouvement est circulaire. Elle ne descend pas, car elle ne vient pas immédiatement de Dieu sur les Synodes, des Synodes sur les pasteurs & des Pasteurs sur le Peuple, mais elle vient de Dieu immédiatement sur le Peuple & du Peuple elle monte aux Synodes & aux Evêques, c'est la manière dont roule l'autorité des Sociétez confédérées." *Ibid.*

societies." Once again Jurieu declares that in civil society there is no form of government established by divine law immediately from God, but men are obligated by divine precept to submit to the powers that be. For example, the French could have chosen a republic instead of a monarchy, but since they established the latter form of government, they and all their posterity must obey a monarch as a religious duty. This same reasoning applies to the church. The separate congregations can freely choose to live either under a bishop or a synod, but once having made their choice they must obey the bishop or the synod "by that divine and apostolic law, which says 'obey your leaders.' " [143]

If individuals can form an ecclesiastical society and establish an authority in it, which can not only preach but also censure them, then several congregations can choose from their churches leaders to whom will be granted the power to control differences as to the faith. If the individuals have to obey these leaders of the congregation or suffer excommunication, then the separate churches which are confederated must obey the authorities of the confederation on the pain of the same penalty. Thus, the ecclesiastical power, though originally in the people, is now in the pastors and confederated assemblies.

But to Dumoulin it was otherwise. The magistrates are masters of the sacerdotal power and the ecclesiastical jurisdiction is the same as the civil. To Jurieu, however, they are to be clearly distinguished. He attempts to show this by pointing out that men are capable of entering into many relationships—that of father, master, doctor, merchant, king, and magistrate; but one particular tie binds them with God and nature "who teach all men to seek their sovereign welfare and to keep themselves in possession of this good by all legitimate means." [144]

In addition to the distinction between the power of the church and that of the state, there is another important question as to whether the former should be submitted to the latter, with the same magistrates giving laws to both state and church. In an attempt to settle this issue Jurieu observes first that magistrates are either of the same religion as the church or a different one. Second, the following principle must be recalled: the authority of the church, that is, the power of the keys, was given to the whole body of the church, which is composed mainly of the

[143] *Ibid.*, pp. 91–94.　　　　[144] *Ibid.*, pp. 116–117.

laity. Since they are unable to exercise this power, they choose pastors to preach and give the sacraments. But kings, counselors, the estates, and in general all Christian magistrates make up "the most considerable part of the laity." [145] Therefore, the power of the church which goes to the pastors by the choice of the people, comes principally from the magistrates "who are the head of the people." But they hold this position not as magistrates but as members of the church—"considerable members whom God has given a character, which distinguished them from all the others." Thus, there is no justification in concluding that the power of the church is a branch of the civil jurisdiction because it emanates from the magistrates. [146]

Jurieu at this point emphasized once more a principle which will be encountered again and again in his political theory. He regarded it as a natural right that those who grant a power to another have the right to scrutinize the manner in which he exercises it. [147] Thus, the body of the church which gives the power of the keys to its pastors has the right to watch over their conduct and observe whether they make a good or bad use of their authority. This right belongs both to the laity of a particular congregation and to the several churches which have entered a confederation. If there is an abuse of power on the part of the leaders, the body of the church has the right either to make them perform their duty or to abandon them and establish new governors. Therefore, the Christian magistrate who is at the head of the people and is clothed with all their rights [148] should supervise the conduct of the pastors of the church in order to see that they preach the pure word of God and exercise discipline carefully. If they overstep their bounds, he has the right to proceed against them. For example, if a faithful person is violently expelled from the communion of the church, the magistrate can

[145] ". . . des magistrats sont devant Dieu la plus considérable partie de ce peuple Chrétien puis qu'il les appelle Dieux." *Ibid.*, pp. 117–125.

[146] "Ils ont virtuellement & originellement ce qu'ils donnent, mais ils ne l'ont pas formellement comme on parle dans les Écoles, tout de même que les Peuples qui élissent un Roy n'avoient pas la dignité Royale formellement, parce qu'ils n'étoient pas Rois, mais ils l'avoient le pouvoir de faire un Roy." *Ibid.*

[147] Locke also considered that he who gives a commission is the best judge of whether it has been well executed.

[148] Furthermore, "en soutenant l'autorité de leurs conducteurs, ils [le peuple] soutiennent leur propre autorité, puisque les Pasteurs de l'Eglise n'en ont point d'autre que celle qu'ils ont reçue du Peuple." *Traité de le puissance de l'Eglise,* pp. 117–125.

hear his complaint and urge the leaders of the church to remedy the evil. Upon refusal he can take such measures as the calling of a new group of pastors to mete out justice in the case. He should always prevent the use of ecclesiastical discipline from elevating the clergy too far above the people. But the magistrate does not have the right to quash the unjust judgment of an ecclesiastical body, which he would have if the power of the church were derived directly from the civil jurisdiction. He should urge the ecclesiastical authority to nullify it itself. As the head of all civil jurisdiction the chief magistrate has the power to impose civil penalties upon those whom the church has excommunicated. Jurieu adds, however, that infidel magistrates have no right to be concerned with sacerdotal affairs.

From this brief analysis of the true nature of the authority of the church, it is evident that the contrast between Jurieu's political theory before and after the Revocation is not as great as it has been supposed. In fact, several years before the repeal of the Edict of Toleration all the elements of his later theory of popular sovereignty were present in more than latent form. In these earlier writings like *Traité de la puissance de l'Eglise* (1677) and *Le Janséniste convaincu de vaine Sophistiquerie* (1682), Jurieu had already argued that on the basis of two natural rights —that of conservation and that of constituting a master—governmental authority lies in the people. The church as a society does not differ from any other community in the world, since the government of all societies, whether ecclesiastical or civil, by natural right is rooted in the *populus*. Although Jurieu may speak in one place of the perpetual parallel he makes of civil with religious societies, his other statements lead to the conclusion that it is just as logical to emphasize the opposite analogy. Furthermore, it is a natural right of those who grant a power to supervise the manner of its execution and, as such, it is common to the people, whether in sacerdotal or secular society. Therefore, with Jurieu there is no direct connection between a critical attitude in the affairs of the state and the principle of free examination in the conduct of the church and no transposition of liberty of conscience from the religious to the political sphere.[149]

149 Thus, the secular right of resistance is not derived from the fact that the synods, receiving their authority from the people, cannot bind the conscience without the legitimate resistance of the faithful. This is an unwarranted conclusion, which Kappler derives from

Finally, with regard to Jurieu's theory of popular sovereignty as a possible solution along Rousseauistic lines [150] of the antinomy between the principle of individual inspiration and the necessity for authority, it is clear that, like his predecessors, the Monarchomachs, Jurieu was not antimonarchical at heart. He developed a theory of popular sovereignty in the state only for religious reasons, rather than in the spirit of an abstract thinker like the great citizen of Geneva, who speculated upon the general philosophical problem of the reconciliation of liberty and authority. As with the Conciliarists in the fifteenth century, Jurieu tends to regard the location of sovereignty in the community not as a result of the autonomy of each of the members of the body politic, but as a result of the ends for which men live in society. Furthermore, as we have already noted, his theory of popular sovereignty was based more upon the ancient Roman maxim *Salus populi suprema lex esto* than upon the conception of individual rights. Such doctrines as these are quite foreign to the theorists of modern democracy, such as Locke and perhaps Rousseau. If, therefore, concern for the true religion was the *raison d'être* of the origin of governmental authority in the people, it is difficult to see how the Rousseauistic explanation can serve as the logical basis or initial reason for the republican ideas of Jurieu in the church. The fact of the matter is that outside of a general attitude of truculence,[151] arising no doubt from the doctrine of predestination, Calvinists like Jurieu did not elaborate revolutionary theories of popular sovereignty because of anything at all inherent in their religion, but rather because they were a persecuted minority within the community. What other explanation can account for the fact that the theorists of the Catholic League and the Jesuits enunciated the same doctrines of rebellion whenever they found themselves in a similarly unfavorable position with regard to the supreme governmental authority in the state?

Jurieu's *Le Vray Système de l'Eglise*, pp. 199–200. This same error seems to have been made by no less than Pierre Joseph Proudhon in his *General idea of the Revolution in the Nineteenth Century*, London, 1923, p. 112, where he comments: "Following Luther, the principle of free criticism was carried by Jurieu, from the spiritual to the temporal. To the sovereignty of divine right, the adversary of Bossuet opposed the sovereignty of the people."

[150] Refer to pages 82–83 of this study.

[151] Alexis De Tocqueville in his *De la démocratie en Amérique*, Paris, 1864, II, Chap. IX, p. 5, made the keen observation that "le protestantisme porte les hommes bien moins vers l'égalité que vers l'indépendance."

Chapter Four

HUGUENOT MODERATES AND ZEALOTS

As we have already noted, the English Revolution divided the Huguenot refugees into two parties—the moderates and the zealots.[1] Jurieu's open eulogy of William of Orange [2] in the *Lettres pastorales* and the *Apologie pour leurs majestés* and his hope that the French Protestant exiles would benefit by the turn of events in England only accentuated the division among the Huguenots, especially in Holland. But it was the appearance in April, 1690, during the second year of the European war against France, of the famous *Avis important aux réfugiés sur leur prochain retour en France, donné pour étrennes à l'un d'eux en 1690,* which separated even more definitely the moderate group of French Calvinists from the extremists.

The *Avis important* was characterized by a great mildness with regard to the King of France. It was presented to the dispersed Huguenots by an anonymous author, Monsieur C.L.A.A.P.D.P., who was Pierre Bayle, without a doubt, although he never dared acknowledge it during his lifetime.[3] The initials can easily be interpreted as Carus Larebonius,

---

[1] This division is nowhere more accurately described than by Gédéon Huet in the preface to his *Lettre écrite de Suisse en Holland* (1690): "Il y a une autre chose dont quelques gens pourroient bien s'étonner encore, c'est à savoir la manière modérée en laquelle je parle du Roy de France. Ces sortes de gens, qui, grâce à Dieu, sont en très petit nombre, s'imaginent que l'on . . . . . n'a ni foy, ni loy, selon eux, à moins que les noms de Tyran, de Pharon, d'Antiochus, etc., ne se trouvent 2 ou 3 fois dans chaque page, pour embellir la pièce & pour inspirer au lecteur une sainte aversion contre nos persécuteurs." Joseph Dedieu in his *Le Rôle politique des protestants français, 1685–1715* attempts to show that the radical group was in the majority but H. J. Reesink after his study of Bayle's *Nouvelles de la république des lettres*, Le Clerc's *Bibliothèque universelle*, and Basnage de Beauval's *Histoire des ouvrages des savants* in his *L'Angleterre et la littérature anglaise dans les trois plus anciens périodiques français de Hollande,* concludes that the moderates are more characteristic of Huguenot refugee thought than the zealots.

[2] Up to 1695 over a dozen histories of the English Revolution were published in Paris itself.

[3] See Georges Ascoli, "Bayle et l'Avis aux Réfugiés," *Revue d'histoire littéraire de la France,* XX (1913), 517–545, and Jean Devolvé, *Religion, critique et philosophie positive chez Pierre Bayle,* pp. 186–194, for the most convincing proof of his authorship. For the denial of his hand in the work, compare Charles Bastide, "Bayle, est-il l'auteur de l'Avis aux Réfugiés," *Bulletin . . . du Protestantisme français* (1907), and Howard Robinson, *Bayle, the Sceptic,* pp. 119 ff. Cf. also a letter of Bayle to Constant dated January 29, 1691, quoted

avocat au Parlement de Paris, which is the pseudonym which Bayle used when writing his *Janua coelorum reserata* in 1692 against Jurieu. Furthermore, the first syllable of each word of this pen name when combined spell Carla, the place of Bayle's birth. The work is supposed to be by a lawyer in France who had been converted to Catholicism. The Huguenot to whom the book was sent also claims in a preface to it that he was scandalized by the indignities against the Protestants therein, but since it would take time for him to prepare an adequate reply, he thinks it best to publish the work so that its character can be publicly known and refuted.

Under the guise of a liberal Catholic, who has disapproved of the persecution of the Huguenots and who should like to see them reestablished in France by the authority of the king,[4] Bayle outlines his arguments with the greatest cogency. He begins by warning the French Protestants to rid themselves of the spirit of satire and republicanism before they can possibly return to France. It is with these two themes that the *Avis* is concerned. As to the first, Bayle declares that instead of the charity preached by Saint Paul the refugees manifest a spirit of revenge against their sovereign. He finds no counterpart in libelous writings in the early church. Attention is also called to the moderation of the English Catholic refugees abroad, while James II is described as a Saul who has been attacked by a David in the person of William of Orange.

As to the second point, Bayle maintains that the cardinal principle of the refugees· is that sovereign and subjects are reciprocally obligated by contract. If the former fails to fulfill his promises, the latter are released from obedience and can set up new rulers, whether the whole people

in Dedieu, *Rôle politique des protestants,* pp. 69–72. Bayle concludes: "Ce que je puis mettre en fait, est qu'il n'y a que le désaveu du dogme de la Souveraineté des peuples qui nous puisse justifier du dessein où nos adversaires nous mettent, pour nous fermer à jamais l'entrée du Royaume de France, comme à des républicains qui mettent les rênes du governement, non seulement entre les notables, mais de la canaille même si les notables ne font pas leur devoir." This evidence seems conclusive for Bayle's authorship in spite of the fact that many of the ideas in the *Avis* are inconsistent with the argument against persecution in his famous *Ce que c'est que la France toute catholique sous le règne de Louis le Grand* (1685). The other authors to whom the *Avis* has been attributed were Daniel de Larroque and Paul Pellisson.

[4] See Charles Read, "Vauban, Fénelon et le duc de Chevreuse sur la tolérance et le rappel des Protestants," *Bulletin . . . du Protestantisme français,* XXXIX (1890), 113–128.

disapprove the action of the monarch or only the most considerable part of them. This same doctrine was the inspiration of the civil wars in the preceding century and of the foreign interventions at that time. It was from the tombs of Buchanan, Junius Brutus, and Milton that Bayle accused the Protestants of deriving this principle of popular sovereignty.

The philosopher of Rotterdam cites with approval Arnauld's *Apologie pour les catholiques*,[5] in which Buchanan, Junius Brutus, and other Protestant writers are severely condemned. The Protestant synods also are reproached for never denouncing the iniquitous books of these men. Only the national synod held at Tonneius in 1614 censured Jesuits like Suarez for their seditious antimonarchical doctrines. Jurieu's reference to this event in his *Histoire du calvinisme et celle du papisme mises en parallèle* is cited together with the following acid comment: "Are kings dependent upon God alone? . . . If it is a question of defaming the Pope and the Jesuits, I affirm it; if it is a question of excluding from the throne some prince distasteful to the Protestants, I deny it." [6]

Bayle next accused the Protestants of passing from white to black in less than ten years. This had also been a "legitimate prejudice" of Nicole against the Calvinists. As evidence Bayle contrasts Jurieu's ideas in his *Politique du clergé* (1681) with his doctrine in the *Lettres pastorales* (1689). He then asserts that the Protestants would return to their position of 1681 if a Catholic ruler, such as the Emperor or the King of Spain, desiring to become a Protestant, should find his subjects ready to depose him. He calls attention also to the treatment of the Irish, who are denied the right to obey James II, at the same time that the people of England are justified in establishing a new king, William of Orange. Moreover, he cleverly points out that the Huguenots desire a victory of the House of Austria over France, but the Hungarian Protestants pray for the very opposite. This proves that the Protestants are not all animated by the same spirit, but by the peculiar circumstances in which they happen to find themselves.

Bayle insists that there must be in every civil society, whether republican or monarchical, a certain authority from whose decisions there is

[5] As Bossuet said in his *Défense de l'Histoire des variations*, the *Avis* is built largely upon the arguments contained in this earlier work by Arnauld, especially Chaps. III and IV of Book I.

[6] *Avis aux réfugiés*, pp. 75–86.

no appeal. If the people reserve the right of free examination and the privilege of obeying or not according to the justice or injustice of the commands of this authority, then public order becomes impossible and anarchy results.[7] But such consequences need not follow from popular sovereignty when parliaments, estates, or magistrates rather than private individuals have the right to control rulers. But Bayle replies with "sed quis custodiet ipsos custodes?" Will not individuals question the action of estates or magistrates and not ratify it, if they judge it to be unreasonable? This would eventually make each individual as independent as he would be without belonging to the body politic at all.[8]

Bayle declared, furthermore, that the doctrines of the Protestants result in the principle that the majority should not prevail over the minority. If this doctrine is adopted, then the Protestants were perfectly correct in refusing to obey the Edicts of Revocation, even though they were verified in all the *parlements* of the realm. But at the same time, if a less numerous sect like the Socinians and the Quietists should refuse to obey the penal laws against them, then logically they could not be condemned either for such action. This, however, is an application of the theory which the orthodox Jurieu would be most unwilling to accept. In the same way the nobility, a province, a city, or even a private individual could resist the laws of the kingdom, if they are considered unjust.

Bayle mentions next the Catholic attack upon the Calvinists with regard to the submission to national synods, which is required by their discipline. The Calvinist reply had been that these disciplinary regula-

---

[7] "Or si une fois on établit pour principe que la souveraineté émane du peuple, on conçoit chaque membre de la société comme un souverain absolu pour le moment qui a précédé son incorporation dans la République. Ensuite s'il n'est plus souverain ce n'est qu'à l'égard des droits auxquels il a renoncé, mais quand aux choses dont il n'a point cédé la souveraineté, il est évident qu'il demeure souverain, donc il le demeure quand au droit d'examiner ce qu'on lui commande & d'y désobéir s'il le juge tirannique & contraire au but qu'on s'est proposé en formant les Sociétez. . . . Chaque particulier étant juge en dernier ressort de la conduite de ceux qui gouverne, il ne manquera pas de définir la tyrannie, l'oppression, le bien public, le salut du peuple (d'après le maxime: *salus populi suprema lex esto*), les commodités de la vie, la liberté, le nécessaire, par rapport à sa sensibilité, à son inclination et ainsi jamais les prétextes les plus spécieux de se dégager de son serment et de changer de maître ne manqueront." *Avis aux réfugiés*, pp. 87–97, 108–119.

[8] In a discussion of Sorbière's translation of Hobbes *De cive*, Bayle indicates that he regards the evil results of "la puissance partagée" as far greater than those which attend "la puissance arbitraire." See his *Réponse aux questions d'un provincial* in *Oeuvres*, 1737, III, 621.

tions could not derogate from the inalienable right of all individuals to examine the decisions of the Councils and only submit to them when they were in conformity with the word of God. In the same way with regard to the oath of fidelity to the king in the temporal sphere, the people, according to this principle, should always reserve the right to examine the king's conduct and only ratify it if it conformed to the laws.

Bayle cites Nicole's *De l'unité de l'Eglise* (Book III, Chapter IV), which demonstrated that the Protestant principle of individual free examination in matters of faith was a doctrine of dissolution, leading to the establishment of as many sects as families in a state. He then asserts that the doctrine of popular sovereignty results in the same disintegration. In fact, he demonstrates that it was not far to go from an overthrow of the authority of the church to a rebellion against the secular power, nor from the equality of pastors to that of temporal magistrates.[9] Bayle points out further that the Catholics are correct when they stress the conformity between ecclesiastical and civil government, since the Protestants give no more authority to the latter than is allowed to the former. In fact, they have modeled the plan of civil society upon that of the church. Therefore, the objection of M. Claude in the preface of his *Conférence* that the Catholics have formed the plan of the infallibility of the church upon that of civil society, which requires a sovereign authority, is to no avail.

Bayle declares that the principal question is whether, according to the Calvinists, all the people, a minority, or each person, can disobey the ruler. He concludes that it is each person, since the preparation of a revolt can be made only by private individuals who become discontented and communicate their dissatisfaction to others. Bayle adds that when he speaks of individuals he understands not only those who hold no office in the state, but also those who do, either in the judiciary or army. When a councilor, a master of requests, or a marshal of France is not acting by commission either of the king, the *parlements,* or the Estates

---

[9] "Croire comme vous avez fait de tout temps que l'Eglise n'a point une autorité à laquelle chaque particulier doive soumettre ses propres lumières & croire comme vous faisiez encore lors de la publication de *la politique du clergé & de la conférence (1683) de M. l'Evêque de Meaux avec M. Claude* que la Société civile est revêtue d'un pouvoir à quoi tous les particuliers doivent obéir, c'étoit joindre ensemble deux systèmes qui n'étoient pas faits l'un pour l'autre." *Avis aux réfugiés,* p. 128.

General, his actions can only be considered to be those of an individual. Since, therefore, he includes all the magistrates acting on their own account in the class of individuals, Bayle argues that his analysis is in agreement with Junius Brutus, who permitted resistance by private persons under the standard of the officers of the realm, representing them. But he cannot help expressing fear for the social order if individuals group themselves under magistrates to resist the king. Would this procedure not result in the production of a thousand tyrants in addition to the ruler?

In connection with an analysis of Beza's *Du droit des magistrats sur leurs sujets* Bayle declares that if sovereignty comes from the people, then it follows that rulers are but the first officers of the people and all the subordinate magistrates are but inferior officers. As first officers of the people the kings are accountable for their administration and the magistrates even more so, since they are subordinates of a still lower rank. If this is true, then it would be absurd to hold that the people can examine the action of kings and resist them when necessary, but that they must follow blindly the orders of the subordinate magistrates. But, if an individual should prefer the command of a minor magistrate to that of the king, would not all subordination be destroyed? Obedience would be directly to the magistrate and only by accident to the head of the state. Furthermore, logically the great officers of the crown will watch over the conduct of the ruler, the minor magistrates will examine the behavior of the officers of the crown, and those who hold no office will control the activities of the minor magistrates. But, asks Bayle, what is to be done if the king dominates all the magistrates and as a result they refuse to resist his tyranny? He concludes that in the end it is necessary for private individuals to have the right of resistance. In Bayle's view, Knox and Goodman were much more logical than the rest of the Monarchomachs, since the former put resistance by the people on the same level as that of the magistrates, while the latter gave the right of rebellion to the people alone, according to our philosopher.

Bayle prays that God deliver Europe from a Huguenot Pope, who has caused more damage to sovereigns since 1517 than the Catholic Pontiff. There is more to be feared from the doctrine of popular sovereignty than from ultramontanism. He is astonished that the life of Julian the

Apostate [10] was published to show that the Christians were obliged to exclude him from the empire and that for more reason the Duke of York should be barred from the throne of England. It was even more audacious of the Huguenot refugees, who complain bitterly over the interdiction of their religion and who await their recall to France, to translate from the English the libel, *Le Triomphe de la liberté; ou, L'Irrévocabilité du Test et autres lois fondamentales des états prouvés par le droit divin, par le droit de la nation & par la mort tragique de Charles Stuward Père du Roi règnant* (1688), in which the king was menaced if he dared change the laws that denied liberty of conscience to his Catholic subjects.

Bayle strongly approved of the treatment of the Vaudois Protestants by the Duke of Savoy, who in 1686 under the influence of Louis XIV had expelled them from their valleys. In 1688 they attempted to return and in the following year they executed this plan by force. For this action they are severely condemned by the *Avis*. Bayle cites the *Esprit de M. Arnaud* (II, 335) by Jurieu as approving the banishment of Catholics from Protestant realms. But he asserts that the Calvinists would be the first to condemn the Socinians, should they attempt to return by force of arms into Poland, from whence they had been driven.

From this whole argument it can be readily seen that Bayle is emphasizing all along the supremacy of the temporal authority over all religious parties in the state.[11] This stress upon secularism, in keeping with the age, was none the less anathema to the orthodox Jurieu, who was championing a lost cause—that of the *Corpus christianum*. It should be

[10] Certain copies of this book are entitled *La Peste du genre humain ou la vie de Julien l'Apostat mise en parallèle avec celle de Louis XIV,* Cologne, 1696. This revision was probably made by Jurieu. See Charles Nodier, *Mélanges extraits d'une petite bibliothèque,* p. 133. One of the principal propositions of this tract is that Christianity does not destroy the natural or civil rights of anyone, but confirms them. "Tous les hommes ont un droit naturel & civil à la propriété de leurs vies, jusqu'à ce qu'ils ayent mérité de les perdre par les loix de leur Pays." *Julien l'Apostat,* 1688, pp. 106–107. This tract was probably a partial translation originally of Samuel Johnson's *Julian the Apostate,* which was issued in England at the time of the Exclusion Bill.

[11] "En effet les auteurs paiens qui ont traité des devoirs de l'homme ont établi pour principe qu'après ce que nous devons à Dieu, la première et la plus sacrée de nos obligations est celle de servir notre patrie; de sorte qu'ils nous ordonnent de la préférer à nos pères et à nos mères. Leur gradation est qu'il faut rendre ses devoirs premièrement à Dieu, puis à sa patrie, ensuite à ceux qui nous ont engendrés." *Avis aux réfugiés,* in *Oeuvres,* 1737, II, 594–595.

recalled, however, that his more famous contemporary Locke had sided with Bayle on this very issue, asserting that "there is absolutely no such thing under the gospel as a Christian Commonwealth." [12]

As can be imagined, this very able attack on the extreme group of the Huguenot refugees burst like a bombshell upon the whole French Protestant colony in the Netherlands. The leader of the zealots, Jurieu, was in a frenzy of anger over this piece of outrageous *Advice*. He was the first to answer the book with his *Examen d'un libelle* (1691). He described it as the most pernicious writing against the Protestants since the Reformation. In another place [13] Jurieu compares it with the letter of Charpentier to Candois, justifying the massacre of Saint Bartholomew. He immediately accused Bayle of being the author, pointing out that he refutes often *La Politique du clergé, L'Esprit de M. Arnaud, La Réponse à Maimbourg, La Plainte de M. Claude,* but never cites nor refutes *La Critique générale contre L'Histoire de P. Maimbourg,* which everyone knew was by the philosopher of Rotterdam. At any rate Jurieu successfully established the Protestant origin of the libel by numerous illustrations of minute details [14] which would not be accessible to a Catholic.

Opening his counterattack he denies that complaints can be considered as libels.[15] Even those writings [16] which attempt to cause an uprising in France by advocating that the Dauphin should bring his father to reason are to be regarded as methods of strategy permissible in wartime.[17] Is it not the tactic of war to attempt to arouse divisions in the

[12] Locke, "A Letter concerning Toleration," in *Works*, VI, p. 38.

[13] *Apologie du Sieur Jurieu*, (1691), p. 25.

[14] For example, Jurieu doubted that a Parisian Catholic would know that in the year 1555 the theologians of Magdeburg published a treatise on the power of kings and on the manner in which they should be obeyed.

[15] Cf. Antoine Coulan, *La Défense des réfugiés contre un livre intitulé Avis important aux réfugiés sur leur prochain retour en France,* pp. 133–134: "C'est un droit que la nature a donné à tous les hommes & que la grâce n'a pas ôté aux Chrétiens de se plaindre des maux qu'ils souffrent & des personnes qui les font souffrir & que si la Religion modère les plaints elle ne les étouffe pas."

[16] See the *Salut de la France*, Cologne, 1690. Since this pamphlet appeared in the Netherlands but two weeks before the *Avis*, Jurieu concluded that the author of the *Avis* must be a Protestant in Holland in order to have knowledge of this tract so soon.

[17] "Or selon toutes les loix de la guerre il est permis de souhaiter, d'approuver & de procurer la destruction de ses ennemis excepté par les assassinats. C'est pourquoy la maison d'Autriche a pu sans rapport à la religion ni au droit des Roys approuver l'action des Anglois qui ont rompu les châines dont Jacques II leur lioit les mains. Et si aujourd'huy pareille

enemy in order to secure victory more easily, asks Jurieu? He admits that such books would not be allowed in peace time yet during hostilities the pen should aid the sword. There were scores of similar libellous tracts in the second and third centuries, but the lapse of time has destroyed these evidences of the impatience of the early Christians,[18] whose virtues are now being constantly extolled by the author of the *Avis*. If the libels of the preceding century on the Protestant side would fill ten volumes, then those of the Catholic League would fill twenty, concludes our minister of Rotterdam.

Jurieu declares that the *Avis* was published for four reasons: first, to alienate the Catholic allies from their union with the Protestant princes, by declaring that the war was a religious struggle in which the Protestants demanded the restoration of their privileges by seeking the disgrace and defeat of France. This explains the accusation of rebellion and sedition against the Protestants. Second, the author attempts to discourage internal movements in France, upon which the Allies were counting heavily, by granting the royal authority unlimited power and demanding complete obedience of subjects. Third, the *Avis* warns the refugees that they will count in vain upon the Allies for the reestablishment of Protestantism in France and that, therefore, the only course open to them is to rely upon the clemency of Louis XIV for their return. But the king will be kindly disposed toward them only if they will retract their antimonarchical doctrines. Furthermore, even if the Allies should be able to force the restoration of the Edict of Nantes upon

---

révolution arrivoit en France, que le Dauphin poussé par les Alliés prit les resnes du gouvernement & rendit à ses Voisins tout se qui leur a été ravi se contentant de l'ancien Domaine de ses Ancêtres, tous les Roys de l'Europe l'approuveroient & le pourroient approuver sans violer aucune des règles de la Religion & de la Morale. Car tout est permis & de bonne guerre contr'un ennemi déclaré." *Examen d'un libelle*, pp. 111–114. It was this last statement which led Bayle to accuse Jurieu of approving tyrannicide as exercised by Poltrot, Clément, Châtel, Ravaillac, etc. Because Jurieu declared that the Prince of Orange, Condé, Coligny, Rohan, and so on, were inspired by God, Bayle was quick to conclude that the same could be said of Poltrot, Clément, and Ravaillac in the mind of our theologian. See Jurieu, *Le Philosophe dégradé* (1692), pp. 83–89.

[18] Jurieu cites the surviving work of Firmianus Lactantius, *De mortibus persecutorum*, which was written after the Emperor Constantine published his edict of toleration in 313, as an example of the fact that the severe morality of the time did not prevent a statement of the truth. This work was translated, after its recovery by Basnage in 1687, as *Récit de la mort des persécuteurs de Lactance*, and created quite a stir in the prophetic atmosphere of an age when the Protestants regarded Louis XIV as the persecutor of the true church.

the king, they could not prevent his again recalling it later. Fourth, the Allies, both Catholic and Protestant, must be persuaded that they can never humble France, which is invincible. As a result, the only way left is to demand peace upon French terms.

A short time before the appearance of the *Avis*, an outline of such a peace had already been presented by a Genevese merchant named Goudet, who wrote *Entretien sur les moyens de faire la paix*. Its terms were on virtually the same conditions as those of France; all that was promised with regard to the Huguenots was a toleration similar to that of the Catholics in Holland. When Jurieu suspected that Bayle was connected with the publication of this *Projet de paix*, the *Avis* became no longer the work of a single person, but of a cabal which extended from the south to the north and had its center in the French Court. Both Goudet and Bayle [19] are indifferent to the advancement of the glory of the Lord and the deliverance of His Kingdom, since they wish to sustain a "prince, the declared enemy of God and the cruel persecutor of his church." [20] How, asks Jurieu, can the authors of the *Avis* and the *Projet* square the conquests of such a monarch with justice? Just conquests come only from just wars, which do not include those of Louis XIV. [21]

But Jurieu hastens to add that he does not seek the ruin of his native land. He only wants to make it more beautiful than ever by the reestablishment of liberty and truth. [22] Although the Huguenots have sworn allegiance to other sovereigns, Jurieu asserts that the feeling of duty to their native land could be reborn if the king would only restore their privileges and cease to wage war upon the Protestant powers which gave them shelter. "In a word, our peace is today attached to that of all Europe," [23] he concludes.

It is important to note that all the while Jurieu was accusing Bayle of intriguing with the French court for peace and the return of the Hu-

[19] A close connection can be noted between the *Projet de paix*, the *Avis*, and the *Réponse d'un nouveau converti*. All three seem to be preparing for the return of the Protestants to France through a pacification of the king.

[20] *Examen d'un libelle*, pp. 69-79.

[21] Jurieu say he does not wish to argue against the right of conquest in general: "Peut-être trouveroit-on que dans la plus exacte morale, ce droit n'est pas mieux fondé que celuy de prendre les armes pour cause de Religion?" *Ibid.*

[22] "On rend toujours service à la patrie quand on procure sa liberté. On n'a nul dessein de la livrer en proye aux étrangers & d'en faire une province d'Allemagne." *Ibid.*, p. 217.

[23] *Lettres pastorales*, XIV, Third Year, pp. 314-315.

guenots through the authority of the king, he himself was engaged in a most extensive fashion in an intricate espionage system in behalf of William, of the Grand Pensioner, Heinsius, and of the Allies against France. According to one authority,[24] he began his espionage activities as early as 1689 and from 1692 or 1693 until his death he directed a committee of secret agents, but his part in this affair was so skillfully guarded by William and Heinsius that his contemporaries never discovered the secret. Of this we can be absolutely certain, since Bossuet, Bayle, and Basnage de Beauval would certainly have exploited such information to the last possible degree, not only in their own defense but in addition as a proof that Jurieu himself was a bad Frenchman.

The one letter of Jurieu's [25] made public in his lifetime, written to Montausier on April 4, 1689, was constantly used against him by his enemies [26] as an example of his inconsistency. His views on the right of resistance and popular sovereignty as expressed in the *Lettres pastorales* (1689) were contrasted with his secret expression of loyalty to the king in the same year. In that letter, wherein he sought the release of a Huguenot pastor from the Bastille in return for the surrender of the monk who intended to assassinate Louis XIV, he had contended that his "respect [27] for the sacred person of His Majesty was still complete in his soul without having received any injury." In the same epistle he protested that he never had advocated insurrection against the royal authority, to which he owed inviolable obedience. Jurieu, however, later defended his action against his critics by frankly admitting that, when

[24] Dedieu, *Le Rôle politique des protestants*, p. 181. This author has published the important correspondence of Jurieu with the English Secretary of State from 1692–1705. See also G. Das, "Pierre Jurieu als Middelpunt van een spionnagedienst (son organisation d'espionage en France, 1689–1713)" in *Tijdschrift voor Geschiednis*, XLI (Groningen, 1926), 372.

[25] This letter was published by E. Griselle, "Louis XIV et Jurieu, d'après une lettre inédite de ce dernier," *Bulletin . . . du Protestantisme français*, March–April, 1906.

[26] See Basnage de Beauval, *Lettres sur les différends de M. Jurieu & M. Bayle*, pp. 35–36 and Bayle, *La Chimère de la cabale de Rotterdam* in *Oeuvres*, 1727, II, 782.

[27] Jurieu preached a sermon in 1694 which advocated hating the enemies of God, such as the King of France. This is contrasted with the letter to Montausier in Bayle's *Nouvelle hérésie dans la morale touchant la haine du prochain, prêchee par M. Jurieu* in *Oeuvres*, 1727, II, 815. Bayle also devoted more than five pages in folio of his famous *Dictionary* to this dispute. See the article "Zuerius Boxhornius" Rem. P. Cf. also Basnage de Beauval, *Considérations sur deux sermons de M. Jurieu*. Jurieu answered this libel in an *Apologie pour les synodes* (1692), to which Basnage replied with his violent *M. Jurieu convaincu de calomnie & d'imposture*.

a favor is desired from a prince, the method to be employed to insure success is not violence but general submission.[28]

In response to that section of the *Avis aux réfugiés* which dealt with the seditious maxims of the Protestants against the power of kings, Jurieu begins by declaring that the matter is very delicate and that when treating it "a golden mean" is to be sought. Too low a regard for the power of sovereigns is to be avoided, for they are to be feared and obeyed not only "because of punishment but also for the sake of conscience." They are "the anointed of the Eternal and the lieutenants of God," and their persons are sacred. This was but a restatement of the same ideas he had proclaimed many times previously.

Furthermore, it is better "for public peace" that the people do not know the true extent of their powers. At this point Jurieu takes violent exception to the accusation of the *Avis* that the Huguenot ideas of the rights of the people against the arbitrary power of sovereigns are only used in order to bring about revolution in those states where the Protestant interest demands it, after which they are immediately abandoned. On the contrary, the rights of the people are "remedies which must not be wasted or applied in the case of minor wrongs. They are mysteries which must not be profaned by exposing them too much before the eyes of the common herd." [29] But when are these remedies to be employed? "When it comes to the destruction of the state or religion, then they can be produced; beyond that I do not think it evil that they should be covered with silence," concludes Jurieu. Even those kings whose power is the most limited by the laws of the state are eager to appear to have arbitrary power and so long as they observe "the laws for the preservation of the state and the church" it is better to let them indulge in this little pretense. Thus, the people are not to be reminded too often of their true powers, since they might make a bad use of them and become disposed to sedition. But at the same time it is equally dangerous to speak to sovereigns of their arbitrary power and independence, since experience shows this to be even more disastrous than too great an emphasis on the rights of the people. Therefore, great precautions should be taken not to be the disciple of anyone on this ticklish question, "neither of

[28] *Réflexions sur un libelle* (1691), pp. 4–5.
[29] Note still another reference of a typically Calvinistic contempt for the multitude.

Buchanan, nor Pareus, nor Junius Brutus." [30] Furthermore, it is unnecessary to discuss such "odious questions" as to whether kings can be imprisoned and punished. The conclusion Jurieu draws is that it is not his task to define precisely the limits either to the rights of the people or to those of the power of sovereigns. [31] From general ideas on this question the particular application must be made according to the circumstances.

But moderation cannot, however, obscure or lead to the renunciation of two fundamental doctrines—first, that there is no power in the world immediately from God, and second, that human authority, whether civil or ecclesiastical, has its limits beyond which people are not obliged to carry their patience. As for the first maxim, both the secular and the spiritual powers have their source in the people. If there is any power which comes directly from God, it would be the ecclesiastical, since God immediately established the sacerdotal power of Aaron and his sons, and Christ sent the apostles. But when the miracles and direct revelation ended, the people reentered into their rights to erect and conserve the ecclesiastical ministry. If this is not admitted, then, first, no matter how corrupt the ecclesiastical ministry should become, the people could not act. Second, should a people find itself on an island far from any churches on the mainland, it could not create for itself pastors and an ecclesiastical government. Moreover, the sovereign independence of the sacerdotal power as emanating immediately from God is combated by the Protestants, since among them the clerical power is subordinated to the civil authority of the magistrate, which is derived only from men. Here is a reference to the Erastian position, which Jurieu adopts with regard to the relations of church and state, a problem to be considered in the second part of this study. Furthermore, if the civil power of sovereigns came from God directly, then God would have to descend in the erection of each monarchy. This whole argument had already been stated in practically the same manner much earlier in his *Lettres pastorales;* in his *Traité de la puissance de l'Eglise;* and in *Traité de l'unité de l'Eglise.*

[30] For this and the previous quotations see *Examen d'un libelle,* pp. 70–75.

[31] Cf., however, the Eighteenth *Lettre pastorale* of the Third Year: "Il me semble pourtant que sans beaucoup risquer on peut dire que ces bornes se trouvent justement où cessent le salut et la conservation du peuple qui est la souveraine loi."

But how was Jurieu to explain away the fact that Huguenot writers like Merlat, Daillé, Saumaise, Bochart, and others had derived the authority of kings directly from God? They could be regarded as speaking prudently, since they lived under absolute monarchies, where it is well for the people to be reminded of their duties by such a principle, argues our theologian. The real reason for the theory of the immediate relation between God and the ruler, however, is that these writers did not by their extreme statements intend to prejudice the rights of the people by not referring to them. They could be left intact in silence. But these authors could also mean that kings do not have a sovereign over them like the Pope, who has been regarded in some quarters as supreme over kings in the temporal as well as for the spiritual sphere. Jurieu asserts that it was principally against this papal encroachment that the Huguenot writers had defended the sovereign independence of kings. Nor is even the people to be regarded as a sovereign [32] above the king. In order to explain this, Jurieu holds that once again the comparison between the ecclesiastical and the civil power must be made. Even though the people is the source of the sacerdotal power, it is not a ministry with the right to administer sacred affairs.[33] Jurieu maintains, therefore, that "there is quite a difference between having power and authority in hand and preserving the right of appeal against the abuse of authority." [34] For example, children have the right to resist the misuse of paternal authority, but because of that they do not have paternal authority in hand. Therefore, concludes Jurieu, there is but one sovereign in the state, who has no one above him but God.

With regard to the other proposition that the power of sovereigns has limits, Jurieu repeats the arguments of the *Lettres pastorales* that the very origin of the power of sovereigns from the people indicates its bounds. But even if kings received their authority directly from God, the people need not be massacred by rulers, since God established kings

---

[32] See an emphatic passage occurring later in the *Examen d'un libelle*, p. 141: "Au contraire, nous l'ôtons aux peuples pour la (la souveraineté) donner aux Roys & nous disons que les peuples en la donnant s'en sont entièrement dépouillés."

[33] "Quand une société se fait un Tribunal de Justice pour la décision des procès, à cause qu'elle a fait le Tribunal de Justice, peut on dire qu'elle a retenu par divers foy le pouvoir de juger les particuliers & les juger mêmes? Parcequ'une Armée a reservé le Généralat à l'un des Capitaines toute l'Armée en Général & chaque soldat en particulier aura-t-il retenu le pouvoir de commander & de donner les ordres." *Examen d'un libelle*, pp. 141–142.

[34] *Ibid.*, p. 84, and see p. 71 of this study, note 96.

"to conserve communities and religion and not to destroy them." Jurieu maintains further that it is not necessary to discover the sentiments of the Huguenot theologians in a few passages extorted by fear and prudence, but rather in the conduct of the Protestants in their resistance by arms to the cruelties of the French and Spanish kings in the past. He refused to abjure either the behavior or the sentiments of his ancestors. Those who do so put themselves in a state of contradiction. This is especially the case with those English who supported the declarations of the University of Oxford [35] in 1622 against the propositions which seek to limit the power of monarchs and to give a right of resistance to the oppressed. How could the English, who are so jealous of their privileges, ever espouse the extreme position of the academies of Oxford and Cambridge, asks Jurieu? Even Turks have deposed their rulers, while the Anglicans, whom Bayle had praised in the *Avis* for their support of the independence of kings, were the first to rebel when religion and liberty were really touched.[36]

As we have seen, among the contradictions of the Protestants which Bayle had pointed out, the most glaring was the difference between the maxims of the French Calvinists on the authority of kings, when they were arguing against the papal power in 1681, and those of the Huguenots, when they were subjecting the ruler to the authority of the people at the time of the English Revolution of 1688–89.[37] In reply to these accusations of contradiction Jurieu held first, that in general all that could be concluded was that the Protestants were divided on the question of the limited or unlimited power of sovereigns, which in his mind decided nothing. Even if a few authors are proved to be contradictory on this issue, the Protestants as a whole are not obliged to answer for these particular cases. As for the statement Bayle had cited from Jurieu's *Politique du clergé* that kings depend upon God alone "for the temporal," our theologian argues first that an author is to be understood

---

[35] This decree was reprinted in *Principes de Messieurs Bossuet et Fénelon sur la souveraineté*.

[36] Jurieu refers here, of course, to the resistance of the seven bishops in 1688 against the king on the occasion of his order for them to read a declaration of liberty of conscience.

[37] It should be recalled that Bayle regarded Merlat's doctrine as very common among the Protestants in 1685, but eight years later in September, 1693, he wrote to Minutoli with regard to Locke's theory of the sovereignty of the people: "Vous savez que c'est l'Évangile du jour à présent parmi les Protestants." See the *Oeuvres*, 1737, IV, 700.

and explained with relation to the subject matter in question, which in this book was the pretensions of the Pope and not the rights of the people. Secondly, with regard to the other principle in the book, namely, that kings cannot be deposed for heresy or schism, Jurieu contended that he was referring to a Protestant theological doctrine, which was directly opposed to the Catholic dogma that the Pope or a Council can dethrone kings when they become enemies of the church. In other words, it was a "religious dispute," and not at all a matter concerning the rights of the people oppressed by tyrants. Furthermore, continued Jurieu, the question of the independence of kings and the rights of the people against tyrants has a purely political aspect in which religion is not involved, whether Protestant or Catholic. It is rather a matter of controversy among all nations and at all times, since all kings have always tried to secure blind obedience from the people. As a result both Protestant and Catholic writers are split on the question. At any rate the issue was not discussed in the *Politique du clergé*. Finally, Jurieu objects to the tactic of seeking contradictions in a book of apology and remonstrance,[38] the object of which was to soften the heart of a king (who was under the domination of a persecuting clergy), by presenting the Huguenot cause in the best possible light. In such a tract it is sufficient to remain within the confines of religion and not be concerned with politics in order to define the respective rights of the peoples and kings.

Jurieu now turns to Bayle's objection that popular sovereignty would result in each member of society having a right of revision over the commands of the Prince, if the magistrates do not act. But Jurieu asks if this has anything to do with the basic question as to whether "nations and communities have the right of self-preservation by resisting an authority which destroys them?" He conceded that the right of conservation is possessed in joint tenancy by the whole society but "there is no individual who is not bound to act for the safety of the republic when those who govern are the instruments of tyranny."[39] Jurieu maintains

[38] Cf. Henri Basnage de Beauval, *Lettres sur les différends de M. Jurieu et de M. Bayle,* in which the author insists that the *Politique du clergé* is not a work of remonstrance but a closely reasoned book to show how the king can depend upon the absolute submission of the Huguenots in preference to his other subjects. If it is regarded only as flattery, which is now to be disregarded, what basis can the king have ever to trust his Protestant subjects again, concludes Basnage de Beauval?
[39] *Examen d'un libelle,* pp. 121–128.

that only by the action of private individuals can a reformation in the church or state be begun and accomplished. Because sailors, seeing a vessel founder, are permitted to rush to its aid, they are not invested thereby with the office of admiral. In the same way, private persons who consult together on the means of resisting tyranny, are not clothed with the right of sovereignty, as Bayle believed. According to the philosopher's theory, Jurieu claims it would be necessary "that an inspiration seize a whole nation in order that at the same time it could conceive the design of remedying the disorder of the state, because if it went from individual to individual, then there would be as many sovereigns, newly created." [40] But Jurieu felt that the action of private persons would never arise, since "it is not possible that the plan of delivering the country from the yoke would not originate first in the mind of some prominent persons." But if, however, "the most accredited officers" [41] should not act, then "everybody has a vocation for awakening those who sleep and for inciting an oppressed society to think of its preservation." [42] True to his word Jurieu approved the revolts of the Protestants in the Cévennes and in Hungary.

Bayle had also accused the Protestants of holding a theory whereby the people could force a ruler to render an account of his administration and then refuse to obey him if they do not find his commands conformable to the laws. But Jurieu denied that either he or the other Reformers had ever held such a doctrine.[43] In reply to the philosopher of Rotterdam he argued that he would again distinguish two types of monarchy, while to Bayle all monarchies are the same, with the power to do anything with impunity. The basis of Jurieu's distinction, it will be recalled, was the amount of authority granted to the sovereign. Where the people reserved certain privileges and the right of revision over the actions of their sovereigns, the rulers are not "properly sovereigns, but governors," [44] since the people are only obliged to obey commands which

---

[40] *Ibid.*, pp. 161–164.

[41] Jurieu also terms them "chefs caractérizés." *Ibid.*, pp. 121–128.

[42] *Ibid.*

[43] It will be recalled that in the Seventeenth *Lettre pastorale* of the Third Year Jurieu had contended that the people could not give to the sovereign "l'administration des affaires publiques sans se réserver ou expressement ou tacitement le droit de pourvoir aux désordres que les souverains pourraient causer à la société par une mauvaise administration."

[44] *Ibid.*, pp. 141–146.

are compatible with the laws. Even Grotius had recognized this type of monarchy, but, according to Bossuet, to reserve any part of sovereign authority is contrary to the indivisibility of sovereignty, which ever since Bodin had been regarded as one of its principal characteristics. Jurieu maintained, however, that most of the sovereign states of Europe at that time, and, formerly all of them, including France, had the English type of government. Such a form divides the legislative power between the king and the people, requires the consent of the estates to grants, and demands that the sovereign rule according to the laws.[45] But Jurieu admits reluctantly [46] that people can also surrender all rights to a sovereign, who then has "an absolute power and without reservation." [47] This means that he has all the legislative power in hand to levy taxes and make peace and war. In fact he can even revoke "the privileges of such and such individuals with respect to temporal matters," without any right of resistance on the part of the people to his will. This idea of a complete alienation is also to be found in Grotius. Because he, in spite of certain exceptions, forbade resistance by subjects, this authority was cited by Bayle as well as by Jurieu, who emphasized those very exceptions to complete obedience.

But there are two rights which the people cannot surrender, since they are inalienable—"the right of conservation for the sake of the community and that of conscience and religion for the church." Grotius and even Barclay, who is quoted by Locke in this connection, agreed that a king who attempts to destroy a whole people can be resisted. With the situation in France obviously in mind, Jurieu maintains that "when a king desolates the state by the sword, by punishments, by exiles, and when he destroys the church and true religion by persecution," then the people are released from obedience. After all, they have only conferred the sovereign power upon the king "for the preservation of the community and the church and not for their destruction." But once again Jurieu warns

<hr />

[45] *Ibid.*, pp. 146–151.

[46] Especially is this reluctance evident with regard to France: "Ainsi en supposant que les Roys de France ayent été mis en possession de la Puissance Arbitraire par des voyes légitimes, ce qui est plus que douteux," still "leurs sujets n'ont plus en partage que l'obéissance." *Ibid.*, pp. 141–146.

[47] *Ibid.* In his Sixteenth *Lettre pastorale* of the Third Year it will be recalled that Jurieu was more liberal, since he could not conceive of a people being so blind as to surrender without condition to a ruler.

that for lesser evils, such as the ruin of a few private individuals or excessive taxes, rebellion is forbidden. He adds, however, another important restriction, namely, that "the devastation of the society and religion should be plain to everybody." [48] In a state where an arbitrary power is not established, "it is necessary that the breaking and the nonobservance of the laws will lead clearly to the subversion of religion and the republic." But the important question now follows: who is to judge whether religion or the republic are on the brink of destruction? Naturally, the prince will deny that the quashing of certain laws will lead to the demolition of the state and religion. Jurieu's answer to this crucial question is clearly put: "It will be public notoriety that will decide." [49] The interpretation hinges on the meaning of "notoriété publique." For example, James II held that the repeal of the Test Act and the establishment of Catholicism did not destroy the fundamental laws of the realm; but, asks Jurieu, is he to be believed "contre la notoriété?" Jurieu thinks it is evident that if the King of England ruins religion, he thereby destroys the laws, since by law and possession during two centuries the Protestant religion had become inseparably attached to the English government. Thus, it would seem that "notoriété publique" is to be defined as public knowledge or opinion. It is interesting to compare a passage in this connection from Jurieu's famous contemporary Locke, the English defender of the Glorious Revolution. "Who shall be judge whether the prince or legislative act contrary to their trust?" "To this, I reply, the people shall be judge." [50]

But Jurieu concludes that it is false to hold that according to his theory the people are the judges of their rulers, for on the contrary they are united "to make kings their judges and not to be made judges of monarchs." Even in England the people do not have the power to judge the

[48] *Examen d'un libelle*, pp. 146–151. Jurieu claims that this was why the Protestants suffered patiently under Francis I and Henry II, but could not under the later Valois, whose tyranny was leading to the destruction of society and religion. On this same principle the Netherlands was justified in revolting against Spain.

[49] *Ibid.*, pp. 152–154. Cf. the contradictory view in Jurieu's Sixteenth *Lettre pastorale* of the Third Year: "on leur [les rois] doit rendre tous hommages et toute obéissance dans toutes les choses qui sont justes, honnêtes, nécessaires. . . . Et c'est à ces puissances souveraines à juger de ce qui est nécessaire ou ce qui ne l'est pas."

[50] *Civil Government*, Chap. XIX, p. 241. Locke also speaks of the people having a "persuasion grounded upon manifest evidence that designs are carrying on against their liberties." *Ibid.*, p. 234.

king, although he does not possess an absolute or arbitrary power. "There is quite a difference between resisting tyranny and judging a king as one judges a private individual." [51]

Bayle had accused the Protestants of applying the same rule with regard to civil submission as was the case concerning ecclesiastical obedience. Each individual is at liberty to conform or not to the laws of the prince, just as he has the right in the church to submit or not to a judgment of a Synod or Council. In his emphatic denial of this charge Jurieu held that the submission of the heart to ecclesiastical decisions is an internal affair reserved to God alone, since the heart cannot be coerced into believing something which does not appear true to it. But obedience to the commands of the sovereign can be forced, since it is an external and visible action. He admitted, however, that sovereigns cannot force their subjects to believe that their commands are just, but "for the sake of order they can obligate them to obey them, even though they believe them unjust." [52]

Bayle had also pointed out, as we have noted, that the Protestant theological position now squared with the political, since all power both civil and ecclesiastical was in the hands of private individuals. In carrying the analogy further, the author of the *Avis* held that just as those persons who refused to submit to the decisions of the synods were excommunicated and permitted to set up another communion, so the Prince could only cut off those who refused to recognize the justice of his commands and permit them to form "a separate society." This would result in breaking the republic into a hundred other states. To this charge Jurieu answered that separation from the church by excommunication is simply "the last resort of the ecclesiastical power," [53] just as the death sentence of the civil authority is an extreme remedy. Thus, just as violent dissidents from the faith can in the last analysis be excommunicated, so extremely disobedient subjects can be put to death, if absolutely necessary. But this is quite different from saying that they can secede from the state.

Jurieu then proceeded to outline his own comparison of the ecclesiastical power with the civil. First, as the origin of the ecclesiastical power is in the *populus*, so also is the source of civil authority. Second, just

---

[51] *Examen d'un libelle*, pp. 146–151.   [52] *Ibid.*, p. 154.   [53] *Ibid.*, pp. 154–161.

as the ecclesiastical tribunals can make false decisions which are contrary to the faith, so can rulers give unjust commands. Third, as the members of the church are not obliged to believe the decisions of a synod to be true, unless they are according to Scripture, so subjects need not believe that the commands of the prince are just, unless they are in conformity with natural law or the law of the state. Fourth, as the members of a church must obey "at least by their silence" a decision of the Council, even though they believe it to be false—provided that it does not touch eternal salvation—so a subject is obliged to obey the commands of the sovereign "for the sake of order," since that cannot affect his eternal welfare. Fifth, as the church can excommunicate individuals and even rely upon the additional aid of the civil power against those who refuse to submit to its decisions, unless by so doing they destroy the fundamentals of the faith, so the sovereign can pronounce the death penalty on refractory subjects, if his commands do not lead to the ruin of religion or society. In that case Jurieu would allow not only disobedience but also resistance, as we have repeatedly seen.

But Bayle also had contended that Protestant principles lead naturally to the doctrine that the majority should not prevail over a minority. Even Grotius,[54] however, laid no blame upon a minority that resisted the oppression of a majority, answered Jurieu. Furthermore, Bayle's attack on this point was obviously a condemnation of the Huguenots, who took up arms in the preceding century when they were persecuted by kings, behind whom were a majority of the people. It was also a censure of the recalcitrant refugees whose exile was secured by the revocation of the Edict of Nantes; the Edict had at least the tacit consent of the majority, and had been verified in the sovereign courts of France. Finally, it was an execration of the Vaudois Protestants, who, though but a handful of people, forcibly returned to their homeland from which the other subjects of the Duke of Savoy had driven them.

To Jurieu an unjust judgment did not become just simply because it had the authority of a majority behind it. Therefore, one is not obliged in conscience and before God to obey it.[55] In fact, an innocent man who

[54] *De jure belli ac pacis,* p. 150.
[55] This same idea is also to be found in less completely developed form in the sixteenth century Huguenot pamphlet *Dialogue d'archon et de politie* (1576) in Simon Goulart, *Mémoires de l'état de France sous Charles IX* (1578), III, 136.

is condemned by a criminal chamber can resist this unjust judgment but only upon two conditions: first, that the "public peace and that of individuals" are not disturbed and, second, that "resistance does not entail the destruction of order, which would inflict a considerable injury on the public." In fact, the majority principle itself is necessary "for the preservation of order." [56] Therefore, in general, a private individual is obliged to submit to an unjust judgment, not "because of the plurality of opinions," but "because of order." However, resistance to an unjust law, made with the authority of a majority, is permissible "when the interest is considerable." [57] From this it follows that the Huguenots in France, both in the sixteenth century and after the revocation of the Edict of Nantes in the seventeenth, are justified in their action, as are the Vaudois Protestants, who are "a people and a nation, an entire and a considerable society." [58]

But Bayle had pointed out that this principle should also apply to the Socinians and the Quietists, who would be justified in not submitting to the penal laws inflicted upon them by the majority. To this clever charge Jurieu retorts that the abuse of a principle does not destroy its use. For example, an innocent person who resists the execution of an unjust judgment does not sin thereby; but a justly condemned criminal who forces his prison is doubly guilty. Thus, the Socinians and Quietists must submit to penal laws, "not because of the plurality of opinions but because of the authority of the sovereign magistrate who is the master of the affairs of religion and especially because these laws are just and because they are true heretics." [59] Jurieu's intolerance is clearly shown here. Those who resist "princes who work to establish true religion are wrong and obstinate, because, being wrong in the heart of the matter and their

[56] *Examen d'un libelle*, pp. 194–199, 167–171.
[57] When it is only a question "des biens & mêmes de la vie d'un particulier ou de quelques particuliers, cela ne vaut pas le dommage qu'apporte la rupture de l'ordre dans un Société, il faut souffrir; mais quand il y va de la perte de la Société par la ruine d'une grande partie, quoy que ce ne soit pas la plus grande, s'il y va de la ruine de la religion & de la damnation éternelle d'une infinité d'âmes qu'on veut engager dans une Religion Idolâtre & qui damne, alors l'intérêt est assez grand pour qu'on n'ait point d'égard à ce règlement humain, il faut suivre la pluralité des voix." *Ibid.*, pp. 171–180. Jurieu argues that since human laws are only made for the conservation of society, when their execution destroys it, they are no longer binding.
[58] *Ibid.*, pp. 194–199.
[59] *Ibid.*, pp. 171–180.

resistance tending to the retention of a false religion, they are wrong in all the consequences." [60]

Bayle had also severely attacked, as we have observed, the action of the Vaudois Protestants. In their defense Jurieu maintained that since their valleys had belonged to them for centuries, the Duke of Savoy did not have the power to seize the property of his subjects. Furthermore, they had been confirmed in their Protestantism by several declarations. It is true that sovereigns have the power to expel people for reason of religion, but when they banish "the true religion and those who profess it, they commit a very great crime before God, and those who are ejected for reason of the true religion have the right to do whatever is possible for the preservation of their property, life, country, and religion, provided it is practicable without violating the rules of Christian charity." But, as Jurieu had asserted before, the rules of Christian charity are not infringed "when one keeps within the limits of a wise and moderate resistance," because "the laws of Christianity have not abolished the laws of nature, which permit a just defense." [61] If the Vaudois Protestants are guilty, then so are the Huguenots of the last century and the Dutch Calvinists, concludes our theologian.

As usual Bayle had referred pointedly to the patience of the early Christians, which Scripture enjoined upon them.[62] Although Jurieu admitted that Christians should cultivate a spirit of moderation, still this Biblical precept should not be taken too literally.[63] The text reads that flight is in order "when you shall be persecuted with authority" and not simply "when you shall be persecuted." Moreover, have not most of the local persecutions committed by the "unruliness of the people" been instigated by the false zeal of priests or a few magistrates?

Furthermore, although it pleased God in the first centuries of Chris-

---

[60] *Ibid.*, pp. 146–151. Anyone who opposed Jurieu was to him either a fool or a knave. Cf. "Qui ne voit le doigt de Dieu dans notre Réformation est aveugle, qui ne le voit dans le retour des Vaudois est stupide." *Ibid.*, pp. 229–234. This typically Calvinistic attitude of arrogant self-righteousness is even more evident in a passage from *Apologie du Sieur Jurieu,* 1691, p. 1: "Les personnes qui essayent de perdre ma réputation sont donc bien moins mes ennemis que ceux de Dieu & de l'église."

[61] *Examen d'un libelle,* pp. 194–199.

[62] "Go ye and preach the Gospel in all nations, if you are persecuted in one city flee into another." Matthew 28.19; 10.23.

[63] "Il ne faut pas renverser l'ordre, la police, les États, les loix de la nature & le droit des gens." *Examen d'un libelle,* pp. 217–222.

tianity to conserve His church without the use of arms, it need not be concluded that the employment of force for the defense of the church should never be resorted to at any time or in any circumstances. Not only was there no reliance upon the sword in the establishment of the Christian religion but also no authority or king intervened. Should it be thought, then, that sovereigns are forever forbidden to use their power to establish Christianity or to reform it?

In addition to references to the historical period of early Christianity, Bayle also was diabolically interested in comparing the English civil wars and the execution of Charles I with the Revolution of 1688 and the deposition of James II. He also drew a parallel between the Catholic James II, who wished to rule over a Protestant people, and Henry IV of Navarre, a Calvinist, who desired to reign over Catholic subjects.[64] As to the first comparison, Bayle had refuted the response of M. Daillé to Cottiby to the effect that the execution of Charles I must be blamed on the Independents and not on the Presbyterians, by showing that Charles's son, James II, was dethroned not by the Independents but by the Anglicans and Presbyterians together. In addition, Daillé was refuted in Bayle's exposé by references to Saumaise, who had held that the Presbyterians had brought Charles to the block and placed the axe in the hands of the Independents. But, according to Jurieu, the Presbyterians have strongly condemned the action of the Independents in that horrible parricide. Furthermore, it was preposterous of Bayle to declare that the Protestants approve the action against Charles I because they applaud the fate of James II, since the two situations are entirely different.

Bayle had concluded the *Avis* by showing that the action of the Protestants against James II deprived them of any right to complain over the conduct of the Catholic League toward Henry IV of France. But to Jurieu there were essential differences between the performance of the

---

[64] Gédéon Huet in his *Lettre écrite de Suisse en Hollande,* p. 29, had argued that James II could be legitimately deposed as an oppressor of his people outside of the question of orthodoxy, for the true "hérésie d'un prince en tant que Souverain ne consiste pas en ce qu'il est d'une autre Religion que ses sujets mais seulement en ce qu'il les veut opprimer & les réduire à l'esclavage. De quelque religon qu'il puisse être, Juif, Mahometan, Payen, on le doit reconnaitre pour légitime souverain tandis qu'il ne fera aucune violence à son peuple & qu'il n'entreprendra pas de changer le Gouvernement de l'état par le renversement des loix."

League and that of the English. The French kings had absolute authority, although Jurieu declares that it was a usurpation, while the English
ruler was limited by Parliament and the laws. Therefore, Henry IV,
because he was above the laws, did not have to give account of his religion, even though there might conceivably be a condition which rendered "the qualification of Catholic monarch inseparably attached to
that of king of France." [65] To Jurieu, the coronation oath of the kings
of France was only a formality and not a fundamental law of the state.
But in England James II was king by laws which attributed the crown
to a Protestant prince, who must renounce the Pope and become head
of the Church of England. Jurieu said also with reference to Henry IV
that he could not blame [66] the French Catholics for wanting a king of
their religion "because there is a true implication of contradiction that
the dominant religion should be on one side and the ruler on the other."
But at that time a considerable part of France was Protestant and the
Huguenots had as much right to desire a Calvinist ruler as the Catholic
party a prince of their own faith.[67]

Bayle was not slow in answering [68] this blistering attack [69] by his

[65] *Lettres pastorales*, IX, Third Year, pp. 208–216.

[66] Henri Basnage de Beauval in his *Lettres sur les différends de M. Jurieu & M. Bayle*
delights in comparing this view with an earlier discussion of the question by Jurieu in his
Histoire du calvinisme et celle du papisme, IV, Troisième Récrimination, Chap. III, where
he attacked the Catholics for their refusal to recognize Henry IV as king so long as he
was a Huguenot. Antoine Arnauld, in order that nothing could be concluded from this
resistance, was hard put to prove that this opinion—that one is not obliged to obey a heretical
king—was not universal. But Jurieu refuted this by insisting that all agree that Henry IV
need not be obeyed as a Huguenot ruler but upon abjuring his religion he should be.
Basnage de Beauval sarcastically observes that Jurieu could have shortened the dispute by
asserting at that time that he would not blame the Catholics for wanting a king of their
own faith.

[67] "Car ces sortes d'affaires où il y va du tout & de la vie & de la Religion ne se doivent
point passer à la pluralité des voix puisque la partie la moindre en nombre ne peut mettre
en compromis les droits de Dieu." *Examen d'un libelle*, pp. 257–265. This principle was
attacked later by Basnage de Beauval, who declared that it would destroy both the hereditary and elective methods of succession to the crown, since if the king should be a heretic,
the orthodox party, even if it is the smallest in number, is not obliged to obey.

[68] *La Cabale chimérique*, 1691.

[69] Compare also *Avis sincère de M. Jurieu . . . par lequel il fait voir que les plus savants
et les plus éclairés Docteurs de cette Eglise ont toujours eu l'esprit Républicain et des sentiments opposés à la puissance absolue des Souverains et Monarques. Tiré de son livre qu'il
intitule Examen d'un Libelle pour combler de honte & de confusion le Sr. Becman* (Johann
Christoph Becman, 1641–1717, a Lutheran theologian) *& ses adhérents qui osent nier ce
que Mons. Masius en avoit avancé avec vérité dans ces écrits, par un de ses amis.* In that

former friend Jurieu, with whom he had been closely associated at the Protestant Academy of Sedan in France and at the famous Ecole Illustre in Rotterdam since 1681. Basnage de Beauval claimed [70] that Jurieu's enmity against Bayle was rooted in the beginning in jealousy over the greater popularity of the *Critique générale de L'Histoire du calvinisme du P. Maimbourg* than his own refutation of the former Jesuit father's attack on Calvinism. But Jurieu had had increasing doubts over the orthodoxy of his colleague with the appearance of such books as *Pensées diverses écrites à un Docteur de Sorbonne à l'occasion de la comète,* and the *Commentaire philosophique* as well as the *Critique générale de L'Histoire du calvinisme du P. Maimbourg.* He had evidently refrained, however, from an open break until the appearance of a writing that he regarded as an open eulogy of the Kings of France and of England (James II) and a condemnation of the English Revolution and its leader, William of Orange. It is the reoccurrence in the late seventeenth century of a controversy reminiscent of other famous quarrels, as those of Luther and Erasmus, Calvin and Servetus, Beza and Castellion. A terrific pamphlet war between the two adversaries was reinforced by the friends of both parties.[71] The result of this disgraceful performance was that, through pressure exerted by Jurieu [72] Bayle was finally deprived of his professorship in October, 1693. This was done, however, on the basis of his treatise on the comet and not because of his connection with the

---

pamphlet the author is inclined to agree with the Danish Lutheran, Hector Gottfried Masius, in his *Interesse principum circa religionem evangelicam* (1688) that both Calvinists and Catholics held maxims dangerous to sovereigns, but not so the Lutherans.

[70] *Lettres sur les différends de M. Jurieu & de M. Bayle,* p. 2.

[71] Jurieu, *Nouvelles convictions contre l'auteur de L'Avis aux Réfugiés* (1691); *Dernière conviction contre le sieur Bayle* (1691); *Remarques générales sur La Cabale chimérique de M. Bayle* (1691); *Courte revue des maximes de morale et des principes de religion* (1691); *Le Philosophe dégradé* (1692); *Factum selon les formes* (1692).

Bayle: *Lettres sur les petits livrets publiés contre La Cabale chimérique* (1690); *Déclaration de M. Bayle* (1690); *La Chimère de la cabale de Rotterdam* (1691); *Entretiens sur le grand scandale* (1691); *Janua coelorum reserata cunctis Religionibus a Celebri admodum viro domino Petro Jurieu* (1692); *Nouvel avis au petit auteur* (1692).

Basnage de Beauval also entered the controversy on the side of Bayle with his *Lettres sur les différends de M. Jurieu et de M. Bayle,* and Gédéon Huet contributed a *Lettre d'un des amis de M. Bayle aux amis de M. Jurieu* (1691).

[72] See J. L. Gerig and G. L. van Roosbroeck, "Bayle Persecuted: an Unpublished Letter about Jurieu," *The Romanic Review,* XXIII (1932), 20–23. Jurieu wrote to Cuper in 1691 that he could endure Bayle's faults "pendant que je l'ay cru honneste payen, mais j'ay découvert qu'il est traistre et méschant." Quoted in Frank Puaux, *Les Précurseurs français de la tolérance au XVIIᵉ siècle,* p. 209.

pacifist cabal and the *Important Advice* to the refugees. It was a clash between secularism and a conception of the state as old as Hildebrand.[73]

At the time of the quarrel between Jurieu and Bayle, several other important refutations [74] of the *Avis aux réfugiés* by the French Protestant exiles appeared. By far the ablest of these was written by Jacques Abbadie, (1654–1727), who had been pastor of the French Protestant church in Berlin, going to London in 1688. In his *Défense de la nation britannique où les droits de Dieu, de la nature et de la société sont clairement établis au sujet de la Révolution d'Angleterre contre l'Auteur de l'Avis important aux Réfugiés* (1693), Abbadie presents many of the ideas of Jurieu in mitigated form.

He begins his answer to the *Avis* with an examination of the question as to whether kings have an absolute and arbitrary power over their subjects. He holds first that the idea of power includes two others, that of right and that of force. But neither right nor force alone makes power. For example, neither a prince unjustly deprived of his estates nor a robber is a power. Power, furthermore, is limited or without bounds either with regard to force or to right. A power circumscribed with regard to force is that possessed by an inferior magistrate, who can put a man to death but who cannot make war. Power without restraint with regard to force is what was enjoyed by a Roman dictator. In the same way power is limited or unrestricted with regard to right. A power confined as to right is any power which does not give the liberty to do with justice whatever is desired; while a power unlimited with regard to right gives the absolute prerogative to do anything. Upon these principles Abbadie distinguishes three kinds of power: first, a power is limited with regard to right and force, such as the power of a minor or subordinate magistrate, who has neither the right nor the force to destroy the republic; second, a power unlimited with regard to right and force, such as the power of God; third, a power unlimited with regard to force but limited as to right, such as that of the Roman dictators, who had

---

[73] As Jurieu phrased it in his *Remarques générales sur La Cabale,* pp. 42–44: "Ainsi M. Bayle en confondant ces deux choses, l'amour de Dieu & l'amour du Roy, fait bien voir que la religion n'est pas ce qui luy tient le plus au coeur."

[74] There was one reply, not written by a French refugee, which relied heavily on Grotius's *De jure belli ac pacis* to refute the *Avis.* It was by G. Nizet and entitled *Réponse sommaire au livre intitulé Avis important,* 1690.

the force to destroy everything but not the power or authority. From this lengthy analysis Abbadie concludes that kings have unrestrained power over their peoples with regard to force, since they have armies and fortresses to execute their commands. But their power is restricted as to right, since they are obliged to defend and conserve their subjects instead of destroying them. Arbitrary power, which is the power to save and destroy without doing injustice to anybody, belongs only to God and not to kings, which is good Calvinist doctrine.

Whatever the origin of the power of kings, Abbadie denies them an unlimited power over their subjects. Patriarchal kings do not have it, since fathers do not by nature have absolute right over their children. A patriarchal government like all others seeks the good of the individuals composing it and avoids both tyranny and anarchy. Even the right of a conqueror is not unrestricted, but is tempered by the law of God, which commands him to spare the lives of his subjects. When the conqueror becomes king he goes even further and contracts with the people he has subjected to protect them. Although he reserves a greater authority in this contract than other kings, still he could not become sovereign over the people he has vanquished without renouncing an arbitrary power.

The third source of power is the law or consent of the people. The terms are synonymous, since the law is originally but the assent of the community. Civil society is composed of individuals who unite to form the body politic. Each individual has a natural right to his property, liberty, children, life, reputation or honor, and conscience. But the right of the individual in these things is not an absolute right. For example, each person can employ his property as he desires, but he cannot willfully destroy it, since he is but the second proprietor, God being the first. As each person found that it was impossible to defend his goods, children, liberty, life, and conscience when living alone and deprived of the aid of others, it was necessary for men to associate with each other "by civil laws for the defense of their natural prerogatives." [75] Men therefore formed a state or community, which they made powerful enough to defend them, by clothing it with the right of all the individ-

[75] "Et c'est Dieu & la nature qui leur en ont imposé la loy par le langage d'une nécessité absolue & indispensable qui est toujours un langage divin."

uals.[76] But "individuals could not communicate to the community the right to destroy without reason and necessity their property, children, lives, etc., since no private person has this right." Since the multitude of persons who are confederated cannot govern itself, it chooses magistrates to exercise the right granted by each individual. These magistrates are either groups of heads of families, who assemble to deliberate on public affairs as in democracies, or a senate composed of the most outstanding persons as in an aristocracy, or a sovereign who represents the rights of the whole nation, as in monarchies. As to the power of these magistrates, "it is evident that the people could not and would not confer absolute right on the sovereign magistrate, because it is impossible to give what one does not have; because the right of the people is only the right which individuals have ceded for their common advantage; and it is true that private persons do not have absolute right over themselves or over the things which belong to them." [77]

Abbadie declares, furthermore, that it is possible to distinguish three fundamental and original laws upon which states and empires are established. The first is the law of society, the second the law of the government, and the third is the law of the empire. The law of the society is that individuals do everything for the conservation of the community to which they belong, and it is founded not only on what they owe to others but to themselves as well. The law of the government consists in the necessity of having certain persons above others in order to secure justice. The law of the empire is comprised of the requirement of having some person possess the legislative and the coercive power. All three of these laws, concludes Abbadie, are opposed to arbitrary power. The law of society is incompatible with it, since the conservation of society is the supreme law (*salus populi lex suprema in civitate*). If this is true, then how, asks Abbadie, can the right to destroy, which makes arbitrary power, be squared with the necessity of preserving the community, which is the first of the laws? The law of the government is also opposed to arbitrary power, since government exists for the protection of men and not for their destruction. In the same way, since the law of empire

[76] "Chaque père de famille a cessé d'être le Magistrat dans sa famille pour former une Magistrature plus autorisé qui pourvent à la seureté de tous; & Dieu s'est servi de cette voye du consentement des peuples pour établir la puissance des Roys."
[77] *Défense de la nation britannique,* pp. 113–118.

or the provision for coercive power in the hands of the sovereign magistrate is only for the purpose of defending the public, it too is opposed to absolute power.

In addition to these general laws, which apply to all governments, there are three others applicable to hereditary monarchical government only—the law of royalty, of succession, and of contract between the king and his subjects. The law of royalty specifies not only that the king is the sovereign magistrate, but also that the inferior magistrates depend upon him for their authority. The law of succession is derived from a double consent—that of the nation which is convened to attach the royalty to a certain family, and that of this family in accepting the royalty for its head and promising to conserve the state. The law of contract consists of the promise made by the prince when he is constituted ruler to observe the laws of the realm and to maintain the liberty and privileges of his subjects. All three of these laws are opposed to arbitrary power. If the king had an arbitrary power over his subjects he could destroy all the magistrates, which would be opposed to the law of royalty. Since the law of hereditary succession is identical with the welfare of the people, it is incompatible with absolute power, which permits the prince to do anything. By its very nature the law of contract points to the conservation of subjects and is opposed to arbitrary power.

Having considered the power which kings receive from the people, Abbadie turns next to that which comes from God. Without doubt God has arbitrary power over men, both with regard to force and right; but even He sees fit not to exercise it, thereby imposing, as it were, a law upon Himself. Abbadie then points out that some hold that kings are absolute because their power is tempered only by the will and the law of God. It can be said that kings are in the same relation to God as the subordinate magistrates are to the king. But just as it would be absurd to say that the subordinate magistrates have an arbitrary power over the people in their jurisdiction because their power is only tempered by the will of the king and the law of the state, so is it extravagant to hold that kings have absolute power because this power is limited only by the will of God and religion. Every right is related to God who communicates it and to men over whom it is obtained. If, then, kings have absolute right over their subjects, it comes from God and has men for its object.

But if this right comes from God, how can it be said that kings do not have arbitrary and unlimited power with reference to Him, since every legitimate right has this double relationship—to God and to men? In general, concludes Abbadie, the language of nature and right reason speak against any such arbitrary power.

With Abbadie as with Jurieu, Christianity controls and sanctifies nature, but does not destroy it. Natural rights remain inviolable, among which are the right to property, life, and the conduct of the family. The magistrate has a natural right to his authority, which Scripture confirms by commanding men to be subject to the powers that be. God is a god of order and not destruction, as He would be if He had abolished this natural right. Christ would never have said that His kingdom is not of this world if He had come to remove the natural right over things belonging to men. When He ordered man to love his enemies, He assumed the existence of such a natural right. There is a great difference between not resenting an injury and renouncing the rights of nature to the point that no injustice can be committed against which a man can defend himself. In certain cases, as when a single person is injured by another but society itself is not affected, there should be no opposition. But if ill-treatment is extended to many persons and the public is concerned, then even the law of charity would advocate punishment.[78]

If sovereigns do not have absolute power over men, then God has reserved certain rights which He has not ceded to men. As a result, men have a right to question and even disobey kings, who encroach upon these privileges of God. But reason, nature, and Scripture exhort that private injustices be suffered, both because of the obedience owed to the powers that be, but also because of the necessity for order in the state. When it comes to the rights of conscience, however, disobedience is permissible. Besides, there is a right according to nature of resisting by force those who attack men by violence.[79]

---

[78] *Défense de la nation britannique*, pp. 149–153: "C'est pourquoi quand on nous prêche ce devoir de la morale, qu'il faut aimer ses ennemis, il est certain que ce devoir s'entend de particulier à particulier & non pas de puissance à puissance; que cela signifie le relâchement du droit naturel & non pas son extinction: que cela regarde le droit particulier & non pas le droit public & que rien ne seroit plus impertinent que de vouloir régler les droits d'une puissance par la loi de la charité évangélique expliquée dans le sens littéral."

[79] "Or la droite raison nous apprend qu'il est raisonable de défendre sa vie contre un injuste aggresseur, elle nous enseigne donc que c'est là nôtre droit naturel." *Ibid.*, p. 172.

Abbadie grants that when society was formed men ceded to the magistrate the right to protect them, but the Revocation is an indication that the government regards the Huguenots no longer as part of the state, hence they recover the possession of their natural right. Grotius, quoting Barclay, is cited to the effect that if a ruler declares himself to be the enemy of the whole people, he deposes himself. But usually this happens only when, as in the case of James II, the prince destroys one people in favor of another. This monarch would ruin England in favor of the Irish and the Protestants in favor of the Catholics.

With his usual moderation, Abbadie wanted to take a middle course between two extreme views: one, that the people reserved sovereignty over all authority granted to the king, and the other, that they retained none of it. How, asks Abbadie, could the community grant everything to the king when individuals reserve certain rights or privileges [80] as against society at the time of the origin of governments? [81] Abbadie warns, furthermore, that men cannot act directly against their conscience, even for the safety of their native land and the conservation of the community.

Thus, the authority of kings comes from God, Who communicates it through the people to them. Moreover, they can be deposed in certain cases—"God, nature, necessity, and the supreme law of the state pronouncing, so to speak, the sentence." [82] Even a father can lose his status, if he tries to destroy his family. But whereas he rules without a treaty or alliance with his family,[83] a king rules by virtue of a contract with his

---

Hobbes is cited as holding that the first principle of natural right is that each person can defend his life and Grotius's definition of the law of nature is quoted.

[80] ". . . quand tous les peuples du monde unanimement s'accorderoient à renoncer à tous leur privilèges en faveur des Princes qui les gouvernent, il y a pourtant certaines loix essentielles & fondamentales du gouvernement dont les peuples ne peuvent se départir parcequ'il n'y auroit plus de Société si ces loix ne subsistoient plus. Il y a une loy commune à tous les Etats qui veut que les biens soient assurés à leur possesseur; que chacun soit maître de ses enfans & en sûreté de sa vie autant qu'il est possible, qu'il ne puisse être déshonoré impunément & qu'il ait la liberté de craindre Dieu." *Ibid.*, p. 296. Cf. "Quand on violeroit toutes les autres loix il faut toujours que celles qui assurent nos biens, notre vie, nos enfans, notre liberté & notre conscience soient entièrement inviolables." *Ibid.*, p. 365.

[81] "Nous nous engageons envers le peuple à donner s'il le faut, nos biens & notre vie pour sa conservation bien entendu qu'aussi nous sommes reçus au droit rejouir chacun selon sa mesure & son rang des privilèges de la communauté." *Ibid.*, pp. 194–207.

[82] *Ibid.*, pp. 211–216.

[83] Compare Jurieu who sees a contract behind all human relationships. *Lettres pastorales,* XVI of the Third Year.

subjects. If the father can be resisted, then so much the more the king. "Men are placed in society not only to avoid death, but also to avoid the loss of their property and their natural advantages." [84] Kings cannot have a power of destruction over their subjects, since society itself does not have such power over individuals. Like Jurieu, Abbadie puts great emphasis on the inalienable natural right of conservation and upon the necessity of the public safety, which is a law that abolishes all others incompatible with it. In fact, so pressing a situation might arise that forcible resistance to the ruler even by individuals and not the magistrates should be employed. The urgency of armed resistance to a despotic prince should be judged "according to the degree of that tyranny and its notoriety." [85] A ruler is "notoriously" the destructor of the people when he violates the laws protecting the property, liberty, life, honor, and conscience of individuals in the state.[86]

From these principles Abbadie has no trouble in justifying the deposition of James II. England had, as a Protestant nation, enacted laws against Catholicism. These laws protected property, liberty, children, honor, life, and conscience from Catholicism. It was the king who sought to abolish these safeguards by abusing the dispensing power, establishing ecclesiastical commissions, destroying the privileges of the cities by taking away their charters and liberty of elections, and by relaxing the penal laws against Catholics. Certainly there was greater justice in transferring the crown from James II to William III than from Childeric to Pepin in France. Therefore, if the Stadtholder is a usurper, then the kings of France are even closer to being *sine titulo*,[87] according to Abbadie.

[84] *Défense de la nation britannique*, pp. 245–264.
[85] *Ibid.*, p. 286. In this connection Knox and Goodman and the dictum of Tertullian, "Contre tyrannum omnis homo miles," are cited.
[86] *Ibid.*, pp. 307–308. Abbadie qualifies this statement by insisting that private injuries must be suffered and even "des injustices notoires qui ne regardent que nous en particulier lorsque nous n'en pouvons avoir satisfaction qu'en troublant l'ordre de la Société & en procurant un mal publique qui est toujours plus considérable que le mal particulier & même jusqu'à souffrir des injustices publiques lorsqu'on ne peut arrêter le mal sans un plus grand mal encore, selon la première loi de la prudence." *Ibid.*, p. 264.
[87] Cf. Tronchin du Breuil, *Lettres sur les matières du temps*, Lettre 13 of July 15, 1689, pp. 213–215. The choice and consent of the estates is the sole title of the French kings. "Et si Charles de Lorraine, le légitime héritier par droit de succession selon la loi fondamentale du Royaume, n'eut pas été exclus par un autre droit supérieur à cette loi (la loi supérieure

Another reply of merit to the *Avis* was the *Défense des réfugiés* (1691),[88] which has been attributed to the pastor, Antoine Coulan, who was a refugee in Switzerland, Holland, and England. It is very similar in tone to Jurieu's answer and the works of the theologian of Rotterdam are cited several times, especially *La Politique du clergé, L'Accomplissement des prophéties* and the *Histoire du calvinisme et celle du papisme.* With regard to the burning issue of popular sovereignty the author elaborates ideas to be found in Jurieu's *Lettres pastorales,* which Coulan does not refer to anywhere, however.[89]

Coulan repeats again and again the assertion that if self-defense is permissible in the case of a massacre of subjects by the king, then it must be granted that there are limits to his authority beyond which he can be prohibited from straying. If, as Grotius holds, a king cannot alienate his state, then it follows that he cannot damage it. If he cannot exterminate a great part of his subjects, then he cannot deprive them of their property,[90] liberty of conscience, or "temporal liberty." Either God has directly prescribed limits to the royal authority or the people have done so when they established their rulers. Since it was the latter, then it is for the people to determine the extent of these restrictions and to keep the king within them. There is a great difference, contrary to the opin-

---

du bien publique) il est vrai de dire selon le cours ordinaire que le Roi Louis XIV ne seroit pas aujourd'hui le possesseur de la couronne ni par conséquent le défenseur de la cause de Jacques II contre les maximes fondamentales des trois races aussi bien que contre celles d'Angleterre."

[88] Cf. a letter of Bayle to M. Constant, dated January 29, 1691: "On a publié depuis peu la Défense des Réfugiés qui n'est qu'une justification la plus étudiée et l'apologie la plus travaillée du dogme de la Souveraineté des peuples, je dis, des peuples en tant que distincts des Rois, des Sénats, des États-Généraux et autres corps représentatifs." It would appear that Bayle could be referring to Coulan's little book rather than to Abbadie's *Défense de la nation britannique,* as Dedieu concludes in his *Rôle politique des protestants français,* p. 71.

[89] Note the reliance upon institutional history: "qu'en France par exemple les Rois ne pouvoient autrefois faire aucune ordonnance ni aucun Edit sans le consentement des Parlemens; qu'ils étoient obligez d'assembler de tems en tems les États généraux du Royaume qui réprésentoient toute la Nation pour délibérer sur les affaires où l'Etat étoit le plus intéressé; & que même le peuple avoit parti à l'élection des Rois dans les deux premières races? *Défense des réfugiés,* pp. 72–102.

[90] ". . . il n'y a point de monarque qui ne puisse disposer absolument de la vie & des biens de chacun de ses Sujets pris séparément, quoi qu'il ne puisse pas les faire mourir ni les dépouiller tout pris conjointement." *Ibid.,* pp. 104–117. Cf. with the Monarchomachs like Junius Brutus.

ion of the *Avis,* between submitting a king to the Pope and submitting him to a larger number of persons, who established him and among whom "there are always several who are eminent by their birth, responsibility, integrity, prudence, or merit." [91] There is no people which does not feel obliged to obey the king, even when he commands injustice. When his laws are extremely harmful to society, however, then all the members of the state, the greatest part or at least a considerable part, can join together to refuse submission to him.

In Coulan's theory all men are naturally free and independent with the exception of the natural dependence between fathers and children and husbands and wives.[92] Although they could keep their liberty by living separately, they need each other for their conservation and their happiness. Therefore, they nearly all concur in forming societies. Each person upon entering one of these societies either expressly or tacitly agrees to work more for the public welfare than for his private interest, and to sacrifice, if necessary, his life, liberty, and property—everything except conscience—to the community. After this event the members of each society found it to their advantage to set up a ruler with a certain extent of power beyond which he was forbidden to go on pain of deposition. Some societies granted more authority than others to their sovereigns. Thus, Coulan makes a clearer distinction than either Jurieu or even Abbadie between the formation of the body politic and the government within that community.[93]

According to Coulan, resistance cannot be engaged in by individuals, unless all or at least a considerable part of those who compose the society consent. With an eye to Junius Brutus and to Beza, the *Avis* had mentioned inspectors of the acts of sovereigns in the form of a *parlement* or Estates General, but Coulan thinks it sufficient that each individual had the right to judge as to whether the ruler is staying within the limits of

[91] *Ibid.,* pp. 79–102.

[92] There is no idea of contract in these relationships as with Jurieu. On this point Coulan agrees with Abbadie.

[93] "Chaque particulier a deux liaisons fort différentes; l'une avec la Société dont il fait partie & l'autre avec son Souverain. La première est plus ancienne que la seconde. Il a formé celle-là pour son bonheur particulier & il a consenti à celle-ci pour le bien général de la Société: mais quoi qu'il en soit dans l'une & dans l'autre il doit avoir plus en vue l'intérêt du publique que son intérêt propre." *Défense des réfugiés,* pp. 117–128.

his authority. When all the subjects of a state agree on the injustice of the prince, there will be no difficulty in finding the means of remedy. If the people cannot congregate in a body, they can form separate assemblies which will communicate to each other their decisions. Furthermore, it is not necessary for everyone to have a part in these resolutions, since tacit consent would be considered sufficient. Coulan wanted it understood that he is not opposing the establishment in monarchies of certain organs, which share sovereignty with the king or which are even above him to the point of giving him laws and condemning him when he violates them.[94] But when the king tries to encroach upon their authority, the people can have recourse to themselves and muster bodies of varying size for their protection.[95] To these instruments the people could entrust absolute power, which they have over themselves,[96] since they can be confident it will not be abused.[97] Here is a faith in a popular assembly and the justice of all its acts, which like Jurieu's, is unbelievably blind and naïve.

Coulan inclined to agree with the *Avis* that Junius Brutus and Beza, in insisting upon the resistance of the people only after the consent of the magistrates, were taking away from the people with one hand what had been granted with the other. It might happen that the officers would attach themselves to the interest of the sovereign, while the body of the people would demand resistance. Therefore, to Coulan, each individual has the right of inspection over the ruler.[98] Just as individuals alone

[94] "Mais il n'est pas nécessaire que ces corps ayent entre les mains la souveraineté absolue des peuples & qu'ils puissent juger sans appel, parce qu'il ne peut arriver que fort difficilement que les membres qui les composent s'accordent tous à trahir les peuples en faveur du Monarque avec qui ils sont d'ordinaire en opposition."

[95] "Il est moralement impossible qu'en montant de cette manière d'un petit corps à un corps plus grand, on n'en trouve bientôt un assez équitable ou assez rigoureux pour soutenir les droits du Peuple contre usurpations du Souverain."

[96] This view opposes that of Jurieu and Abbadie, who denied that the people have absolute power over themselves.

[97] "Il est fort naturel & fort aisé à un monarque d'abuser de son pouvoir . . . mais il est fort difficile & presque impossible qu'un corps qui est composé d'un nombre considérable de personnes choisies par le Peuple même abuse de l'autorité qu'on luy a donné à son préjudice." *Défense des réfugiés*, pp. 117–128. Henry Parker advanced the same argument while defending the supremacy of the English Parliament in 1642.

[98] "Les peuples sont selon nos principes autant ou plus autorisez à s'opposer à la tyrannie des magistrats & des Seigneurs subalternes qu'à résister à des Souverains tyrans; & par conséquent ils n'ont pas besoin des ordres ni de la conduite d'un Magistrat ou d'un grand pour pouvoir

cannot establish a king but only together in a body, so all the individuals in a state taken separately do not possess the right to depose the
sovereign, but taken together they do.[99]

Coulan's defense of the right of minorities to prevail over majorities
is most interesting. He declares that every state is composed of several
separate societies or groups—religious, professional, and provincial.
These bodies have a particular interest outside of the general interest
of the state of which they are a part. When the interests of these various
groups conflict, which is to be preferred over the others? Should the
choice be made on the basis of numbers? To Coulan it was better to inflict a slight injury on a large number of persons in order to bring good
to a smaller number of people with whom there are stronger ties, than
to do evil to this small number in order to bring a minor good to the
larger group. Everyone is obliged to deprive himself of good and suffer
evil for his family, religion, city, and state. When one has to choose between two societies of which one is larger than the other, it is essential
to compensate the size of the first by the strength of the relationship one
has with the second, and "especially by the justice of its cause." [100] This
whole idea of compensations reminds one strongly of Calhoun's doctrine of the concurrent majority. But Coulan never extended it to the
individual from a minority within the state.

Another book which was inspired by the *Avis,* if not directly a reply
to it, was written by the grandson of Duplessis-Mornay, La Combe de
Vrigny, entitled *Défense du parlement d'Angleterre dans la cause de
Jacques II où il est traité de la puissance des rois et du droit des peuples*
(1692).[101] It was dedicated to the Estates of Holland and West Frisia.
The author tells us that he hopes to revive France from the supine state
brought upon her by her long period of servitude. In fact, during her

---

prendre les armes contre leur Roy lorsque l'obligation où ils sont de se conserver les y
contraint."

[99] "Et lorsqu'il se trouve que tous les membres d'une Société sont justement mécontens
ils aquirent en se joignant ensemble, un droit qu'ils n'avoient pas étant séparez; je veux
dire le droit de se pourvoir par les moyens qu'ils ont en main contre l'injustice & la
violence." *Ibid.,* pp. 141–146.

[100] *Ibid.,* pp. 128–136.

[101] There is also a refutation of the *Avis* appearing at about this time in the *Lettres sur les
matières du temps* of May 1, 15, June 1, and Sept. 1, 1690, which relies heavily on Grotius.
These letters were issued by Tronchin du Breuil every two weeks from February 10, 1688,
to December 15, 1690.

bondage she has lost all the sentiments of nature and renounced all those of the grace of Jesus Christ.

In the Preface De Vrigny informs us that in any discussion of this momentous question of the power of kings and the rights of peoples the best order would be to commence with the proofs of Scripture, continue with the reasons drawn from the law of nature and nations, and conclude with the testimony of various learned authorities of all ages. But he has proceeded in a directly opposite manner, since "Holy Scripture not having exactly pronounced on this matter, it is sufficient to show that it has left the laws of nature and nations in their entirety." [102] He points out, furthermore, that in general all Protestant authors reject the arguments based on the examples either of the Councils or Doctors of the Catholic Church and employ only Protestant authorities. This is unnecessary, however, since the early Councils were not composed solely of ecclesiastics as were those of the last centuries but of all the estates of the nation where they assembled. Therefore, their decisions on political questions drew their authority from the king, who almost always attended the councils along with the magnates of the realm. In addition, the Latin church was not as corrupted in doctrine and discipline in the first centuries as in later times. Also the citation of Catholic Doctors simply demonstrates that all Christians, whether Catholic or Protestant, have always agreed that the power of princes over their subjects is not absolute either in spiritual or in temporal matters. But De Vrigny hastens to add that he does not want to go on record as attacking the legitimate power of kings, since he is convinced of the superiority of monarchical government when it is confined to just limits. He is only defending the conduct of the English parliament because it changed the governor, James II, and not the government, putting in the place of the oppressor the legitimate heir to the crown, William of Orange, who was being deprived of his rights to the throne.[103]

In the first two chapters of his book De Vrigny attempts to show that his ideas on the limitation of the power of princes are common not only to all Christians but also to all humankind. In addition to citing decrees of the councils in order to combat the absolute power of kings, he refers

[102] *Défense du parlement*, Preface.
[103] Grotius' *De jure belli ac pacis*, Book I, Chap. IV, is cited as presenting seven causes for which a tyrannical ruler can be deposed.

to the testimony of Popes, as Zacharius who was instrumental in the deposition of Childeric. He also quotes Catholic Doctors like Aeneas Sylvius, St. Thomas, Gerson, Du Perron, and Bellarmine, especially in his reply [104] to Barclay, but he omits such proponents of regicide as Mariana and Suarez as unworthy of inclusion.

The largest section of the book, however, is devoted to the proof that according to the law of nature and of nations, the power of kings over their subjects is not absolute. To many the illumination of right reason is far more potent than all other examples and authorities, since nature is a veritable arsenal of evidence against tyranny. It is generally believed, continues De Vrigny, that if Adam had remained innocent there would have been no need for laws or for magistrates. Man would have been a law unto himself with no other government than his reason. There was no dominion among men who were perfectly equal, unless it was the rule of fathers over their children, until they attained the age of reason themselves. But sin corrupted reason with the result that disorder arose, which calamitous state God remedied by allowing the introduction of laws and magistrates.

Now absolute power has no basis in natural law because it is not nature which creates kings, but the consent of the people. In fact, absolute power is contrary to the law of nature, since all men are naturally equal. But what about the contention that absolute power is a necessary result of sin, which has placed all human nature in slavery? De Vrigny is forced to admit that, with the entrance of sin into the world, human nature has become enslaved, "but in bondage to sin and death and not to men." Monarchs like all other types of magistrates are the result of wickedness; but this does not sanction absolute power. Since all human nature is corrupted by sin, then kings as men are not immune from the ravages of iniquity and death.[105]

Absolute power is not derived from the law of nations any more than from the law of nature, for all peoples do not live under kings and all monarchies do not have the same constitution. In fact, the first govern-

---

[104] *Tractatus de potestate summi pontificis in rebus temporalibus adversus Gulielmum Barclaium,* Rome, 1610.
[105] "D'où l'on peut inférer que ni par le droit de la nature intègre ni par celui de la nature corrompue un homme n'a aucun droit sur un autre, si l'on en excepte le droit des pères sur leurs enfans." *Défense du parlement d'Angleterre,* pp. 38–94.

ment which was instituted by God directly was democratic or aristocratic. Furthermore, absolute power cannot be grounded in civil law, which would be nothing but injustice if it were contrary to the law of nature and nations. Besides, since the whole is greater than its parts, the state is greater than the prince. The state does not need the prince in order simply to exist but only for "the good life." Thus, when the state has ceased to supply it, it has become a tyranny, a condition that can rightfully be remedied. Besides, if there is any absolute power, it belongs not to man but to God alone. This is clearly an idea implicit in all Calvinistic doctrine.

It is also generally agreed that laws are established to restrain human cupidity, but absolute power only increases the desires of princes; therefore, it cannot be legitimate. Furthermore, all power is ordained of God for the advantage and welfare of society, but absolute power destroys the community; it cannot, therefore, have divine sanction.[106] It is also clear that if any power is derived from another, it is dependent upon it, especially in moral causes. Monarchical power is derived from the people; therefore, it is dependent upon them. But certain authors like Du Pin, Saumaise, and Richer have argued that this does not always follow, since the Pope, though selected by the College of Cardinals, is entirely independent of them after his election. De Vrigny answers that in choosing the Pope the cardinals represent the Church, which always remains the superior of the supreme pontiff and which could grant to the cardinals the power of deposition as well as of election.

If the power of kings is absolute, then the difference between subjects and slaves is obliterated, because the authority of masters over their slaves cannot be greater than the absolute predominance of kings. In fact, subjects under an absolute power may be in worse condition than slaves, since even slaves can resist their masters for extreme cruelty. If that is the case, then subjects can oppose manifest tyranny. De Vrigny also cites the feudal relation to show that in certain instances lords can lose their rights over vassals and fathers can forfeit their control over their children for ill treatment.

---

[106] De Vrigny cites the coronation of the French kings, in which the Archbishop who consecrates the ruler speaks as follows: "Conservez le poste que vous occupez par la succession de votre père de droit héréditaire, par la providence Divine & par notre présente tradition." "Mémoire de Du Tillet au chap. du couronnement des Rois," *ibid.*

De Vrigny points out next that even extreme defenders of absolute power like Barclay, Grotius, and Saumaise agree that the people have never granted all their rights to the prince. For example, the people have never given to the ruler the right to choose a successor when the royal line is extinguished or the privilege of alienating the royal domain.[107] De Vrigny concludes: "When, then, the public safety is in danger, it cannot be doubted that the people have reserved the right to maintain and uphold it with all its power." [108] If kings can be excommunicated by the Catholic Church for acts against the faith and morals, then why cannot the estates of a nation depose a tyrant? There is no divine law which prohibits the overthrow of despots. In fact, nature sanctions it.[109]

There are only two sources of a monarchy—conquest and election. If a prince who has conquered the realm by arms should force his subjects to commit injustices against the law of nations and nature, the people can restrain him within the limits of legitimate government.[110] If the ruler obtains the realm by election, certain conditions will be laid down that will be binding upon both prince and subjects, "according to the principles of religion as well as those of nature." Even God binds

[107] See the examples cited from the history of France. Charles VI passed over his son Charles VII in favor of Henry of England, his son-in-law, but the people reinstated Charles VII. The instance of the alienation of the domain by Francis I, in order to pay the ransom to the Emperor, is also described.

[108] Even Saumaise admits that if the prince becomes an enemy of his people, he can be dethroned: "Or un Tyran est toujours l'ennemi de son Peuple non seulement quand il répand le sang à tors & à travers de ses sujets; mais aussi quand il opprime leur Religion, qu'il corrompt leurs femmes & leurs filles, qu'il les dépouille de leurs biens, qu'il viole sa foi & sa promesse; qu'il casse & annulle tous leurs privilèges & toutes leurs immunitez; en un mot lorsqu'il foule aux pieds tout droit divin & humain . . . Et à dire le vrai il n'y a point ou peu de Tyrans d'exercice, c'est à dire de gouvernement que l'on nomme ainsi pour les distinguer des usurpateurs qui ne soient couverts de tous les crimes." *Défense du parlement*, pp. 38–94.

[109] "Au contraire la coûtume reçue de tout temps & par toutes les Nations de chasser les Tyrans prouve invinciblement que de maintenir & défendre le salut public & de ne point épargner un seul homme pour l'intérêt & le bien de toute la nation, est une loy que la nature a gravé profondément dans le coeur de tous les hommes. Or quand les Loix divines se taisent qui est-ce qui peut douter que l'on ne doive écouter la nature comme une espèce de divinité?" *Ibid.*

[110] This is, "selon et axiome de la nature qu'il est permis de repousser la force par la force & que ce qui est arraché par la violence peut être repris par la même voye. . . . Il ne peut y avoir de prescription dans les droits de la nature & des gens, comme il y en a quelque fois dans le droit civil, parceque les premiers sont les fondemens inébranables du corps de la Société & que ce dernier ne regardant que les membres particuliers de cette même Société peut souffrir quelque changement sans qu'elle en soit altérée dans son tout." *Ibid.*

Himself by His promises. Hereditary right adds nothing to the right of conquest or election, since the successor is invested only with the prerogative of his predecessor. Furthermore, the royal power in an hereditary monarchy is no more extensive than in an elective realm, since both originate in the concessions of the people. The prince renews his obligations to his subjects at his coronation, swearing to conserve the rights and privileges of the nation as they were at the beginning of the monarchy and the right of subjects is revived whenever the ruler fails in his duty.

De Vrigny goes on to show in the last chapters that there is nothing in the Old or New Testament which supports the absolute power of kings. But when tyrannical kings are resisted, action must be taken by the estates of the realm rather than by private individuals.[111] With special regard to the passages in the New Testament which prescribe the duty of obedience to magistrates, De Vrigny explains that these precepts apply to all types of government. That is to say, obedience should follow according to the laws of each country. Furthermore, these Apostolic commands apply only to individuals and not to the body of the nation, otherwise war would not be permitted among men, nor would resistance by force to a violent aggressor. The early Christians did not revolt because they did not have the force at hand and God wished to make known that the reign of Christ should be purely spiritual and attainable only by supernatural means.

Absolute power belongs only to God. Therefore, an individual does not have it over himself, since he cannot take his own life or even destroy his property. Nor does society as a whole have absolute power, free of the laws, to put an innocent person to death without being responsible to God for such a crime. Therefore, the community cannot give to the prince an absolute authority independent of the laws, since it does not have it, nor has God granted such power to kings. De Vrigny concludes that absolute and arbitrary power is nothing but pure usurpation.

The last answer to the *Avis* appeared many years later by Isaac de Larrey (1638–1719) in his *Réponse à L'Avis aux réfugiés,* written in 1709. Even though the controversy is no longer so timely, the author

[111] "Car nous ne prétendons pas qu'il appartienne à aucun particulier ni même à plusieurs particuliers de changer l'état de la République mais seulement à toute la nation ou à la meilleure partie." *Ibid.,* pp. 25–104.

feels that it is never too late to justify the conduct of the refugees against a libel, the object of which was to legitimize the Revocation in the same way that Charpentier justified the massacre of Saint Bartholomew. He takes the position that it was not strange that the refugees looked upon the English Revolution as a prelude to their own and upon the general peace of Europe as including their own conservation.[112] He insists, however, that they never intended the destruction of their native land but only the restoration of their liberty.[113]

Isaac de Larrey does not regard a preference for true monarchy over tyranny as an exhibition of a feeling of partiality for republican government. Many Catholic writers like Pibrac,[114] de Thou, and Mezeray wanted a return to the reign of Louis XII who was known as "the father of his country" rather than to the rule of Louis XI, under whom a monarchy tempered by the fundamental laws of the state was unknown and absolute or arbitrary government was in force. Two maxims must be observed: the first, *salus populi suprema lex esto,* and the second, *Imperium est regum in proprios greges.* Only a despotic ruler can encroach upon the one and the spirit of rebellion on the other. The passage from Grotius, who refers to Barclay, declaring that if the king becomes the enemy of the whole people he is rightfully to be deprived of his authority, is quoted again. Like Jurieu and Abbadie, de Larrey maintained that Christianity does not destroy nature. In fact, "the right of the people is that of nature itself (which has engraved it on the hearts of all men)."[115] Kings are not created to oppress or destroy, but to govern according to the laws, express or tacit, by which they are elevated to their thrones. The people cannot be deprived of their original right, which

---

[112] See the pamphlet, *L'Europe esclave si l'Angleterre ne rompt ses fers,* 1685.

[113] "Nous en demandons plûtot la liberté & en soupirant pour notre délivrance nous soupirons pour celle de tous nos compatriotes que nous croions encore plus malheureux que nous." *Réponse à l'Avis aux réfugiés,* pp. 21–23.

[114] See his little poem: "Je hai ces mots de puissance absolue
                    De plein pouvoir, de propre mouvement
                    Aux saints Décrêts ils ont premièrement
                    Puis à nos Loix la puissance tollue."

[115] ". . . il consiste à prendre soin de son salut & le peuple reprend ce droit toutes les fois qu'on le veut détruire. Quelqu'indépendans que soient les Rois ils ont faits pour les peuples, & non les peuples pour les Rois. Les peuples naissent peuples; les rois ne naissent pas tels originairement; ce sont les peuples qui ont premièrement crées & quelque longue suite de siècles que puisse compter la Race qui est sur le trône il faut remonter à un tems où elle a commencé de régner par le consentement des peuples."

comes from God and nature, to the conservation of their life, liberty, and conscience. Furthermore, sovereignty can reside only in the community and not in each individual.[116]

In connection with these various replies to Bayle's famous *Avis* it is interesting to consider the views [117] of the celebrated historian of the Edict of Nantes, Elie Benoit, (1640–1728) who was publishing in the years 1693–1695 his great five-volume work. According to this zealot, the word of God does not destroy the rights of natural justice, since these are founded on divine justice. All the precepts of patience in the Scriptures do not negate the natural right which authorizes men to defend their lives when attacked. It is not necessary to wait for the decision of some jurisconsult or royal judge in order to act, since nature itself speaks and takes the place of doctor and magistrate.[118]

Benoit admits the inconveniences of a right of resistance, but he believes that the practice of unlimited patience is subject to even more troubles. Revolt, however, should never extend to the execution of kings, but only to the point of restraining them within the bounds which the laws place upon their authority. The ruler usurps gradually the liberty reserved by the people, but there are few examples of such assumption by the people of the power it has granted to the sovereign.

To Benoit the best method of understanding the respective rights of king and subject is to discover what is allowed by natural right to each party. With regard to the origin of societies he finds, first, that the purpose of these unions is mutual conservation rather than destruction. Conquest is a usurpation, which lasts only so long as the application of force endures. Second, good faith is the spirit of all governments and societies. Third, in all relations among men there is a reciprocal element

---

[116] When the Huguenots speak of the right of the people "ils en parlent comme font les Etats d'Arragon, de Castile, d'Angleterre, de la France elle-même." *Réponse à L'Avis aux réfugiés,* pp. 170–221.

[117] Benoit's discussion of the right of peoples and the power of kings is to be found in the preface of the second volume of his *Histoire de l'Edit de Nantes.*

[118] "De même en supposant le cas d'une oppression évidente où chacun voit les fers qu'on luy prépare; où il s'agit non seulement des biens & des privilèges de quelques particuliers; où il n'est pas question de simples droits de bienséance & de commodité; mais où tout l'état souffre ou au moins une partie nombreuse & digne de n'être pas méprisée; où il va de ce que la liberté a de plus naturel & de plus précieux; où il y a raison de craindre que la patience des opprimez n'autorise l'oppression d'aller plus avant; dans ces cas, dis-je, il n'y a personne qui doive mieux juger de la nécessité de se défendre que ceux qui voyent & qui sentent le progrès de la servitude qu'on leur impose."

and especially is this true in the relation of ruler and subject. From these principles it follows that in certain cases [119] resistance is not criminal, for not even divine law deprives men of the right of self-defense, which is born with them. It can be readily seen from this brief analysis that Benoit adds little to the stock of ideas already more competently expressed by the leader of the zealots, Jurieu.

[119] "Quand un Prince travaille à détruire sans cause légitime des peuples qu'il est obligé de conserver; quand il viole évidemment la bonne foy, qui est le sceau des obligations mutuelles de ses peuples envers luy & de luy envers ses peuples; quand il se sert de leur patience & de leur soumission pour les exterminer plus à son aise; quand il les poursuit à force ouverte."

Chapter Five

THE HUGUENOT ATTACK ON
ROYAL ABSOLUTISM

O N THE first of July, 1689, Jurieu discontinued [1] his *Lettres pastorales* with which he had attempted to console and guarantee from seduction the Huguenots remaining in France. In these letters, which were placed on the Index [2] in 1700, 1703, and 1709, he had for three years refuted many eminent Catholic authors. These included the great Bossuet, whose *Exposition de la foy catholique, Lettre Pastorale aux nouveaux catholiques de son diocèse* [3] and *Histoire des variations des églises protestantes* received special examination; Nicole, whose *Les Prétendus Réformés convaincus de schisme* and *De l'unité de l'Eglise* [4] were answered in briefer scope than in the particular treatises which he later devoted to each; and even Pellisson, whose *Réflexions sur les différends en matière de religion* [5] was given more attention than the merits of the book would seem to justify. In addition to matters of controversy the *Lettres pastorales* also contained comments upon the incidents of the persecution and the state of his coreligionists in France, together with an analysis of European events in general after William of Orange's expedition to England.

[1] According to Bayle in his *Nouvelles Lettres,* II, 351 (January 27, 1695) and 363 (November 7, 1695), Jurieu took up the *Lettres pastorales* again in November, 1694, when he wrote the Twenty-second, but he only issued three or four more. In *Lettre XXII* Jurieu had inserted at the end some *Réflexions sur la longueur de la persécution & sur le delay de la délivrance,* which he had predicted would materialize at an early date.

[2] All the works of Jurieu were put on the Index by the decrees of January 14, 1737, and May 10, 1757, at the same time as those of Bayle and Basnage.

[3] It was this letter of Bossuet which gave Jurieu the idea of addressing his own pastoral letters to the faithful under persecution in France. Fénelon attests to their success.

[4] The very important controversy over the nature of the church was treated elaborately beyond the *Lettres pastorales,* (especially numbers 10–24 of the year 1687) in Jurieu's *Le Vray Système de l'Eglise* (1686); in his *Traité de l'unité de l'Eglise* (1688) and in the opening pages of his *Préjugez Légitimes contre le papisme,* Part I.

[5] Paul Pellisson was a former Protestant who abjured his religion. He had charge after 1676 of the administration of the revenues secured by conversions. See his *Les Chimères de M. Jurieu.* Jurieu countered with his *Réponse à l'auteur des Chimères* (1691).

On the tenth of August, 1689,[6] a little more than a month after the appearance of the last *Pastoral Letter* there appeared anonymously the first *Mémoire* of the fifteen contained in *Les Soupirs de la France esclave qui aspire après la liberté,* which was concluded on September 15, 1690, after having been released, like the *Lettres pastorales,* every two weeks. Here was a collection destined to attain even more fame than the bi-monthly *Letters* which preceded it. It was not until the period of hate and recrimination occasioned by the appearance of the *Avis aux réfugiés* that much attention was focused, in Holland [7] at least, upon this most important writing in that small but extremely significant literature of protest [8] against the despotism of Louis XIV, which was published in the last twenty-five or thirty years of his long reign. In the heat of contro-versy the *Soupirs* was now attributed to the leader of the violent party among the Protestant refugees, Pierre Jurieu. Since the *Soupirs* com-bines not only the Protestant attack upon the government but also many of the arguments of disillusioned Catholics, whether officials like Vau-ban and Boisguillebert, clergymen like Fénelon, or nobles like Saint-Simon and Boulainvilliers, it is imperative that its authorship be estab-lished. This is particularly essential when there is such a dispute [9] over its relation to the political ideas of Jurieu himself.

It was in his *La Cabale Chimérique ou réfutation de l'histoire fabu-leuse qu'on vient de publier malicieusement touchant un certain projet de paix dans l'examen d'un Libelle* that Bayle, in the face of Jurieu's

---

[6] In some editions of this work the first *Mémoire* is dated September 1, 1689, and the last October 1, 1690.

[7] The work was strenuously suppressed in France. See the editor's note to the reprint of the *Soupirs* in 1788 with the new title *Les Voeux d'un patriote.* This reissue of the *Soupirs* was accomplished by Jean-Paul Rabaut Saint-Etienne on the eve of the French Revolution as a plea for a meeting of the Estates General.

[8] The failure of this opposition to obtain institutional expression made the whole move-ment abortive, and after the suppression of Calvinism and Jansenism in France skepticism and free thought became the sole weapons left against the despotism of the government.

[9] This whole question has now reached the proportions of a special study of Gotthold Rie-mann, *Der Verfasser der "Soupirs de la France Esclave qui aspire après la liberté"* (1689–90). *Ein Beitrag zur Geschichte der Politischen Ideen in der Zeit Ludwigs XIV,* Berlin, 1938. Riemann attempts to establish the authorship of Michel Levassor, who was never mentioned in connection with the *Soupirs* by contemporaries, however. He was a priest of the Oratory exiled in Holland, who was later converted to Protestantism. See especially his *Histoire générale de l'Europe sous le règne de Louis XIII,* Amsterdam, 1700–1711, and *Lettres d'un gentil 'Homme français sur l'établissement d'une capitation générale en France,* Liége, 1695.

violent accusations, put forth the counter charge that his enemy was the author of the seditious *Soupirs*. In his counterdefense Bayle declared that rumor has it that Jurieu was given to understand that he would have to discontinue his *Soupirs*, since the last *Mémoires* had been displeasing to William of Orange and indiscreet [10] with regard to the possibility of the French landing on the Dutch coasts during the war. These indiscretions are only explainable to Bayle by recalling Jurieu's passion for prophesy. For example, the attempt made in the fourteenth *Mémoire* of the *Soupirs* to give a favorable interpretation to the unfavorable event of the victories by Louis XIV in the war caused Bayle to ridicule Jurieu as the "Prophète Tant-Mieux," since there is no event he does not include or explain away in his system. To save that reputation he is now seeking the defeat and the desolation of France, for only by such means could the triumph of Protestantism be secured, which he had long since been predicting.

In response to these accusations, Jurieu in a pamphlet, which served as a *Dernière conviction contre le sieur Bayle* (1690), declared that the *Soupirs* was attributed to him "rashly and without proof." He adds, however, that if he were the author, he would not be ashamed of it. According to Jurieu, Bayle is opposed to the *Soupirs* because it supported the cause of the Allies against the king of France. In addition, this work is the cause in Jurieu's mind of a renewed attack against him by one of Bayle's friends, Henri Basnage de Beauval. In fact, declares Jurieu, the *Soupirs* produced the same effect as *Les Véritables Intérêts des princes de l'Europe,* which appeared at the beginning of the war and which was also ascribed to him. He recalls the attack of Basnage de Beauval at that time in a letter [11] against the "little Prophets." According to Beauval,

[10] It was these indiscretions which seemed so strange to Bayle, since Jurieu "se tuoit d'assurer par tout où il voioit de bonnes gens allarmez, c'est à dire selon le sentiment cuisant de son coeur qui lui reprochoient la fausseté de ses promesses, que nos côtes & nos ports étoient trop bien gardez & trop avantageusement situez pour devoir rien craindre. S'il le croioit, pourquoi publioit-il le contraire: Un ministre fait-il bien de dire une chose pour soutenir sa réputation chancellante de Prophète & d'en publier une toute opposée pour médire ses ennemis?" *La Cabale Chimérique,* pp. 125–164.

[11] *Lettre d'un ministre aux catholiques au sujet des petits prophètes de Dauphiné,* 1689. For the ascription of this letter to Beauval, see also the *Avis de l'auteur des Lettres Pastorales à M. de Beauval* (1690), whom Jurieu charges with ridiculing his prophecies as to the imminent deliverance of the church and with opposing "les véritables intérêts des Princes." Cf. also the *Réponse de M. . . . Ministre à une Lettre écrite par un catholique*

because the *Véritables Intérêts* had urged the Allies to unite against France, Jurieu was raising "a hue and cry" against his native land in order to destroy it.

Bayle, in turn, replied to Jurieu's defense in his *La Chimère de la cabale de Rotterdam démontrée* (1691). He offers the following proofs of our theologian's authorship of the *Soupirs:* first, that public opinion ascribes it to him, and second, his best friends do not deny it nor do those at his home. In fact, they all give the air of certainty when explaining his authorship. But Bayle hastens to add that he would retract if Jurieu would declare publicly that he was not the author. Although Jurieu had an opportunity to give such a denial, it is significant that he did not, either in *Le Philosophe dégradé* or in *Factum selon les formes ou disposition des preuves contre l'auteur de l'Avis aux réfugiés,* which appeared in 1692.

Now one of the principal objections to Jurieu's authorship of the *Soupirs* is its Catholic character, which is ultramontane and not Jansenist or Gallican, as has been mistakenly held.[12] This is joined with the fact that in several of his writings Jurieu adopts like many other Huguenots an extreme Gallican position. Although we possess evidence that Jurieu was accustomed at this time to writing various political pamphlets [13] under the mask of a Catholic,[14] no one has linked this fact with his authorship of the *Soupirs.* Basnage de Beauval in his *Réponse de*

---

romain sur le sujet des petits prophètes du Dauphiné & du Vivarets, 1689, which was also probably written by Basnage de Beauval.

[12] See Charles Nodier, *Mélanges tirés d'une petite bibliothèque,* pp. 356–361, and Antoine Barbier, *Dictionnaire des ouvrages anonymes et pseudonymes composés, traduits ou publiés en francais et en Latin,* Paris, 1822–1827, IV, 537–539.

[13] In the *Défense du Sr. Samuel Chappuzeau contre une satire intitulée L'Esprit de M. Arnaud* it is stated that Jurieu is "déguisé sous toutes sortes de figures pour débiter ses médisances ou ses speculations politiques." Cf. also a letter of Bayle to M. Constant in the *Oeuvres diverses,* 1727, IV, 640, where he writes that Jurieu should limit himself to his theological profession and not meddle in politics in such writings as the *Lettre . . . à Bourgmestre de Soleure,* which he ascribes to Jurieu without a qualm. Cf. also *Réponse de M. . . . Ministre* in which Jurieu is accused of distributing "certain écrits politiques où l'on contrefait le Catholique," pp. 2–3.

[14] "Notre auteur oubliant sa qualité de Ministre de S. Evangile a eu beau se travestir en Papiste outré pour faire des Rémonstrances aux Magistrats de Soleure; il a beau se flater de la chimère que ce petit Écrit feroit du mal à la France & démonteroit toutes ses intrigues; ni cet Écrit ni tant d'autres confrères qu'il luy a donnez pour faire des soulevemens en France n'ont été que de l'encre versée sur le papier qui n'ont servi de rien à la Ligue." Bayle, *La Cabale chimérique,* pp. 81–82.

M . . . Ministre à une lettre écrite par un catholique romain sur le sujet des petits prophètes connects the Catholic [15] nature of a certain *Lettre de B. D. S. C. à M. D. Bourgmestre de Soleure* (a Catholic canton) *sur les intérêts des cantons suisses* (1689) with *Les Véritables Intérêts des princes,* both of which he ascribes to Jurieu. Furthermore, as we have noted, Jurieu links in his *Dernière Conviction* against Bayle the *Soupirs* with the *Véritables Intérêts,* declaring the former was attributed to him rashly and without proof, which is not a complete denial while there is no repudiation at all of the second ascription. Both pamphlets certainly seek to unite the allies against France and both stress the internal discontent within the French kingdom.

So much for the external evidence in support of Jurieu's authorship. Internally it is necessary, first, to begin with an analysis of *Les Véritables Intérêts.* The pamphlet opens with a description of the external situation in which France finds herself, facing a formidable alliance of both Protestant and Catholic states. Not only are there movements of the "new converts" within her borders, but the whole country is discontented, since all the orders of the realm are ruined. The *parlements,* which formerly were the guardians of public liberty, are now completely enslaved. In fact, the king had long since planned their destruction, because of their activities during the *Fronde.* The nobility no longer retain their privileges, such as the immunity of their lands from the *taille.* The people are in misery under heavy taxes.[16] The towns and cities are ruined. "Can one believe that a people in this state do not aspire after liberty?" asks Jurieu. The Catholic subjects, furthermore, are dissatisfied with the manner in which the Papacy has been treated by Louis XIV and the Jansenists are another body of malcontents.[17] France must be humiliated [18] by a continuation of the war, so that it will be forced to

---

[15] Cf. also the Catholic tone of *Le Salut de la France,* which on the basis of the *Apologie pour leurs majestés* is certainly by Jurieu.

[16] In the *Cabale chimérique* Bayle ridicules Jurieu, the theologian, for attempting to write about the finances of the realm.

[17] "Tout cela considéré on peut croire que la France est dans une disposition prochaine à une grande révolution. Quand des Princes entreront en France sous le titre & avec la conduite de libérateurs, en observant une bonne discipline militaire & en levant l'enseigne de la liberté, en promettant remise de taille aux Peuples, la restitution de leurs privilèges à la Noblesse & aux Parlements, le rétablissement des états libres; on doit espérer que tout le monde se rangera sous cette enseigne."

[18] In the *Lettres pastorales,* XXI of the Third Year, Jurieu said that the author of the

return its conquered territories to their rightful owners and restore the edicts which protected Calvinism in France.

In practically identical language with the *Lettre de B. D. S. C. à M. D. Bourgmestre de Soleure,* Jurieu speaks of the struggle between Austria and France for the domination of Europe and how at the present time France is the terror of its neighbors, as Austria was formerly. In order to restore the balance, France must be reduced to its ancient limits. He then attempts to dispel the misgivings of the Catholic princes with regard to an alliance with the Protestant William of Orange, the conqueror of the Catholic James II. He argues that the conduct of the King of France has closed the gap between Protestant and Catholic princes, effecting an alliance between even the Pope and the House of Austria and Protestant rulers. He insists that it is not a war of religion to restore Protestantism which is being waged. But if James II is reestablished on his throne, then France would only be strengthened so that she could further destroy the liberty of Europe.

The pamphlet closes on an extreme Catholic note.[19] There is a complaint that the authority of the Holy See has been disputed in such assemblies as that of 1682 and that French writers "speak against the rights of the Holy Father with almost as much insolence as Luther and Calvin." As a result, the action of the Pope against France is to his own best interest.

These passages, as we have seen above, are placed in juxtaposition to the Catholic[20] statements of the *Lettre . . . à un bourgmestre de Soleure* and both ascribed to Jurieu by the *Réponse de ministre à une Lettre . . . sur le sujet des petits prophètes.* This letter to the Swiss cantons, urging them, whether Catholic or Protestant, to abandon their neutrality and to join the Allies against France requires some further attention in this connection. The same argument is employed as in the *Véritables*

Véritables Intérêts did not intend to "sonner le tocsin pour la ruine de la France mais seulement pour son abbaisement qui est d'une souveraine necessité pour la paix & pour la religion."

[19] "Estant de la Religion dont je suis, ce n'est pas mon affaire d'entreprendre l'apologie des Anglois, des Hollandois, & du Prince d'Orange qui ont dépossédé le Roy d'Angleterre." *Les Véritables Intérêts des princes de l'Europe,* pp. 30–32.

[20] "Je suis aussi bon Catholique que vous." See also "Si le Roi de France par la persécution pouvoit convertir les Hérétiques, cela vaudroit bien la peine d' y concourir avec lui," and "au monde de Dieu ne vous piquons point d'être plus Catholique que le Pape, le chef de l'Eglise." *Lettre à un bourgmestre de Soleure,* pp. 3–7.

Intérêts that the invasion of England and the union of the Protestant princes were accidental circumstances which were not favored by Pope or Emperor, but of which they should take advantage. As for the profit accruing to the Huguenots from the war, it is to the interest of Catholics [21] that there should be more than one religion in France, since the existence of several religions would cause civil wars, which would prevent external conquest by France. Furthermore, "it is certain that it is to movements for the sake of religion that Europe is indebted for the happy conjuncture which it finds favorable to the recovery of its liberty."

Now, like the *Véritables Intérêts,* the *Soupirs* stresses simultaneously the internal discontent within France and the external pressure by the Allies, which, it is hoped, will force Louis XIV to his knees. But it has been suggested [22] that, if, as Bayle believed, the *Soupirs* is a modification, occasioned by the events of the time, of the prophecy of Jurieu (that is, if the English Revolution and the European war caused him to visualize the reestablishment of Protestantism in France through the humiliation and defeat of Louis XIV at the hands of William of Orange and the League of Augsburg) then it would follow that Jurieu would have projected any program other than the Catholic and reactionary plan of reform as outlined in the *Soupirs*. In fact, it would appear that such a design would be in definite contradiction to the conversion of France to Protestantism. Such an interpretation is, however, to misunderstand completely the temper of Jurieu's thought and action. The inconsistencies of Protestants, which Bayle and Montaigne before him had delighted in pointing out, are not fairly to be labeled as such if we only remember that the all-consuming purpose of the Calvinists everywhere was to establish absolute truth. A sympathetic understanding of this conception could not be expected of a complete skeptic like Bayle, but we must attempt to grasp the idea before we hasten to condemn the Huguenots in the sixteenth or the seventeenth centuries either for a lack of patriotism or for complete opportunism. They felt that loyalty to their religion was greater even than that to their native land. In a word, the Calvinists were inconsistent in their politics because they held to absolute consistency in their religion. With regard to the apparent contra-

---

[21] Jurieu points out that the policy of persecution has really made atheists rather than Catholics.

[22] Riemann, *Der Verfasser der "Soupirs de la France Esclave,"* pp. 44 ff.

diction of parts of the *Soupirs* with his other writings, if we simply recall that religion is the motivating force of Jurieu's thought, then it matters little that these *Mémoires* do not square in every respect with his prophecies. In fact, his prognostications were regarded by Jurieu himself as only another weapon against the enemy—a stimulus to the realization of the events therein predicted.

Under the guise of a Catholic as in *Les Véritables Intérêts,* the *Lettre . . . à un bourgmestre de Soleure,* the *Soupirs de la France esclave,* and later in the *Salut de la France,* Jurieu was simply trying to appeal to all the dissatisfied elements, and this would not have been possible if he had revealed his Calvinistic origin. On the external side, the Catholic states must be convinced that it was to their true interest to oppose a Catholic country by joining an alliance headed by a Protestant prince who had just seized the throne from a Catholic ruler. On the internal side, Jurieu, under the mask of a liberal Catholic, attempted to appeal to all the discontented groups in France—Huguenots, Jansenists, ultramontanists, nobility, the aristocracy of the robe, the provinces and cities, the people, and, last but not least, the Dauphin himself. But it was not so easy as in the preceding century for the Calvinists to give force to their cause by allying with other powerful elements in the state opposed to the royal authority. These groups had all been pretty well suppressed by the government, although in the Cévennes the rebels did include not only the "new converts" but also other bodies, which were protesting against the burden of taxation, and so on. As Jurieu said in his Eighteenth *Lettre pastorale* of the Third Year, the defeat of France was absolutely necessary "for peace and religion." He was ready to employ any means [23] at hand to secure this end, even though logically and taken by itself the permanent encouragement, for example, of ultramontanism would be anything but favorable to the Protestant cause. With these factors in mind Jurieu's authorship appears certain from both internal and external evidence.

But let us now turn to the examination of the *Soupirs* itself, making further comparison of the ideas therein elaborated with other works of Jurieu of known authenticity. The *Soupirs* opens with the impassioned

---

[23] This would even account for the remarks in the last *Mémoires,* which are disparaging of William of Orange.

pronouncement that the loss of liberty is the greatest calamity imaginable.[24] The happy outcome of the English Revolution is then cited as an example for France to follow in seeking to recover her lost freedom,[25] since she alone is subject to an unlimited power. Such action by France is to the interest not only of the people but also of the heir to the crown, who will inherit a mere skeleton of a kingdom if the monarchy is not reformed.[26]

At this point the plan of the *Soupirs* is outlined. There is to be, first, a sketch of the oppression of all the orders of France under the despotical regime; second, a consideration of the means by which the French court sustains its absolute power; third, a description of the difference between the present government and the ancient form of the French monarchy; and fourth, an analysis of the methods by which the favorable circumstances of the time can be used to restore the monarchy to its pristine condition.

Beginning with the oppression of the various orders of France, the *Soupirs* cites the church. This should be regarded as the most noble of all parts of the state, having the greatest privileges and the utmost liberty, and yet today it is subject to the tyranny of the government. The king makes himself absolute in ecclesiastical affairs to the detriment of the Pope.[27] Even the faith depends upon the will of the sovereign. In

---

[24] "Entre tous les biens dont on a sujet de pleurer la perte la liberté sans doute est des principaux." *Mémoire* I, p. 1. Cf. *Lettres pastorales,* XVIII of the Third Year: "Parceque les biens sont infiniment moins chers que la liberté, la vie & la religion quand il n'y va que de la perte des biens il ne faut point résister lorsqu'il n'y a peril que le repos public & le salut des particuliers pourroyent souffrir."

[25] "Et le bonheur que l'Angleterre vient d'obtenir en voyant rompre les fers qu'on luy mettoit sur les bras, doit faire renaître dans l'âme de tous les bons Francois l'amour pour la Patrie les désirs pour le retour de la liberté & le dessein de sortir de dessous cet épouvantable joug qui repose sur leurs épaules." *Mémoire* I, p. 4. Cf. Jurieu's *La Religion des jésuites* (1689), p. 4: "J'ai été bien aisé d'apprendre par votre lettre aussi bien que par celle du Jésuite que la liberté n'est pas encore tout à fait éteinte & que l'idolatrie pour le Roy portée au comble n'est pas encore bien établie dans tous les coeurs . . . il suffit que cela est vrai que les Francois ne sont pas encore tous montée au point d'Idolatrie & d'Impiété où sont arrivés il y a longtemps les esclaves & les adulateurs de la Cour . . . ce petit germe de liberté qui est caché dans le fonds des âmes pourra quelque jour produire de bons effets pour rompre le joug qu'on a posé sur nos épaules."

[26] Cf. *Le Salut de la France* where this theme is elaborated on the basis of the *Apologie pour leurs majestés.*

[27] "Il soumet le Pape au Concile, il luy ôte le pouvoir d'excommunier les Rois, il déclare qu'il est sujet à erreur." *Mémoire* I, p. 8, and see also pp. 5–8, 9–10; *Mémoire* III, pp. 30–32; *Mémoire* IV, pp. 54–57.

addition, the ruler has forced the church to take part in the persecution of the Calvinists.[28] The affair of the five propositions of Jansenius should have been left to the province of the church; instead, the court had this controversy defined at Rome according to its own desires and then persecuted the disciples of Saint Augustine who refused to comply with the decisions thus obtained from Rome. In the famous *Formulaire* the Court prescribed an oath by which the five propositions were not only pronounced heretical but also regarded as to be found in Jansenius. This made the Pope infallible not only in matters of right but also of fact. In the affair of the *Régale* the king established his supreme power over the bishops in a further attempt to secure an unlimited empire over the church.

The opposition of the *Soupirs* to the Gallican position [29] is even more clearly revealed in the twelfth *Mémoire*. The Gallican church must be regarded as the tool of the court in its ambitious designs, and both are in opposition to the legitimate authority of the Pope. Therefore, the true interest of the Papacy [30] is to support the League of Augsburg until France is forced "to renounce in all forms and by a general council of the nation that theology so fatal to the legitimate authority of the Holy Pontiffs." [31]

Shortly after the opening of the war in 1689 Louis XIV resumed diplomatic relations with the Papacy in an attempt to split the League of Augsburg by drawing off the Catholic princes. The *Soupirs* attempts to forestall any such development, declaring that only by external defeat would the king consent to internal reform. The method employed to

---

[28] Although this assertion may seem contradictory to the passages in the *Politique du clergé* where Jurieu accused the Catholic clergy of instigating the kings to the persecution of the Huguenots, it should be recalled that in his *L'Esprit de M. Arnaud,* II, 274, the king alone is blamed for the plight of the Calvinists.

[29] "Mais je comprends pourtant bien qu'il est nécessaire pour la conservation de l'Eglise que l'autorité du Saint Siège demeure en son entier comme elle est. Le Pape n'est pas de droit Divin empereur des Rois pour le temporel, je l'avoue, mais sa possession là-dessus est ancienne, il est périleux de remuer les bornes de nos ancestres. Et il y a beaucoup plus de danger pour l'Eglise de diminuer l'autorité de son Chef que de l'augmenter."

[30] The Holy See is indebted to the Calvinists, argues Jurieu, for if the English and Dutch had not caused the war, the Emperor would have still been alone at war against France and the Turk. As a result the rights of the Pope would still be infringed in France.

[31] "Théologie de rébellion qui a pris son origine dans les Conciles de Constance & de Bâle & dont on s'est servi pour combattre les Papes depuis le règne de Charles VII, Roy de France." *Mémoire* XII, pp. 179–184.

interfere with any understanding between the Pope and Louis XIV is to question the sincerity of the apparent readiness of the king to renounce the liberties of the Gallican church. It is argued that self-interest alone is the motivating force of the religion of the court of France. When France is victorious over its neighbors, then "Catholics, heretics, Holy Pontiff,[32] and church . . . are sacrificed to its arrogance." The principle of the Gallican church [33] may be held in abeyance for a time but it stands ready to be revived by the King of France whenever it is feasible.

In addition to the church, other orders in the state such as the *parlements,* the nobility, the cities, and the people have felt the evil effects of the despotic regime, which has diminished, if not abolished, their privileges. The aristocratic antipathy to this leveling of the various orders is manifested in bitter fashion.[34] There is no realm except France where privileges are not regarded as irrevocable once granted. The Calvinists relied upon this principle when they protested the revocation of their edicts. But the people, warns Jurieu in the *Soupirs,* will never be persuaded that such despotic action can be taken as a matter of right without resistance.[35]

[32] "On alloit le grand chemin de mettre en France les Droits sacrés du Saint Siège au même état que les privilèges accordés aux Calvinistes." *Mémoire* XII, pp. 176–179.

[33] "La Théologie de l'Eglise Gallicane ne vaut pas mieux à cet égard que celle de Calvin puis qu'elle ne donne au Pape qu'une primauté d'ordre de droit divin sur les autres Evêques." *Ibid.*

[34] "Il est bon d'apprendre . . . que dans le Gouvernement présent tout est Peuple. Un ne sait plus ce que c'est que qualité, distinction, mérite, naissance. L'autorité Royale est montée si haut que toutes les distinctions disparoissent, toutes les lumières sont absorbées, car dans l'élévation où s'est porté le monarque tous les humains ne sont que la poussière de ses pieds. Ainsi sous le Nom de Peuple on a répandu l'oppression & la misère jusque sur les parties les plus nobles & les plus relevées de l'état." *Mémoire* II, p. 17. Cf. "Elle (la cour de France) foule les Peuples, les grands, les petits, les Nobles par des nouvelles charges." *Mémoire* III, p. 32.

[35] "Il (le peuple) conserve dans le coeur les desseins de se vanger & de secouer le joug & cela devient la sémence des révoltes. C'est de qui se voit aujourd'huy dans ceux qu'on appelle nouveaux convertis. . . . Les Calvinistes persécutés ont ému toutes les puissances de l'Europe de leur Religion. Ces puissances Protestantes ont fait jouer des machines pour remuer le reste de l'Europe. Le Roy d'Angleterre en est déjà tombé par terre, La France est émue." *Mémoire* III, pp. 33–35. Cf. Jurieu's *Réflexions sur la cruelle persécution que souffre l'Eglise reformée de France,* pp. 44–46: "La persécution rendra & rend dés à présent la France l'horreur de tous les étrangers particulièrement de tous les Protestants. Les Alliances avec la France ne dureront qu'autant qu'on se verra en état de luy courir sus . . . quand les guerres étrangères s'éleveront les millions d'hommes dont on tiendra la conscience en une cruelle servitude ne manqueront pas de chercher les moyens de briser leurs fers . . . on jette les sémences des guerres civiles."

The exercise of this despotic, arbitrary, and unlimited power has changed the very conception of the state. "Formerly the state entered everywhere; one spoke only of the interests, needs, conservation, and service of the state. Today to speak thus serves literally as a crime of high treason. The king has taken the place of the state. It is the service and interest of the king, it is the preservation of the provinces and property of the king. Finally, the king is everything, the state is no longer anything." [36] The true doctrine, on the contrary, is "that the welfare of the state and the public should be the sovereign law." [37] Louis regards himself as the absolute master of the life, liberty, persons, property, religion, and conscience [38] of his subjects, whereas the *Soupirs* holds that "the people have established kings to conserve the persons, life, liberty, and property of individuals." [39] The close similarity of such ideas to Jurieu's other pronouncements is quite remarkable, but nowhere is it more in evidence than in the following summary:

And for those . . . who say that the nations established kings to be their fathers and not their tyrants; that the right of the peoples is imprescriptible; that one is obliged in conscience to work for his own preservation against the oppressions of whatever class there may be; that kings cannot have more power over their subjects than fathers have over their children, since they are created to be the fathers of the people; that kings have their limits, not only in the rules of justice and equity but also in the rights which have been

---

[36] *Mémoire* II, pp. 23–26. Cf. Jurieu's *La Religion des jésuites*, pp. 15–20: "Quels Francois, dit on . . . prendre les armes contre son Roi: conspirer avec toute l'Europe pour la ruine de sa patrie, au contraire nous cherchons sa délivrance. Ne confonds pas je vous prie le Roi avec le Royaume. Pour le Royaume tout autant que nous sommes des Réfugiés nous voudrions verser comme nous avons fait autrefois le plus pur de notre sang pour la gloire & pour la conservation de la couronne. Mais quant au Roi nous ne concevons pas que nous soyons dans le même obligation . . . nous croyons obligés de regarder comme notre ennemi celui que nous devons regarder comme le plus cruel ennemi que Dieu, sa vérité & son Eglise ayent jamais eu."

[37] *Mémoire* II, pp. 26–28. This phrase occurs constantly in Jurieu's other works.

[38] "Un pauvre Janséniste . . . ou un pauvre Huguenot . . . croient faire un grand effort de liberté en disant mes biens & ma vie sont au Roy mais ma conscience n'est qu'à Dieu." This maxim is from Daillé. In general in the *Soupirs*, because of its Catholic tone, the persecution of the Calvinists is regarded as damaging the Catholic Church which is forced to give the sacraments to hypocrites, rather than as injuring the souls of the unwilling Protestants.

[39] *Mémoire* II, pp. 17–18. Cf. *Lettres pastorales*, XVIII, "Les peuples ne donnent à leurs souverains la souveraineté que pour la conservation de leurs biens, de leurs vies, de leur liberté & de leur religion."

conserved; that fathers are the sacred heads for their children just as kings are the anointed of the Lord and all laws, divine and human, pagan and Christian, permit resistance to the violence of fathers; that the prince has power to levy taxes for the preservation of the state and not for its destruction . . . those, I say, who utter such maxims are treated in France as detestable people, enemies of the king.[40]

In opposition to the claim that French monarchs possessed an arbitrary, absolute, and unlimited power, the *Soupirs* maintains first that the crown of France was not successive but elective during the first two lines of kings and even for a time under the third. Under elective monarchy the prince is limited by the laws. Every nation which establishes its king has the right to depose him when he exceeds his authority and when he destroys rather than conserves the state. Therefore, an elective king cannot have an arbitrary power. The conclusion is reached that the French crown has become successive by a pure usurpation, since the Salic Law is "one of the greatest myths which history has ever invented." Therefore, since the arbitrary power of French kings is not of the same age as the monarchy, the royal authority can be reduced to its just limits without violating the fundamental laws of the state.

The second means employed to prove that the absolute power of the rulers of France is usurped is to show that the estates have always been the principal depositaries of sovereignty [41] and are superior to kings. In short, "the government of France was aristocratic rather than monarchical, or at least it was a monarchy tempered by aristocracy, exactly as it is in England." [42] In certain respects the estates are superior to the

---

[40] *Mémoire* IV, p. 53. Note also the passage: "Que la puissance des Rois est sans condition, que les devoirs du Roy & du sujet ne sont pas respectifs comme ceux du maître & du serviteur, du mari & de la Femme, du Père & de l'enfant, parceque le Roy de sa part n'est obligé de rien." Cf. *Lettres pastorales*, XVI of the Third Year: "Il est donc certain qu'il n'y a aucune relation de maître, de serviteur, de père, d'enfant; de mari, de femme qui ne soit établie sur un pacte mutuel et sur les obligations mutuelles."

[41] "Le peuple, c'est à dire cette partie qui est distinguée des grands & de la Noblesse composoit avec les Seigneurs les Assemblées générales entre les mains desquels étoit le souverain Pouvoir de la Monarchie." *Mémoire* VII, pp. 100–102. Cf., *ibid.*, the low view of the mass of the people: "La sagesse & les bons conseils se trouvent rarement dans la multitude." Cf. with the many other passages in Jurieu which are disparaging of the *vulgus.*

[42] *Mémoire* VII, p. 95. See *Mémoire* IX, p. 134: "Nous reconnoistrons que le gouvernement de France & de celuy d'Angleterre étoient absolument semblables. La différence est

king, as when they elect, depose, or judge him; while in others,[43] such as legislation and the giving of grants, they share all parts of the sovereignty with the monarchs, who "were greater than any of the members of the assembly taken as individuals but less than all the individuals taken as a body." [44] With regard to the power of the estates to depose the prince, "it is necessary that a power be unlimited when it comes to deposing him who is the principal depositary of sovereignty. And it is easy to understand that those who take such action against the royal person and dignity should have the same power everywhere and in all things." [45] It can readily be seen that this again places no less than an arbitrary power in the estates, which is something that Jurieu had absolutely denied to the monarch.

From this arbitrary assembly of the estates the author of the *Soupirs* derived the power of the *parlements* under Philip the Fair and the authority of the *Grand Conseil*. The *parlements* are no longer consulted about affairs of state, while many governmental matters are now settled in "the great council" which were formerly determined in the assembly

---

que les Anglois sont demeurés dans leurs anciens Loix & Privilèges. Et nous avons misérablement laissé perdre les nôtres."

[43] Jurieu claims that action on the destruction of Calvinism should have been considered in the estates and not by the king alone. *Mémoire* III, p. 35. Cf. the view in his *Tableau du socinianisme* (1690), pp. 491–492: "Nous ne disons pas qu'un seul homme à cause qu'il se dit Roy & qu'il s'arroge une puissance absolue ait pouvoir de ruiner le salut temporel & éternel de ses peuples. Il faut donc pour changer la Religion d'un pays avoir consentement du peuple tacite ou formel: tacite quand le peuple laisse faire le Prince & ne s'oppose pas; formel quand on assemble les États & les sages d'un pays & que l'on change la Religion de leur consentement."

[44] *Mémoire* VII, pp. 102–104. Cf. the passages from the *Vindiciae contra tyrannos* cited earlier in this study. Jurieu concludes that kings should be held "dans une médiocrité de puissance" by the people, so that their liberty will not be jeopardized. Cf. the Scotch Calvinist, Samuel Rutherford, who in his *Lex Rex* (1644) speaks of "measuring out by ounce weights" the king's authority.

[45] *Mémoire* VII, pp. 102–104. Cf. *Lettres pastorales,* XVIII and XXI of the Third Year: "Il faut qu'il y ait dans les sociétés certaine autorité qui n'ait besoin d'avoir raison pour valider ses actes; or cette autorité n'est que dans les peuples. . . . Cette maxime ne peut avoir de mauvaise conséquence qu'en supposant qu'on veut dire que tout ce qu'un peuple fait par voie de sédition peut valoir, mais c'est bien peu entendre les termes; qui dit un acte, dit un acte juridique, une résolution prise dans une assemblée de tout un peuple, comme peuvent être les Parlements & les États. Or il est certain que si les peuples sont le premier siège de la Souveraineté ils n'ont pas besoin d'avoir raison pour valider leurs actes, c'est à dire pour les rendre exécutoires. Car encore une fois, les arrêts, soit des cours Souverains, soit des Souverains, soit des assemblées souveraines sont exécutoires quelque injustes qu'ils soient."

of the estates. But the liberty of the people had already begun to diminish when the *parlements* were established. Both the *parlements* and the Great Council have been subjugated. They only served to augment the encroaching despotism because they tended to place in oblivion the assembly of the estates in which alone rests the fundamental powers of the nation.[46]

Jurieu derives other proofs in the *Soupirs* against absolute royal power from the history of the independent role in the ancient government of the realm of "the nobles" and "the princes of the blood," [47] who, being established by the people and by the kingdom, cannot be deposed by the king alone. This whole historical and institutional portion, in which the former government is described, is richly illustrated with authorities such as Pasquier, Budé, Charles Du Moulin, Claude de Seyssel, and Bernard de Girard, Seigneur du Haillan.[48] Special attention is given to the famous phrase "car tel est notre plaisir" to prove that this was formerly written in Latin as "tale est Placitum nostrum," which does not refer to the personal will of the ruler but to the action of the estates of the realm.

Having set forth the contrast between the present government and the ancient form of the French monarchy, Jurieu in the *Soupirs* urges the return to its pristine glory by taking advantage of the combination of internal discontent and the external war against the League of Augs-

[46] Jurieu summarizes the powers of the estates as including "le droit d'élire & de déposer les Rois" and "le pouvoir de changer la forme du Gouvernement, de faire de nouvelles Loix, de confirmer le partage entre les enfants des Rois, de transporter la couronne de l'un à l'autre. De créer des Tuteurs aux Rois. De nommer des Régents & des Administrateurs du Royaume durent la Minorité des Rois, leur absence ou leurs Maladies. De condamner à la mort des Têtes Couronnées, de châtier les plus grands Seigneurs du Royaume par la privation de leurs Biens, de leur liberté & même par la perte de la vie." *Mémoire* IX, p. 126. In the *Lettres pastorales,* XVIII of the Third Year, Jurieu had condemned the death penalty for the monarch, so this is an important change.
[47] He calls them "Conseillers nés du Roy & de la couronne." *Mémoire* V, pp. 74–77.
[48] Both Hotman in the *Franco-Gallia* and Jurieu in the *Soupirs* wanted to return to the ancient French constitution. Although numerous passages are lifted from the *Franco-Gallia* (Mémoire VI of the *Soupirs* is largely based on Mémoire II of the great work of Hotman, pp. 406–411 of Vol. II of the *Mémoires de l'état de France*) to prove that "le souverain pouvoir (est) entre les mains du Peuple & des Assemblées composées de ses Députés" (Mémoire VIII, p. 111), Hotman is not cited. The Catholic Du Haillan, however, is referred to as supporting the election of kings by the people. He borrowed this idea from Hotman, the Protestant jurist, whom the *Soupirs* cannot cite because of its ultramontane position. For French legal thought in general see William F. Church, *Constitutional Thought in Sixteenth Century France.*

burg, since the king will never consent to a reformation of the realm
without being forced by the overwhelming number of his enemies.[49]
But Jurieu declares that he does not wish to incite a civil war or deliver
the kingdom to foreigners. Instead, "if our Frenchmen wish to embark
in a unanimous fashion upon legitimate means of reforming the state,
as the English nation has entered upon the plan of favoring the designs
of the Prince of Orange when he invaded England, it will not be necessary to go as far as the English have done." [50] The government can
be restricted without bloodshed and even without removing Louis XIV
from the throne.[51] In fact, even the Calvinists will limit themselves to
"humbling the tyrants who have persecuted them," [52] without ravaging
their native land to which they are as much attached as any other Frenchman.

This historical, legal, and institutional approach of the *Soupirs,* written in the same vein as the *Franco-Gallia,* supplements the philosophical,
natural law arguments of the *Lettres pastorales* which bear great similarity to the *Vindiciae contra tyrannos.* The result of both attacks is the
insistence upon an arbitrary authority in the estates; and this is the most
conclusive bit of internal evidence in support of Jurieu's authorship of
the *Soupirs.* Certainly it cannot be admitted, as Barbier contends, that
as a theologian Jurieu lacked the knowledge necessary for such a remarkable analysis of French constitutional development. In the seventeenth century, erudition extended beyond the limit of one's vocation,
to put it in Calvinistic terms. Furthermore, Jurieu's other writings reveal a vast background in profane as well as in ecclesiastical history.[53]

[49] "C'est pourquoy sans avoir des pensées opposées aux véritables intérêts du Royaume
on peut souhaiter beaucoup d'ennemis du Roy." *Mémoire* XIV, p. 216. Here again is that
same distinction between the king and the realm which Jurieu had made in his *La Religion des jésuites* which, contrary to Rieman, is definitely from the pen of Jurieu. For
conclusive evidence of his authorship of this tract as well as of *L'Esprit de M. Arnaud* which
is closely connected with it, see the anonymous *Réponse des fidèles captifs en Babylone*
(1695), pp. 23–24, which was probably written by Basnage de Beauval.

[50] *Mémoire* XII, pp. 186–189.

[51] *Ibid.,* pp. 186–187. Under the mask of a Catholic, Jurieu holds that if foreign enemies
enter the realm to join the internal discontent, both the Catholic church and the crown
will be endangered.

[52] *Mémoire* XV, p. 224.

[53] Jacques LeLong in his *Bibliothèque historique de la France,* II, 19, cites an interesting
item in manuscript, entitled *Receuil de mémoires curieux concernant le progrès de la
puissance des rois de France sur tous les corps de l'état.* X *Mémoires,* 1690. "Il parait que
c'est une partie du receuil que P. Jurieu a intitulé les *Soupirs de la France.* Il l'a sans doute
arrangé et augmenté selon ses idées."

Closely connected with the *Soupirs* is a little tract entitled *Le Salut de la France à Monseigneur le Dauphin,* which appeared in April, 1690, about fifteen days before the *Avis aux réfugiés.* On the basis of the *Apologie pour leurs majestés britanniques* which Jurieu certainly wrote,[54] there is every reason to believe that he is the author[55] of *Le Salut de la France* just as he was of the *Soupirs.* The *Salut* urges Louis XIV to retire from the throne as the Emperor Charles V had done for his son. In other words, there should be a Glorious Revolution in France.[56] If it cannot be accomplished peaceably, then the use of force is justifiable.[57] Besides "there is a supreme law which emanates from nature which rulers cannot violate without losing their title of king; this law is the safety of the people."[58] All these ideas are identical with those expressed in Jurieu's *Apology* for William and Mary and in his *Pastoral Letters.* There is also the same consideration of the abolition of the Estates General, which formerly elected and deposed kings, of the *parlements,*[59] and of the power of the cities and the nobility.

The *Salut* is written in the ultramontane vein of the *Soupirs,*[60] but

---

[54] See the *Dernière conviction contre le Sieur Bayle,* p. 32.

[55] This opinion is expressed in the face of a recent study which regards Jurieu's authorship of the *Salut* as improbable as of the *Soupirs.* See Friedrich Kleyser, *Der Flugschriftenkampf gegen Ludwig XIV zur Zeit des pfälzischen Krieges,* p. 45.

[56] Cf. the song sung at Dijon which advises the French to follow the example of the English Revolution:

> Pour bien défendre le royaume
> Il nous faudroit un roi Guillaume.
> Louis ne fait que radoter;
> Et quoi que l'on puisse en dire,
> Le plus court est de l'enfermer
> Avec sa megère à Saint-Cyr.

Quoted in Marcel Bouchard, *De l'humanisme à l'encyclopédie,* p. 283.

[57] There are certain circumstances "où la Religion & la conscience nous obligent à traiter un Père comme un Payen & Peager. En un mot la nature inspire qu'il faut extirper la Tyrannie & que celuy qui est en droit de le faire doit s'estourdir sur les relations qu'il peut avoir avec le Tyran." *Salut de la France,* pp. 71–133.

[58] Cf. "Les Rois sont leurs pères & leurs Pasteurs comme les anciens les appellent & du moment qu'ils cessent de l'être ou qu'ils en deviennent incapables les peuples les doivent dégrader & en élire d'autres à leur place." *Ibid.,* pp. 134–181. The opposite view, which would give a universal impunity to the prince, is mentioned as derived from Hobbes's *Corps Politiques,* Part II, Chap. VIII, Art. 6.

[59] "Les vérifications aujourd'huy ne sont que de pures notifications comme l'a fort bien remarqué un grand ennemy de la Tyrannie (L'auteur des *Soupirs,* Mémoire 8)." *Salut de la France,* pp. 134–181.

[60] "Et pour porter la tyrannie à son plus haut point il s'en est pris au Vicaire de Jesus Christ à celuy que nous devons regarder comme un Dieu & qui est véritablement un Dieu sur la terre. Que ne l'excommuniez-vous, O Sainte Père. . . . Vous n'êtes plus qu'un

with far more force and detail than in the *Soupirs,* the example of England and the Prince and Princess of Orange is here set before the Dauphin of France. If the heir apparent does not act, then the people or foreign princes will depose Louis XIV, for a "king who usurps the rights of God is a thousand times more criminal than a subject who seizes unjustly the crown of his prince." [61] Jurieu urges the calling of the Estates General and he demands the aid of the Allies and the Pope.[62] The Protestants should be recalled and their edicts reestablished if there is to be a general peace.[63] In spite of the Catholic tone of this pamphlet, the typically Calvinistic view is advanced that the Catholic prince does not really persecute Protestants for the sake of religious truth but for the purely secular reason of political unity.[64]

But peace in the European war, which had begun in 1688, was not in sight until 1696. As the cessation of hostilities approached, the Huguenots became very active in pressing their cause, confident that William of Orange, whose fortunes they had aided in Holland, England, Ireland, and on the Continent, would demand that their liberties in France should be restored to them by the treaty of peace. These fervent hopes of the refugees and the role of Jurieu, who was assisted by Benoit and De Vrigny at the time of the peace negotiations, are clearly shown in a letter to the King of England written on August 18, 1696. In this document Jurieu seeks further assurance from William in order to allay the fears of the refugee pastors.[65] He suggests that since the Protestant

Phantome de Pape à l'égard de l'Eglise Gallicane. . . . Vos enfants n'ont qu'à recourir à vous pour encourir l'indignation de ce Prince & être traitez avec la même rigueur qu'il a accoutumé de traiter les Hérétiques." See also the same emphasis on the profanation of the Catholic church by the policy of constraint toward the Protestants. *Le Salut de la France,* pp. 184–186.

[61] *Le Salut de la France,* pp. 216–226.

[62] Along with the *Salut,* mention should be made of another refugee pamphlet, *Les Sept Sages de France à leur Roi Louis XIV sur les moyens de la paix,* Rotterdam 1692, which urges that peace can be made only on condition that the Protestants be restored to their former liberty of conscience. The author also demands that the Estates and the *Parlements* be restored to their ancient liberties.

[63] For a description of the persecution he cites *Les Plaintes protestantes* of Claude, *L'histoire apologétique ou déffence des Libertez des Eglises réformées de France* of Fr. de Gaultier, sieur de Saint-Blancard and *Les Lettres pastorales du Ministre Jurieu.*

[64] "Le roi veut qu'on soit de sa religion non parceque sa religion est la véritable mais parce que c'est la Religion qu'il professe; c'est à dire que quant il seroit Mahometan . . . il exigeroit la même chose de ses peuples." *Le Salut,* pp. 216–226.

[65] "Ils voyent que les affaires tendent à une paix générale et on s'efforce de leur persuader

states will receive no territory in the peace settlement, the Catholic princes should not object to the restoration of Protestantism in France. In fact, such action would "favor the interests of all those states which fear the power of France, since good politics demands that as many seeds of partition and division as possible be left in the state, whose power is dreaded because of too great a union of its members." [66]

At the same time that the extreme party of the refugees, represented by such figures as Jurieu, Benoit, and De Vrigny, was seeking the reestablishment of Protestantism in France through the influence of William of Orange and the Protestant powers in the coalition which had waged the war against France, another group of refugees, the moderates, were, in the tradition of the *Avis aux réfugiés,* seeking relief in a direct application to the grace of the king himself. On the third of September, 1697, there appeared a *Requête présentée au roi de France par les protestants qui sont dans son royaume, que l'on a contraints ci-devant d'embrasser la religion romaine,* which was probably written by Bayle. The tone of this request was of complete submission to the king.[67] In a letter [68] of September 20/30, 1697, Jurieu refers to this document, viewing it as the product of a party [69] similar to the English Jacobites, but

---

que dans cette paix du monde ils ne trouveront pas la paix de cette église persécutée dont ils sont les debris. Ils craignent que les autres États qui s'intéressent peu ou point du tout à nos malheurs en détournent les favorables intentions que votre Majesté pourroit avoir pour eux. Quant à moi à qui Votre Majesté a donné tant d'assurances par écrit et de vive voix que son grand but est de travailler à la gloire de Dieu et au rétablissement de son Eglise, je ne saurois avoir ces déffiances."

[66] This letter has been only partially published in the *Bulletin . . . du Protestantisme Français,* June–September, 1902, p. 485, and in Et. Charavay, *Lettres autographes,* Paris, 1887.

[67] "Ils (vos Sujets qui professent la Religion que les Edits nomment prétendue Réformée) sont persuadez qu'après ce qu'ils doivent à Dieu ils sont obligez de rendre à Votre Majesté une obéissance sans bornes. Ils ne connoissent aucun Homme sur la terre qui puisse les dispenser de la fidélité qui vous est due. Craindre Dieu & honorer Votre Majesté, employer à son service leurs biens & leurs propres vies; c'est parmi eux une maxime inviolable qu'ils ont soin d'inculquer à leurs enfans. On ne peut qu'avec la dernière injustice leur imputer quelques troubles des Règnes précédens. . . . Permettez, Sire, permettez à un grand nombre de vos Sujets que leur Religion a contrainte à sortier hors de vos Etats d'y retourner pour y finir leurs jours sous Votre autorité royale afin d'invoquer Dieu avec vous comme nous faisons ci-devant."

[68] This letter is published by P. Fonbrune-Berbinau, "Deux lettres inédites de Pierre Jurieu, 1697," *Bulletin . . . du Protestantisme Français,* November–December, 1905.

[69] "C'est le même parti que nous combattons depuis dix ans qui a toujours taché à nous retirer de la confiance que nous avions en la protection du roy d'Angleterre pour nous tourner du côté du roy de France."

he ascribes its authorship to Jacques Muisson, Isaac Jaquelot, and Henri Basnage de Beauval rather than to Bayle.

In spite of all these efforts [70] by the Huguenots of both extremes in 1697–1698, the Peace of Ryswick was signed without the inclusion of any provision benefiting the French Protestants. William of Orange forsook the cause of the refugees in exchange for the recognition by France of the results of the Revolution of 1688 and the abandonment of the cause of James II. Jurieu has left his own account of the whole affair in his *Relation de tout ce qui s'est fait dans les affaires de la religion réformée et pour ses intérêts depuis le commencement des négociations de la paix de Ryswyck* (1698). He recalls his labors of a decade to free the Huguenots and, especially, his unsuccessful efforts at the time of the English Revolution of 1688.[71] Now that once again his endeavors have failed, Jurieu concludes in deep discouragement that the reestablishment of the Protestants is not to be secured by force of arms but by some other method yet to be revealed by God.[72] He attempts to console his coreligionists, in what amounts to three pastoral letters which have been printed along with the *Relation*.[73]

France had only three years of peace after the conclusion of the war of the League of Augsburg in 1697 before she became engaged in the War of the Spanish Succession in 1701. In the midst of this struggle that was soon to become European in scope, the Huguenots of the Cévennes staged various uprisings in the revolt of the Camisards, which continued

[70] The best account of these negotiations is to be found in Dedieu, *Le Rôle politique des protestants;* Charles Bost, *Les Prédicants protestants des Cévennes et du Bas-Languedoc, 1684–1700;* Charles Read, "Les Démarches des réfugiés huguenots auprès des négociateurs de la paix de Ryswick pour leur rétablissement en France, 1697," *Bulletin . . . du Protestantisme Français*, April 15, 1891; Charles Read, "Les Réfugiés huguenots lors du traité du Ryswick," *ibid.*, July 15, 1891; and Frank Puaux, "Essai sur les négociations des Réfugiés pour obtenir le rétablissement de la religion réformée au traité de Ryswick," *ibid.*, June 15, July 15, 1867.

[71] "Comme on prévoyoit que cette révolution auroit de grandes suites on fit tout ce que l'on put pour en tirer des avantages & pour disposer de loin les affaires à une autre espèce de révolution." *Relation de tout ce qui s'est fait.*

[72] According to Dedieu, in *Le Rôle politique des protestants,* p. 99, Jurieu even conceived of a heavy infiltration of the Huguenots in France under the protection of the ambassadors of the Protestant powers at the court of Louis XIV.

[73] *Première suite ou description de l'état lamentable où se trouve l'Église de France depuis la paix.* Cf. also Basnage's fourteen *Lettres pastorales sur le renouvellement de la persécution,* 1698, which urge patience and faith in God, since the trust in the Allies for deliverance had proved to be useless.

spasmodically from 1702 until 1711. On March 15, 1703, during these disturbances there appeared in Holland, certainly with the approval if not the inspiration of Jurieu, a *Manifeste des habitans des Cévennes sur leur prise d'armes*.[74] The tract argues that the Edict of Nantes could not rightfully be revoked, since a king must keep not only his own word and faith but also that of his predecessors, "when it has become a condition inseparably attached to the succession." The author of the pamphlet contends that since violence has been used against the Huguenots, they in turn have the right to use arms to defend themselves, to conserve life and liberty, and to oppose force with force, "which is a right of nature, authorized by divine and human laws." But the appeal is addressed to all good Frenchmen to restore justice where a "tyrannical and military government" now reigns. To revolt against such oppression is not "a religious matter only, but a right of nature common to all nations and all religions of the world to oppose the violence of those who rob us of our property without cause and who devastate our homes and families." In conclusion there is a demand for foreign aid, and, at home, the princes, the *parlements,* and the Dauphin are called upon for support in reestablishing order, reason, and humanity in the state.

In the last writing in which he indulged in political speculation, Jurieu likewise devoted attention to this question of foreign assistance to the Camisard revolt in the Cévennes. He begins his *Avis à tous les Alliés protestants et catholiques romains, princes et peuples, Souverains et sujets sur le secours qu'on doit donner aux soulévés des Cévennes* (1705) by declaring that, to those who awaited the deliverance of the Huguenots, the opening of the war of the Spanish Succession was regarded as a last opportunity to humiliate their persecutors. He regrets, however, that at the time of writing (1705) the Allies had not taken advantage of the situation. He recalls a brochure of 1685, the title of which was in the nature of a prophecy—*L'Europe esclave si L'Angleterre ne brise ses fers*. It was unfulfilled at the time and only partially accomplished by William of Orange, who did not carry the work to its conclusion. Providence has decreed that this happy event should be completed under Queen Anne. Jurieu therefore urges the Allies of both

[74] This tract has been reprinted by Frank Puaux in the *Bulletin . . . du Protestantisme Français,* July–August, 1912.

religions to follow the tactics of arousing so many disturbances in France itself that the king will be unable to prosecute a successful campaign outside the country. Jurieu laments the fact that for more than forty years the only interests considered in the treaties of peace were political rather than religious. In the present uprising in the Cévennes God has once more given men a chance to think of His truth and its preservation. The persecuted Huguenots in that region must be aided by entering the realm from the south. During the last three years the Camisards have been joined by other groups feeling the yoke of tyranny in the form of excessive taxation. Both Protestant and Catholic subjects "long for liberty." Therefore, it is to the interest of both religions outside of France to reestablish not only the Huguenot liberties in France but also liberty in Europe.

In defending the right of the Camisards in the Cévennes to take up arms against their sovereign, Jurieu declared that they had "the law of nations and nature" on their side, since "just defense is always permitted by the law of nations." Furthermore, "people who submit to a monster, whatever name he bears, whether king or prince, do not sell either their property or their lives." In fact, it is for "their preservation that men form societies and choose masters." [75] Therefore, if the ruler violates the laws of justice and humanity, he is not to be obeyed.

Jurieu especially attacks that maxim of Daillé that the king is the master of life and property but that conscience belongs to God. The first part of the maxim, particularly, is the source of tyranny and "unlimited power." Jurieu deplores this attempt to justify and defend the Huguenot cause by the method of attributing an arbitrary power to the king. Furthermore, the second part of this maxim destroys the first, since kings have no power over property and life when they desire to encroach upon the rights of conscience, which alone belongs to God, because "our property and our lives are attached to our consciences"; [76]

---

[75] *Avis aux alliés*, pp. 18–23.

[76] *Ibid*. Jurieu does not deduce from this that only Calvinists can enjoy rights of property and life, which could follow logically, however, since the Reformers held that the only conscience which has any claim to consideration is a right conscience. Cf. "Le droit de la conservation à l'égard de l'âme est incomparablement plus inaliénable que celuy de la conservation de la vie & des biens." *Le Janséniste convaincu*, p. 311. Cf. Locke's secular view in his treatise *Of Civil Government*, Chap. XII, pp. 158–159: "man . . . hath by nature a power not only to preserve his property . . . that is, his life, liberty, and estate."

therefore, they should be forsaken only for the "preservation of the true religion of God." [77] It is often necessary to submit to the violence of tyrants and make a voluntary sacrifice to God of one's life but it does not follow at all that the tyrant has power over life. For example, argues Jurieu, if an enemy should seize a person and oblige him to blaspheme or die, then it is necessary to forfeit one's life; but because of the operation of such brute force, is it to be concluded that this enemy has a right over life and property? On the contrary, an individual has always the right to resist the oppression of conscience and the seizure of his property and life.

The next problem to which Jurieu turned his attention was the old question of the character of that resistance when once it is admitted to be permissible. It was argued by some that only the entire nation by unanimous consent had the right to resist a tyrannical sovereign. Therefore, individuals, either a few or several, who take up arms are to be classed as rebels. Jurieu replied that he would like the supporters of this view to indicate the exact number necessary before action can be taken and to enumerate the instances of the orderly abdication of tyrants. Jurieu believed that "solemn abdications" had always been begun "by particular assemblies." In fact, "the decision to get rid of a tyrant begins with resolutions taken by families, cities, and communities. They assemble by groups; they take secret measures; and if possible they unite for their execution." [78] But to some, these acts and determinations are not those of the whole body of the nation and are therefore to be regarded as so many acts of rebellion. Only when these "diverse groups" are assembled can they force a legitimate abdication. But Jurieu thinks it is absurd that several acts of rebellion joined together result in a legitimate act of abdication, as if black added to black would make white.

Finally, Jurieu comes to the distinction between a true king and a tyrant, which even his opponents, the strict observers of the Scriptural laws, would recognize. He uses the example of Nero to trace the stages in the degeneration of kingship into tyranny and asks if the same obedience should be rendered to a legitimate prince turned tyrant as was due

[77] *Avis aux alliés,* pp. 18–23. Jurieu, like Calvin, seems to encourage a form of "this worldly asceticism."
[78] *Ibid.,* pp. 24–25.

him when he was the "observer of the laws and the preserver of his subjects." The reference from the Epistle of Saint Paul to the Romans which
commands obedience to the higher powers was, as Jurieu mentioned,
one of the principal weapons in the hands of those who oppose resistance to the prince, but he tries to show that these passages do not support
"arbitrary power." First, with regard to Verse 3—"For rulers are not a
terror to good works but to evil"—it is necessary, according to Jurieu, to
add the words, "good" and "legitimate," before the word, "rulers,"
which makes the verse read: "For good and legitimate rulers are not a
terror to good but to evil." Therefore, it follows that the princes who are
a terror to good works are not true and legitimate sovereigns.[79] "Wilt
thou then not be afraid of the power? Do that which is good and thou
shalt have the praise of the same," continued Saint Paul, which indicates
the princes who are to be obeyed. They are those who command the
good, while those who command evil are not to receive any submission
whatsoever.

Furthermore, Saint Paul said (Verse 4) that the prince "is the minister
of God to thee for good." Therefore, he is not the minister of God
"when he damns you, when he forces you into a religion that you believe to be idolatrous; when he torments you cruelly; when he robs you
of your property and life; in a word when he has become a tyrant." "But
if thou doest that which is evil," continued Saint Paul, "be afraid, for
he beareth not the sword in vain." God, therefore, has only given the
sword to princes to do good; that is, to secure the maintenance of the
laws and the conservation of the people. "When, then, a prince is armed
with the sword against the laws and the life of his subjects, it is clear
that according to the definition of Saint Paul he becomes a tyrant to
whom no obedience is due." "For he (the Prince) is the minister of God,
a revenger to execute wrath upon him that doeth evil." The ruler, therefore, is not ordained of God to do just as he pleases, "to commit enor-
mous injustice, to take away both the property and life of his subjects." [80]

[79] "Le vrai Prince n'est pas à craindre pour les bonnes oeuvres; ainsi celui qui se fait
craindre à ceux qui veulent obéir à Dieu & le servir selon sa Parole (that is good works)
ne doit pas être obéi & ne peut être considéré comme un vrai Prince, car il faut obéir à Dieu
qu'aux hommes," as Saint Peter enjoined.
[80] *Ibid.*, pp. 25–29.

When he acts in such a manner he becomes a minister of the Devil rather than God. As a result, the rights of sovereigns as established by Saint Paul in this text do not belong to him.

In his *Avis,* Bayle had cited the admonition of Paul in Titus 3.1— "Put them in remembrance that they be subject to the principalities and powers"—in his condemnation of the violent group of the refugees. Jurieu, however, had explained that this precept (phrased in Romans 13, that every soul should be subject to the higher powers) did not signify a blind obedience and an unlimited power. According to him, all these maxims of obedience to the powers that be are not to be construed in any more generous terms than those Scriptural passages which ordain the obedience of children to their parents and servants to their masters. It does not follow that paternal authority and the power of masters is unlimited to the point that a father can massacre his children or a master his servants. All obedience on the part of men, concludes Jurieu, is circumscribed "by nature, the rights of the conscience, and by conservation itself," [81] which explains why Saint Paul did not express its limits himself.

From this discussion Jurieu held that he had established three propositions in his *Avis à tous les alliés:* first, that there is a real distinction between a king and a tyrant; [82] second, that true kings can become tyrants; and, third, that according to Scripture no obedience is due to tyrants and ministers of the Devil. But with regard to the last principle, the admonition of Peter—"Servants be subject to your masters with all fear, not only to the good and courteous but also to the froward"—was cited as being in direct contradiction to it. Jurieu replied that "a vexatious sovereign" can act without becoming a tyrant, "without violating the divine and human laws, without arming himself against the life, honor, and conscience of his subjects." Obedience to a sovereign should be pushed as far as possible for the peace of the world and the honor of the church, but not so far as to include tyranny, which arises from the

---

[81] Jurieu, *Examen d'un libelle,* pp. 251–252.
[82] Jurieu puts all the emphasis on the tyrant "exercitio" with no mention of the tyrant "sine titulo." Cf. *Lettres pastorales,* Third Year, XVII, p. 392: "Il y a des souverains qui se sont faits par usurpation, par une injuste conquête, par un attentat sur la liberté de leurs pays. Nous ne parlons pas de ces rois-là."

abuse of power on the part of a true king. Resistance by men to such violence is permitted by the laws of nature and nations as well as by Scripture, concludes our pastor.

It should be noted that the opponents of the Cevennois relied, as had all other advocates of arbitrary power of the ruler, upon the practice of the early Christians. Jurieu again held, however, that books could be written on this experience to show that the principles of the conduct of men change according to the times and places; that God had his reasons for not permitting human passions to enter into the establishment of the Gospel; that the prudence of the early Christians kept them from exciting the fury of their persecutors by resistance; and that there was a great difference between establishing a religion by arms and defending it from oppression once it has been established. Therefore, the conduct of the first Christians had no application to the revolt of the Cevennois. As a result, our theologian concluded that no scruple of conscience should prevent the giving of aid to their cause, which is that of God, liberty, and peace.

Chapter Six

JURIEU AND TOLERANCE

STRANGE as it may seem, the corollary to the Huguenot theories of resistance was in most cases intolerance, although the right of defense for religion would seem to imply both civil and ecclesiastical tolerance. In fact, the continued existence of Protestantism, as the first successful heresy, should have served as a denial of the theological theory of persecution. Furthermore, the very germ of tolerance was inherent in one of the fundamental principles of the Reformation—justification by faith. From this tenet it can be concluded that although a man may be coerced to outward works, faith can be demanded by God alone. But as Tillich has said, the Reformation "never submitted the doctrine of justification by faith to the experience of justification by faith." [1]

In the sixteenth century Theodore Beza is the author not only of the *De jure magistratuum in subditos* (1574), in which the right of revolution is set forth, but also of the *De haereticis a civili magistratu puniendis libellus* (1554), which was written against the *De haereticis an sint persequendi . . .* (1554) of Castellion.[2] It contains one of the most elaborate statements in existence of the Protestant theory of persecution. In the seventeenth century the most violent advocate of rebellion, Pierre Jurieu, was the principal defender of orthodoxy against the Castellions of his time—Elie Saurin, Noel Aubert de Versé, Isaac Papin, De la Con-

---

[1] Reinhold Niebuhr, *The Nature and Destiny of Man*, Vol. II: *Human Destiny*, New York, 1943, p. 226. Cf. *ibid.*, p. 231. "The intolerance of the Reformation is the consequence of a violation of its own doctrinal position. Its doctrine of justification by faith presupposed the imperfection of the redeemed. Logically this includes the imperfection of redeemed knowledge and wisdom."

[2] See also the case of Lambert Daneau in the sixteenth century. His *Politices christianae libri septem* is one of the last of the political works of the Huguenots of the Monarchomach school. This same author was also engaged during his sojourn at Leyden, Holland, in violent attacks upon the heresies of Coornhert and other theologians. See the *Antwoort Lamberti Danaei wijlen Professeur in de hooghe Schoole tot Leyden* (1613); his *Ad libellum ab anonymo quodam libertino* (1582); and his *Calx viva* (1583).

seillère, Henri Basnage de Beauval, Gédéon Huet,[3] Jean Le Clerc, and Pierre Bayle.[4]

Although Saint Bartholomew's Night was the touchstone of all the theories of resistance by the French Calvinists in the sixteenth century, it aroused few theories of tolerance among its victims,[5] even though they were an insecure minority whose very existence within the state was threatened. However, the Revocation precipitated among the refugees, especially in Holland, a dispute over the nature and limits of religious tolerance which has scarcely received as a whole the attention it deserves in the history of that important principle. Perhaps this is due to the fact that the discussion was not political as in England under Locke, but rather philosophical in nature as with Bayle, who, however, may be said to have had a considerable influence upon the English philosopher. But several years before the Revocation the ground was prepared even in France for the later controversies, since the Huguenots began to show the effects of the influence of the great Dutch struggle over Arminianism, which raged in Holland in the first half of the seventeenth century.[6]

[3] Gédéon Huet, however, demonstrated his approval of the English Revolution in his *Autre lettre écrite de Suisse en Hollande* and at the same time he advocated toleration in his *Lettre écrite de Suisse en Hollande* as well as in his *Apologie pour les vrais tolérants* and *Apologie pour l'apologiste des tolérants*. The more secular thinker, John Locke, easily combined the theories of the *Two Treatises on Civil Government* with the *Letters on Toleration*, since he discards the idea of the glory of God as the end of all human society. See also the grudging approval of toleration in Johannes Althusius, in whose rather secular *Politica methodice digesta* the Monarchomachs are summed up.

[4] Bayle tended to adopt much the same attitude toward the French monarchy as his spiritual descendant, Voltaire. Such tolerance in politics can lead to indifference toward the question of political justice, however. Bayle's description of the close connection between revolt and persecution is to be found in his *Réponse aux questions d'un provincial,* Quatrième Partie, in *Oeuvres diverses,* 1737, III, pp. 1011–1012. Cf. Voltaire, *Essai sur les moeurs et L'Esprit des Nations,* Chap. CLXVIII, p. 153, in Vol. XX of the *Oeuvres complètes,* 1785: "Cette proposition: Tout prince doit employer sa puissance pour détruire l'hérésie et celle-ci: Toute nation a droit de se soulever contre un prince hérétique sont les conséquences d'un même principe."

[5] To men who had just experienced such terrible persecution, tolerance is not a speculative problem. In fact, practically the only book in France advocating a toleration on the basis of a minimum of truths for which men alone should be held responsible, was that of Innocent Gentillet, *Apologia pro christianis gallis religionis evangelicae seu reformatae,* 1588.

[6] For an excellent modern discussion see Douglas Nobbs, *Theocracy and Toleration.* For very brief but also very good accounts see the few pages in W. K. Jordan, *The Development of Religious Toleration in England,* II, 319–349, and E. M. Wilbur, *A History of Unitarianism,* pp. 535–559. In the case of the Huguenots compare the judgment of Locke

Thus, the gradual liberalization of French Calvinism in this period was not an indigenous development but an importation from the Netherlands. As early as 1634–1635 a bitter dispute raged between the Academies of Saumur and Sedan over the modified doctrines of grace and predestination, which the theologian of Saumur, Moise Amyraut, was teaching against his opponent Pierre Dumoulin, a professor at Sedan. But Amyraldism was a half measure between Calvinism and Arminianism. It is amazing, however, that the Huguenots should be torn in a desperate fight over orthodoxy at the very time that they were opposing the intolerance of their Catholic persecutors. It is also interesting to note that about the same time the Calvinists were feeling the effects of the struggle between Gomar and Arminius the Catholic camp was wracked by the controversy between Jansenius and Molina over the same problem—grace, with the result that Arminians corresponded to Jesuits and Gomarists to Jansenists. But as in the preceding century the majority of the Huguenots condemned the doctrine of universal tolerance. "They were contending for the liberty of their own consciences, not for those of other people. . . . So far as they were concerned it was merely an accident in the vast process of things that their efforts to free themselves helped to enlarge human freedom." [7]

According to Jurieu, who was a product of the orthodox academy of Sedan, the spirit of religious indifference was unknown among the Huguenots before the year 1669.[8] In that year, Jurieu reports, a pastor at the Protestant Academy of Saumur, Isaac d'Huisseau, had published a book under the title of *La Réunion du christianisme ou la manière de rejoindre tous les chrétiens sous une seule confession de foy.* The influence of Cartesian philosophy [9] is apparent throughout this little treatise.

(*A Letter concerning Toleration* in *Works,* VI, 20), that when religious groups "are not strengthened with the civil power, then they can bear most patiently and unmovedly the contagion of idolatry, superstition, and heresy in their neighborhood."

[7] J. W. Allen, *A History of Political Thought in the Sixteenth Century,* p. 209. As John Robinson wrote in the early years of the seventeenth century, "Protestants living in the countries of papists commonly plead for toleration of religions: so do papists that live where Protestants have sway: though few of either, especially of the clergy . . . would have the other tolerated, where the world goes on their side." Cited by Jordan, *The Development of Religious Toleration,* II, 246.

[8] Jurieu, *Lettre pastorale aux fidèles de Paris* (1690), p. 13.

[9] "On a proposé depuis quelque temps dans la Philosophie un moyen de bien raisonner et de faire de sures démarches vers la verité. On tient que pour cela il faut absolument

As Jurieu was quick to observe, this method of theological inquiry was the same as that followed by the Arminians and Socinians.[10] This made D'Huisseau's argument far more dangerous to the fundamental body of absolute truth than errors over grace, such as those which approached Pelagianism.[11]

As the title suggests, the general plan of D'Huisseau's book is to re-unite all Christians, whether Greek or Roman, Catholic or Protestant, since these divisions lead only to a state of irreligion and atheism and are the source of such disorder in both the state and the church. Such an appeal was somewhat ill-timed; it was introduced at a period when both the court and the clergy were seeking a reunion by the forcible return of the Protestants to the fold of the Catholic Church. Isaac d'Huisseau argues, like Castellion before him, that the origin of these partitions lies in the fact that what is essential and fundamental in the Christian religion has never been distinguished from the nonessential. His project of reunion follows from this distinction. It is based upon the selection of certain fundamentals to which all Christians can adhere and which are to be found in express and clear terms in Scripture and in abridged form in the Symbol of the Apostles and the crucifixion of Jesus Christ. Everything else, such as a difference over the mystery of the Trinity and

détacher de toutes opinions préconcues. Ne pouvons-nous pas imiter ce procède dans la Religion? Ne pouvons-nous laisser à part pour un temps toutes opinions que nous défendions auparavant avec tant de chaleur, pour les examiner après avec liberté et sans aucune passion, nous tenant toujours à notre principe commun qui est l'Ecriture Sainte." d'Huisseau, *Réunion du christianisme*, pp. 117–119.

[10] As Jurieu later said in his *Traité de la puissance de l'église* (1677), p. 215: "ce qui nous donne le plus aversion pour ces Églises Arminiennes c'est la criminelle tolérance qu'elles ont pour toutes sortes d'erreurs puisqu'elles nourrissent dans leur sein des Pelagiens & des Sociniens." Since at the end of the century the leader of the Arminians, Limborch, held unorthodox opinions with regard to the Trinity and since the Socinians themselves considered the great Arminian theologians, such as Episcopius, Courcelle, and Grotius as their own, it is not astonishing that the distinction between Arminianism and Socinianism came to be blurred in the public mind, which came to regard the Arminian sect as "l'égout de tous les Athées, Déistes et Sociniens de l'Europe." See *Lettre de M. Bayle à M. Lenfant*, dated July 6, 1685 in *Oeuvres*, 1737, IV, 623. Cf. L. A. Guichard, *Histoire du socinianisme*, Paris, 1723, Part I, Ch. XXXIV, p. 166. ". . . qu'être Arminien & être Socinien, c'est aujourd'hui presque la même chose."

[11] "Mais les temps m'a tout appris & m'a fait connoître que les oeuvres d'Episcopius, de Courcelle & des Sociniens qu'on fit venir de Pays étranger par curiosité firent de grands maux particulièrement du côté du Nord de la France." *Apologie du Sieur Jurieu* (1691). Grotius was also included along with the above. See *Lettres pastorales*, XI of the Third Year, p. 257. Cf. also *L'Esprit de M. Arnaud* II, 307–308, where Jurieu accuses Grotius of Arminianism, Socinianism, Papism and even atheism.

the Incarnation, whether in dogma or in cult, is to be tolerated so long as it does not destroy the articles of this Symbol.[12]

Jurieu's first important work, published in 1671, was an answer to this plan of D'Huisseau who had been condemned by the Synod at Saumur in 1670. It was entitled *Examen du livre de La Réunion du christianisme; ou, Traité de la tolérance en matière de religion et de la nature des points fondamentaux.*[13] He begins by saying that the tolerance which D'Huisseau allows is the same as that demanded by the Arians of the past and the Socinians of the present. It is the fashion of all Latitudinarians to declare that "it suffices in order to be saved in all religions to believe in crucified Jesus." Jurieu accuses D'Huisseau of deriving his ideas from Hobbes, since he claims that Christians must accommodate themselves to the religion of the state in which they find themselves, so long as it follows the fundamentals. In addition, Jurieu holds that in time even these few essentials will be questioned by some heretic, who if not successful in the persuasion of others, will at least demand toleration for himself. This process will continue *ad infinitum* until the Christian religion itself is destroyed. Such a price is too great to pay for peace within the state, which, Jurieu is forced to grant, such a policy of toleration would undoubtedly bring.

As we have seen, among D'Huisseau's criteria for a fundamental article was its location in Scripture in express terms and its reception by all Christians. To Jurieu, however, there are other means whereby a fundamental can be recognized. First, there is the agreement of sense and reason. Although faith, sense, and reason are different, they are never opposed because of their common origin in God. Second, there is the evidence of revelation. It is not necessary, however, that a fundamental truth be couched in express terms in Scripture. Jurieu asserts that he has no intention of making articles of faith out of every prophecy in the Bible. The third character of an essential truth is its weight and impor-

---

[12] *Réunion du christianisme*, pp. 160–161. There is an appeal also to the authority of the prince in this matter of reunion. "Surtout j'estime que ceux qui peuvent frapper les plus grands coups dans cette occasion sont les Princes et touts ceux qui ont la conduite des États et le maniement des affaires. Ils peuvent appuyer de leur autorité toutes les raisons qu'on emploiera dans cette haute entreprise et leur pouvoir sera très efficacieux pour faire valoir les exhortations des autres." *Ibid.*, p. 173.

[13] D'Huisseau answered Jurieu's attack with his *Réponse au livre intitulé Examen du livre de la réunion du christianisme*, Paris, 1671.

tance. A principle might be conformable to the judgment of reason and sense and be expressly revealed in the word of God, but still not be significant enough to be made an article necessary for salvation. There is a certain rule, furthermore, whereby this importance can be judged. Anything which establishes or destroys the ends of religion is important. Religion has three ends and the glory of God is the chief. Therefore, anything which effaces this glory demolishes a fundamental truth. The second end of religion is the salvation of man in another life. Consequently any belief or act which tends to ruin this salvation is an essential error. The third end of religion is the sanctification of man in this life, so anything which destroys that is also a fundamental heresy. By the application of these rules Jurieu thought it would be difficult to make a mistake as to the fundamentals of religious belief.[14]

The most significant part of the *Examen de La Réunion du christianisme* is Jurieu's outline of the extent of his own ideas on tolerance. He makes several distinctions, the first of which is between dogma and cult. He would allow a much wider measure of toleration to the former than to the latter, since most dogmas are only for the erudite to discuss. Second, it is necessary to distinguish societies from individuals. Toleration should be much greater when a people espouse a certain belief than when an individual does so,[15] since union and peace among Christian societies is highly important. Furthermore, it is not necessary to show as much indulgence for "infant communions" as for those already formed. On this basis Jurieu justified the action of the Synod of Dordrecht against the establishment of the Arminian doctrine in Holland.

---

[14] Jurieu repeats these distinctions in his *De pace inter protestantes* (1688), pp. 160 ff., where he tried to show the Lutherans that the toleration of Calvinistic "Particularisme" or the five articles of the Synod of Dordrecht would not destroy the fundamental truths. Jurieu, as we shall see, considered the essence of the Christian religion to be in the belief of a God in three persons, redemption by Christ, a last judgment, and so on, which elements were violated in one way or another by both Catholicism and Socinianism, according to our Rotterdam theologian.

[15] In his *Eclaircissement de quelques passages condamnés dans le livre de L'Examen de la réunion du christianisme* (1671), Jurieu defends the case of Servetus as follows (p. 124): "Jamais l'Église n'a fait profession de répandre le sang. Et les supplices d'un Servet dans ces derniers siècles, d'un Priscillien dans les premiers . . . ne peuvent être tirés à conséquence à cause de leur rareté & des circonstances qui s'y rencontrent. . . . Or il est certain tout au moins que si l'Église a eu quelque fois de la sévérité pour les hérétiques, ce n'est que pour les hérésiarques & les chefs de parti: elle ne s'est jamais armée contre le vulgaire engagé dans l'erreur, par malheur & par ignorance."

The tenuous and contradictory nature of these distinctions was later conclusively revealed by Jurieu's opponents. Huet pointed out [16] that the distinction between an individual heretic and a whole society of heretics is ridiculous, since the latter, being more numerous, can do much more damage and there is therefore greater reason for its extermination. Bayle showed [17] in addition that if the heresiarch is to be the more severely punished, then penalties against Luther, Calvin, Saint Paul, and Saint Peter should have been praiseworthy. If "nascent communions" are not to be tolerated, then, concludes Bayle, it follows that the first persecutions of the Christians and those of the Huguenots under Francis I and Henry II, centuries later, were legitimate.

Returning to the idea of the cult, Jurieu would extend much less liberty here, since it is the visible part of the church. But even though he desires uniformity of cult, he would not quarrel over ceremonies, vestments, and forms of prayer. In fact, in his later plan for the reunion of Lutherans and Calvinists he asserted that rites, church polity, and discipline were matters indifferent. In such things toleration should be far greater than that exercised between Presbyterians and Anglicans in England. With regard to church government he concludes that it is best to follow the custom of the country and the laws of the sovereign.

Jurieu makes one more distinction as to time. When a nation is beginning to come out of error, opinions and cults may be tolerated which would not be later on in a period of greater enlightenment. This idea of evolution is, as we shall see later, contrary to the usual notion of fundamentalism among Calvinists. In place of D'Huisseau's tolerance Jurieu would "tolerate everything which does not destroy the glory of God, when it cannot be suppressed without destroying the peace of the church." [18]

Jurieu tells us that these liberal ideas of moderation and tolerance in D'Huisseau made their reappearance shortly afterward under the name of Pajonism, after Claude Pajon,[19] who came under the influence of

---

[16] Gédéon Huet, *Lettre venue de Suisse*, p. 113.

[17] Pierre Bayle, *Commentaire philosophique sur ces paroles de Jesus Christ "Contrains les entrer"* in *Oeuvres*, 1737, II, 422.

[18] *Examen de La Réunion du christianisme*, pp. 143–156.

[19] Cf. Pajon's answer to Nicole's *Préjugez légitimes contre le Calvinisme—Examen du livre qui porte pour titre Préjugez légitimes contre le Calvinisme*, 1675.

the school of Saumur and the *Réunion du christianisme,* which directly inspired him. Pajon had simply endeavored to soften the rigor of the Calvinistic doctrine of predestination, which was enough to subject him to the charge by Jurieu of leanings toward Pelagianism and Arminianism. Through the insistence principally of our theologian these doctrines of Pajon were condemned in the synod of Paris in 1676. Several years later after Pajon's death in 1685 Jurieu attempted to state the orthodox theory of grace in his *Traité de la nature et de la grace; ou, Du concours général de la providence et du concours particulier de la grace efficace contre les nouvelles hypothèses de M. Pajon et de ses disciples* (1688).[20]

Not satisfied with keeping the Reformed Churches free from religious latitude, Jurieu accused the Catholic Church itself of promoting heresy. Citing the preface of Bishop Pierre Daniel Huet's *Demonstratio evangelica* as proof,[21] he charged that Catholic France was overrun with deists, Socinians, and free thinkers who were to be found even among the Jansenists noted for their austere morals.[22] If, as Jurieu asserted, there was difficulty in preserving orthodoxy in both the Catholic and the Calvinist churches in France, it became almost impossible after the Huguenot dispersion to Holland. In fact, an act of uniformity was designed for the refugee ministers by the synod of Rotterdam in 1686.

Here in the Netherlands great strides toward religious toleration had already been made. After 1630, due to the success of the Remonstrants in weakening orthodoxy, even the Socinians were granted a large measure of liberty.[23] In theory the problem was constantly discussed in all the journals of the time.[24] But ever since the controversy over Arminianism in the early part of the century, religion and politics were very closely connected. The struggle between the Remonstrant Arminians and the Counter-Remonstrant Calvinists was at the same time the reverse side of the fight between the Estates General and the Stadtholder, William

[20] Cf. also Jurieu's *La Juste Idée de la grâce immédiate,* 1689.
[21] See *L'Esprit de M. Arnaud,* I, 194.
[22] *La Politique du clergé,* pp. 90 ff.
[23] See Bayle, *Dictionnaire,* article "Socinus," notes k and l.
[24] Jean Le Clerc in his famous *Bibliothèque universelle* of May, 1687, p. 188, declared that tolerance was "une matière de grande importance dans le temps où nous vivons." In fact, "il parait tant de livres de controverse et il y a si longtemps qu'on n'entend presque parler d'autre chose," July, 1687, p. 257. See also Le Clerc's statement in his *Bibliothèque choisie,* Vol. XIX, Avertissement: "Il n'y a rien dont on parle plus aujourd'hui que de la tolérance et des principes de la société civile."

of Orange. In other words, the Republican party favored the new religious tendencies and, as we saw in the first part of this study, an alliance with France, while the Orangists were orthodox and partisans of England against France. In fact, many of the Dutch felt that any relaxation of orthodoxy would mean a return to the oppression of Rome which had been especially severe in the Netherlands.

These relationships are clearly revealed in a letter written by Jurieu in 1695. In it he recalls that Adrian van Paets, who brought him to Rotterdam, had as a representative of the Arminian and Republican party urged that Jurieu should exert his influence upon William of Orange to secure the reentrance of the Arminians into the orthodox Reformed Church. The Stadtholder, however, had warned, Jurieu recalls, that this would mean that the Arminian party would become the stronger and might even become the master of the government if any such plan were adopted.[25] As the leader of the intolerant party of the Huguenots, Jurieu sided with the growing powers of William against the Republicans and with his general position of strict orthodoxy, which, as we have seen, was characteristic of our pastor of Rotterdam long before he left France. In general, his opponents in the tolerant group of the refugees lined up with the Arminian and Republican party in Holland.[26]

Even before he went to Rotterdam, Jurieu had given an expression of his views on the situation in the United Provinces of Holland with respect to toleration. In the *Politique du clergé de France* he had declared that he did not regard such a wide freedom for every kind of sect as according to the principles of religion. "According to the rules of politics," however, the Dutch practice of a general toleration was responsible for the strength of that state, since all groups, although holding different religious beliefs, have the same interest in seeking to conserve the state.

[25] Jurieu concluded the letter: "Depuis ce temps là l'union de Mr. Paets et de moy ne fit que languir et cessa enfin entièrement à l'occasion de ses maximes sur l'indifférence des religions et sur la necessité d'un Stadthouder dans cet état." See R. N. L. Mirandolle, "À propos d'une lettre de Pierre Jurieu," *Bulletin de la Commission de l'Histoire des Églises Wallonnes*, VII (1899), 237–270. See also H. V. P(aets) *ad B(ayle) de nuperis angliae motibus epistola in qua de diversum a publica religione circa divina sentientium disseritur tolerantia*, 1685. For a review of this letter see Bayle's *Nouvelles de la république des lettres*, October, 1685, in *Oeuvres diverses*, 1737, I, 385.

[26] Mirandolle, "À propos d'une lettre de Jurieu," p. 244, claims, however, that the Dutch quarrels affected the Huguenots in the Walloon churches in Holland very little until after Jurieu's arrival.

It was the event of the sixteenth century civil wars in France, of course, which was responsible for the view among the Catholics that the toleration of several religions in a state is most dangerous. Jurieu denied this as a *non sequitur*. He admitted, however, that there is nothing more desirable than for all subjects to live in the true religion.[27] Toward this goal all legitimate means of persuasion, which are sanctioned by Christian morality, are permitted but these methods do not include violence and bad faith in order to secure a reunion of religions. But this principle is true only "in morality" and not "in politics," [28] where a diversity of religions is just as conducive to the conservation of the state as a single religion. To make the contrary assumption is to justify persecuting princes, as for example, the pagan emperors who attacked the Christians. In refutation, on the political side, of this maxim of the need for uniformity of religious belief, Jurieu relied upon the Roman maxim of *divide et impera*. By this means he maintained that when there are several parties in a state, if the ruler avoids the espousal of any one, then each becomes attached to the interests of the prince in order to have his protection. Therefore, conspiracies are unknown since each party is continuously watching the other.

In spite of this apparent approval of diversity in religious belief, Jurieu again makes one exception in favor of enforced uniformity on the part of the ruler. This occurs upon the first appearance of a schism.[29] In the initial stages a rift can be suppressed by an edict of the prince, but once the schism is accomplished and the new sect has become numerous, it

[27] Jurieu especially condemns the idea, however, that the prince is the absolute master of the religion of his people, for that is the position of Hobbes and Spinosa, who are "l'objet de l'exécration des théologiens," since they are the enemies of religion. If the prince is the master of religion, then Catholics must become Protestants in England and Christians, Mohammedans in Turkey. See his *Suite de la Politique du Clergé*, pp. 72-73. But Aubert de Versé claimed that Hobbes and Spinosa did not go farther than Jurieu in granting the magistrate authority over religion. See Aubert de Versé, *Traité de la liberté de la conscience ou de l'autorité des souverains sur la religion des peuples opposé aux maximes impies de Hobbes et de Spinosa adoptées par le sieur Jurieu*, Cologne, 1687, p. 55.

[28] *Politique du clergé*, pp. 226–230, 237–240.

[29] "Je ne saurois blamer les Suisses qui ne peuvent souffrir que de nouvelles Sectes prennent naissance chez eux; la Hollande est pleine de différentes religions, il eut été à souhaiter qu'ont eut étouffé ces désordres dans leur naissance." *Ibid.*, pp. 237–240. But this idea of tolerating sects, which had become numerous and suppressing those which were weak, is not quite the same as that held by the party of the *Politiques* in France in the sixteenth century. See page 236 of this study.

would be contrary to the spirit of Scripture to crush it either by violence or bad faith, especially when the king upon assuming the crown finds the sect already established and tolerated.[30] This reference to Louis XIV and the Edict of Nantes is transparent.

Second to this, Jurieu's most complete treatment of the issue of tolerance is in his answer to the Catholic Maimbourg. That author, balancing Saint Bartholomew with Servetus, had asserted that Calvin in his action toward Servetus had defended the right to condemn heretics to the stake.[31] Jurieu is, therefore, forced to admit that in the preceding century it was common among Protestants to advocate the death penalty for certain heretics. He adds, however, that "this was a vestige of papism which remained with them." [32] It was not possible, in other words, to abolish immediately a practice of five hundred years standing. Furthermore, the Protestants distinguished between heretics and heresies. This means that they condemned to death only those who denied the principal articles of the Symbol of the Apostles, while the Catholics in the Inquisition burned heretics for trivial errors. In addition, of all the heretics to be found in those countries where the Reformation is dominant, only five or six were condemned to the stake. Furthermore, never once had a Catholic been put to death for his religious beliefs alone. Therefore, among the Protestants this error is tolerable because it does not have dangerous consequences. It is intolerable among the Catholics, however, because it is the cause of horrible cruelties.[33] It must be admitted that

---

[30] Cf. *L'Esprit de M. Arnaud*, II, 335. But when rulers are obliged to tolerate different sects, their tolerance must not extend to those which destroy "les fondemens du Christianisme."

[31] Maimbourg, *Histoire du calvinisme*, p. 33.

[32] Jurieu, *Histoire du calvinisme et celle du papisme*, IV, Chap. IX, 130. Cf. his *Parallèle de la persécution d'Antiochus* (1687), pp. 114–115: "Que l'opinion des premiers Réformateurs touchant la violence qu'ils prétendent pouvoir & devoir être faite aux hérétiques étoit un faux préjugé qu'ils avoient pris de l'Église Romaine comme les Apôtres avoient recu de la Synagogue celuy où ils étoient: que l'Evangile ne devoit être prêché qu'aux Juifs." (Cf., however, Lord Acton's judgment in "The Protestant Theory of Persecution," in *The History of Freedom and Other Essays*, p. 166: "To say, therefore, that the Protestants learnt persecution from the Catholics is as false as to say that they used it by way of revenge.") This *Parallèle* was the Protestant answer to the almost official justification of the Protestant persecution probably written by the Archbishop of Paris, Monseigneur Francois de Harlai de Champvallon, as *Conformité de la conduite de l'église de France pour ramener les protestants avec celle de l'église d'Afrique pour ramener les donatistes à l'église catholique*, Paris, 1685.

[33] In both his *Parallèle de la persécution d'Antiochus* and his *Préjugez légitimes contre le*

this whole line of argument is exceedingly weak and not always even truthful.

It is against the spirit of Scripture, which condemns the shedding of blood, to pronounce the death penalty upon heretics, continues Jurieu. The conduct of Christ and the Apostles disproves such stringent measures for dealing with those who refuse to submit to the laws of the Evangile. Besides, why burn heretics and not idolators or infidels? If it is necessary to burn all those who poison souls, then libertines and profane persons of all kinds should be burned. Reason and common sense work against this conclusion, according to our theologian. Furthermore, there is a great difference between crimes committed from ignorance and those which result from a spirit of rebellion. Jurieu concludes: "I do not claim that this good faith, in which heretics are, excuses them absolutely before God, as some say. But at least it diminishes their sin before men. It is not necessary to be persuaded that it is right to burn on earth all those whom divine justice can burn in hell." [34]

In the following chapter Jurieu goes on to show that the doctrine of the ancient church of the first three centuries also condemned the punishment of heretics by death. If it had taught that heretics who blaspheme against the mysteries of religion could be executed, then it would have had no reason to complain over the same treatment at the hands of the pagans.[35] Jurieu was later to regret bitterly this type of argument against the death penalty for heretics, for it was turned against his own intolerance by those who would not control the actions of heretics at all, so long as they did not disturb civil society.[36]

---

papisme Jurieu contrasts the cruelties of Catholicism with the exemplary conduct of the Calvinists.

[34] *Histoire du calvinisme* IV, Chap. VIII, 144–145. Jean Delvolvé in his *Religion critique et philosophie positive chez Pierre Bayle*, p. 62, interprets the statement that sin is diminished rather than removed by ignorance as following from the fact that the Calvinists suffer Catholic intolerance in France but wish to mete out intolerance themselves in England and Holland.

[35] "On ne doit pas répondre que ce que les chrétiens disoient contre les mystères du paganisme n'étoient pas des blasphèmes; mais de justes reproches. Cette réponse, dis-je, ne vaut rien, car il est certain qu'à l'égard des payens ces justes reproches étoient des blasphèmes et que les payens dans leurs principes les devoient regarder comme tels. De plus si cette réponse étoit bonne pour les chrétiens des premiers siècles elle seroit aussi fort bonne pour les hérétiques d'aujourd'hui qui diroient dans leur principes nous ne blasphemons point contre vos verités, mais nous faisons de justes reproches à vos erreurs." *Histoire du calvinisme*, IV, 150.

[36] See Gédéon Huet, *Apologie pour les vrais tolérants*, pp. 33–73, 77–141: "A-t-on jamais

But if heretics are not to be burned, what action if any should be taken against them? At this point Jurieu makes three distinctions. First, heretics and heresies are to be differentiated. More drastic measures should be taken against serious heresies which destroy souls, such as Arianism and Socinianism, than against those which only disfigure the beauty of the church, such as Pelagianism. Jurieu now enters into a digression concerning a current opinion that errors of belief of whatever nature do not lead to damnation. That is to say, all heresies are tolerable whenever they are accompanied by good faith. Only a denial of such essentials as a belief in God, His Providence, and the Evangile will bring damnation, according to this view. But, protests Jurieu, such a conception of universal tolerance leads only to an attitude of indifference toward religion: "If good faith prevents errors from being grievous, why does that not excuse also an atheist, a Jew, an idolater, an infidel, who believes in good faith that our Jesus is an impostor and our God a myth?"[37] Many were holding that only by such a policy of universal toleration would it be possible to conserve the peace of the church.[38] To Jurieu such an opinion is the opposite extreme from the principle that heretics should be burned. He concludes that both extremes are bad and therefore, are to be avoided.

Granting that all heresies are to be condemned, since they are to be distinguished as to degrees of seriousness, still another important problem remains. Should the magistrate intervene in the matter or should he leave the issue to the church alone, whose weapons are spiritual only? The reply of Jurieu to the second alternative is in the negative. In his mind "the Christian magistrate is obliged to work for the peace of the church as well as for that of the state. That is why he must interpose his authority to arrest the consequences of division. He is obliged to preserve the truth and to defend it and thus he must not abandon it to the dis-

---

mieux établi le dogme de la Tolérance? . . . puisque selon M. J. ces reproches d'être des Hérétiques & des blasphémateurs mettent toutes les religions du monde en droit de se les faire réciproquement; n'est-il pas de la dernière évidence ou qu'il faut tous s'égorger ou qu'il faut tous se tolérer de quelque religion que l'on puisse être?" "Car qui ne voit que tout cela une fois posé comme M. J. expose . . . voilà les infidèles & les hérétiques autant en droit de s'opposer à l'introduction de la véritable religion & de l'orthodoxie; que les Chrétiens & les orthodoxes à l'introduction du Paganisme & de l'Hérésie?"

[37] *Histoire du calvinisme*, IV, Chap. XI, 182–183.

[38] Jurieu makes reference to the *Traité de la raison humaine traduit de l'Anglois* for many of the arguments supporting toleration.

quietude and arrogance of heretics." But in the exercise of his authority there is a difference between condemning a heretic to death and preventing him from spreading his heretical doctrines. According to the laws of the Evangile the prince cannot do the former. But "he must impose silence upon a heretic and prevent his dogmatizing by penalties. And if the heretic violates this prohibition, he can be very legitimately punished, no longer as a heretic but as a violator of the commands and the laws of the sovereign." [39] Jurieu admits that the magistrate has no power over the spirit and heart. Furthermore, he has no right to punish a heretic because of his heresy, since the empire over conscience belongs to God alone. "But he does have power over the tongue [40] as over hands, so that he has the right to punish a heretic who dogmatizes against the prohibition just as he has the right to chastise a man who steals or kills." [41] For example, if a man believes and even publishes abroad that all things should be held in common, the magistrate cannot punish him unless he tries to put his theory into practice. To Jurieu it is the same in this matter of heresy. So long as a man who holds erroneous opinions keeps them to himself and does not seek to establish them, the magistrate has no right to punish him. [42]

A second distinction Jurieu makes once again is that the same severity should not be exercised against a heresiarch and those whom he has corrupted. The former can be exiled from a country in order to abolish heresy but not a whole people. The banishment of one or a few may prevent the seduction of the people, but once they have all been debased there is nothing left to be done. But as to the heresiarch, there are cases

---

[39] *Histoire du calvinisme*, IV, Chap. XI, 184–185. Cf. Chapter VIII, p. 140: "Malgré les barbaries du papisme on n'a pas laissé d'y retenir cette maxime l'église ne met pas sa main au sang. C'est cette maxime qui fait le fondement de l'impertinente comédie des inquisiteurs, qui après avoir condamné les hérétiques au feu, les donnent à brûler au bras séculier: comme si celui qui condamne et donne la sentence de mort n'étoit pas celui qui tue, et non pas le bourreau qui n'est que l'exécuteur. C'est là l'horreur que l'église romaine fait aux rois et à ses magistrats, elle en fait ses bourreaux."

[40] This led Aubert de Versé in his *Traité de la liberté de conscience* to accuse Jurieu once again of adopting the maxims of Hobbes and Spinoza, maintaining that even the latter did not extend the authority of the magistrate as far as words.

[41] *Histoire du calvinisme*, IV, Chap. XI, 185.

[42] "Il est donc clair qu'un hérétique qui s'en tiendra à dire sans mystère ses opinions ne peut être puni comme coupable; mais s'il travaille à persuader les autres, parceque cela gâte la société religieuse dont le magistrat est conservateur, le magistrat sans doute aura le droit de la châtier. Et même il pourra être puni d'avoir communiqué simplement sa pensée sans travailler à la persuader si cela lui a été défendu." *Ibid.*, p. 187.

like that of Servetus in which the death penalty is pronounced by the magistrate against an extremely dangerous person.[43] But Jurieu believes that the circumstances which call for such severity are very rare.

The third distinction with regard to the action necessary toward heretics is whether promises have been made to them. If treaties have been entered into, they must be maintained, since good faith is inviolable. This allusion to the Huguenots needs no further comment, since we have already noted this type of argument.

It is evident from even this cursory survey of Jurieu's tenuous distinctions that his position with reference to tolerance was especially vulnerable, and his enemies lost no time in pointing out the contradictions in his theory. One of the most devastating criticisms was by Bayle in his *Réponse d'un nouveau converti à une lettre d'un réfugié*. The philosopher of Rotterdam contended that it was in vain for Jurieu to denounce the death penalty for heresy, since those who favor such an extreme measure could find ample justification in those very principles outlined in Jurieu's reply to Maimbourg. In fact, he approved the burning of Servetus on one page but on another in the same book he declared that such action was a vestige from Catholicism—a pardonable and tolerable error, to be sure, but nevertheless an error. What contradictions!, exclaims Bayle. Furthermore, since Jurieu grants to the sovereign magistrates the same authority over the tongues as over the hands of their subjects, then it follows that there are certain crimes of speech, such as calling upon subjects to revolt against the king, which are punishable by death. Therefore, the discourses of Servetus can bring the same penalty.[44] If then the magistrates have jurisdiction over heresies whenever they find them more dangerous than the crime of assassination, they can mete out a punishment more severe than for a civil crime. In other words, if the dogmatizing of a heretic can be punished at all, the penalty

---

[43] "Une sévérité contre un particulier peut servir à quelque chose et bien qu'à la rigueur du droit il y eut quelque injustice à le punir, cependant le salut du peuple étant la souveraine loi, on peut arrêter le mal en sa source par quelque remède violent." *Ibid.*, p. 189. Note the use of the maxim, *salus populi suprema lex esto* in connection with the problem of tolerance as well as the question of popular sovereignty.

[44] "En un mot ou les Hérésies proférées de vive voix selon l'instinct de la conscience & par le seule envie d'avancer ce qu'on croit être la vérité & de désabuser ceux qu'on croit dans des mortelles erreurs, sont soumises au Tribunal des Juges criminels, tout de même que les discours d'un Séditieux . . . ou elles n'y sont pas soumises." *Réponse d'un nouveau converti*, in *Oeuvres*, 1727, II, 567.

can be extended even to death, in proportion to the gravity of the blasphemous discourses. From Jurieu's maxims it follows, according to Bayle, that the early Christians and the Huguenots had no reason to complain over their treatment. At least in the latter case they could not grumble until after the promulgation of the Edict of Nantes, which granted them toleration, "because it is certain that they . . . preached their opinions against the edicts of their sovereign and thus they were punishable, if not as heretics, at least as violators of his commands." [45]

In addition to Bayle's severe critique there was an even more detailed attack upon Jurieu's position on tolerance in the fourth volume of his reply to Maimbourg. The attack was launched by Noel Aubert de Versé [46] in *Le Protestant pacifique; ou, Traité de la paix de l'Eglise dans lequel on fait voir par les principes des réformez que la foy de l'Eglise catholique ne choque point les fondemens du salut: et qu'ils doivent tolérer dans leur communion tous les chrétiens du monde les sociniens & les quakres mêmes, dont on explique la religion contre Monsieur Jurieu,* which was published in 1684. Aubert de Versé takes special exception to Jurieu's attempt to condemn the death sentence for heresy at the same time that he grants the magistrate the right to prevent a heretic from dogmatizing on the pain of death for a violation of this prohibition. He very easily demonstrates that it is impossible in this way to distinguish heresy from civil disobedience, since the proscription against dogmatizing is made by the magistrate on the subject of heresy and the cause of the death penalty for disobedience to this order is clearly the heretical opinions of the victim.[47]

The comparison which Jurieu made between a person who believed and attempted to persuade others that all things should be held in com-

---

[45] *Ibid.*

[46] This author later ridiculed Jurieu's prophecies in *Le Nouveau Visionnaire de Rotterdam,* 1686, and *La Véritable Clef de l'Apocalypse . . . en particulier l'illusion des prédictions de J(urieu) F(aux) P(rophete) D(e) R(otterdam),* 1690. See his *Manifeste de Maitre Noel Aubert de Versé . . . contre l'auteur anonyme* (that is, Jurieu), 1687, and his *Tombeau du Socinianisme,* 1687, also directed against Jurieu.

[47] "Et voilà le procède de tous les Papes, de tous le Rois & de tous les Princes qui ont fait autrefois & font encore brûler les Calvinistes, les Luthériens, les Anabaptistes & tant d'autres, hautement justifié. . . . Voilà toute la persécution présente des Protestants de France que M. J. exagère si tragiquement hautement justifiée." *Le Protestant pacifique,* pp. 1–20. This reminds one of the opinion of Grotius that the burning of Servetus was a very bad example for the French Protestants.

mon and a heretic who sought to corrupt others with his dogmatizing was regarded by Aubert de Versé as completely false. The former action would destroy civil society and should, therefore, be punished, while the latter is merely the expression of speculative opinions, which would by no means ruin the community. Although he admits that the magistrate has the right to punish a man who sets forth principles which destroy both morality and society, yet he refused to class heresy alone along with such a crime as murder. But Beza in his answer to Castellion in the preceding century had argued that if heresy cannot be punished, then neither can homicide.

It can be readily seen that the clash between Jurieu and Aubert de Versé comes on this old question of whether the magistrate has a duty to conserve the church or not. If with Jurieu the answer is in the affirmative, then persecution is the inevitable result, especially in a period when religious uniformity in fact is gone forever. But the late seventeenth century was with Aubert de Versé, who believed that "the magistrate has no right of magistracy in the character of Christian and member of the church" but only "in relation to civil society." [48] With such a principle there is only one result—the toleration in the state of all religions which do not destroy civil society. This is certainly the position of Locke in his famous *Four Letters on Toleration*.

In the Second *Lettre pastorale* of the First Year, Jurieu replies to a letter of Bossuet, dated April 3, 1686, in which the bishop had defended the persecution of heretics against a member of his Diocese who had reproached him with the persecution in France as the mark of a false church. The Roman Church is the very spirit of persecution according to both its principles and its practice, argues Jurieu. He recalls the burning of Jean Hus and Jerome of Prague and the action taken against the Albigensians, Waldensians, and Bohemians, to say nothing of the Inquisition as to practice. For theoretical justification there are those writers such as Saint Augustine who interpreted a passage from Luke (14.23) [49] to mean persecution against the Donatists. But Bossuet had contended that the Catholic Church did not make use of force itself. It called upon the secular authorities to fulfill that function. Therefore, the

---

[48] *Ibid.,* pp. 19–20.
[49] "And the Lord said unto the servant, go out into the highways and hedges and compel them to come in, that My house may be filled."

church is innocent of persecution. Furthermore, how can Jurieu dare to assert that Bossuet's doctrine is bloody and cruel, when the republic of Geneva condemned Servetus to the stake for having denied the divinity of Christ!

Jurieu again showed great irritation at the mention of Servetus, since the Catholics at this time always justified their treatment of the Calvinists upon the basis of this incident.[50] His explanation of the affair contains the familiar but untenable distinction between heresy and blasphemy,[51] which had been employed by the early Reformers against the Anabaptists. He continues that Protestant doctors never held that those who confess God and Christ according to the three symbols should be burned. In fact, Catholics have never been put to death because of their religion. Even if the early Protestant writers did go too far in advocating severe penalties for heretics, it must be remembered that such authors are not binding authorities, since Christ alone is the only savant.

But Bossuet had declared that heretics are not exceptions to the number of those malefactors against whom Saint Paul said God had armed princes.[52] Jurieu answers that there is a difference between "evil thinkers" and "evildoers." Just because the prince has the right to punish the latter, whose actions might lead to the destruction of the public, it does not follow that he has also the right to chastise the former, whose crime is in their conscience, which belongs to God alone. Besides, if the church has the right to seek the secular arm for the punishment of here-

[50] Bayle's remark on this controversy over Servetus in the *Dictionnaire*, article "Bèze," is worth noting: "Dès que les Protestants se veulent plaindre des persécutions qu'ils souffrent on leur allégue le droit que Calvin & Bèze out reconnu dans les Magistrats. Jusqu'ici, on n'a vu personne qui n'ait échoué pitoiablement à cette objection ad *hominem*." Bayle's praise of Protestant remorse over the fate of Servetus was enough in itself to arouse the ire of Jurieu. As Niebuhr says, "the greatest teachers of the Reformation doctrine of the sinfulness of all men used it on occasion as the instrument of an arrogant will to power against theological opponents." *The Nature and Destiny of Man*, Vol. I: *Human Nature*, p. 202.

[51] "Cet homme étoit non seulement ennemi de toute divinité de Jesus Christ mais il étoit ennemi de toute divinité; il étoit impie, il étoit blasphémateur. Et quoi qu'il fit profession de croire un Dieu la manière atroce dont il parloit des mystères, faisoit bien connaitre qu'il avoit renoncé à toute Religion comme à toute pudeur. Il doit être permis de se défaire de telles gens." Gédéon Huet in his *Apologie pour les vrais tolérants*, pp. 35–73, delights in calling attention to the fact that in the *Histoire du calvinisme*, IV, Chap. VII, 128–129, Jurieu had condemned Cranmer for his part in condemning Jean of Kent to death, while he now approved a similar punishment for Servetus.

[52] *Romans* 13.4.

tics, then why did Saint Paul say simply, "A man that is an heretic, after the first and second admonition, reject." [53] Why did the Apostle not command instead that he be delivered to the secular authorities for execution?

Bossuet, of course, was trying to prove that the action taken in France against the Calvinists was purely an exercise of the legitimate authority of the ruler over the punishment of criminals. Jurieu disputes this position as follows: first, rulers do have as an objective in the use of the sword against evildoers the protection of society against criminals. It was on this basis that Charles IX ordered the massacre of Saint Bartholomew, but today the end in view is not the punishment of heretics but their conversion. Thus, even if it be true that heretics should not be excepted from those evildoers against whom God arms princes, only their punishment can be attempted, not their conversion. Secondly, "the use of the sword which God has placed in the hand of princes has the exercise of justice and the maintenance of good faith as its basis." But Jurieu argues that the treatment of Calvinists is injustice and bad faith by the contravention of their edicts. Thirdly, "the use of the sword in conserving and avenging the rights of God preserves also the rights of man; it has for its end the glory of God and the salvation of souls." But, according to Jurieu, the present persecution is directed solely toward the glory of the king. Furthermore, if each prince has the right to exterminate by fire and the sword all those who are not of his religion, then it must follow that the Turks have the right to massacre Christians wherever the Moslems are the masters.

Jurieu once again did not lack for critics of the reasoning employed in his refutation of Bossuet. Bayle argued in the *Réponse d'un nouveau converti* that the Catholic and the orthodox Protestant positions on the question of toleration were practically the same. If the death sentence for heresy was rarer among the Protestants, it was only "by accident." Both sides agree that a heretic who denies the fundamental truths of the faith should be punishable by death. The reason the Catholics have condemned more heretics to death is that they have a clearer means of distinguishing fundamentals. With them all doctrines opposed to the decisions of oecumenical councils are fundamental errors, while the Protes-

[53] Titus 3.10.

tants hold as essential only such dogmas as the Trinity, the Incarnation, and so on.

An even more telling criticism came from the anonymous *Lettre de quelques nouveaux convertis de France à M. Jurieu sur ses Lettres pastorales* (1687). This tract was actually from the pen of Richard Simon, whose *Histoire critique du Vieux Testament,* published in 1678, was regarded as a scandalous treatment of Scripture by both orthodox Calvinists and Catholics. In it, the author asks, is there really any difference between Servetus, who is called impious and blasphemous by Jurieu, and "the Evangelical Protestants" who confess God and Jesus Christ according to the three Symbols? [54] Obviously there is none, when Jurieu could write in the Second *Lettre pastorale* that the Protestants have only one doctor, who is Jesus Christ, speaking through his prophets and Apostles. But this is the very same response which Servetus made to the Senate of Geneva. Since he claimed that his belief was based on the word of God, to accuse him of impiety is to prefer the traditions of men to the divine pronouncements. This criticism raised the whole question of the unmistakable clarity and infallibility of Scripture, which lies at the very foundation of Calvinism itself in its Bibliolatry.[55] Does it exist when Socinians as well as orthodox Calvinists employ it to achieve opposite results? The conclusion some drew was that it was necessary to be either a Catholic or a Socinian, the middle position of orthodox Calvinism being looked upon as completely untenable. It is interesting to note here that both Jurieu and Bossuet draw quite close together on the question of persecution. In fact, both authors severely condemn the Socinians who reject that principle.[56]

[54] See Guichard, *Histoire du socinianisme*, pp. 177 ff.: "S'il (d'Huisseau) s'appuye sur son bon sens & sur son habileté dans l'étude des livres sacrez; Servet, Luther, Calvin, Socin & les autres novateurs des derniers siècles se sont prévalus de cette même habileté & cependant ils sont différens les un des autres dans leurs explications."

[55] As Niebuhr puts it, "the certain conviction of the faithful that the Bible gave them the final truth, transcending all finite perspectives and all sinful corruptions, thus contributed to individual spiritual arrogance, no less intolerable than the collective arrogance of the older church. This pride expressed itself despite the fact that contrary interpretations of Scripture against which the arrogance was directed contradicted the pretension of an absolutely valid interpretation." *The Nature and Destiny of Man,* Vol. II: *Human Destiny,* p. 229.

[56] Jurieu regarded tolerance as "le dogme Socinien, le plus dangereux de tous ceux de la Secte Socinienne puisqu'il va ruiner le Christianisme et à établir l'indifférence des religions." See his *Des Droits des deux souverains en Matière de religion* (1687), p. 14.

Very closely connected with the general problem of tolerance was the question of the true nature of the church.[57] According to Jurieu, the controversy between Protestants and Catholics over the character of the church eclipsed all others. This struggle could be reduced to two questions—whether the church possesses infallibility and whether the church universal lies in different communions or only in one. In a very important work, *Le Vray Système de l'église* (1686), written against Nicole's *Les Prétendus réformés convaincus de schisme,* Jurieu considered these issues [58] at great length.

It has been argued by the Catholics, including the Jansenists, that only by recognizing the authority of the church, its unity, and its infallibility, could there be found any firm basis for the faith. "The path of (free) examination" of the Protestants could lead but to progressive dissolution.[59] But Jurieu attempts to show that in spite of the divisions of the Protestants there is unity in the church universal and á traditional continuity of faith.[60] To our minister of Rotterdam the problem of heal-

---

On his part Bossuet declared: "Il (Jurieu) permet l'exercice de la puissance du glaive dans les matières de la Religion et de la conscience; chose aussi qui ne peut être revoquée en doute sans enerver et comme estropier la puissance publique, de sorte qu'il n'y a point d'illusion plus dangereuse que de donner la souffrance pour un caractère de vray Eglise et je ne connais parmi les chrétiens que les Sociniens et les Anabaptistes qui s'opposent à cette doctrine." See his *Histoire des variations* II, 107–108.

[57] For a discussion of the thought of writers other than Jurieu in this period see John T. McNeill, "The Church in Post-Reformation Reformed Theology," *The Journal of Religion,* April, 1944.

[58] Jurieu also discussed the nature of the church in identical fashion in the first part of his *Préjugez légitimes contre le papisme* and in his *Lettres pastorales,* especially of the Second Year. Cf. also his *Traité de l'unité de l'église et des points fondamentaux contre M. Nicole,* who in his *De l'unité de l'église; ou, Réfutation du nouveau système de M. Jurieu* attempted to show that there is only one unique visible communion, the Catholic Church, which to the exclusion of all others bears the character of the true church in authority, infallibility, visibility, and perpetuity.

[59] This was the general argument of Nicole's *Préjugez légitimes contre le calvinisme,* which attacked the Protestants on doctrinal grounds by asking what authority was the basis of their church and faith. Cf. also the dispute of Bossuet with Claude in Bossuet, *Conférence avec M. Claude touchant l'infaillibilité de l'Église,* 1682, and Claude, *Réponse au livre de Monsieur l'Evêque de Meaux,* 1683.

[60] Jurieu's book is intended not only as a reply to Nicole but also to Bossuet, Maimbourg, and Arnauld. It was intended especially as an answer to Book VII of the latter's *Le Renversement de la Morale de J. C. par la doctrine des calvinistes touchant la justification,* 1682. See also Jurieu's *Apologie pour la morale des réformés,* 1675, and his *Justification de la morale des réformés contre les accusations de Mr. Arnaud,* 1685. He also attempts to refute the charge of Bossuet and Maimbourg that the Protestants attribute infallibility to their ecclesiastical assemblies.

ing the divisions of Christendom was very acute. In fact, "the ideal of Christian unity was a pronounced characteristic of Protestantism" [61] ever since the ecumenical efforts of Luther, Melanchthon, Bucer, Calvin, and Beza. It was always the contention of the Protestants that it was the Pope and not they who had destroyed the *Corpus christianum* or *Respublica christiana*. The methods proposed by irenic advocates in the seventeenth century to restore "the common corps of Christendom" excluded, of course, a unity through one pastor but included a revival of the principle of conciliarism, confessional agreement, comprehension, and adherence to a universal law. Rulers were interested in reunion of the churches for political reasons but in the last analysis it was the great Leviathan in addition to Catholic and Protestant scholasticism which prevented uniformity.[62]

According to Jurieu's idea of the church, it is composed like a man of body and soul. The soul of the church is faith and charity, while the body is the profession of the faith and the external practice of charity, that is, the Sacraments. The true faith is invisible, while the profession is visible. Therefore, with regard to the question of visibility and invisibility, they are but two attributes of the same church and not of two churches. The body of the church is composed of all the Christian societies in the world. In this body there are healthy parts, which retain in their entirety all the truths taught in the word of God. There are other portions which are more or less sick. Although they have retained the fundamental truths, corruptions have arisen which have destroyed the full beauty of the vigorous faith.[63] But some parts have become so de-

[61] J. T. McNeill, *Unitive Protestantism*, p. 15. For other accounts of the various plans of reunion see M. T. Tabaraud, *De la réunion des communions chrétiennes*, Paris, 1808; C. W. Hering, *Geschichte der kirchliches Unionsversuche seit der Reformation bis auf unsere Zeit*, Leipzig, 1836–1838; G. J. Slosser, *Christian Unity, Its History and Challenge*, New York, 1929; J. Minton Batten, "Political Factors in Movements toward Christian Unity in Seventeenth Century Europe," *Church History*, September, 1943; Gunnar Westin, *Negotiations about Church Unity, 1628–1634*, Uppsala, 1932 and J. Minton Batten, *John Dury*, Chicago, 1944.

[62] See Franklin Le Van Baumer, "The Church of England and the Common Corps of Christendom," *The Journal of Modern History*, March, 1944, p. 21.

[63] Niebuhr thinks that the "Reformation gave little indication of any consciousness that error might be mixed with the truth which it possessed; though the truth which it possessed contained the recognition of this very paradox." *The Nature and Destiny of Man*, Vol. II: *Human Destiny*, p. 226.

graded that they have abandoned even the essential truths of Christianity. Since they have retained only the most general beliefs, they are dead, although still a part of the body of Christianity as a withered arm is still a part of the body of a living man. Socinianism is a religion of this last category, while Catholicism is one in which numerous conceptions have been added to the pristine purity of the faith but at least the fundamentals have not been abandoned. Thus, according to Jurieu, the universal church includes all sects which keep the essentials of Christianity, even though these various sects go so far as to excommunicate one another.[64]

If the church is in all Christian communions which in all centuries have retained the three symbols, then the church has endured without interruption, since the establishment of Christianity. But not only was the church perpetual; it was also perpetually visible, since there have always been visible Christian societies which have preserved the fundamentals. The Catholics had argued that since the church of Luther and Calvin was not visible until the Reformation, it cannot be the true church. But Jurieu insists that the qualities of visibility and of perpetuity apply only to the universal church, which exists in all communions retaining the essentials and never to a particular church, since individual churches either come no longer to exist or are yet to appear.[65] If the church is composed of separate societies, then the church councils,[66] except perhaps the very first, represent but a part of the visible church,

[64] "L'Église est demeuré visible durant tous les siècles dans les communions qui malgré leur séparation & les anathèmes qu'elles ont mutuellement prononcé les unes contre les autres ont toujours conservé les vérités principales & qui font l'essence du Christianisme." Jurieu, *Le Vray Système de l'église,* p. 226. Perpetual visibility of the church, then, consists in the perpetual subsistence of Christian communions and not of just one entity, as the Catholics were claiming.

[65] "Avant notre Réformation l'Église n'étoient pas visible dans notre société qui n'étoit pas encore mais elle étoit visible dans l'Église Grèque, Armenienne, Cophte, Abyssine, Ethiopienne, parce que toutes ces Eglises ont conservé le Christianisme entier dans les trois Symboles. Quand nous sommes venus au monde, l'Église est devenue visible dans notre Société comme elle étoit auparavant dans les autres." *Lettres pastorales,* XXIII, August 1, 1687, pp. 111–114. The visibility and perpetual existence of the particular churches consists only in the perpetuity of this adherence to the essentials of the faith.

[66] "Conciliarism had a drawback as a solution to the problem of Christian unity. In the absence of one clearly recognized head of Christendom, the chances of convening a truly general council were negligible." Baumer, *Church of England and Common Corps of Christendom,* p. 11.

the Roman Catholic. Therefore, they are not infallible even in the Gallican sense.[67] Furthermore, since the church is composed of all Christian societies, including those in error, it cannot be infallible, since many of its parts have erred. Moreover, if the church is composed even of societies which excommunicate each other, it can have no visible head as the Pope but only a visible center of unity in Jesus Christ. The essential truths, to which all Christians agree, are the bonds of unity with Christ. Thus, Christian societies which retain the fundamental truths can be in schism with regard to each other but never with regard to the universal church, which includes them all. Therefore, there can be general schism, which is a separation from Christ and the universal church, and a particular schism, which is between two churches that are both parts of Christianity and retain the essential truths. A church can be guilty of the former only when it has renounced the fundamental truths. Thus, to Jurieu, the Protestants were not outside the church and not, therefore, schismatics.

But the Catholics maintained that the infinite variations of the Protestants demonstrated their spirit of schism. In his *Histoire du calvinisme et celle du papisme* Jurieu had conceded that peace in the church was to be desired but that it was a feature of heaven and not of this earth. In fact, there must be divisions in the church, since God has willed that His church be composed on earth of the elect and the damned. The human passions of the latter serve to defend the church against the mortal desires of the enemies of God. The damned are, therefore, the cause of schisms and heresies in the church. These shadows of diversity, however, serve the purpose of making more brilliant the role of the elect in the realm of the church.[68]

---

[67] ". . . il n'y a que deux idées de l'unité qui soyent compatibles avec la raison: la nôtre qui pose Jesus Christ pour centre unique & qui définit le schisme & les Schismatiques par rapport à ce centre. Et celle de la cour de Rome & ses adhérents qui pose le Pape pour centre de l'unité. Le sentiment de l'Église Gallicane tient un milieu incompatible." Jurieu, *Traité de l'unité de l'Église*, 1688, p. 334. One of the reasons for this reaction toward Gallicanism, which was simply an attempt to restore the old Gelasian dualism in the relationship between the spiritual and temporal authorities, was that Jurieu tended more toward Erastianism than toward the collateralism of the Gelasian theory.

[68] "Les armes, les ménagements de la politique du monde, la prudence humaine, les alliances avec les ennemis de Dieu ne sont point du tout de l'esprit du christianisme. Il est pourtant vrai que Dieu a souvent tiré des secours de ces sortes de choses pour empêcher la ruine de ses églises. Quand même l'Église ne seroit appellée qu'à souffrir et jamais à se

It is obvious that this whole theory of the church is in direct opposition to the Catholic view of a writer like the Jansenist Nicole, who conceived the church as existing in one Christian society alone—the Roman Catholic—apart from all the others. Jurieu fully realized that he was treating the most important aspect of the question here. For if the Catholic Church is the sum of all Christian societies, which retain the fundamental truths, then the Roman Church and all its dogmas as to infallibility, whether in Pope or Council, perpetuity, visibility, schism, and unity are without authority.

In the body of the church, then, which to Jurieu is composed of all the Christian societies in the world, the faithful and the elect are scattered. They are the soul of the church and invisible, since no one knows with certainty who are the true faithful. But just as a man is not invisible, although his soul is, so the church is visible, even though it has its invisible portion. Thus, Jurieu tried to modify that fundamental distinction between Catholics and Protestants, which Cardinal Bellarmine [69] had perceived long before. The two churches are no longer divided on this question of visibility.[70] In fact, both Claude and Jurieu considered the theory of the invisible church as a means used by the early Protestant writers to mask the innovations of their religion.[71] They, therefore, disapproved of it, since still other innovators could employ it in a similar fashion in order to justify their own heretical doctrines. But what had made the earlier perception of Bellarmine so remarkable was the fact that, although the basis of the Reformation had been rooted in the

---

défendre, le mélange de réprouvés ne lui seroit pas inutile pour sa conservation." *Histoire du calvinisme*, 1683, I, Chap. IV, 184.

[69] ". . . non enin possunt vera membra Ecclesiae vocari Lutherani, & Calviniste, etiam si in Symbolo nobiscum convenirent. Nam praeter illam fidem, requiritur subjectio ad legitimum caput Ecclesiae vocari a Christo constitutum & communicatio cum aliis membris: Ecclesia enim est unum corpus visibile & proinde caput & membra visibilia nec potest dici membrum, quod a capite & corpore reliquo separatum est." Robert Bellarmine, *Disputationes de controversiis christianae fides*, Vol. II, Book III, Chap. XIX (non posse conciliari Catholicos cum haereticis), p. 385, of the edition of 1628 (four tomes in one folio). Cf. a statement of Cardinal du Perron later: "le nom de Catholique n'est pas un nom de simple créance, mais de communion." *Lettre de Mons, le Card. du Perron envoyée au Sieur Casaubon* quoted in A. O. Meyer, "Charles I and Rome," *The American Historical Review*, October, 1913, p. 16 n.

[70] "Nous ne voulons pas dire que l'Église ait cessé d'être au monde ni même qu'elle ait cessé d'être visible." Jurieu, *Le Vray Système de l'église*, p. 229.

[71] See Rébelliau, *Bossuet, Historien du protestantisme*, p. 39.

conception of invisibility, still the original Reformers themselves had set up visible churches on earth. This action no doubt resulted from the doctrine of exclusive salvation, whether in the church visible or invisible. The real point was whether those outside the visible church could really belong to the invisible.

This whole question of visibility is obviously connected with the problem of religious tolerance. It is difficult for the magistrate to persecute an invisible church, which implies a personal relation between the individual and God. Therefore, any form of nonconformity which is a visible act is not apparent. Thus, in general it can be said that those who believe in a visible church are intolerant, while tolerance and the conception of the invisibility of the church go together. It is interesting, therefore, to note in this connection that John Locke's theory of tolerance is based upon his conception of the church as "a voluntary society of men joining themselves together of their own account in order to secure the public worshipping of God in such manner as they judge acceptable to Him and effectual to the salvation of their souls." [72] Furthermore, only when the importance of the visibility or invisibility of the church is fully grasped can one be in a position to understand the reason for such prolonged disputes over the Eucharist.[73]

Jurieu's enemies lost no time in pointing out that since Cardinal Bellarmine had distinguished the body and the soul of the church, it is not legitimate for a Protestant to employ the same distinction. But there is a great difference, argued Jurieu in his *Seconde apologie,* between the conception of the great Jesuit and his own. To Bellarmine it is enough to belong to the body of the church in order to be a true member of the spiritual community, while, according to Jurieu, one must also be a member of the soul of the church in order to be a true member of Jesus Christ. With Bellarmine, to be separated from the body of the church is to be no longer a member. Therefore, members who have been unjustly excommunicated are completely outside the church. With Jurieu they

[72] *A Letter Concerning Toleration,* in *Works,* 1812, VI, 13.
[73] See Jurieu's *Examen de l'eucharistie de l'Eglise romaine,* 1682, which was an attack upon Arnauld's *Perpétuité de la foi de l'Eglise catholique touchant l'eucharistie.* Cf. also *Les Trophées de Port-Royal renversés,* 1688; this has been attributed to Jurieu by Kaeppler and to Aubert de Versé by Haag. Note also the anonymous *De l'adoration de l'eucharistie pour répondre aux faux raisonnements de MM. de la religion prétendue réformée dans leur Préservatif contre le changement de religion,* Toulouse, 1683.

would still be of it, both of the soul and of the body. Finally, the attributes of perpetuity, infallibility, and so on, belong only to the body of the church according to Bellarmine, while to Jurieu they are all attached to the soul of the church. Jurieu concludes from this analysis that the only novelty in his "system of the church" is to be found in his distinction between the body and the soul of the church. But, he asks, is this not the same thing as the differentiation between the visible and the invisible church, which is common to all Protestants? He only changed the terms because the division of the church into visible (body) and invisible (soul) portions imparts the idea of two churches in one. There is, however, but one church, visible by its exterior part (body) and invisible by its internal segment (soul).

But it was argued that if all sects are a part of the universal church, then salvation can be obtained anywhere and toleration should be extended indifferently to all faiths.[74] Jurieu strenuously denied any such implications of his theory. "God forbid then that we have the design of establishing that dangerous maxim that salvation can be secured in all religions which confess Jesus Christ, the son of God, the Messiah, crucified, dead, and resurrected from the dead. On the contrary we regard it as one of the most deadly heresies of Socinianism, the most capable of destroying from top to bottom the Christian religion." [75]

But what are those fundamental truths of the Christian religion,[76] the adherence to which determines membership in the true church universal? Not even Castellion had defined them exactly but it had been attempted by one Protestant writer before Jurieu—Innocent Gentillet, in

[74] "Il y a dans le Système quelque chose qui plaisait à mes censeurs c'est que j'ai prouvé d'une manière invincible contre Nicole, que l'Église renfermoit des Communions toutes opposées & qui même s'excommunioyent les unes les autres; & même que l'Eglise Chrétienne renfermoit dans son étendue générale cette grande diversité de Sectes qui la divisent dans l'Orient & dans l'Occident. Ils croyoient que cela les aideroit à établir leur dogme pernicieux qu'on peut être sauvé en toutes religions." *Seconde apologie pour M. Jurieu*, 1692, p. 30. Outside of Bayle in the Preface to his *Supplément du commentaire philosophique* and in his *Janua coelorum reserata cunctis religionibus*, 1692, the principal attack of this nature on the *Vray Système de l'église* was by Allix in his *Réflexions critiques & théologiques sur la controverse de l'Eglise*, 1686, which Bayle commented on in *Déclaration de M. Jurieu au sujet d'un Livre intitulé Réflexions critiques & théologiques sur la controverse de l'Eglise* in the May issue, 1686, of his *Nouvelles de la république des lettres* in *Oeuvres*, 1737, I, 551.
[75] Jurieu, *Le Vray Système de l'église*, p. 147.
[76] Locke spoke of those nonessentials which "breed implacable enmities among Christian brethren who are all agreed in the substantial and truly fundamental part of religion." *Works*, London, n.d., III, 15.

the preceding century.[77] Jurieu interprets these essentials as the belief in "one adorable God in three persons, incarnate in the second; one Jesus Christ, eternal son of God of the same essence and substance as the Father; Jesus Christ who died and rose again for the redemption of men, who ascended into heaven and who will come there to judge the living and the dead."[78] But he admits that Scripture does not reveal precisely a fundamental truth from one which is not. It does, however, supply the rules whereby the essential truths can be distinguished. "What destroys the glory of God and what ruins the sovereign end of man, that is, his sovereign beatitude, is a fundamental error. But Scripture reveals to us sufficiently what is the glory of God and the sovereign blessedness of man and lets us know what demolishes them."[79]

It is important to note at this point that Jurieu's theory of certain fundamental truths should not be confused[80] with the attempts of Pajon and D'Huisseau to reconcile the various branches of Protestantism with Catholicism on this basis. Even Calvin had distinguished the essentials from the nonessentials. Among the fundamentals are belief in one God, in Christ as God's son, and in salvation from God's grace. As a result Calvin would pardon error which does not touch the essential articles of the faith. In his system, however, everything is subordinate to the honor and glory of God. Thinkers like Pajon and D'Huisseau had en-

[77] Cf. Gentillet's *Apologia pro christianis gallis religionis evangelicae seu reformatae,* 1588, Chapter XIX (entitled, "De Ratione Componendarum Religionis Christianae controversarium"), pp. 263–266: "Et articulos quidem Fidei in tria Symbola quasi compendia contraxit, ad populi commodiorem usum (nec enim cuique darum est omnem sacram Scripturam intelligere fideque complecti) in Symbolum videlicet Apostolorum Niceni concilii patrum Symbolum & Symbolum D. Athanasii."

[78] Jurieu, *Le Vray Système de l'église,* p. 150.

[79] *Ibid.,* p. 209. Cf. *De pace inter protestantes ineunda consultatio,* p. 164. For a further discussion of fundamental and nonfundamental truths see Jurieu's *Traité de l'unité de l'Eglise et des points fondamentaux contre M. Nicole,* 1688, Part VI, p. 529. As against Nicole, Jurieu insists that nothing can be made into a fundamental point by the power of the church, which is not such by its very nature. He sums up the whole matter in the *Tableau du Socinianisme* by declaring: ". . . il y a trois caractères pour distinguer ces vérités fondamentales 1) Le premier est la révelation. 2) Le second est le poids & l'importance (dont le bon sens & la raison seule" and "le consentement de tous les chrétiens," even of Catholics, "peuvent en juger"). 3) Le troisième est la liaison de certaines vérités avec la fin de la Religion." *Lettre,* III, p. 116. The Biblical basis for the distinction between fundamentals and nonfundamentals is to be found in the third chapter of the First Epistle to the Corinthians.

[80] Delvolvé makes this mistake in his *Religion critique et philosophie positive chez Pierre Bayle,* p. 206.

deavored to arrive at a minimum number of articles of faith that would be common to all sects; for Jurieu, however, the truth remains always the same in its entirety. It is simply a question of what errors God will tolerate and what sects can contain the elect. For example, Jurieu points out [81] that by means of separation God saves souls in communions that have been corrupted. That is, He grants the communions power to separate the good from the bad. He accomplishes the same end by means of tolerating certain nonfundamental errors. All essential errors can be clarified by the reading of Scripture and the study of revelation with a spirit of humility and good faith. But this tolerance of God varies at different times. Since all are now in a position to know the true church, it is a crime not to enter it.[82] Thus, there is a great difference between Jurieu and the liberal Protestants on this question of fundamental truths. It is more than a difference of degree. Since it is not a problem of the number and extent of the fundamental points, it is an issue of principle. For the rational Protestant thinkers from Castellion to Bayle [83] the question is to arrive at a minimum set of truths. For Jurieu the problem is the limitation of the tolerance of God, the truth remaining always unchanged as a whole. The sovereignty and awful majesty of God is the fundamental doctrine behind everything in his mind. Not even reason is to be trusted in a matter of faith.[84]

With such a view of the authority of God it is not surprising that Jurieu insisted upon the most rigid orthodoxy. Such a position was especially vulnerable, however, since it was claimed by Bossuet, Maimbourg, Arnauld, and Nicole that the Calvinists had no right to attack the infallibility of the Catholic Church when they reversed themselves and substituted in its place Protestant infallibility in their synods, which exercised the same power of excommunication as the Catholics employed. In fact, Nicole claimed that the Protestants made each individual infallible. As

---

[81] Jurieu, *Le Vray Système de l'église,* 1686, Chap. XX, pp. 152–162.

[82] *Ibid.,* Chap. XXI, pp. 163–171.

[83] The liberal Protestants like Jean Le Clerc were only rationalists before certain articles of belief. Bayle, however, was skeptical of belief and truth itself. As we shall see, Bayle's idea of tolerance was founded not on a minimum of fundamentals but on the principle of the superior right of the moral reason. He was the first to shift the argument for tolerance from the plan of agreement on a minimum of fundamentals.

[84] "Il n'y a qu'un fondement capable d'assurer le coeur dans les matières de la foy: c'est l'authorité de Dieu: car la foy ne se repose que là-dessus." *Le Vray Système de l'église,* 1686, p. 381.

one of the proofs for the first charge the treatment of the Remonstrants at the Synod of Dordrecht, which was a sort of oecumenical council of Protestantism, is cited.

As Jurieu had declared in his *Traité de la puissance de l'Eglise,* in order to appraise the nature of the authority of the synods it is necessary to realize that the source of this power lies in the Christian people— the laity. But what authority could the people confer upon the councils? Jurieu answers that the councils can do three things. First, they judge controversies over the dogmas and the truths of religion. Second, they make regulations of discipline and government of the church. Third, they excommunicate heretics from the church. But the councils do not perform these three functions under the same character but under three different characters. The first is that of an assembly of wise and learned persons, who share each other's knowledge. The second is that of dele- gated legislators who assemble to form a government or to conserve one. The third is that of judges established by their churches to handle of- fenses against the law of God.[85]

Of this triple character or nature a triple right is to be derived. From the first character is derived the right which nature and reason give to learned persons to decide difficult controversies. From the second char- acter is derived the right which belongs to all confederations to require submission to those persons established to govern them. Finally, from the last character is derived the natural right to expel those who violate the laws of a society. The church cannot be deprived of this right of ex- communication, since it is rooted by nature itself in all societies.

The Roman Church makes its mistake in ignoring the first two char- acters of the councils and in stressing only the third, making them judges in everything, as much in points of doctrine as in discipline. The Independents in England emphasize only the first character or function, that of a body of learned persons, not recognizing the role of judge under any conditions. As usual, Jurieu claims that he finds the truth in between these extreme positions. He thinks that the councils play the role of an assembly of experts in certain matters and as such they need not be obeyed, unless they are regarded as rendering a correct decision. In other matters, whether their judgments are just or not, submission must be

[85] *Ibid.,* p. 243.

forthcoming or departure from the communion of the councils must follow. This is essential because it is absolutely necessary for the sake of order, even though in certain cases innocent persons will be unjustly condemned.

Thus, in matters of faith the councils act only as experts [86] and not as judges with authority to bind the conscience, which belongs to God alone. In questions of faith then each person is freely to judge as against a whole council.[87] But in matters of discipline and ecclesiastical government, which do not concern the conscience, the synods can enforce their decisions, since they receive their authority from the people, who have agreed together to submit to certain regulations for the conservation of the confederation or to suffer excommunication from the communion for disregarding its laws.[88] But an individual can quit a discipline he does not like without risking his salvation. These matters of discipline are for the most part indifferent,[89] since they are not clearly decided by Scripture. In addition to violations of discipline, the synods acting as judges can excommunicate those who have fallen into fundamental error and those who are guilty of other errors. For example, Jurieu cites the errors of the Lutherans and Arminians on grace, which, although not fundamental, are nevertheless important and serious. But the synods cannot act in the capacity of judges in all cases. Since they are not infallible, they cannot be judges in matters of faith. Furthermore, since the councils receive their authority from the people, they cannot be infallible.

---

[86] The decisions of these experts in matters of doctrine oblige the conscience not because of the source from which they come but because they are in conformity with the word of God. *Traité de la puissance de l'Eglise,* 1677, p. 243. Therefore, the Remonstrants were excommunicated not because they refused to submit to the decisions of the Synod of Dordrecht but because they did not wish to submit to a doctrine which was conformable to the word of God and which the Calvinists were obliged to sustain "par une confession confédérée" against the Pelagianism of the Roman Church. *Le Vray Système de l'église,* p. 305.

[87] ". . . nous soutenons avec un très grand zèle contre l'Eglise Romaine qu'aucune assemblée d'hommes n'est en droit de faire des loix ou des décisions qui obligent la conscience." *Traité de la puissance de l'Eglise,* p. 225. But if freedom of conscience and examination are to be preserved before the councils, then what is to prevent the disintegration of Protestantism to the stage of complete indifference of religion? In default of a religious authority Jurieu is forced to adopt the authority of the magistrate as the supreme guardian of religion.

[88] Jurieu, *Le Vray Système de l'église,* p. 253.

[89] Things neither prohibited nor commanded by the word of God are indifferent. *Traité de la puissance de l'Eglise,* p. 291.

Since the people lack that quality, they cannot confer it upon the synods.

Jurieu concludes, then, that in matters of faith submission to councils need not be blind. In matters of discipline obedience should be pushed much farther than in articles of faith. But in cases of censure or excommunication obedience is to be carried to the highest degree, since "in cutting off from their communion those whom they judge unworthy, they (the councils) exercise properly the right of nations, the natural right common to all men." But national synods do not have the power to decide controversies upon fundamental points. It is never in their power "to examine whether Jesus Christ is the son of God, the redeemer of the world, whether we are saved by the sole grace of Jesus Christ, whether men are born in original sin, whether the dead are resurrected, if there are more than two sacraments, if the body of Jesus Christ is in the Eucharist by transubstantiation, whether it is necessary to adore images and other similar matters." [90] In fact, a council should never banish a man from the church because his opinions are not in agreement with its decisions but because he has denied a truth revealed in the word of God.

But Bossuet had argued that if all were not required to submit to the judgment of the synods, then the door would be left open to the possibility of the establishment of as many religions as parishes. He cites, for example, the Independents in England who believed that each faithful individual should follow the dictates of his own conscience and that each organization should be governed by its own laws without any dependence upon other authorities in ecclesiastical matters. Jurieu replied that one is not obliged to submit his judgment to the synods but his tongue. If a man is heterodox in his heart but does not preach heresy, then there will be no danger of the inconveniences of Independency. This authority of the synods over speech and not over the heart results from the fact that synods and councils are assemblies of men who have no empire over conscience. Furthermore, when the congregations confederated under certain laws and confessions of faith, they did not promise to believe certain doctrines. They did obligate themselves, however, to profess to believe and teach them.

In the *Préservatif contre le changement de religion* (1680), Jurieu in

[90] Jurieu, *Le Vray Système de l'église,* 1686, pp. 263–264.

arguing against Bossuet had said that there was a great difference between a considerable authority in the church and an infallible power—
between a blind dependence and a conditioned dependence. "The faithful must be in dependence but they should examine by the word of God
the decisions upon which they must depend, not in order to establish a
new religion, if that seems good to them, but in order to submit to decisions by a principle of reason, enlightened by divine faith and founded
on the word of God." [91] Jurieu admits that if individuals judge the decision of a council to be false, then they must follow the dictate of their
hearts. They should be silent, however, and take no action in case the
error is not fundamental. But if it is a question of their salvation, even
then their conscience would oblige them not to form a new religion. Instead, they should choose the existing one which they believe most in
conformity with the truth of the Scriptures.[92] As to matters of discipline
Jurieu repeats that there must be an order, which means each society has
a right to judge the controversies in its midst. Those members who do
not wish to submit to this judgment can be expelled. In fact, Jurieu does
not blame the Council of Trent for the expulsion of the Calvinists, since
they employed a right belonging to every society.[93] The only trouble
was that the Calvinists were unjustly condemned by that Council, according to our theologian.[94] Such are the broad outlines of the long controversy between Catholics and Protestants in this period over the nature
and authority of ecclesiastical assemblies.

[91] *Préservatif*, pp. 325–332.

[92] For support and further elaboration on this point Jurieu cites Claude's *La Défense de la
réformation contre le livre intitulé Préjugez* (1673), which was an answer to Nicole's
Préjugez légitimes contre le calvinisme.

[93] See Jurieu's *Abregé de l'histoire du Concile de Trente*, 1682.

[94] Bayle in his famous *Dictionnaire historique et critique*, article "Maimbourg," concludes
as follows: "Il n'y a point d'autre différence entre l'Eglise Romaine & l'Eglise Réformée
à l'égard de l'autorité si ce n'est que l'une déclare qu'elle est infaillible & qu'il n'est point
permis aux particuliers d'examiner des Décisions; au lieu que l'autre se reconnoit faillible
& permet aux particuliers d'examiner tout pourvu qu'enfin ils se soumettent à ses arrêts;
je sais bien dis-je que l'on objecte qu'à ce compte le voie de l'Autorité n'est pas moins le
dernier réfuge pour les Protestants que pour les Papistes."

Chapter Seven

THEOCRACY AND THE MENACE
OF BAYLE

Ever since Voltaire the judgment of history has been with Bayle rather than with Jurieu on the question of tolerance.[1] Of course, the spiritual descendant of the famous philosopher of Rotterdam, writing in the period of the Enlightenment on the eve of the French Revolution, would hardly be expected to have much sympathy for an orthodox Calvinist who claimed to be so certain of the absolute truth. But the time has finally come for a revaluation of Jurieu's ideas on tolerance and his part in the celebrated quarrel with Bayle.

According to Henri Basnage de Beauval, as we have already observed, the beginning of the estrangement between Jurieu and Bayle can be dated from the appearance of Maimbourg's attack on Calvinism. Bayle's *Critique générale de L'Histoire du calvinisme de M. Maimbourg* in reply to the Jesuit father appeared before the *Histoire du calvinisme et celle du papisme mises en parallèle* of Jurieu and was destined to have the greater success.[2] This probably aroused the jealousy of the theologian of Rotterdam. But Jurieu did not openly criticize the *Critique générale* until the period of the bitter controversy over the *Avis aux réfugiés,* almost a decade later.

During that bitter struggle the quarrel between Jurieu and Bayle extended beyond the immediate question of Bayle's authorship of the *Projet de paix* and the *Avis aux réfugiés.* It included the whole thought of the philosopher of Rotterdam, whom Jurieu now accused of atheism,

---

[1] "Qu'a servi contre Bayle une infame cabale?
    Par le fougueux Jurieu Bayle persécuté
    Sera des bons esprits à jamais respecté
    Et le nom de Jurieu son rival fanatique
    N'est aujourd'hui connu que par l'horreur publique"
    "Discours en vers de l'Envie" in *Oeuvres complètes,* 1785, XII, 27–28.

[2] According to Desmaizeaux, *Vie de Bayle,* I, 84, Gilles Ménage in his *Menagiana,* Paris, 1694, II, 22–23, made the contemporary comment: "Le livre de M. Bayle est le livre d'honnête homme et celui de M. Jurieu celui d'une vieille de prêche. C'est un méchant rechaussé de tout ce que Dumoulin & les autres ont dit de plus fade contre la Religion Catholique."

which was a terrible charge at the time. In the *Courte revue des maximes de morale et des principes de Religion de l'auteur des Pensées diverses sur les comètes et de La Critique générale sur L'Histoire du calvinisme de M. Maimbourg* (1691), Jurieu calls attention to two especially dangerous features of Bayle's reply to Maimbourg. First, he is scandalized by the skepticism which Bayle showed toward historical treatments of the Reformation. The philosopher of Rotterdam had said that he could only adopt an attitude of Pyrrhonism after observing the great contradictions between the histories of the Reformation which were written by Catholics and Protestants. How, asks Jurieu, can such an author be rightfully called the defender of the true faith? But Jurieu was even more disturbed over the Ninth Letter of the Third Tome of the *Critique générale*. It was here that Bayle first set forth the doctrine of the erring conscience which he elaborated in the *Nouvelles lettres de l'auteur de la Critique générale de L'Histoire du calvinisme de M. Maimbourg* and especially in his *Commentaire philosophique sur ces paroles de Jésus Christ: contrains les d'entrer*.[3]

Bayle's theory of the erring conscience was based upon the inviolability of conscience that was strongly emphasized among the Calvinists. It should be remembered, however, that they held that the only conscience which has any claim to consideration is a right conscience. In simplest form the doctrine of the erring conscience meant that all errors which are of good faith have the same right over the conscience as orthodoxy. In other words, those who are persuaded wrongly that a certain doctrine is true are obliged to sustain it just as though they were justly convinced. Whenever error is disguised in the appearance of truth it succeeds to all the rights of truth, since it is only opinion which makes up the essence and basis of such rights. This means that a murder committed according to the promptings of conscience is a lesser evil than the refusal to kill when the conscience commands it. It follows, therefore, that heretics are obliged to disseminate their errors in the same way that the orthodox seek to extend and preserve the doctrine which is true.[4]

---

[3] Jurieu considered the Ninth Letter of the *Critique générale* and the *Commentaire philosophique* as "les plus forts" and "les plus pernicieux livres qui ayent jamais été faits pour le Pyrrhonisme." Bayle had stated that it is impossible to know for certain that what appears to be the truth really is. See *Courte revue des maximes de morale*.

[4] Locke expresses these same ideas of Bayle in the dictum that "every church is orthodox to itself; to others erroneous or heretical." *A Letter concerning Toleration*, in *Works*, VI, 19.

In the *Courte revue des maximes de morale* Jurieu calls attention to
the nefarious results of such a conception of the conscience. First, it
means that the pagans are obliged to worship their false gods and in doing so they do not sin. Second, it follows that everything is opinion in
religious matters and that everything is equally good in religion, false
or true, provided that one holds it to be veritable. Third, heretics are
not guilty in defending their heresies or in dogmatizing in spite of pro-
hibitions against it. They believe their heresies to be true and are obliged,
therefore, to act upon the dictates of their erring consciences. Even atheists, when in good faith, are excusable, and all religions are equally pleasing to God. Furthermore, it follows from this concept of the erring conscience that the most dreadful crimes can be committed without offending God, provided the criminals believe that they are doing right. In
this manner not only all religious but also all moral standards are destroyed.

But the objections Jurieu made to the Ninth Letter of the Third Tome
of the *Critique générale* were much more cogently stated in Chapters
XXII to XXIV of Book I of his *Le Vray Système de l'église*. One of the
very methods of attack upon Jurieu's conception of the church was that
it would lead to indifference of religions, since it permitted a general
toleration of all religions by the fact that all communions which are
Christian make up the church. Now Jurieu had admitted that his idea
of the church did imply some degree of toleration,[5] but he denied that
it implied "a Socinian indulgence." In the first place, Jurieu would not
tolerate, as we have seen in his "system of the church," those sects which
destroy the fundamental truths such as the Socinians. Secondly, he declared his idea of the church did not lead even absolutely to the toleration of those sects which, although not destroying the essentials of religion, disfigure its beauty by various false opinions and superstitious
practices. It follows, however, from his view of the church that when
these sects are established in a country they should not be uprooted by
fire and the sword. For if they retain the fundamental truths, they are
to be regarded "as sick and weak parts but not to be cut off as dead portions." It does not follow that these sects are to be permitted to establish

5 "Nous ne voudrions pas regarder commes des réprouvés tous ceux qui s'écartent le moins
du monde de la vérité; ni même tous ceux qui nous excommunient." Jurieu, *Le Vray
Système de l'église*, 1686, p. 176.

themselves in places where they did not exist before. In fact "that shameful deformity which always arises from the diversity of religions" [6] must be avoided at all costs. Jurieu acknowledges, however, that different sects can get along well in a country if they submit to the civil authorities.

According to these principles, it was held by those who desired a general toleration for all sects in all circumstances that the Calvinists had no cause to complain about the violent means taken in Europe to prevent the establishment of their religion. To this Jurieu replied that the Calvinists had every reason to object to such methods as fire and the sword, since they do not hold it permissible to use force to establish a sect. Besides, these measures were taken against a sect already settled in France. Finally, Jurieu answered that the advocates of a general freedom did not understand the maxim "For we can do nothing against the truth, but for the truth." [7] They had contended that since Jurieu would have the magistrate use his authority to prevent heretics from dogmatizing and spreading their doctrines by speech and by writing,[8] in Catholic countries the government could prevent Calvinists from instructing their peoples. But to Jurieu this made as much sense as to argue that because rulers have the right to punish criminals with death they also have the right to execute innocent persons as well. A sovereign has the right to levy taxes on his people but no right to pillage his provinces. The one is just and necessary for the good of the state and the other is most unjust. Therefore, it can be concluded that "it is then justice and truth which give the right." [9] Thus a prince has the liberty of silencing heretics without violence within his realm, but it does not follow that he has the privilege of crushing those who wish to preach the truth.

It was objected that the Catholic magistrates believed they had truth and justice on their side when they persecuted Calvinists. At this point Jurieu admits that there are errors of fact which excuse since they are insurmountable. But the matter of heresy is an error of right which can never enter into the rights of the truth. The reason for this is as follows: "The truths of right bear on the face their distinctive character and those

---

[6] *Ibid.*, p. 177.   [7] II Corinthians, 13.8.

[8] "Le magistrat a donc droit de supprimer les hérésies par la déffence de dogmatiser mais non pas par l'effusion du sang des hérétiques . . . car son Evangile n'est point un Evangile de sang." Jurieu, *Le Vray Système de l'église*, p. 181.

[9] *Ibid.*, p. 179.

who do not see them are not worthy of being pardoned, because it is cupidity, the corruption of the heart, prejudice, arrogance—these are the human passions which cast their shadows of darkness." [10] The truths of fact are not visible by themselves; their evidence depends upon external things which can be separated. But every truth "of right sufficiently revealed to the spirit has the privilege of requiring its consent, and if the spirit (mind) refuses this approval, God has the prerogative of punishing man for this denial." [11] Furthermore, the sufficiency or insufficiency of the revelation cannot be argued, since even an atheist could claim toleration on the ground that the truth has not been adequately disclosed to him.

Bayle's doctrine of the erring conscience was regarded by Jurieu as especially dangerous since it was based on the Protestant conception of the conscience as the lieutenant of God. If, therefore, it is impossible to sin in following the movements of one's conscience, then a man who believes that tyrants can be put to death is innocent. Moreover, if this doctrine of the erring conscience is detestable in moral questions and in those of the social order, it must be also in questions of dogma, that is, heresy. In fact, obedience is no more due to a criminal conscience than to "a wicked legislator who commands what is contrary to the law of God, because the conscience is a true legislator." [12] When the conscience is corrupted it becomes the lieutenant of the Devil rather than of God, and disobedience to it is to sin not against God but against the Devil. Such arguments were employed by Jurieu to destroy Bayle's thesis that since heretics believe that they are obliged by conscience, which belongs only to God, to preach their doctrines, then the magistrate has no power to prevent heretics from dogmatizing.

But Jurieu was accused of arming the persecutors of the Calvinists by enunciating such theories in answer to Bayle. Do not the Catholics believe they have the truth and that the Huguenots are heretics and that, therefore, they are obliged in conscience to prevent the spread of Protestant doctrine? But Jurieu thought it was not enough to suppose that one had the right. In addition "it is necessary to have actually the right that one thinks he has." But who is to judge between the magistrate and the heretic on the question of who has the right? "I answer," con-

[10] *Ibid.,* p. 187.   [11] *Ibid.,* p. 190.   [12] *Ibid.,* p. 191.

tinues Jurieu, "that it is the sovereign magistrate himself who will be damned if he judges wrongly." [13] But if a heretic takes a false religion for the true one, his crime does not deprive the magistrate, who defends the true religion, from using his authority to prevent the establishment of a fraudulent faith. Besides, according to the principle of the erring conscience, the magistrate would not only have no control over heresy but also none over crime of any sort. For example, if conscience dictated that all property should be held in common, then the magistrate could not prevent a man from seizing the possessions of another. Finally, the evil usage of a good principle does not remove the right to a correct application of that precept. For example, the Protestants regard only what is clearly contained in Scripture as fundamental and necessary for salvation. The Socinian puts an incorrect interpretation upon this doctrine by asserting that nothing can be regarded as an article of faith except what is contained word for word in the Bible. This does not prevent, however, the use of this rule against the Catholics. In the same way it is a tenet of orthodoxy that tolerance is not universal and that the magistrate has the right to prevent a heretic from preaching his dogmas. The Catholics misuse this concept by burning heretics and restraining the ministers of truth, but this bad application does not prevent the true church from correctly employing the maxim.

It was in his *Des droits des deux souverains en matière de religion: la conscience et le prince* that Jurieu attacked at length the doctrine of the erring conscience [14] as set forth by Bayle in his *Commentaire philosophique*.[15] In fact Jurieu contended that Bayle sought to establish a "tolerance and general indifference of all sects and even of all religions." Such a position was in Jurieu's mind a "deism, pure and simple," [16] since it resulted in the relativity of truth. In contrast our pastor believed

[13] *Ibid.*, p. 197.

[14] Jurieu declares that this doctrine has been set forth also in a *Traité de la raison humaine*, which had been translated from the English, and in a treatise of that libertine, Thomas Hobbes. It was the principle of the Socinians and Arminians as well. They hate persecution because they do not love the truth.

[15] Although in the Preface to the *Supplément du Commentaire philosophique* Bayle denied a knowledge of Jurieu's *Le Vray Système de l'église* before writing the *Commentaire*, it would appear that the book is a direct answer to Jurieu's "system of the church." The last four chapters of the second part of the *Commentaire* are described by Jurieu as the core of the work, since they set forth the concept of the erring conscience.

[16] *Des droits des deux souverains*, 1687, pp. 12, 85.

that "God himself is the absolute truth, that his understanding is the source of all truths and therefore it is impossible to be orthodox with respect to God without being so with regard to the reality of things." [17]

In opposition to the doctrine of the erring conscience, Jurieu presents his own idea "of the nature, duties, and rights of the conscience." [18] He finds it composed like the soul of which it is the expression, of two parts; "the spirit and the heart, the understanding and the will." These elements are united but those who are advocates of the doctrine of the erring conscience separate them, since "they bind the heart to everything and the spirit to nothing." This is to claim that the heart should seek the good but that the spirit is not obliged to know the truth. It is true, of course, that the conscience is a legislator but it has a superior legislator, namely, God. The libertines hold that these two legislators are always in agreement and that God always orders what the conscience commands, since it is His law that one should follow its dictates. But if the conscience commands a crime, then this places God in a state of contradiction. To Jurieu, when the two different legislators are in opposition, that of the conscience cannot prejudice that of God. Since, as we learned in *Le Vray Système de l'église,* justice and truth and not the appearance of them are the one source of all right, therefore, the conscience can only command with justice and truth when it orders what is compatible with divine law. Ignorance of right or heresy, to Jurieu, is simply the result of the baser elements in human nature, or corruption.[19] But Jurieu concedes that people must be notified of God's truth in order to be bound by it. Once the word is preached, however, no one can plead a lack of understanding.

In contrast to Jurieu's theory, Bayle had held, as we have noted, that the appearance of truth and justice give the same right as actual truth and justice. Therefore, he argued that if an orthodox prince had the right to suppress heresy and sustain truth, then a heretical ruler, who believed himself to be orthodox, had the same right to suppress the

[17] *Ibid.,* pp. 32–38.   [18] *Ibid.,* Chap. VIII.

[19] "Toutes les erreurs sont du nombre de ces opinions qui naissent de la paresse, de la negligence, de l'opiniatreté, de l'amour-propre et de l'attache à son propre sens, ou de l'amour pour la sensualité. Il est à remarquer qu'une erreur de bonne foi peut partir de ces principes de corruption comme les autres s'il y en a." *Ibid.,* pp. 227 ff.

truth which he regarded as heresy. From this he concluded that universal tolerance was the only solution to the problem. But Jurieu contends that it was in vain to write a book against persecution on the basis of the right of the erring conscience, since the persecutors are in this ignorance of good faith when they apply their various constraints. Therefore, they are to be exonerated, since it is a crime not to follow the dictates of conscience. This very telling rejoinder greatly embarrassed Bayle.[20]

As usual, Jurieu declared that he would take a middle position between Bayle's extreme of universal tolerance and the stand of the Catholic Church, which would allow no toleration at all. He begins in Chapter XIII his analysis of the measures that the magistrate can legitimately take to destroy the false religion in favor of the true. In typically Calvinistic fashion he declares that "each one in his place is bound to work for the glory of God, to establish the truth, to ruin error, to conserve religion in its purity, and restore it when it is lost." Should the prince, then, be exempt from this same duty? Certainly the prince has even greater obligations toward God than private individuals for the establishment of His truth.[21] Numerous examples are cited from sacred history, while profane history teaches that paganism fell under the authority of the Roman Emperors. In fact, "three quarters of Europe would still be pagan if Constantine and his successors had not employed their authority to abolish it."[22] Furthermore, he declares that the rulers of Sweden, Denmark, Scotland, England, Switzerland, Holland, and cer-

[20] Jacques Basnage in his *Traité de la conscience . . . avec des réflexions sur le Commentaire philosophique,* 1696, I, 74 ff. made the same point.

[21] "Chacun est obligé de servir à delà selon le caractère dont Dieu l'a revêtu. Le savant est obligé d'y faire contribuer son savoir, le sage sa sagesse, l'éloquent son éloquence, le riche sa richesse." Chap. XIII of *Des droits des deux souverains.*

[22] *Ibid.,* pp. 273–298. L'Abbé Novi de Caveirac in his *Apologie de Louis XIV et de son conseil sur la Révocation de l'Edit de Nantes,* 1758, p. 552, cited this passage in support of his own opposition to the reestablishment of Calvinism in France in the eighteenth century. Cf. however, the following passage from Jurieu's *Préservatif contre le changement de religion,* pp. 9–10: "Elle (l'église) ne s'est pas servie de l'autorité des Constantins & des Théodoses pour ensanglanter les Temples des faux Dieux, du sang de leurs adorateurs, comme les Payens avoient employé les épées des Nérons, des Maximins, des Decides & des Diocletiens pour baigner la terre du sang des Chrétiens. Il faut être peu savant dans l'Histoire de l'Eglise pour ignorer que dans les démelez qu'elle a eus avec les Arriens, les Eutychiens & les autres Hérétiques elle ne s'est servi que d'Exhortations que de raisons, que de conciles & d'autres semblables armes." Bayle delighted in pointing out this flagrant contradiction in his *Dictionnaire,* article "Arius."

tain German states had used their authority to overthrow "Papism." [23] With the exception, then, of the first institution of Christianity, in which God ordained a miracle instead of the aid of secular power, He has always employed that authority to establish the true religion and to destroy the false. In fact, Jurieu warns against the view that it would be better for the Huguenots, because of their persecution in France, to adopt the position that would exclude the secular arm from any interference in affairs of religion. He concedes that they would profit by it for the moment, but the church would be the greater loser in the end because there might conceivably come a time when the kings of France and Spain could use their authority to abolish Catholicism, as the kings of England and Sweden had already done.[24]

But as Jurieu had stated before, there are limits to the authority of the ruler over religion. The death penalty is forbidden, as well as all constraint over conscience which only makes hypocrites instead of sincere believers. The closing of the churches and public services of the false religion is permissible, however. Does this mean that if the Catholic monarchs had only gone this far and no farther there would be no reason for complaint? Not at all, replies Jurieu. Because the prince has the privilege of levying reasonable taxes for the support of the state does not mean that he has the right to ravage the public with exorbitant charges. In the same way, although a prince has the right to advance the truth and thus serve God, he does not have the liberty of establishing heresy and thereby serve the Devil. But Jurieu thinks that in sustaining the authority of orthodox princes to suppress the false religion he is not giving

[23] Denis de Sainte Marthe in his *Réponse aux plaintes des protestants touchant la prétendue persécution de France,* 1688, pp. 236–238, retorts that in that event the king of France has a perfect right to revoke the Edict of Nantes: "Certainement si les Rois ont droit de changer une Religion aussi ancienne que la nôtre, pourquoy n'auroient ils pas droit de casser tout ce qui s'est fait en faveur d'une Secte aussi nouvelle que celle de Calvin & de remettre les choses dans l'Etat où elles étoient encore il y a cent cinquante ans."

[24] "C'est l'autorité des Rois de l'Occident qui a bati l'Empire du Papisme, ce sera leur autorité qui le détruira." *Des droits des deux souverains,* pp. 273–298. Gédéon Huet in his *Apologie pour les vrais tolérants* and Bayle in his *Dictionnaire,* article "Augustin" claimed that because Jurieu expected through his study of the Apocalypse that the ruin of Catholicism was imminent and that it would be accomplished by princes, he therefore condemned those who did not believe that the sovereign should extirpate heresy by the use of his secular authority. Bayle, of course, delights in contrasting this attitude with Jurieu's condemnation of persecution in his *Politique du clergé de France,* his *Préservatif contre le changement de religion,* and *Histoire du calvinisme et celle du papisme.*

the heretical Catholic rulers even the occasion to persecute the true church but instead a specious ruse. In the first place, the institution of the true religion is not the inspiration behind the action of the French court and the House of Austria. Secondly, these persecutors burn at the stake and constrain persons in an excessive manner. Finally, he did not give the right even for the orthodox magistrate to break treaties and faith with heretics.

Therefore, Jurieu could see nothing illogical in denouncing the persecutions of Louis XIV, while at the same time he himself was advocating that the Protestant princes did well to abolish Catholicism. What separates him from Bossuet, then, is not a difference over the principle of tolerance, which they both condemn, but over a question of fact. Lord Acton has disagreed with this conclusion by attempting to show that Protestantism is even more intolerant than Catholicism. Catholics justified persecution only for the defense of the church, as in cases of apostasy, while the Protestants demanded the persecution of all error and idolatry, whether Jewish, pagan, or Christian. In Acton's own words, "Catholic intolerance is handed down from an age when unity subsisted and when its preservation, being essential for that society, became a necessity of State as well as a result of circumstances. Protestant intolerance, on the contrary, was the peculiar fruit of a dogmatic system in contradiction with the facts and principles on which the intolerance actually existing among Catholics was founded. . . . The only instance in which the Protestant theory [placing the necessity of intolerance on the simple ground of religious error] has been adopted by Catholics is the revocation of the Edict of Nantes." [25] But however great the difference in theory it is difficult to see any distinction as to the practical results of the two systems.

Although Bayle made no direct answer to Jurieu's attacks upon the *Commentaire philosophique* in the *Traité des droits des deux souverains,* he gave what amounts to a reply in the preface to the *Supplément du Commentaire philosophique.* In his usually devastating manner, he at-

[25] Acton, *Protestant Theory of Persecution,* pp. 169–170. On this point cf. E. W. Nelson, "The Theory of Persecution," in *Persecution and Liberty. Essays in Honor of George Lincoln Burr,* pp. 12ff. See also Niebuhr, *The Nature and Destiny of Man,* Vol. II: *Human Destiny,* p. 228: "The intolerance of theologians of the orthodox Reformation was the more reprehensible because the sectaries, against which their fanaticism was particularly directed, emphasized the very truths which supplemented the insights of the Reformation."

tempted to show that his own ideas on the erring conscience were the same as those expressed by Jurieu in *Le Vray Système de l'église*. The passage cited as proof of this contention was the following: "Conscience always binds the individual to the course which is certain to involve less crime. But there is less sin for a heretic to separate from than to remain in the orthodox church, when he judges it to be heretical and idolatrous. This demonstrates that those who remain in the Roman Communion without believing in the real presence sin much more than if they had withdrawn, even if the real presence is true and its adoration necessary." [26] Gédéon Huet in his *Apologie pour les vrais tolérants* held that it followed from this passage that if the orthodox magistrate was obliged to use his authority against heretics, then the heretical magistrate would be forced to act against the orthodox; since he thought himself to be orthodox, he must, in order to avoid the greater sin, proceed against the orthodox whom he regarded as heretics.[27]

But it was during the quarrel over the *Avis aux réfugiés* and especially after Jurieu's attack upon him in the *Courte Revue des maximes de morale et des principes de religion* that Bayle found his real vengeance.[28] He accomplished this in a work which carried on the argument of the preface to the *Supplément du Commentaire philosophique* and which was a cruel and sarcastic criticism of the theologian's conception of the church as outlined in his *Le Vray Système de l'église* and in his *Traité de l'unité de l'église*.[29] Bayle wrote it in Latin under the title *Janua coelorum reserata cunctis religionibus a celebri admodum viro, Domino Petro Jurieu*, which gives an indication of the general nature of the book. The author pretends to be a defender of orthodoxy against the attempt on the part of Jurieu to open the gates of heaven to all religions, whether Catholic or Socinian, on the basis of a common denominator of certain fundamental truths of Christianity.[30]

---

[26] *Le Vray Système de l'église*, 1686, p. 308. Bayle finds this to be in direct contradiction to a passage in *Des droits des deux souverains*, p. 245, where Jurieu had declared: "Un hérétique caché qui est dans l'église n'est pas obligé à rompre avec elle parceque sa séparation seroit un nouveau crime ajouté à son Hérésie; quoique sa conscience lui dicte qu'il se doit séparer, il n'est point obligé à cette conscience parce qu'elle est erronée."

[27] *Apologie pour les vrais tolérants*, pp. 77–141.

[28] Bayle replied to this libel in 1694 with his *Addition aux Pensées diverses sur les comètes*.

[29] Bayle in his article on Nicole in the *Dictionnaire* again attacked the books of Jurieu on the church, which were written against the great Jansenist.

[30] According to Bossuet who came to the aid of Bayle on this point: "si l'on veut maintenant

But Bayle in his *Commentaire philosophique* had given an even more crushing criticism of the idea of tolerance based upon certain fundamental truths of Christianity. He described as demi-tolerationists those who would tolerate only sects that do not destroy the essentials. The question as to what is a fundamental is never answered. Is it something that is fundamental by its own nature, or something which is believed to be such by the accuser and not by the accused? These questions prepare the way for a dreary debate, in which the accused will deny that he is destroying a fundamental which only exists as such in his accuser's brain. "Such a thing appears to me as a fundamental; then it is, which is a pitiable reasoning." If it is enough, in order not to tolerate a religion, to believe that it destroys essentials, then pagans should not tolerate Christians nor should there be any tolerance between Protestants and Catholics. The former believe that the fundamentals of Christianity are not to be found in the Roman Church except accompanied by a dangerous poison; while the latter are convinced that in denying the infallibility of the Roman Catholic Church, the Protestants destroy the very basis of Christianity. In despair Bayle concludes: "Each side uses the dictionary to suit its fancy in beginning to seize upon this hypothesis: 'I am right and you are wrong,' which is to throw the world into a chaos more frightful than that of Ovid." [31]

Jurieu never answered the *Janua coelorum reserata* except to cite it contemptuously in his *Seconde apologie*. Because of Bayle's *Pensées sur les comètes*, Jurieu was instrumental in having him deprived of his position at the Ecole Illustre in 1693, as we noted earlier.[32] It is little wonder that Bayle exclaimed at this time, "God deliver us from the Protestant inquisition; it will be so dreadful in five or six years that one will long

---

savoir l'histoire & le progrés de cette opinion la gloire de l'invention appartient aux Sociniens. Ceux-ci à la vérité ne conviennent pas avec les autres Chrétiens sur les articles fondamentaux: car ils n'en nottent que deux, l'unité de Dieu & la Mission de Jésus Christ. Mais ils disent que tous ceux qui les professent avec des moeurs convenables à cette profession sont vrais membres de l'Eglise universelle; & que les dogmes qu'on surajoute à ce fondement n'empêchent pas le salut." *Histoire des variations des Eglises protestantes*, II, Chap. XV, 392. For further evidence of the Socinian leaven among Catholics in France see the Abbé Louis de Cordemoy, *Traité contre les sociniens*, 1697, and *L'Eternité des peines de l'enfer contre les Sociniens*, 1707. Aubert de Versé returning to Rome wrote *L'Anti-Socinien, ou, Nouvelle apologie de la foi Catholique, contre les Sociniens et les Calvinistes*, 1692.

[31] *Commentaire philosophique*, in *Oeuvres diverses*, 1737, II, 421–422.

[32] See Bayle's letter to Minutoli of March 2, 1694, in *ibid.*, IV, 707–709.

for the Roman as after a blessing."[33] Certainly Jurieu was coming
around to the point of censoring even conversations, contending that one
should not wait to act until heresies had been preached or written.[34] In
fact his enemies compared him with Ishmael, whose hand was against
everyone and the hand of all against him.[35]

Even after Bayle was deprived of his teaching position, Jurieu continued to attack his former friend. In 1697, he condemned the *Dictionnaire historique et critique* with his *Jugement du public et particulièrement de l'Abbé Renaudot sur le Dictionnaire de M. Bayle*.[36] It is curi-
ous to see the staunch Calvinist Jurieu supplementing the French Catholic Abbé Renaudot, to whom the duty of censor of the *Dictionnaire*
had been intrusted and whose negative decision prevented the publication of Bayle's great work in France. Religion as well as politics makes
strange bedfellows. A few months before Bayle's death in 1706, Jurieu
published a final condemnation of his former colleague and friend in
Le Philosophe de Rotterdam accusé, atteint, et convaincu. In this libel
Jurieu goes so far as to approve the attacks upon Bayle by Jacques Bernard, Isaac Jaquelot, and Jean Le Clerc, even though these men had
been his deadly enemies on the question of tolerance and, in Jaquelot's
case, on the issue of resistance to France and her ruler as well. The usual
accusations of atheism are made from an analysis of writings like the
Pensées sur les comètes and the *Commentaire philosophique*. So ended
a dispute, which not only was instrumental in pushing the orthodox
Protestants into abandoning the doctrine of the visible church but also in
hastening the dissolution of Protestant orthodoxy itself.

[33] See Bayle's letter of December 17, 1691, to M. Silvestre in *ibid.*, 671.
[34] See the *Examen de la doctrine de M. Jurieu pour servir de réponse à un libelle intitulé
Seconde apologie de M. Jurieu*, 1691, which was probably written by Basnage de Beauval,
p. 29. Cf. *Apologie du Sieur Jurieu*: "Il en est de l'Eglise comme de l'Etat. On n'attend pas
à découvrir une conjuration qu'elle soit achevée & mise en évidence. On l'arrête des les
commencements. L'hérésie & la conduite des Hérétiques est une vraye conspiration contre
la vérité. C'est une negligence criminelle d'attendre à s'en plaindre que le mal soit entièrement formé."
[35] "Cependant il (Jurieu) fait toutes les fonctions d'un Inquisiteur Général . . . Il allume
la dissention en tous les lieux: il met tout en combustion, il arme les Eglises les unes contre
les autres . . . il est toujours l'aggresseur & au lieu d'emploier ce qui reste de forces contre
l'ennemi commun, il les consume à persécuter ses collègues & à exciter des guerres civiles
au milieu de nous. Jurieu a converti la Religion en Fanatisme & livre le Christianisme pieds
& poins liez aux Libertins & aux impies." *Examen de la doctrine de Mr. Jurieu*, p. 6.
[36] Bayle answered this in 1697 with *Réflexions sur un imprimé qui a pour titre Jugement.*

We have already mentioned Jurieu's controversy with Noel Aubert de Versé, who was an intimate of a certain Isaac Papin. It was with this nephew of Claude Pajon that Jurieu had an especially bitter quarrel. Papin's *Essais de théologie sur la providence et sur la grâce où l'on tâche de délivrer M. Jurieu de toutes les difficultés accablantes qu'il rencontre dans son système* (1687) was a refutation of two works of our theologian, his *Jugement sur les méthodes rigides et relâchées d'expliquer la providence et la grâce* and *Traité de la nature et de la grâce; ou, Du concours générale de la providence et du concours particulier de la grâce efficace contre les nouvelles hypothèses de M. Pajon et de ses disciples.* But this was only a dispute over grace, which, although dangerous to the truth, did not shake the very fundamentals of the faith. It was the appearance in the same year, however, of a second book by Papin, *La Foi réduite à ses véritables principes et renfermée dans ses véritables bornes,* with a preface by Bayle, which stirred Jurieu into action. Both the book and the author were condemned by the Synod of The Hague in 1688. His objections to this treatise were set forth two years later in a *Lettre pastorale aux fidèles de Paris,* and in the *Factum de l'affaire de Monsieur de la Conseillère.*[37] In the latter tract Jurieu maintains that Papin's purpose is to establish universal toleration all the way from Catholics to Socinians. He contends that Papin claims that in order to be saved it is enough to believe that Jesus Christ is dead; that He is risen and ascended into heaven; that the dead will arise; and that Christ will return to judge the living and the dead, rendering to each according to his works. This is to demand no more as a basis for the faith than the Socinians. One is not obliged to believe that God is infinite; that man is born in original sin; that without the grace of God men can accomplish nothing; that Jesus Christ is God, equal to His father; that there are three persons in the divinity; and that Jesus Christ died for our sins in order to demonstrate the justice of God. On the contrary, Papin maintained that one needs to regard as fundamental only what is in Scripture in express terms. At this point Jurieu observed that Papin was pretending to be relying on the general principle of all Protestants, namely that Christians need only receive as articles of faith those things which are in the Bible. This

37 M. de la Conseillère is accused by Jurieu of maintaining the same principles as Papin. Cf. M. de la Conseillère, *Factum de M. de la Conseillère, demandeur, en réparation contre M. Jurieu défendeur,* 1690.

conception has been employed ever since the Reformation against the Catholics, who relied so extensively upon ecclesiastical tradition. But, retorts Jurieu, "this principle has nothing in common with that of M. Papin, who claims that one is only bound to hold as an article of faith the express words of Scripture without any interpretation and that each person is permitted to construe these words as he thinks proper [38] . . . a doctrine as pernicious as ours is excellent." [39] Jurieu feared that once the principle that nothing is fundamental which is not clearly revealed in Scripture is granted, there would be no limit to the variety of interpretations and variations of faith. Bossuet, of course, in his *Histoire des variations des Eglises protestantes* used this argument against the very principles of the Reformation itself. As Richard Simon observed at the time of the condemnation of D'Huisseau, many Protestants were convinced that Calvin and the other original Reformers had only established a "demi-Reformation." [40]

But even more dangerous in Jurieu's mind was the tendency in Papin to regard the great mysteries of Christianity, such as the Trinity and the Incarnation, as obscurely revealed in Scripture. This opinion drives men either to Catholicism,[41] where there is a visible authority to determine these matters, or to complete religious indifference. But to Jurieu, "the word of God is clear as to these articles as the sun. If in Scripture one finds difficulties, it is not necessary to advance proofs against the mysteries. One should explain these perplexities and in truth these difficulties are only great in minds prejudiced by heresy." [42]

But if the obstacles in the way of finding the truth were not numerous according to Jurieu, the number of heretics was increasing in spite of the attempt to enforce orthodoxy by the Synodal Act of Uniformity

---

[38] Cf. Hobbes, *Behemoth*, in *Works*, VI, 190: "After the Bible was translated into English, every man, nay every boy and wench that could read English, thought they spoke with God Almighty . . . and every man became a judge of religion and an interpreter of the Scriptures himself."

[39] *Lettre pastorale aux fidèles de Paris*, p. 9.

[40] Richard Simon, *Lettres choisies*, III, 13.

[41] This was the result in Papin's own case. In his answer to Jurieu in *La Tolérance des protestants et l'autorité de l'Eglise,* Papin argued that the principle of free examination of Protestantism leads inevitably to the toleration of all sects. Universal tolerance in turn results in the destruction of Christianity. Therefore, the Reformation ends in the ruin of Christianity. Consequently Catholic Christianity must be intolerant.

[42] *Lettre pastorale aux fidèles de Paris*, pp. 13–16.

of 1686. As a result, in August, 1690, the Synod of Amsterdam attempted once again to conserve orthodoxy by condemning a list of nine heretical propositions.[43] In that same year, Jurieu himself marshaled in his *Tableau du socinianisme* all the possible arguments against the onrushing tide of universal tolerance of all sects and the mounting wave of religious indifference. This was the spirit and design of those disciples of Socinus and Episcopius [44] whose Pelagian attack upon the orthodox doctrine of grace was but a screen for much more heretical views—views that endanger Christianity itself. Furthermore, as we have noted before, in Jurieu's opinion, wherever Arminianism has penetrated, Socinianism [45] had also become established. This is due to the attitude of tolerance on the part of Arminians for heretical sects in which it is believed men could be saved. But it must be remembered, however, that the term Socinian should be used with caution. At this time it was a term of reproach which often corresponded to no definite theological conception. Any innovation was likely to be labeled as Socinianism. In fact, it may be said that in the late seventeenth century the term had connotations similar to those of the word communism in the mouth of a member of the middle class today.

This idea of universal civil tolerance was so distasteful to Jurieu that

---

[43] 1) Que le Socinianisme est une Religion tolérable et dans laquelle on se peut sauver 2) Que l'on se peut sauver en toutes Religions à la faveur de la bonne foy ou de la bonne intention. 3) Qu'on ne pêche point en suivant les mouvements de sa conscience quelque mauvais que soit l'action. 4) Qu'il n'y a point d'autre hérétiques que ceux qui combattent la vérité contre leur conscience. 5) Qu'on n'est point blasphémateur si l'on ne blasphème contre ses propres principes. 6) Que la piété et la raison obligent à la Tolérance tant civile qu'ecclésiastique de toutes les hérésies. 7) Que le Magistrat n'est point en droit d'employer son authorité pour abattre l'idolatrie et empêcher le progrès de l'hérésie. 8) Que tout particulier a droit non seulement de croire mais aussi d'enseigner tout ce qu'il veut sans que le souverain magistrat le puisse empêcher. 9) Que la grace consiste uniquement dans le proposition de la parole et il n'y a point d'opération interne du Saint Esprit." These theses, which Jurieu was commissioned to draw up, are printed in his *Tableau du Socinianisme,* p. 565.

[44] Jurieu marks Episcopius as "le plus dangereux ennemi de la Religion chrétienne & de ses mystères qui ait paru dans notre siècle." Cf. the Arminian answer to this accusation by Jean Le Clerc in his *Lettre à M. Jurieu sur la manière dont il traite Episcopius dans son tableau du socinianisme,* 1690.

[45] The defense of Socinianism was undertaken by Isaac Jaquelot in the *Avis sur le tableau du socinianisme,* 1690. Jacques Philipot answered Jaquelot with his *Les Justes Bornes de la tolérance,* 1691. Socinianism can be defined as a supernatural rationalism or as a rational supernaturalism, leading to freedom, reason, and tolerance in religion. See Wilbur, *History of Unitarianism,* pp. 5, 586.

he regarded anyone who upheld it as suspected of heterodoxy upon that basis alone. Furthermore, he believed that the advocates of civil tolerance are the same as the defenders of ecclesiastical latitude, since religious indifference is the real aim of both. As in the sixteenth century, the problem of mutual toleration among the various sects was closely linked with the question of the acceptance of diversity of religious belief by the civil authorities.

Jurieu begins his argument in the *Tableau* by stating the various views of those who advocated this hateful toleration.[46] The magistrate should not meddle in the affairs of religion, since men are associated in civil society under rulers not in order to be constrained in their consciences, which belong to God alone, but solely for temporal considerations. By toleration alone can peace be secured in civil society; for if each man is free in his religious beliefs he will work for the conservation of the government which grants him that peace. If the truth has the right to suppress error forcibly, then error will have the same right against the truth.[47] If heretics are persecuted, then how can the Huguenots complain of their treatment, since the King of France believes he has the true religion? Error, whether in the form of Socinianism or Catholicism, can only be combated by preaching and reasoning. All these arguments are the result of the advantage taken of his own liberal stand on the question, contended Jurieu. He admits that he had asserted that the death penalty should not usually be meted out to heretics, except in a case like Servetus, and that conscience should not be constrained. But our theologian never expressed anything but horror for the belief that society has been formed exclusively for temporal interests and not primarily for God and His glory. The magistrates are the protectors of the church as well as the temporal state. They have the care over the purity of souls as well as the conservation of the body. Nothing contributes more to this end—the glory of God—than the protection of the true

---

[46] Jurieu condemns the *Epistola de tolerantia* by Locke, thinking from the analysis of it in the *Histoire des ouvrages des savants* of September, 1689, pp. 20–26, that M. Bernard was the author.

[47] Cf. Locke in his second *Letter concerning Toleration*, VI, 64: "The truth would certainly do well enough if she were left to shift for herself. She seldom has received and, I fear, never will receive, much assistance from the power of great men . . . If truth makes not her way into the understanding by her own light, she will be but weaker for any borrowed force violence can add to her."

religion and the destruction of idolatry. The toleration of a damnable heresy means an attitude of indifference toward religion, a belief that all cults are agreeable to God.

But the advocates of toleration, complains Jurieu, equate "persecution and restraint," yet these are entirely different. Forced confessions and corporal punishments are forbidden, but in general the treatment of Catholics in Protestant countries like Holland is permissible in his theory. This treatment included the denial of the liberty of the public exercise of their religion and the privilege of holding public office. In other places Catholics are prohibited from having priests or from dogmatizing on their religion. But in depriving heretics of the privileges which other subjects enjoy, everything can be removed except "what belongs to them . . . by the law of nations and nature; liberty, life, children are among those things which must not be taken away from them." [48] If heretics assemble and dogmatize in spite of the prohibition of the magistrate, then he has the power to impose corporal punishment upon them for violating his laws. In this case they are punished not as heretics but as disturbers of the public peace. If, however, a whole society of heretics were to assemble against the command of the prince, such extreme measures would be unwarranted, because of the difference between societies and individuals. All this is but an elaboration of ideas Jurieu had presented earlier.

In general, it can be said, continued Jurieu, that the magistrate is the absolute master of the degree of toleration to be shown toward heretics. This is a secular concern. The church can only advise in the matter, since its jurisdiction extends only to ecclesiastical toleration. There are occasions when intolerance can cause more evil to the church than a moderate degree of sufferance. It would be foolish, in order to secure a small benefit for the church by intolerance of heretics, to affect thereby the state adversely. "As the magistrate is born the father of the state and the church, he should weigh the interest of each and not destroy the state against its proper and true concerns to satisfy the church. Because when the state is demolished, it is impossible that the church should not be buried beneath its ruins." Thus the magistrate can tolerate heretics for reasons of conscience or for reasons of state. In the latter case, which

[48] *Tableau du socinianisme*, pp. 413–425.

is that of the Huguenots, they were tolerated in France "by means of authority"; that is, by edicts, privileges, and treaties, but Catholics are tolerated in Holland only "by means of connivance," [49] since the laws of the state do not permit the exercise of their religion, nor are they permitted to hold public office in the state.

For over a century, declares Jurieu, the question of the power of the sovereign magistrate in the affairs of the church has been hotly debated. On the one side the Pope has completely deprived kings of power over ecclesiastical matters, while on the other the Presbyterians, by removing the ecclesiastical jurisdiction not only from the Pope but also from the bishops, have transferred it entirely to the Presbytery and Synods. In fact, without their direction the magistrate cannot act in religious concerns. Now the separation of the ecclesiastical and secular fields along the lines of the theory of Pope Gelasius in the fifth century had been adopted in England not only by the Calvinists but also by the Jesuits. In fact James I had gone so far as to declare that "Jesuits are nothing but Puritan-papists." [50] This very claim of an ecclesiastical independence from the authority of the civil government "is the special contribution of Presbyterianism to the theory of political freedom." [51] Both these groups, Jesuit and Presbyterian in England and Counter-Remonstrant in Holland, which held that the church and the state were collateral or coordinate, granted the secular authority the power to punish dissidents. But the Remonstrants or Arminians and the Socinian groups proclaimed the superiority of the state over the church, while at the same time they accompanied their Erastianism with the principle of religious tolerance. It is interesting to note further that intolerance was the motive even of Anabaptists or collegialists in desiring separation of church and state.

Jurieu reacted against collateralism, tending toward an Erastian view that the prince was born the chief of the church as well as of civil society. In his plan for the reunion of the Calvinist and Lutheran churches, his method of realizing this accord was to employ the authority of the princes of each party, since the very Reformation itself was accomplished

[49] *Ibid.*, pp. 426–434.
[50] "A Premonition to all Most Mightie Monarchies," in *The Political Works of James I,* ed. McIlwain, p. 126.
[51] Harold J. Laski, *Studies in the Problem of Sovereignty,* p. 49.

by their power.[52] He expresses surprise that the advocates of tolerance, drawn mostly from the Arminians, do not approve of the interference by the magistrate in matters of heresy. In fact, the Arminians, when in the ascendancy in the early part of the century,[53] had no scruples against using the authority of the magistrate to control differences of religion even in doctrinal matters.[54] It was the authority of Grotius,[55] however, that Jurieu employs at great length in order to support his Erastian position. He refers to the posthumous work, *De imperio summarum potestatum circa sacra* (1646), in which Grotius showed that magistrates have power equally over ecclesiastical and civil affairs. Jurieu asserted that he had two reasons for giving a close analysis of this book.[56] First, Grotius was the idol of the Remonstrants, who advocate toleration, and in addition Grotius himself was indifferent to religion. Second, his posi-

[52] Speaking of union he writes: "Primo hoc magnum opus nec incipi nec perfici potest sine consensu, auxilio . . . Principum Protestantium utriusque partis . . . Omnis reformatio in Ecclesia facta est Authoritate principum nec sine iis ulla spes est tantum opus perficiendi." Jurieu, *De pace inter protestantes ineunda consultatio*, Part II, Chap. XII, pp. 260–263. Bossuet in an addition to Book XIV of his *Histoire des variations* concludes that princes are made sovereign arbiters of religion and judges of the essentials of the faith.

[53] A law of the Estates of Holland of January, 1614, which was obtained by the Arminian party is cited. Grotius had added notes to this decree.

[54] But as Jordan shows in his *Development of Religious Toleration in England*, II, 457: "Erastianism was a sword which could be wielded to cut both ways. The government could arrogate religious power to itself to extirpate heresy, control morals and advance the true faith; or it could, quite as logically, once the basis of its sovereignty had been granted, frame and enforce an ecclesiastical order which would impose a tolerant and comprehensive system, employing coercion against those individuals or sects which refused to abandon the ancient ideal of religious uniformity." Jurieu would fall in the first case and Grotius in the second. As Figgis states in his *Divine Right of Kings*, p. 318, "A great deal of so-called Erastianism is little more than the extravagant support of the one power that could carry through or maintain the particular religious views of the writer."

[55] "Comme Grotius est devenu depuis quelque temps le grand auteur de M. Jurieu & son oracle dans le droit civil qu'il prend toujours pour modèle du droit ecclésiastique." Elie Saurin, *Réflexions sur un libelle intitulé Information pour nos seigneurs les états*, 1692.

[56] Jurieu's summary of the *De imperio* is to be found on pp. 467–477 of his *Tableau*. Figgis points out in his *Divine Right of Kings*, p. 311: "Grotius, however, like Erastus is guarded. He will grant to the magistrate no power to contradict the word of God, to promulgate new articles of faith, or to prohibit preaching or the sacraments. This would assuredly have seemed a poor and ecclesiastical view to Hobbes and perhaps Selden. Further, Grotius though he cites many supporters . . . does not cite Erastus nor do the views of the two about excommunication agree." See also Edward A. Whitney. "Erastianism and Divine Right," *Huntington Library Quarterly*, July, 1939. Also as McNeill puts it in *Unitive Protestantism*, pp. 263–264, "there is, of course, a world of difference between the theocratic Erastianism of Zwingli, Erastus, and Hooker and the secular Erastianism of Hobbes and the Enlightened Despots, for whom not only the church organization but religion itself is subordinated to the omnicompetent state."

tion is the same as that of the states in Holland which control the orthodox church. Although they may tolerate other sects "by connivance," it
is never according to the principle of universal civil tolerance. From
Grotius, reason, and usage, Jurieu concludes "that the magistrate has
the right to settle religious disputes; that dogma only has the force of
law in a country when it is upheld by the authority of the sovereign;
that the magistrate is the director of ecclesiastical affairs; that he should
establish by his authority the religion which he prefers; that he has the
power to expel and banish the religions which offend him; and that he
has inspection over the elections and expulsions of ministers, so that in-
trigue, favor, and passion do not enter there; in a word, that he is bound
to watch over the eternal salvation of the community as well as its temporal well being and the former more than the latter." [57]

It was objected that if the sovereign magistrate is the master of religion in a country, then the state would change its religion with every
new prince. Of course, this would not matter if the new ruler were of the
true faith, but what if he should be an idolater, a pagan, or a heretic?
After Grotius, Jurieu responds that no form of government, ecclesiastical or temporal, is free from inconveniences; but "that should one
abandon the disposition of religion to the people, one would see what
would happen. This monster of a hundred heads would create as many
religions." [58] If, on the other hand, the ordering of religions is turned
over to the clergy to the exclusion of the ruler, one has only to look at the
history of Catholicism to see the sad results. By giving this power to
the sovereign magistrate Jurieu insisted that he did not wish to exclude
the people or their rights: "We do not say that one man, because he is
king and assumes absolute power, has the authority to destroy the temporal and eternal welfare of his people. It is necessary, then, for changing
a religion that a country have the consent of the people, tacit or formal:

[57] *Le Tableau du socinianisme,* pp. 461–481. Cf. Jurieu's reply to Maimbourg, who had objected to the action of the Senate of Zurich in judging ecclesiastical affairs and in establishing the Reformation there. Also Jurieu asserts that the Gallican church does not receive the decrees of the Council of Trent because the king and the *parlements* refuse their
consent. *Histoire du calvinisme et celle du papisme,* II, 16–20. Jurieu applies here the
principle of *cuis regio eius religio,* which in the sixteenth century had a far wider application than to German states or to Lutheranism alone. It was the theory not only of the
English settlement of religion but also lay behind the French maxim, "une loi, une foi,
un roi."
[58] *Tableau du socinianisme,* p. 491.

tacit, when the people lets the prince do it and does not stand in the way; formal, when the estates and the wise men of a country are assembled and religion is altered with their approval." It was in this manner that the Reformation took place in England, Scotland, Sweden, Denmark, Switzerland, Holland, and Germany.[59] But if a prince should become a heretic and desire to change the true religion, he can be opposed legitimately.[60] "The right of conservation itself is inalienable and above the right of kings.[61] . . . But the preservation of the soul is more precious than that of the body." [62] Thus, the king has no right to damn his subjects, but if in agreement with him they choose a false religion, then Jurieu admits no one has the right to resist their decision. God, however, will be the judge in the end.

This is the same type of argument that Jurieu already had employed in his answer to Maimbourg, who had condemned the Calvinists in Scotland for establishing the Reformation by force of arms against the will of the sovereign. But, contended Jurieu, it is absurd to imagine that the nobility and the people of a whole realm do not have the right to change their religion simply because the ruler is unwilling. Should a people bring damnation on itself and act against conscience in order to obey a single man? Suppose either England or Sweden by unanimous consent of their peoples decided to return to Catholicism, would the king alone have the right to oppose and to check the determination of the whole realm? "A prince represents the people and speaks for the people and has no other rights than those which the people have ceded to him. When the greatest and sanest part of the people [63] desires a religion, the prince should consent to it or at least not oppose its establishment, for this is according to the law of nations." [64] Furthermore, when a Catholic prince persecutes the true religion, he does it on the basis of

---

[59] Although in France the Reformation came about without royal assistance, nevertheless, "elle ne s'est point établie sans l'authorité des grands." *Ibid.*, pp. 484–508.

[60] Cf. the *Examen d'un libelle*, p. 151: "Les peuples n'ont pas le droit de s'opposer aux princes qui veulent établir la vraie religion."

[61] This is following Grotius.

[62] *Tableau du socinianisme*, pp. 491–492.

[63] Cf. however Jurieu's opinion in his *Examen d'un libelle* that an unjust judgment did not become just simply because it had the authority of a majority behind it. But at least the majority here is qualified along the lines of the medieval *major et sanior pars* of a cathedral chapter.

[64] *Histoire du calvinisme*, II, 79–81.

faulty information, received from wicked and blind ecclesiastics, who refuse to examine the question upon the rules which the Reformation demands, namely, the word of God. To Jurieu, as to Calvin, those who do not accept Calvinism are either knaves or fools. In fact, when Calvinists say to Catholics " 'You are wrong because we know we are right' they really mean 'You are wrong, because you know we are right.' " [65]

Now the advocates of tolerance claimed that it was not diversity of religions in a state which disturbed the peace, but intolerance. In reply, Jurieu asserted that in order to have universal tolerance there must be universal indifference, that is, the belief that one can be saved in all religions, whether good or bad. Only then can there really be any peace between different religions. So long as the Catholics and Socinians regard each other as damned,[66] it is impossible to have tranquility.[67] Jurieu declared that the peace in Holland, where so many sects live side by side, is not due to a policy of toleration, but because, in spite of it, the Reformed religion is the dominant one and the various sects are suppressed.

In addition to a consideration of the political or civil aspects of tolerance, Jurieu once more summarizes in the *Tableau* his objections to Bayle's *Commentaire philosophique* but has added nothing really new

[65] Allen, *History of Political Thought in the Sixteenth Century*, p. 86. See *Tableau du socinianisme*, pp. 319–336: "L'erreur aussi bien que le crime est un effet de la cupidité & d'une cupidité à laquelle notre volonté consente librement. Les lumières de l'Ecriture Sainte & même celles de la nature seroient suffisantes si les hommes n'étoient pas negligens ou aveuglés par leur passions." Cf. Niebuhr, *The Nature and Destiny of Man*, Vol. II: *Human Destiny*, p. 231: "The authority of the Bible was used to break the proud authority of the Church; whereupon the Bible became another instrument of human pride." And *ibid.*, Vol. I: *Human Nature*, p. 202: "The fact is that the Protestant doctrine of the priesthood of all believers may result in an individual self-deification against which Catholic doctrine has more adequate checks."

[66] Jurieu had conceived earlier of a reunion between the Calvinist and Gallican churches "par voye de tolérance mutuelle, C'est à dire que sans partir de sa place on se considéreroit mutuellement avec charité & l'on ne se damneroit pas de pleine autorité comme on fait." *Préservatif contre le changement de religion*, 1680, p. 33.

[67] See the interesting discussion in Rousseau's *Social Contract*, Bk. IV, Chap. VIII, pp. 121–122. "Those who distinguish civil from ecclesiastical intolerance are to my mind mistaken. The two forms are inseparable. It is impossible to live at peace with those we regard as damned; to love them would be to hate God who punishes them; we positively must either reclaim or torment them. Whenever theological intolerance is admitted it must inevitably have some civil effect and as soon as it has such an effect the Sovereign is no longer Sovereign even in the temporal sphere; thenceforth, priests are the real masters and kings only their ministers."

in the way of argument. He cites the *Lettre écrite de Suisse en Hollande* by Gédéon Huet as simply an abridgment of Bayle on the rights of the erring conscience, in spite of the fact that Huet in his *Apologie pour les vrais tolérants* attempted in vain to defend himself by contending that he did not understand that the erring conscience had the same rights as the truth "in relation to grace and eternal life but only with regard to persecution." [68]

Besides a refutation of Bayle and Huet in his *Tableau,* Jurieu also answered the arguments of Episcopius for the toleration of Socinianism. The first contention of Episcopius had been that since the mysteries of the Trinity, the Incarnation, and Satisfaction are not clearly revealed in Scripture, it is not necessary to accept them. Now Jurieu agreed with the general proposition that one need not believe anything which has not been revealed at all. It is necessary, however, to receive things that may have been only obscurely disclosed. In this connection the criteria are the importance of the truths and their relation to eternal salvation. Although it is a Protestant principle that everything essential to salvation is contained in Scripture, Jurieu maintains once again that this never implied that a truth had to be found there in express words. Since God never intended to extend his grace to every man, he has purposely left certain parts of his revelation obscure. But the elect will be able to discover the articles necessary for salvation as announced in the Holy Word.

But the great argument of Episcopius for tolerating the Socinians was the variance among the ancient doctors concerning the mystery of the Trinity and the Incarnation. This proves that the doctrine is not certain. Moreover, if the ancients have differed and erred on this mystery and have been tolerated, then why cannot indulgence be extended to the Socinians today? [69] Now Jurieu could have very easily refuted this reasoning by claiming that the faith had never varied if it had not been for the appearance in 1688 of Bossuet's magistral *Histoire des variations des églises protestantes.* In fact, in his *Le Vray Système de l'église,* which he had published in 1686, Jurieu himself had held that the church had

<hr />

[68] *Le Tableau du socinianisme,* pp. 319–336.
[69] This conclusion was cogently presented by Bayle in his *Janua coelorum resserata,* Part II, Section VII, No. XXVII, in *Oeuvres diverses,* 1737, II, 844–846.

never varied in the fundamental articles.[70] At that time he had contended that one of the characteristics of a fundamental truth was the fact that it had always been recognized with no aberrations. But after the publication of the *Histoire des variations,* Jurieu altered his principle. In order to justify the mutations of the Protestants, which Bossuet had pointed out at great length, it was necessary to find them in the ancient church, even in the essential or fundamental articles of the faith.

The thesis of Bossuet's attack on the Protestants was that variations in the exposition of the faith are a mark of falsity and that, from the very first, (Catholic) truth came from God in its perfection. On this basis Bossuet proceeded to condemn the Protestants for their innumerable deviations. But Jurieu, possibly because of his conception of the church as including all sects which retain the fundamentals,[71] was prepared to deny constancy as a necessary criterion of religious truth. Certainly before the appearance of the *Variations* both Catholics [72] and Protestants had insisted upon the principle of invariability and perpetuity of doctrine and faith. In fact, Jurieu himself in his earlier *Lettres pastorales* had attempted to show that modern Catholics had forsaken the doctrine of the primitive church. In his last important writing, *Histoire critique des dogmes et des cultes* (1704), Jurieu went so far as to claim that even the fathers of the church were heretics according to existing Catholic orthodoxy. Certainly, then, it is justifiable, as we noted before, to regard Bossuet's epoch-making book as one of the important factors in the evolution of Protestant controversy after 1688.[73]

In his reply to Bossuet, Jurieu declared that no group had varied more than the Catholics and that there had been many variations in the doctrine of the Christian church from the very beginning. Even the most essential doctrines of Christianity up until the fourth and fifth century of the church changed in form and exterior. Instead of arriving in perfection, the truth of God has been disclosed only in parts. These revelations were not perfectly understood until after the labors of several centuries; and heretics had helped to perfect the knowledge of the divine

---

[70] *Le Vray Système de l'église,* pp. 253 ff., 256 ff., 296–298, 453.

[71] Rébelliau, *Bossuet historien du protestantisme,* pp. 544 ff.

[72] See Antoine Arnauld and Pierre Nicole, *La Perpétuité de la foy de l'Eglise catholique touchant l'eucharistie,* 1664.

[73] Rébelliau, *Bossuet,* pp. 550–551.

truths. This was especially true of the mysteries of the Trinity and the Incarnation. The former dogma remained unformed until after the first Council of Nicea and even until that of Constantinople. The truth, therefore, only reached its final form by a long and attentive reading of Holy Scripture.[74] Consequently, it is not necessary to tolerate in modern times what was suffered in ancient.

The advocates of tolerance were quick to take advantage of the variations of the ancients. They argued that the mysteries of the Trinity and the Incarnation were not so clearly couched in Scripture as had been claimed, since the first fathers of the church had differed over them. Thus, in introducing the Cartesian idea of progress and evolution into theology in order to oppose Bossuet, Jurieu found himself caught between the great Gallican and libertines like Bayle.[75] Jurieu hastened to maintain that the ancient fathers had not varied in the essential parts of these mysteries, which proves that Scripture is clear on these articles. Moreover, he distinguished the faith of simple persons from the theology of teachers. The faith of the former never has deviated from the fundamental articles of the Christian religion.[76] But the doctors have created a theology which is an explication of the mysteries beyond that given in Scripture. In these explanations they have differed, since they employed a false philosophy which entered into their theology. Articles of faith must never, therefore, be made out of theological interpretations. Thus, with the attack of the advocates of tolerance Jurieu is forced to retreat in his assault on Bossuet. He must now hold that the church has varied in the elucidation of certain mysteries but that fundamentally the mysteries have remained unchanged as revealed.[77]

[74] "Ainsi la Théologie Chrétienne s'est assurément perfectionnée avec le temps & par l'étude comme toutes les autres sciences." *Lettres pastorales,* VII of the Third Year, pp. 145–152. It was in the Sixth and Seventh *Letters* dated November 15 and December 1, 1688, that Jurieu made his general observations on this principle of variation, but the answer to the book of Bossuet extended through the Eleventh *Letter* of February 1, 1689.
[75] See Alfred Rébelliau, "Les Affaires Religieuses, 1683–1715," in Ernest Lavisse, *Histoire de France,* VIII, 407–408.
[76] *Apologie pour le sieur Jurieu,* p. 17.
[77] *Le Tableau du socinianisme,* Lettre VI, Article 4: "Examen du I Avertissement de Bossuet," pp. 277–310. The title of the Sixth *Letter* was as follows: "Dissertation pour éclaircir la Théologie des Pères qui ont précédé le Concile de Nicée, sur le Mystère de la Trinité & celui de la Génération du fils contre les Sociniens, les Tolérants, M. l'Evêque de Meaux & l'auteur de l'histoire des ouvrages des savants." Jurieu answered the *Premier Avertissement aux protestants sur les Lettres du Ministre Jurieu contre L'Histoire des vari-*

Bossuet's conclusion to the whole question presents a succinct summary of both sides.

Thus the state, in which the Protestant party finds itself, is that the intolerant and the tolerant alike are pushed to the last absurdities, each according to his principles. The tolerant wish to conserve the liberty of their opinions and remain free of any kind of authority capable of restraining them, which, in effect, is the true spirit of the Reformation and the charm which so many people attribute to it; Mr. Jurieu pushes them as far as indifference toward religion.[78] On the other hand, in spite of the maxims of the Reformation, this minister feels the need of a constraining authority on earth and not being able to find it in the interior of his church or in its synods, he is forced to resort to that of the princes and at the same time that the advocates of tolerance drive him from precept to precept to the most odious and discredited excesses in the Reformation.[79]

In addition to these criticisms of Bossuet, there was an extensive attack upon Jurieu's *Tableau du socinianisme* by Gédéon Huet in his *Apologie pour les vrais tolérants. Pour opposer aux fausses idées que M. J. en a voulu donner dans quelques uns de ses écrits; mais particulierement dans son Tableau du socinianisme.*[80] The principal contention of Huet was that fundamentally the source of all his ideas on tolerance is to be found, strange as it might seem, in the writings of Jurieu himself. The error of Jurieu was simply that he had confused, in Huet's mind, tolerance with religious indifference. Toleration signifies nothing

ations in Article 4 as we have just noted above. He was especially irritated at Henri Basnage de Beauval for his favorable review of *Quatre Avertissements aux protestants sur les Lettres du Ministre Jurieu contre L'Histoire des variations* in his *Histoire des ouvrages des savants* for May, 1690. It should be noted also that Beauval had written a treatise in 1684 on the *Tolérance des religions* which had aroused the anger of the orthodox Jurieu. According to Puaux, this is the first book in which the word tolerance appeared in the title. Beauval answered the attack in the Sixth *Letter* of the *Tableau* in his journal for July, 1690, p. 501. Bossuet's reply to the Sixth and Seventh *Letters* of the *Tableau* is contained in the *Sixième Avertissement aux Protestants.*

[78] Jurieu's principal method of attack on these moderates who believed in a limited tolerance was to insist that there could be no half measures which would exclude the toleration of atheists, Mahommedans, pagans, and Socinians. This was a position from which many honest men shrank at the time, including even John Locke, who would not tolerate atheists since "promises, covenants, and oathes, which are the bonds of human society, can have no hold on an atheist." See his *Letter concerning Toleration* in *Works*, VI, 47.

[79] *Sixième Avertissement aux protestants*, p. 255.

[80] See also Isaac Jaquelot, *Avis sur le Tableau du socinianisme*, 1690, and the anonymous *Lettre d'un intolérant à un théologien intolérant aussi*, 1690, and Huet's *Apologie pour L'Apologiste des tolérants*, 1690.

more or less than impunity. It is at best a half measure, since it implies
that what is tolerated is of its very nature bad.[81] It is entirely otherwise
with indifference; there it is to be inferred that the things among which
a choice is to be made are equally good and salutary. Furthermore, there
are two types of toleration—ecclesiastical and civil. How, asks Huet,
can Jurieu oppose the latter when he himself favors a reconciliation of
Lutheran and Calvinist in the same religious communion, in which case
the spirit of indulgence would be much more dangerous than in political society.[82] Jurieu is only justified in opposing "the indifferent," who
believe that salvation can be obtained in all religions, but not "the truly
tolerant," who advocate a purely civil toleration. Ironically enough, the
latter oppose the Protestant inquisitors, such as Jurieu, with the very
same arguments which he himself employs in his attack upon the Catholic persecutors.

Huet concludes from this, as did Bayle in the *Réponse d'un nouveau
converti à une lettre d'un réfugié,* that either all power of constraining
heretics must be relinquished or the Catholic solution of punishment
according to the gravity of the case must be accepted. Jurieu's half measure of a toleration which forbade the death penalty for heresy is shown
to be untenable logically. There can be no middle ground between an
extreme severity against and an extreme support of heresy.[83] If, as Jurieu

[81] On this point compare Thomas Paine's *Rights of Man,* p. 325 in Vol. II of his *Writings:*
"Toleration is not the opposite of intolerance but is the counterfeit of it. Both are despotisms.
The one assumes to itself the rights of withholding liberty of conscience and the other
of granting it. The one is the Pope armed with fire and faggot and the other is the Pope
selling or granting indulgences. The former is church and state and the latter is church
and traffic." Mirabeau also distinguished liberty and tolerance when he asserted in the
Assembly of 1789: "I do not come to preach tolerance. The most boundless liberty of religion
is in my eyes a right so sacred that the word tolerance which tries to express it seems
to me in some manner tyrannical in itself, since the existence of the authority which has
the power to tolerate strikes at the liberty of thought by the very fact that it tolerates and
that, therefore, it would be able not to tolerate." Quoted in M. Searle Bates, *Religious Liberty,* New York, 1945, p. 194.
[82] Jurieu's ideas on this question were expressed in his *Jugement sur les méthodes rigides
et relâchées d'expliquer la Providence et la grâce . . . Pour trouver un moyen de réconciliation entre les protestants qui suivent la confession d'Augsbourg et les Réformés,* Rotterdam,
1686. This book was answered by a Hamburg theologian by the name of Daniel Severinus
Scultetus: *Animadversiones ad nuperum scriptum de Petri Jurieu unionem ecclesaiae lutheranae et reformatae concernens . . . 1687* to which Jurieu responded with his *De Pace
inter protestantes ineunda consultatio sive disquisitio circa quaestiones de gratia quae
remorantur unionem protestantium utriusque confessionis Augustanae et reformatae,* 1688.
[83] *Apologie pour les vrais tolérants.* pp. 25–77

himself admits, both heretics and the orthodox should be punished when they disturb society, then it follows that they should be equally tolerated when they do not trouble the community.

Jurieu added little to his ideas on tolerance after his indictment of Socinianism in the famous *Tableau*. In fact, many of his conceptions on this problem had been presented in outline form in his very first book attacking D'Huisseau's plan of reunion. But from 1691 to 1697 he again analyzed the foundation of the faith in his controversy with Elie Saurin in *Défense de la doctrine universelle de l'Eglise et particulièrement de Calvin et des réformés sur le principe et le fondement de la foi contre les imputations et les objections de Mr. Saurin* (1695).[84] In the Preface, Jurieu warned that it is very easy to confuse the controversy between Protestants and Catholics with that of Protestants and Socinians. In the one case there is a dispute over the clarity and sufficiency of Scripture for the conviction of heretics, while in the other there is an argument over the evidence of the faith and its object. He opposed the founding of faith upon the demonstration of reason and philosophy, contending that the only true basis is the testimony of the Holy Spirit, since sin had corrupted reason. The Cartesian method of approach to faith results in the evil of Socinianism and Spinosism. It is the principle of theology followed by the Manicheans, Pelagians, Remonstrants, Pajonists, and Latitudinarians everywhere. Right reason as a theological approach is to be particularly condemned. "It is faith which makes right reason, and not right reason faith." [85]

In addition to the *Défense de la doctrine universelle de l'Eglise* Jurieu continued his answer to Saurin's *Examen de la théologie de Mr. Jurieu* in *La Religion du latitudinaire* (1696).[86] He accepts De Beaulieu's [87] definition of a latitudinarian as a man who attempts to enlarge the road

---

[84] This was an answer to Saurin's *Examen de la théologie de Mr. Jurieu*, 1694. Saurin answered Jurieu's *Défense* with a *Défense de la véritable doctrine de l'Eglise*, 1697.

[85] *Défense de la doctrine universelle de l'Eglise*, p. 11. Cf., however, Jurieu's approval of right reason outside of theology. "Il y a certains principes qui ont leur racine dans la droite raison qu'on ne peut arracher par ces sévéritez de morale trop poussée & mal entendue." *Relation de tout ce qui s'est fait*, 1698, p. 53.

[86] A few months earlier Jurieu had published *Suite de la Réponse de Mr. Jurieu*, 1695. Saurin answered both books with his *Justification de la doctrine du Saurin*, 1697. See also the anonymous *Latitudinarius orthodoxus*, 1697.

[87] Louis Le Blanc, Sieur de Beaulieu (1614–1675), was a professor of theology at Sedan, who wrote in 1675 in favor of union between Calvinists and Catholics.

to salvation and who saves as many persons as possible. He recognizes the English origin of the term and describes the principle of the group as the reduction of the articles of faith to belief in God, Providence, heaven, hell, and perhaps the crucified Christ. But belief in the Trinity, the Incarnation, original sin, the satisfaction, efficient grace, and others, are excluded, which is the same position as that taken by the Socinians.

Now when the latitudinarians find that their conception of the basis of the faith is in practical agreement with heretics like the Socinians, they reply that such is the case with Protestants in general. But Jurieu calls attention to the fact that this answer is really based on the arguments of Nicole, in his *Préjugez légitimes contre les calvinistes* and in his *Les Prétendus Réformés convaincus de schisme*. The great Jansenist had attempted to prove that the Protestants with their belief in individual reason and inspiration had opened the door to Socinianism when they renounced the authority and the tradition of the Catholic Church.

Jurieu concludes by rejecting the principal conception of Elie Saurin,[88] which in his mind is the same as that advocated by D'Huisseau years before: "It is only necessary to receive as an article of faith what is evident and incontestably accepted by all Christians; that is, the Symbol of the Apostles without any determination of meaning . . . nor need one take as an article of faith anything which is not in Scripture in so many words." [89] It is revealing to note that Jurieu's final repudiation of such a theory is identical with the position of Cardinal Bellarmine in his famous reply to the Catholic George Cassander's plan for the reunion of the Protestant and Catholic churches in the sixteenth century.[90]

---

[88] Saurin attempted to find a middle ground between the intolerant position and religious indifference in his *Réflexions sur les droits de la conscience*, 1697.

[89] Saurin, *La Religion du latitudinaire*, pp. 389–424. According to Guichard, *Socinianisme* Part II, Chap. XLV, Jurieu could be convicted of Socinianism by the same principles by which he accused others, such as Saurin, of the same leanings.

[90] George Cassander (1513–1566) wanted a reunion on the basis of "quod semper, quod ubique, quod ab omnibus creditum est." Bellarmine answered his *De officio pii ac publicae tranquillitatis vere amantis viri in hoc religionis dissidio* (1561). See also Cassander's *De articulis religionis inter catholicos & protestantes controversis consultatio* (1564), in *Opera*, Paris, 1616. "Dicit Cassander sat est, quod omnes fateamur, Symbolum esse verum & illud recipimus. Contra, Primo, Symbolum, unum est & non in verbis, sed in sensu est fides, non ergo habemus idem Symbolum si in explicatione dissidemus: praeterea si sufficeret verba Symboli recipere, nulli fere haereticorum iure damnati fuissent. Nam Ariani, Novatiani, Nestoriani & alii fere omnes verba Symboli Apostolici recipiebant, sed quia in

Jurieu's controversy with Saurin marked the end of the struggle over tolerance. The cause of intolerance was lost for the moment. Its most ardent defender devoted the last years before his death in 1713 to the publication of books like the *Histoire critique des dogmes et des cultes* [91] (1704). But in the middle of the eighteenth century when the Abbé Novi de Caveirac published his defense of intolerance against the Calvinists in the form of an *Apologie de Louis XIV et de son conseil sur la révocation de l'Edit de Nantes pour servir de réponse à la lettre d'un patriote sur la tolérance civile des protestants de France* he included several passages from Jurieu in support of the authority of the civil magistrates over the suppression of heresy. With the spread of rationalism, however, France finally secured an Act of Toleration in 1787. The medieval idea of a Christian Commonwealth, whether Catholic or Protestant, passed from the scene.

---

sensu dissensio erat, ideo damnati & ab Ecclesia Catholica ejecti fuerunt." Bellarmine, *Disputationes de controversiis christianae fidei,* Vol. II, Book III, Chap. XIX, p. 385.

[91] In a letter to Cuper, 1704, in *Supplément à L'Histoire critique des dogmes et des cultes,* 1705, Jurieu said he had been forced to renounce this type of study when persecution drove him into exile.

Chapter Eight

CONCLUSION

FROM this study of the political literature of the Huguenots of the Dispersion we can safely conclude that "reluctantly and in spite of themselves, religious societies were led by practical necessities to employ upon their own behalf doctrines which are now the common heritage of the Western World." [1] Because that precious heritage has just been in such mortal peril today, it is more essential and important than ever before for us to understand and appreciate its long development in one of its most significant ideological phases, namely, the struggle of religious groups to survive.

Furthermore, this very struggle for existence by ecclesiastical entities helps to throw light upon the controversy over the political results of the Reformation. As we have seen, any religious group, whether Protestant or Catholic, made use of such weapons as the theory of popular sovereignty whenever it found itself as a minority on the defensive against the government of a majority of the opposite faith. But in spite of this fact, it has long been the fashion to draw an unbroken line from Calvin to the Declaration of the Rights of Man.[2] In fact, as we have already noted, Jurieu himself has been regarded as one of the precursors of the French Revolution. But this traditional view received an important modification when the judgment was advanced that "modern democracy is the child of the Reformation, not of the Reformers." [3] Finally, the pendulum has swung to the extreme opinion that there is no

---

[1] Figgis, *Gerson to Grotius*, p. 5.

[2] See Emile Doumergue, *Les Origines historiques de la Déclaration des droits de l'homme et du citoyen;* George Jellinek, *The Declaration of the Rights of Man and of Citizens,* tr. by Max Ferrand and David G. Ritchie, *Natural Rights.* Cf. the opinion of Guido de Ruggiero in his *History of European Liberalism,* p. 24, that "jusnaturalism is . . . a kind of legal Protestantism."

[3] See Borgeaud, *The Rise of Modern Democracy in Old and New England,* p. 2. Note also the new study of R. B. Perry, *Puritanism and Democracy;* Winthrop Hudson, "Democratic Freedom and Religious Faith in the Reformed Tradition," *Church History,* XV (September, 1946); and Charles Mercier, "L'Ésprit de Calvin et la démocratie," *Revue d'histoire ecclésiastique,* XXX, (1934), 5-53.

spiritual relationship whatsoever between the Reformation and modern democracy, and, instead, that the state rather than the individual was to profit from the rise of Protestantism.[4] As usual, the truth would seem to lie in the middle position. Protestantism, in insisting upon the isolation of the individual soul before God—an isolation intensified by the Calvinistic doctrine of election—is a spirit that inevitably resulted in setting the individual man against society, whether religious or secular. The very existence of the numerous sects, which the Reformation could not overcome, is an indication of its liberating power. Moreover, the intolerant attitude of the Protestants toward these sects does not nullify the results, since it was a considerable advance to have three intolerant churches in the place of one. Furthermore, it was in the competition of religious bodies with their rival claims to absolute truth that the mood of religious intransigeance was finally shifted to the realm of the secular.

Now, Jurieu and the other Huguenots of the Dispersion have an important place in this gradual transmission of political ideas from the religious plane to the temporal. When it is argued that the Reformation is the antithesis of the rationalism of the French Revolution, great emphasis is placed on the fact that between the birth of Protestantism and the Revolution of 1789 there came Descartes.[5] It is this very opinion which lends itself to a better understanding of Jurieu and the other Huguenot exiles. Since they made their contributions after the great advent of Cartesianism, it is to be expected that their political theories should have many points of difference not only with the original Reformers but also with the Monarchomachs, both of whom they always recognized, however, as their spiritual ancestors.

When a Calvinist like Jurieu can say that Christianity does not abolish nature and the privileges inseparable from human nature as such, and, further, that there are certain principles which have their root in right reason, it is evident that here is an influence quite different from normal Calvinistic thought.[6] Although Jurieu, unlike Locke, by no means com-

---

[4] Georges de Lagarde, *Recherches sur l'esprit politique de la réforme* and Marc-Edouard Chenevière, *La Pensée politique de Calvin*.

[5] De Lagarde, *Recherches sur l'esprit politique, passim.*

[6] Cf. "There is no real discontinuity between the teaching of the Reformers and that of their predecessors with repect to natural law. Not one of the leaders of the Reformation

pletely removes the idea of the glory of God as the end of the state, nevertheless, the strand of Calvinism is being intermingled with another force. This is the rationalizing ferment of natural law, which stems from Grotius, who contributed so much to the secularization of that concept.[7] Of course, natural law had been the basis of the argument in the *Vindiciae contra tyrannos*[8] and Beza had justified tyrannicide on the same foundation. In general, however, orthodox Calvinists tended to distrust the rational arguments embodied in the law of nature. Protestantism "has too strong a sense of the individual occasion and the uniqueness of the individual who faces the occasion to trust in general rules."[9] Calvinism also resisted democratic ideas based on the conviction of the goodness and innate rights of the natural man. Instead the Calvinistic doctrine of popular sovereignty and the right of resistance stressed legitimacy. It was not concerned with the rational construction of the state from the standpoint of the rights of the individual but with the aim that both the ruler and the people should obey God. But in the last analysis "the right of self-government . . . was the fruit of many secular as well as religious movements. But the secular movements were inclined to libertarianism in their reaction to the evils of government; or to base their democratic theories upon the idea of the goodness of human nature; and consequently to underestimate the perils of anarchy; while they directed their attention to the perils of tyranny."[10]

If this theory of the sovereignty of the people was completely secularized in England in the struggle between king and parliament from 1640–

---

assails the principle." J. T. McNeill, "Natural Law in the Teaching of the Reformers," *The Journal of Religion*, XXVI (July, 1946), 168. See also the judgment of Marc Chenevière in his *Pensée politique de Calvin*, p. 66: "Calvin rompt donc tous les biens qui rattachaient la connaissance de la loi naturelle à la raison et faire reposer cette connaissance de voix intérieure qui n'a pas besoin de la raison pour s'exprimer."

[7] See Karl von Kaltenborn, *Die Vorläufer des Hugo Grotius auf dem Gebiete des ius naturae et gentium sowie der Politik im Reformationszeitalter*. G. Gurvitch in "L'Idée du droit social," and in "Natural Law," in *Encyclopaedia of the Social Sciences*, Vol. XI (New York, 1933), traces the beginnings of the secularization of natural law to Aquinas.

[8] Otto von Gierke, *Natural Law and the Theory of Society, 1500–1800*, tr. by Barker, II, 231.

[9] Niebuhr, *The Nature and Destiny of Man*, Vol. I: *Human Nature*, p. 60. See also A. Lang, *Die Reformation und das Naturrecht*; De Lagarde, *Recherches sur l'Esprit politique*, pp. 134 ff.; and A. Passerin d'Entrèves, *The Medieval Contribution to Political Thought*, pp. 94 ff.

[10] Niebuhr, *The Nature and Destiny of Man*, Vol. II: *Human Destiny*, pp. 283–284.

1689, it had also tended in the same direction on the Continent through the influence on the Huguenots of the Dispersion of the modern school of natural law under Grotius. If, in England, Latitudinarianism and natural law form a union, it was in the parallel of English Latitudinarianism on the Continent, namely, Arminianism, that the modern evolution of natural law originated.[11] In fact, it has been held [12] that it was among the opponents of orthodox Calvinism, such as Hugo Grotius and Richard Hooker, that natural law ideas reach their fullest development. It should not be forgotten that Hooker was, along with the Monarchomachs and Philip Hunton, the great formative influence upon Locke; in Jurieu's case, Grotius played the same role, along with the teachings of the *Vindiciae*. Furthermore, both Locke and Jurieu substantiate the dictum of Emerson that the mark of genius is receptivity and not originality.

This process of the secularization of the doctrine of popular sovereignty was never carried as far, however, among the Huguenot exiles as in Locke, who concluded that when the people are convinced that "their laws, and with them, their estates, liberties, and lives are in danger and *perhaps their religion too,*" [13] they cannot be restrained from revolt. This no doubt accounts for the fact that although the Huguenots through their polemical writings and literary journals had first popularized English political institutions, it was through the more secular English theorist that eighteenth century France before the time of Montesquieu and Voltaire became indoctrinated with English political ideas. Even as the first part of the *Vindiciae* was devoted to the question of obedience to princes when they command against the law of God or ruin the church, so in a thinker like Jurieu the emphasis is even greater upon the maintenance of the true religion than upon secular injustice. Recall his unusual assertion that property and life are annexed to conscience.

In general, it can be concluded that the Huguenots of the Dispersion, like the Whigs, enunciated this doctrine of popular sovereignty with the view of securing the support of the people without giving them

---

[11] A. Lang, "The Reformation and Natural Law," *Princeton Theological Review*, VII (1909), 177–218. English translation by J. G. Machen.
[12] De Lagarde, *Recherches sur l'esprit politique*, pp. 188–192.
[13] Locke, *Civil Government*, Chap. XVIII, p. 223. Italics mine.

actual power. A mixed monarchy like England's with sovereignty divided between the prince and the estates is their ideal. For Jurieu as
well as for the Monarchomachs the members of the Estates need not
be necessarily elected by the people. Along with the princes of the blood,
the nobility and other dignitaries of the realm, they are regarded as its
natural representatives. Even though some concessions are made to direct
resistance by the people among the Huguenot exiles, the old Calvinistic
tendency of resistance only by the constituted authorities still prevails.
The people or nation is still regarded as a collective and corporate whole
—the *populus universus*. Moreover, even majority rule [14] must be qualified by the justice of its cause.

Jurieu was prepared to endow the monarchy with a far more absolute
character than his contemporary, Locke, since it must be powerful
enough to establish the true faith in both France and England. If the
English thinker restricted the government through the doctrine of inalienable, individual natural rights, the Huguenot pastor found his governmental limitations principally in the maxim *Salus populi suprema lex
esto*. But, as we have observed, the theologian of Rotterdam in his passion for restraining the authority of the monarch is unaware that he
himself grants an unlimited power to the people. This, the most flagrant
of all the contradictions in Jurieu, can, like all the other variations and
hesitations in his thought, be only understood with reference to his all-
consuming passion for the true religion. But in this one case he failed to
see that the logic of his theory could only result in the very evil he so
strenuously attempted to avoid—the possible persecution of the faith.
However, many of Jurieu's vacillations can be explained as a sign of
the times—as a part of "the crisis of the European conscience."

As we have noted, the reverse side of these various doctrines of revolution in defense of the true religion was theocracy in all its overtones
of both civil and ecclesiastical intolerance. For the first time since Lambert Daneau in the preceding century we find in the person of the fiery
Pierre Jurieu an author who went far toward advocating the Genevan
ideal of the state for France. It is interesting to note that both these Hu-

---

[14] For an interesting discussion of this question see John G. Heinberg, "Theories of Majority
Rule," *The American Political Science Review*, XXVI (1932), 452–469; Willmoore Ken-
dall, *John Locke and the Doctrine of Majority Rule* (Urbana, Ill., 1941); Tocqueville,
Démocratie en Amérique, Vol. I, Chap. XV; Mill, *On Liberty, passim*.

guenot writers published their works outside of France—in Holland. From the point of view of such thinkers there is no inconsistency between the theory of popular sovereignty and intolerance or between an extreme support of royal authority at one time and violent opposition to princes at another. Only an all-consuming passion for the establishment of absolute truth can explain Jurieu's statements, for example, that the people should resist a king who attempts to set up a false faith and that conversely the people must not rebel against a sovereign who is trying to erect the true religion. If we but remember this religious point of reference, it is not difficult to understand why a man like Jurieu was the unconscious apologist of the Revocation. This is something that complete skeptics like Montaigne, Bayle, and Voltaire never could comprehend in their study of the political implications of religion. To them it was simply—"a plague o' both your houses." But since the atmosphere of eighteenth century France was distinctly Baylian, it is not surprising that it was the more tolerant English philosopher Locke, rather than the intransigent theologian Jurieu, who had the greater influence upon the development of French political ideas in the eighteenth century.

Difficult indeed was Jurieu's position on this all-important problem of toleration. As a victim of Catholic persecution, which he attacked, he supported the repressive measures of Protestant states against Catholics. But he was also faced at the same time with members of his own faith, who were struggling against both Catholic and Protestant repression of any kind whatsoever. As Bayle said, "in France he took it very badly that the secular power should be used, and in Holland he takes it very badly that it should not be employed." [15] The very same arguments which he employed against the Revocation of the Edict of Nantes, however, were turned against him by the liberal French Protestants, who wished to escape the effects of the various synodal acts of uniformity which Jurieu had engineered in Holland. Furthermore, our theologian also left himself open to the accusation that in his arguments condemning the liberal Protestants he was but arming the Catholic persecutors of the Calvinists. At least when opposing the Catholics, Jurieu had one thing in common with his enemy: both were in fundamental agree-

[15] Bayle, *Dictionnaire*, 1720, article "Arius," I, 330, G.

ment upon the idea of a Christian Commonwealth. In his struggle with the Latitudinarians or liberal Protestants, however, he was attacking a different principle altogether, namely, secularism. Here it is clear that "liberty of conscience . . . springs from the theory that the final object of the State is man, that man is responsible for his own actions, and that the State assumes no responsibility for his thoughts or beliefs." [16]

It was this lay spirit, according to which the emphasis is placed upon the temporal concerns of man, that seemed most pernicious to a thinker like Jurieu who still clung to the concept of the state as founded on the glory of God. To such a man, universal tolerance simply means universal indifference toward religion, which is the worst of all evils in this world of sin. Furthermore, it is implicit in his thought that the line between skepticism and cynicism is very thin. In the last analysis tolerance in religion can be pushed to an irresponsible attitude towards ultimate epistemological questions. But Jurieu was not willing to go so far as to allow no measure of toleration at all. He condemns, as we have seen, the death penalty for heresy. He adopts the pragmatic procedure of tolerating groups that are considerable in size and already established, but he advocates the suppression of "nascent communions." Furthermore, he grants to the magistrate the authority to silence heretics, who, if they disobey such commands of the sovereign, are punishable for the violation of the civil laws rather than for heresy. As we have observed, however, Jurieu's enemies had little difficulty in showing that heresy cannot be distinguished from civil disobedience in this way, since the magistrate's ban is upon the subject of heresy, which really makes the reason for punishment the heretical opinions advanced. Moreover, as was easily shown at the time, if the dogmatizing of heretics may be punished at all, the penalty may be as inexorable as death. The choice is between either an extreme severity against or an extreme support of heresy.

But the heart of the argument over tolerance centered in the interrelated question of the nature of the church and of the fundamental truths of Christianity. As we have seen, Jurieu conceived of the church as a visible organization on earth, while to his contemporary John Locke it was invisible. According to this interpretation, herein lies the explana-

[16] Jordan, *The Development of Religious Toleration*, I, 18.

tion of their respective positions with reference to tolerance. In spite of the intolerance which attends a conception of the visibility of the church, Jurieu acknowledged that his idea of the universal church as comprised of all sects that retain the fundamentals of the Christian faith did lead to a degree of toleration. It never included, however, an acceptance of the extreme Socinian view that salvation can be obtained in all religions. This is to be explained by the great difference over the conception of fundamentals or essentials between the Socinians and our theologian. Jurieu's theory of fundamental articles of the faith was not the principle of comprehension of the liberal Protestants. It was not a minimum of articles of belief on which all can agree; instead, it was the limitation of the tolerance of God, the truth remaining always the same, completely unchanged. Furthermore, his criterion of a fundamental truth was not, as with the Latitudinarians, its location in Scripture in express terms but its relation to the end of religion, which is the glory of God. In fact, the Lord has purposely introduced some obscurity in Revelation because His grace is not to be given freely to all men but only to the elect.

Whatever measure of toleration Jurieu allowed, whether for reasons of conscience or reasons of state, the beneficiary was always the church; for did not our theologian definitely contend in one place that extreme intolerance might destroy the state, which in turn would have evil repercussions on the church? Therefore, it is clear that Jurieu's pragmatism or expediency with regard to the toleration of groups already established is not quite the same as that of the *politiques* in the preceding century. Their argument was that intolerance was ruining the state, while Jurieu was only concerned over the destruction of the secular side of life because of its evil effects upon the ecclesiastical sphere. It is a question of *ratio ecclesiae* as against *ratio status*.

With regard to the authority of the magistrate over sacerdotal affairs, because of his peculiar conception of the "power of the church," Jurieu's Erastianism, like that of Prynne in England, is logical. Both these thinkers viewed the presbytery merely as a suitable form of church government and not as directly divine in nature, in the manner of a Cartwright, who could not possibly have reconciled Erastianism with Presbyterianism. It was, however, difficult for Jurieu to square with Erastianism the Calvinist principle of the sole authority of the Scriptures in matters of religion. Following Grotius, his was an Erastianism that fell far short of that of Hobbes and Spinoza or, perhaps, Selden.

Even as Calvin and Beza with reference to Castellion, so Jurieu, with respect to Bayle, perceived that the acceptance of the new doctrines would act as a solvent of all religious systems of thought. But Jurieu was faced with an even greater danger. Bayle was skeptical of all belief and truth; he was not, like Castellion, rationalist only before certain articles of faith. It is little wonder, then, that both Jurieu and Bossuet felt that what was at stake was Christianity itself. They feared above all else the perils of the skepticism that was to culminate in Voltaire, who thought as Gibbon that "all religions were equally true in the eyes of the people, equally false in the eyes of the Philosopher, and equally useful to the magistrate." [17] As fundamentalists they dreaded a rising tide of relativism and nihilism, which might put civilization itself in jeopardy. On the other hand, neither Jurieu nor Bossuet understood that revolt against the authority of the church may arise not from "hatred of God or Christ but by resentment against the unjustified use of Christ as a cover for the historical relativities of culture and civilization in which it happens to be involved." [18]

If the Huguenot refugees once again in human history placed great emphasis upon an inviolable something in man, calling conscience or faith that which to the more secularly minded has been named reason, it was only because of their conviction that this inviolable something in man, whether divine or natural, is a part of the pattern of the universe. Therefore, to violate conscience, faith, or reason in man is nothing less than to attack the universal law of life, to bring about the very destruction of being itself.

[17] Quoted in Kingsley Martin, *French Liberal Thought in the Eighteenth Century*, p. 131.
[18] Niebuhr, *The Nature and Destiny of Man*, Vol. II: *Human Destiny*, p. 224.

BIBLIOGRAPHY

WORKS OF PIERRE JURIEU [1]

Manuscripts

Letters to M. de Lisle du Guat. 1686 *et seq.*
Letter to Montausier. April 4, 1689.
Letter of September 1, 1690.
Letters to Cuper. 1691–1705.
Letters to the English Secretary of State, 1692–1705, especially that of Sep
tember 20/30, 1697.
Letter of 1695.
Letter to William III. August 18, 1696.

Writings Significant for Political Theory

Examen du livre de la Réunion du Christianisme; ou, Traité de la tolérance
en matière de Religion, et de la nature et de l'étendue des points fondamentaux. Avec une courte réponse à L'Apologie pour le livre de la réunion.
Orleans, 1671.
Eclaircissement de quelques passages condamnés dans le livre de l'Examen
de la réunion du christianisme. Sedan, 1671.
Apologie pour la morale des réformés; ou, Défense de leur doctrine touchant
la justification, le persévérance des vrais saints et le certitude que chaque
fidèle peut et doit avoir de son salut pour servir de réponse au livre de M.
Arnaud intitulé Le Renversement de la Morale de J.C. par la doctrine des
Calvinistes touchant la justification. Quevilly, 1675.
Traité de la puissance de l'Eglise, dans lequel on découvre la source de cette
Puissance, et de quelle manière elle se répand sur les sujets dans lesquels
elle est; on traite de l'autorité des Synodes et par occasion on répond aux
difficultés que M. l'Evêque de Condom et le P. Maimbourg forment contre

---

[1] Listed chronologically. For Jurieu's more purely theological writings, see E. Kaeppler-
Vielzeuf, "Bibliographie chronologique des oeuvres de Pierre Jurieu," *Bulletin de la
Société de l'Histoire du Protestantisme français,* July–September, 1935, pp. 391–440. Although this compilation is punctuated with numerous errors, it is the most complete in
print. Kaeppler has attributed to Jurieu works that he could not possibly have written,
and has omitted from his list several important items, among them the collection of
Jurieu's letters to Cuper, in the Royal Library at The Hague. It should also be mentioned
that a very careful search revealed that no letters of Jurieu to William of Orange survive
in the Royal Archives at The Hague, although it is known that they were in correspondence.

les Réformés sur l'autorité qu'ils donnent à leurs Synodes. Lettres écrites à Louis Dumoulin à l'occasion de ses écrits contre la juridiction ecclésiastique. Quevilly, 1677.

Seconde réponse à M. de Condom où l'on réfute l'avertissement et les pièces qu'il a fait mettre à la tête de la nouvelle éd. de son traité de la Doctrine de l'Eglise catholique. n.p., 1680.

Préservatif contre le changement de religion; ou, Idée juste & véritable de la religion catholique romaine opposée aux portraits flatteurs que l'on en fait et particulièrement à celui de M. de Condom. Rouen, 1680 and The Hague, 1682.

La Politique du clergé de France; ou, Entretiens curieux de deux catholiques romains, l'un parisien et l'autre provincial, sur les moyens dont on se sert aujourd'huy pour détruire la religion protestante dans ce royaume. Cologne, 1681; Amsterdam, 1682.

Moyens sûrs et honnêtes pour la conversion des hérétiques et avis et expédiens salutaires pour la réformation de l'Eglise. Cologne, 1681.

Suite de La Politique du clergé de France; ou, Les Derniers Efforts de l'innocence affligée. The Hague, 1682; Amsterdam, 1682.

Abrégé de l'histoire du Concile de Trente avec un discours contenant les réflexions historiques sur les conciles, et particulièrement sur la conduite de celui de Trente, pour prouver que les protestants ne sont pas obligés à se soumettre à ce dernier Concile. Geneva, 1682.

Le Janséniste convaincu de vaine sophistiquerie; ou, Examens des réflexions de M. Arnaud sur Le Préservatif contre le changement de religion. Amsterdam, 1682 and 1683.

Examen de l'eucharistie de l'Eglise romaine. Rotterdam, 1682.

Histoire du calvinisme et celle du papisme mises en parallèle; ou, Apologie pour les réformateurs, pour la réformation et pour les réformés, divisée en quatre parties contre le libelle intitulé L'Histoire du calvinisme par M. Maimbourg. Rotterdam, 1683. The edition of 1823 has been used in the present study.

Suite du Préservatif contre le changement de religion; ou, Réflexions sur l'adoucissement des dogmes et des cultes de l'Eglise romaine presentée par R. Brueys, avocat de Montpellier. The Hague, 1683.

L'Esprit de M. Arnaud tiré de sa conduite et des écrits tant de lui que de ses disciples, particulièrement de L'Apologie pour les catholiques. Deventer, 1684.

Réflexions sur la cruelle persécution que souffre l'Eglise réformée de France, et sur la conduite et les actes de la dernière assemblée du clergé de France. Avec un examen des prétendues calomnies dont le clergé se plaint au roy dans sa profession de foy à deux colonnes, que les réformés ont répandues dans leurs ouvrages contre l'Eglise romaine. Le tout pour faire voir à ceux qui sont exposés à la tentation de révolte, quelle est la religion qu'on les force ou qu'on les veut forcer d'embrasser. n.p., 1685.

Justification de la morale des réformés contre les accusations de M. Arnaud. The Hague, 1685.

Avis aux protestants de l'Europe tant de la Confession d'Augsbourg que de celle des Suisses. 1685. Printed along with Préjuges légitimes contre le Papisme.

Préjugez légitimes contre le papisme, ouvrage où l'on considère l'Eglise romaine dans tous ses dehors et où l'on fait voir par l'histoire de sa conduite qu'elle ne peut être la véritable Eglise à l'exclusion de toutes les autres communions du christianisme comme elle le prétend. Amsterdam, 1685.

Lettre de quelques Protestants pacifiques au sujet de la réunion des religions à l'assemblée de messieurs du clergé de France qui se doit tenir à Saint-Germain-en-Laye le . . . du mois de May, 1685. n.p., 1685.

Entretiens sur les conférences que messieurs du clergé de France proposent aux Réformés. Cologne, 1685.

Le Balance du sanctuaire, où sont pesées les afflictions présentes de l'Eglise avec les avantages qui lui en reviennent pour la consolation de tant de personnes qui sont pénétrées de douleur par la persécution présente que souffre l'Eglise. The Hague, 1686.

Réflexions sur deux écrits publiés sous le nom du feu roi Charles II. London, 1686.

Lettres pastorales addressées aux fidèles de France qui gémissent sous la captivité de Babylone. Rotterdam, 1686–1689.

Le Vray Système de l'église et la véritable analyse de la foi. Où sont dissipées toutes les illusions que les controversistes modernes, prétendus catholiques, ont voulu faire aux public sur la nature de l'Eglise, son infaillibilité et le juge des controverses; pour servir principalement de responce au livre de M. Nicole intitulé Les Prétendus Réformés convaincus de schisme, etc., avec une responce abbrégée au livre de M. Ferrand contre l'autheur. Dordrecht, 1686.

Réflexions sur l'écrit de M. Ferrand, intitulé Responce à L'Apologie pour les réformateurs, pour la réformation & pour les Réformés. 1686. Printed in Le Vray Système de l'église.

L'Accomplissement des prophéties; ou, La Délivrance prochaine de l'Eglise. Ouvrage où il est prouvé que le papisme est l'empire anti-chrétien et qu'il n'est pas éloigné de sa ruine. Rotterdam, 1686.

Jugement sur les méthodes rigides et relâchées d'expliquer la providence et la grâce. . . . Pour trouver un moyen de réconciliation entre les protestants qui suivent la confession d'Augsbourg et les Réformés. Rotterdam, 1686.

Suite de L'Accomplissement des prophéties; ou, Amplification des preuves historiques qui font voir que le papisme est l'anti-christianisme. Rotterdam, 1687.

Apologie pour L'Accomplissement des prophéties où on répond aux objections qui on été faites contre cet ouvrage. Rotterdam, 1687.

Deux traités de morale, la balance des afflictions présentes avec la gloire à venir et l'anéantissement de l'homme devant Dieu. The Hague, 1687.

Rome anti-chrétienne; ou, Conformité de l'horrible persécution qu'Antiochus exerce contre l'ancienne Eglise avec celle que le clergé de France fait souffrir aux Réformés. Cologne, 1687. Also published under the title Parallèle de la persécution d'Antiochus l'illustre contre les Juifs avec celle qu'on exerce à présent contre les Protestants. Cologne, 1687.

Des droits des deux souverains en matière de religion, la conscience et le prince. Pour détruire le dogme de l'indifférence des religions et de la tolérance universelle. Contre un livre intitulé Commentaire philosophique sur ces paroles de la parabole: Contrains les d'entrer. Rotterdam, 1687.

Parallèle de la persécution d'Antiochus. See Rome anti-chrétienne.

Factum pour demander justice aux puissances contre Noël Aubert de Versé atteint et convaincu des crimes d'impureté, d'impiété et de blasphème. n.p., 1687. No copy is known to exist.

De pace inter protestantes ineunda consultatio sive disquisitio circa quaestiones de gratia quae remorantur unionem protestantium utriusque confessionis Augustanae et reformatae. Ultrapecti [sic], 1688.

Traité de la nature et de la grâce; ou, Du concours général de la providence, et du concours particulier de la grâce efficace, contre les nouvelles hypothèses de M. Pajon et de ses disciples. Utrecht, 1688.

Traité de l'unité de l'Eglise et des points fondamentaux contre M. Nicole. Rotterdam, 1688.

Les Trophées de Port-Royal renversés; ou, Défense de la foi des six premiers siècles de l'Eglise touchant la sainte eucharistie contre les sophismes de M. Arnaud. Amsterdam, 1688. Also attributed to Noël Aubert de Versé.

Prévarications du Père Lachaise, confesseur du roi, au préjudice des droits et des intérêts de sa majesté. 1688. Printed in La Politique des jésuites.

La Politique des jésuites. Cologne, 1689.

La Décadence de l'empire papal par laquelle il est menacé d'une prochaine ruine pour faire place à la réformation. Amsterdam, 1689. Printed in La Politique des jésuites.

La Juste Idée de la grâce immédiate; ou, Réponse à la critique de la doctrine de P. Jurieu sur les habitudes infuses et la grâce immédiate. The Hague, 1689.

Lettre de B.D.S.C. à M.D. bourgmestre de Soleure sur les intérêts des cantons suisses. The Hague, 1689.

Les Véritables Intérêts des princes de l'Europe dans les affaires présentes;

ou, Réflexions sur un écrit venu de France sous le titre de Lettre de monsieur à monsieur sur les affaires du temps. Cologne, 1689.

Lettre de Genève contenant une relation exacte au sujet des petits prophètes de Dauphiné. Rotterdam, 1689.

Apologie pour leurs sérénissimes majestés britanniques contre un infâme libelle intitulé Le Vray Portrait de Guillaume Henri de Nassau, nouvel Abçalon, nouvel Hérode, nouveau Cromwell, nouveau Néron. The Hague, 1689.

Les Soupirs de la France esclave qui aspirent après la liberté. Amsterdam, 1689. Also published as Les voeux d'un patriote, Amsterdam, 1788. This is a reedition of the first thirteen Mémoires on the eve of the French Revolution.

La Religion des jésuites; ou, Réflexions sur les inscriptions du P. Ménestrier et sur les écrits du P. Le Tellier pour les nouveaux chrétiens de la Chine et des Indes contre la 19e obs. de L'Esprit de M. Arnaud. The Hague, 1689.

Le salut de la France à Monseigneur le dauphin. Cologne, 1690.

Lettre pastorale aux fidèles de Paris, d'Orléans et de Blois sur le scandale arrivé à Paris le 15 janvier 1690 par l'apostasie de M. Papin, qui a renoncé à la religion réformée entre les mains de l'Evêque de Meaux dans l'Eglise des Pères de l'Oratoire. Où l'on voit les tristes suites de l'esprit d'indifférence sur les régions. The Hague, 1690.

Le Tableau du socinianisme où l'on voit l'impureté et la fausseté des dogmes des sociniens et où l'on découvre les mystères de la cabale de ceux qui veulent tolérer l'hérésie socinienne. The Hague, 1690.

Avis de l'auteur des Lettres pastorales à M. de Beauval, l'auteur de l'histoire des ouvrages des savants. n.p., 1690.

Factum de l'affaire de Monsieur de la Conseillère. Rotterdam, 1690.

Examen d'un Libelle contre la religion, contre l'état et contre la révolution d'Angleterre intitulé Avis important aux réfugiés sur leur prochain retour en France. The Hague, 1691.

Nouvelles convictions contre l'auteur de L'Avis aux réfugiés avec la nullité de ses justifications. n.p., 1691.

Réflexions sur un libelle ou feuille volante intitulé Nouvelle hérésie dans la morale touchant la haine du prochain prêchée par M. Jurieu et dénoncée à toutes les Eglises réformées. n.p., 1691.

Apologie du Sieur Jurieu, pasteur et professeur en théologie, addressée aux pasteurs et conducteurs des églises wallonnes des Pays-Bas. The Hague, 1691.

Dernière Conviction contre le Sieur Bayle, professeur en philosophie à Rotterdam, au sujet de L'Avis aux réfugiés, pour servir de factum sur la plainte portée aux puissances de l'état. n.p., 1691.

Courte revue des Maximes de morale et des principes de religion de l'auteur des Pensées diverses sur les comètes et de La Critique générale sur L'Histoire du calvinisme de Maimbourg, pour servir de factum aux juges ecclésiastiques s'ils en veulent connaître. n.p., 1691.

Remarques générales sur La Cabale chimérique de M. Bayle. Rotterdam, 1691.

Réponse à l'auteur des Chimères de M. Jurieu. n.p., 1691.

Le Philosophe dégradé; ou, Réponse à La Chimère de la cabale de Rotterdam. Amsterdam, 1692. Also published as Le Philosophe dégradé pour servir de troisième suite aux remarques générales sur la Cabale Chimérique de M. Bayle.

Factum selon les formes ou dispositions des preuves contre l'auteur de L'Avis aux réfugiés selon les règles du barreau, qui font voir que sur de telles preuves dans les crimes capitaux on condamne un criminel accusé. n.p., 1692.

Seconde apologie pour M. Jurieu; ou, Réponse à un libelle sans nom présenté aux synodes de Leyden et de Naerden sous le titre de Lettre à messieurs les ministres qui composent le synode assemblée à Leyden le 2 de May 1691. Rotterdam, 1692.

Informations pour nos seigneurs les états, et instruction sur ce qui s'est passé au synode de Ziericzée pour les églises qui doivent composer le synode suivant. n.p., 1692.

Apologie pour les synodes & pour plusieurs honnêtes gens, déchirez dans la dernière satyre du Sr. de Beauval, intitulée Considérations, etc., n.p., 1692.

La XXII Lettre pastorale de la III année, Nov. 1, 1694. Careful search failed to make this item available.

Défense de la doctrine universelle de l'Eglise et particulièrement de Calvin, et des réformés sur le principe et le fondement de la foi contre les imputations et les objections de M. Saurin. Rotterdam, 1695.

Suite de la réponse de M. Jurieu: Idée des sentiments de M. Saurin sur les mystères de la Trinité et de l'incarnation. n.p., 1695.

L'Ame Affligée dans le silence; ou, Sermon sur Ps 36, 10 prononcé sur la mort de la reine d'Angleterre. London, 1695.

La Religion du latitudinaire avec L'Apologie pour la sainte trinité appelée l'hérésie des trois dieux. Rotterdam, 1696.

La Peste du genre humain; ou, La Vie de Julien l'Apostat, mise en parallèle avec celle de Louis XIV. Cologne, 1696. (Cf. the anonymous Julien l'Apostat; ou, Abbrégé de sa vie . . . avec une comparaison du papisme et du paganisme . . . et une autre idée générale du papisme avec un petit traité de l'Antichrist, 1688.)

Jugement du public et particulièrement de M. l'abbé Renaudot sur Le Dictionnare critique de Sr. Bayle. Rotterdam, 1697.

Relation de ce qui s'est fait dans les affaires de la religion réformée et pour

ses intérêts depuis le commencement des négociations de la paix de Ryswyck. Rotterdam, 1698.

Apologie de l'amour qui nous fait désirer véritablement de posséder dieu seul,
par le motif de trouver notre bonheur dans sa connaissance et dans son
amour avec des remarques fort importantes sur les principes et les maximes
que M. l'Archévêque de Cambrai établit sur l'amour de dieu dans un livre
intitulé Explication des maximes des Saints. Amsterdam, 1698.

Traité historique contenant le jugement d'un protestant sur la théologie
mystique sur le quiétisme et sur les démêlés de l'Evêque de Meaux avec
l'Archévêque de Cambrai, jusqu'à la bulle d'Innocent XII et l'assemblée
provinciale de Paris du 13 de May, 1699, inclusivement. Avec le problème
ecclésiastique contre l'Archévêque de Paris. n.p., 1699.

Histoire critique des dogmes et des cultes bons et mauvais qui ont été dans
l'Eglise depuis Adam jusqu'à Jésus-Christ, où l'on trouve l'origine de
toutes les idolâtries de l'ancien paganisme, expliquées par rapport à celles
des Juifs. Amsterdam, 1704.

Supplément à L'Histoire critique . . . ; ou, Dissertation par lettres de M.
Cuper sur quelques passages du livre de M. Jurieu. Amsterdam, 1705.

Avis à tous les alliés protestants et catholiques romains, princes & peuples,
souverains & sujets sur le secours qu'on doit donner aux soûlevez des
Cévennes. n.p., 1705.

Le Philosophe de Rotterdam accusé, atteint, et convaincu. Amsterdam, 1706.

RELATED WORKS

Abbadie, Jacques. Défense de la nation britannique, où les droits de dieu, de
la nature et de la société sont clairement établies au sujet de la révolution
d'Angleterre contre l'auteur de L'Avis important aux réfugiés. The Hague,
1693.

Allix, Pierre. Réflexions critiques et théologiques sur la controverse de l'Eglise
où l'on fait voir la fausseté des sentiments de l'Eglise romaine sur ce sujet
par l'écriture sainte et les pères. 1686.

Althusius, Johannes. Politica Methodice Digesta, ed. Carl J. Friedrich. Cambridge, 1932.

Amyraut, Moise. Discours de la souveraineté des roys. Charenton, 1650.

Ancillon, Charles. L'Irrévocabilité de l'édit de Nantes prouvée par les principes du droit et de la politique. Amsterdam, 1688.

Arnauld, Antoine. Apologie pour les catholiques contre les faussetés et les
calomnies d'un livre intitulé La Politique du clergé de France. Liége, 1681.

—— La Morale pratique des jésuites représentée en plusieurs histoires
arrivées dans toutes les parties du monde. Cologne, 1669–1695.

—— Réflexions sur un livre intitulé Préservatif contre le changement de religion. Antwerp, 1682.

Arnauld, Antoine. Le Renversement de la morale de J.C. par la doctrine des calvinistes touchant la justification. Paris, 1682.

—— Le Véritable Portrait de Guillaume-Henri de Nassau, nouvel Abçalon, nouvel Hérode, nouveau Cromwell, nouveau Néron. n.p., 1689.

Arnauld, Antoine, and Pierre Nicole. La Perpétuité de la foy de l'Eglise catholique touchant l'eucharistie. Paris, 1664.

Aubert de Versé, Noël. L'Anti-socinien; ou, Nouvelle Apologie de la foi catholique contre les sociniens et les calvinistes. Paris, 1692.

—— Manifeste de Maître Noël Aubert de Versé . . . contre l'auteur anonyme d'un libelle diffamatoire intitulé Factum pour demander justice aux puissances contre Noël Aubert de Versé atteint et convaincu des crimes d'impureté, d'impiété et de blasphème. Amsterdam, 1687.

—— Le Nouveau Visionnaire de Rotterdam; ou, Examen des parallèles mystiques de M. Jurieu. Cologne, 1686.

—— Le Protestant pacifique; ou, Traité de la paix de l'Eglise dans lequel on fait voir par les principes des réformés que la foi de l'Eglise catholique ne choque point les fondements du salut et qu'ils doivent tolérer dans leur communion tous les chrétiens du monde les sociniens, les quakres mêmes dont on explique la religion contre Monsieur Jurieu. Amsterdam, 1684.

—— Tombeau du socinianisme. Frankfort, 1687.

—— Traité de la liberté de conscience ou de l'autorité des souverains sur la religion des peuples, opposé aux maximes impies de Hobbes et de Spinosa adoptées par le sieur Jurieu. Cologne, 1687.

—— La Véritable Clef de l'Apocalypse . . . en particulier l'illusion des prédictions de J(urieu) F(aux) P(rophète) D(e) R(otterdam). Cologne, 1690.

Barclay, William. De regno et regali potestate adversus Buckananum, Brutum, Boucherium, et reliquos monarchomachos libri sex. Paris, 1600.

Basnage, Jacques. Examen des méthodes proposées par messieurs de l'assemblée du clergé de France en 1682. Cologne, 1684. This has been incorrectly attributed to Jurieu.

—— L'Histoire de la religion des Eglises réformées . . . pour servir de réponse à L'Histoire des variations. Rotterdam, 1690.

—— Lettres pastorales sur le renouvellement de la persécution. Rotterdam, 1698. This has been incorrectly attributed to Jurieu.

—— Récit de la mort des persécuteurs de Lactance. Utrecht, 1687. A translation of Firmianus Lactantius, De mortibus persecutorum.

—— Traité de la conscience . . . avec des réflexions sur Le Commentaire philosophique. Amsterdam, 1696.

Basnage de Beauval, Henri. A Messieurs les ministres et anciens qui composent le synode assemblé à Leide le 2 de May, 1691. n.p., 1691.

—— Considérations sur deux sermons de M. Jurieu touchant l'amour du prochain où l'on traite incidemment cette question curieuse, s'il faut haïr M. Jurieu. n.p., 1694.

—— Examen de la doctrine de M. Jurieu pour servir de réponse à un libelle intitulé Seconde apologie de M. Jurieu. n.p., 1691.

—— Histoire des Ouvrages des Savans. Rotterdam, 1687–1709.

—— Lettre d'un ministre aux catholiques au sujet des petits prophètes de Dauphiné. n.p., 1689.

—— Lettres sur les différends de M. Jurieu & M. Bayle. n.p., 1691.

—— M. Jurieu convaincu de calomnie et d'imposture. n.p., n.d.

—— Réponse à L'Apologie de M. Jurieu. Amsterdam, 1692.

—— Réponse de l'auteur de l'histoire des ouvrages des savants à L'Avis de M. Jurieu, auteur des lettres pastorales. Rotterdam, 1690.

—— Réponse de M. . . . Ministre à une écrite par un catholique romain sur le sujet des P. Prophètes du Dauphiné & du Vivarets. n.p., 1689.

—— Réponse des fidèles captifs en Babylone à la Lettre pastorale de M. Jurieu qui est dattée du 1 Novembre 1694 & qui a pour titre la XXII de la III année. n.p., 1695.

—— Tolérance des religions. Rotterdam, 1684.

Bayle, Pierre. Choix de la correspondance inédite de Pierre Bayle 1670–1706 publié d'après les origineaux conservés à la Bibliothèque Royale de Copenhague par E. Gigas. Copenhagen, 1890.

—— Dictionnaire historique et critique. Rotterdam, 1720; Amsterdam, 1740.

—— Lettres choisies de Bayle. Rotterdam, 1714.

—— Lettres de M. Bayle publiées sur les origineaux avec des remarques par Desmaizeaux. Amsterdam, 1729.

—— Nouvelles Lettres. The Hague, 1739.

—— Oeuvres diverses de Pierre Bayle . . . contenant tout ce que cet auteur a publié . . . excepté son Dictionnaire historique et critique. The Hague, 1727–1731, and 1737.

Addition aux Pensées diverses sur les comètes; ou, Réponse à un libelle intitulé Courte Revue des maximes de morale et des principes de religion de l'auteur des Pensées diverses sur les comètes. 1694.

Avis important aux réfugiés sur leur prochain retour en France. Donné pour Estrennes à l'un d'eux en 1690. 1690. (A separate copy of this work published in Amsterdam is cited here.)

La Cabale chimérique; ou, Réfutation de L'Histoire fabuleuse. Et des calomnies que Mr. J. vient de publier malicieusement touchant un certain projet de paix & touchant le libelle intitulé Avis important aux réfugiés sur leur prochain retour en France dans son Examen de ce libelle. 1691. (An edition published at Rotterdam was used for the present study.)

Ce que c'est la France toute catholique sous le règne de Louis le grand. 1685.

La Chimère de la cabale de Rotterdam démontrée par les prétendues convictions que le sieur Jurieu a publiée contre M. Bayle. 1691.

Commentaire philosophique sur ces paroles de J.C. contrains-les d'entrer. 1686.

Critique générale de L'histoire du calvinisme de M. Maimbourg. 1682.

Déclaration de M. Bayle touchant un petit écrit qui vient de paraître sous le titre de Courte Revue des maximes de morale. 1690.

Entretien sur la grande scandale causé par le livre intitulé La Cabale chimérique. Cologne, 1691.

Janua coelorum reserata cunctis religionibus a celebri admodum viro domino Petro Jurieu, 1692.

Lettres Choisies de Bayle. 1672–1706.

Lettres sur les petits livrets publiés contre la Cabale chimérique. 1690.

Nouvel Avis au petit auteur des petits livrets concernant ses lettres de M. Jurieu et de M. Bayle. 1692.

Nouvelle Hérésie dans la morale touchant la haine du prochain prêchée par M. Jurieu dans l'Eglise wallonne de Rotterdam les dimanches 24 de Janvier et 21 de Février. 1694.

Nouvelles de la république des lettres. 1684–1687.

Nouvelles Lettres de l'auteur de La Critique générale de L'Histoire du Calvinisme du P. Maimbourg. 1685.

Pensées diverses écrite à un docteur de Sorbonne à l'occasion de la comète. 1682.

Réflexions sur un Imprimé qui a pour titre Jugement du public et particulièrement de l'Abbé Renaudot sur le Dictionnaire de M. Bayle. 1697.

Réponse aux Questions d'un provincial. 1706.

Réponse d'un nouveau converti à la lettre d'un réfugié pour servir d'addition au livre de Dom Denis de Sainte-Marthe intitulé Réponse aux plaintes des protestants touchant la prétendue persécution de France où l'on expose le sentiment de Calvin et tous les plus célèbres ministres sur les peines dues aux hérétiques contenant des réflexions sur les guerres civiles des protestants. 1689.

Supplément du Commentaire philosophique. 1688.

—— Quelques Lettres de Bayle et de Baluze. Toulouse, 1891.

—— Requête présentée au roy de France par les protestants qui sont dans son royaume que l'on a contraints ci-devant d'embrasser la religion romaine. The Hague, 1697.

Bedé de la Gourmandière, Jean. Le Droit des roys contre le Cardinal Bellarmin et autres jésuites. Franckenthal, 1611.

Bellarmine, Robert. Disputationes . . . de controversiis christianae fidei ad-

versus hujus temporis haereticos. . . . Coloniae Agrippinae [*sic*], 1628.
—— Tractatus de potestate summi pontificis in rebus temporalibus adversus Gulielmum Barclaium. Rome, 1610.

Benoit, Elie. Avis sincères à MM. les prélats de France sur les lettres qui leur sont addressées sous le titre de prélats de l'Eglise gallicane. n.p., 1698.
—— Histoire de la révocation de l'édit de Nantes. Delft, 1693–1695.

Bernard, Jacques, Henri Basnage de Beauval, and Jean Dumont.
—— Lettres historiques contenant ce qui s'est passé de plus important en Europe et les réflexions convenables à ce sujet. The Hague and Amsterdam, 1692–1728.

Beza, Theodore. De haereticis a civili magistratu puniendis libellus. n.p., 1554.

Bochart, S. Lettre de M. Bochart à Mr. Morley, chapelain du roy d'Angleterre pour répondre à trois questions. Paris, 1650.

Bossuet, Jacques Bénigne. Avertissement aux protestants sur les lettres du ministre Jurieu contre L'Histoire des variations. 1689–1691. The Paris edition of 1740 was used.
—— Conférence avec M. Claude touchant l'infaillibilité de l'Eglise. 1682.
—— Défense de L'Histoire des variations contre La Réponse de M. Basnage. 1689.
—— L'Exposition de la foy de l'Eglise catholique sur les matières de controverse. 1671.
—— Histoire des variations des Eglises protestantes. 1688. The Paris edition of 1740 was used.
—— Lettre pastorale aux nouveaux catholiques de son diocèse. 1686.
—— Oeuvres complètes. Paris, 1856.
—— La Politique tirée des propres paroles de l'écriture sainte. 1709.

Boucher, Jean. De justa Henrici Tertii abdicatione e Francorum regno, Paris, 1589.
—— Sermons de la simulée conversion . . . de Henri de Bourbon. Paris, 1594.

Brueys, R. Examen des raisons qui ont donné lieu à la séparation des protestants. Paris, 1683.
—— Histoire du fanatisme de nôtre temps et le dessein que l'on avoit de soulever en France les mécontens des calvinistes. Paris, 1692.

Buchanan, George. De jure regni apud Scotos. Edinburgh, 1579.

Burke, Edmund. Correspondence of the Right Honorable Edmund Burke. London, 1844. 4 vols.

Cassander, George. De articulis religionis inter Catholicos & Protestantes controversis consultatio. 1564.
—— De officio pii ac publicae tranquillitatis vere amantis viri in hoc religionis dissidio. 1561.

Cassander, George. Opera. Paris, 1616.

Castellion, Jean Sebastien. De haereticis an sint persequendi. Magdeburg, 1554.

Chaufepié, J. Nouveau Dictionnaire historique et critique pour servir de supplément et de continuation au Dictionnaire de Pierre Bayle. Amsterdam, 1750–1756.

Claude, Jean. La Défense de la réformation contre le livre intitulé Préjugez légitimes contre le calvinisme. Paris, 1673.

—— Les Plaintes des Protestants cruellement opprimés dans le royaume de France. Cologne, 1686; Paris, 1885.

—— Réponse au livre de M. Arnaud intitulé La Perpétuité de la foy de l'Eglise catholique touchant l'eucharistie défendue. Quevilly and Rouen, 1670.

—— Réponse au livre de Monsieur l'Evêque de Meaux intitulé Conférence avec M. Claude. Charenton and Paris, 1683.

Constant de Rebeque, Henri Benjamin. De l'esprit de conquête et de l'usurpation dans leurs rapports avec la civilization européenne. Paris, 1814.

Cordemoy, Abbé Louis Géraud de. L'Eternité des peines de l'enfer contre les sociniens. Paris, 1707.

—— Lettres des nouveaux catholiques de l'Isle d'Arvert en Saintonge à l'auteur des Lettres prétendues pastorales. Paris, 1688.

—— Traité contre les sociniens . . . en parlant de la trinité & de l'incarnation. Paris, 1697.

Coulan, Antoine. La Défense des réfugiés contre un livre intitulé Avis important aux réfugiés sur leur prochain retour en France. Deventer, 1691.

Daillé, Jean. Réplique aux deux livres de MM. Adam et Cottiby. Geneva, 1662.

Daneau, Lambert. Ad libellum ab anonymo quodam libertino recens editum hoc titulo: De externa seu visibili Dei Ecclesia, ubi illa reperiri possit et quaenam vera sit etc seu potius adversus externam et visibilem Ecclesiam, utilis et necessaria responsio. Geneva, 1582.

—— Antwoort Lamberti Danaei Wijlen Professeur in de hooghe Schoole tot Leyden, op drie voorghestelde vragen, nopende het Ampt der Overheydt in de regeeringhe der kercken; wat haer toe coemt, ofte niet toe coemt. Delft, 1613.

—— Calx viva, qua Theod. Coornhartii sapo facile consumitur et in fumos evanescit. Geneva, 1583.

—— Politices Christianae libri Septem. . . . In quibus ea ex Dei verbo primum post autem ex que aliis quoque scriptis collecta sunt, quae ad optimam Reipublicae administrationem pertinent . . . Geneva, 1596.

De La Conseillère. Factum de M. de la Conseillère, demandeur, en réparation contre M. Jurieu défendeur. 1690.

Desmaizeaux, Pierre. La Vie de M. Bayle. The Hague, 1732.

De Vrigny, La Combe. *See* La Combe de Vrigny.

Donneau de Vizé, Jean. Affaires du temps. Paris, 1688–1692.

—— Le Mercure galant, contenant plusieurs histoires véritables et tout ce qui s'est passé depuis le premier janvier 1672. Paris, 1672–1710.

Dumoulin, Louis. Fasciculus epistolarum latine et gallice. Eleutheropoli [*sic*], 1676.

Dumoulin, Pierre. Regii sanguinis clamor ad coelum adversus parricidas anglicanos. The Hague, 1652.

Duplessis-Mornay, Phillipe. Mémoires, correspondance et vie de Duplessis-Mornay pour servir à l'histoire de la réformation et des guerres civiles et religieuses en France depuis l'an 1571 jusqu'en 1623. Paris, 1824–25.

—— Le Mystère d'iniquité c'est à dire l'histoire de la papauté, par quels progrez elle est montée à ce comble, et quelles oppositions les gens de bien lui ont fait de temps en temps. Où aussi sont défendus les droits des empereurs, rois et princes chrétiens contre les assertions des cardinaux Bellarmin et Baronius. Saumur, 1611.

Emery, J. A. Principes de messieurs Bossuet et Fenélon sur la souveraineté: tirés du 5ᵉ Avertissement sur les lettres de M. Jurieu et d'un Essai sur le gouvernement civil. Paris, 1791.

Ferrand, Louis. Réponse à L'Apologie pour la réformation. Paris, 1685.

Fétizon, Paul. Apologie pour les réformés, où l'on voit la juste idée des guerres civiles et les vrais fondements de l'édit de Nantes: entretien curieux entre un protestant et un catholique. The Hague, 1683.

Gauthereau. La France toute catholique sous le règne de Louis le grand. Lyon, 1684.

Gentillet, Innocent. Apologia pro christianis gallis religionis evangelicae seu reformatae. Geneva, 1588.

Goudet. Huits Entretiens où Irène et Aristote fournissent des idées pour terminer la présente guerre par une paix générale. 1690.

Goulart, Simon. Mémoires de l'estat de France sous Charles IX. Meidelbourg, 1578. Contains 1. Theodore de Bèze, Du droit des magistrats sur leurs sujets, 1574; 2. Dialogue d'Archon et de politie, 1576; 3. Francois Hotman, La Franco-Gaule, 1573.

Gousset, Jacques. Examen des endroits de l'accomplissement des prophéties de M.J. qui concernent la supputation des temps et de quelques autres endroits considérables par lequel il paroit que l'on ne peut conter sur ses explications. n.p., 1687.

Grotius, Hugo. Appendix ad interpretationem locorum N. Testamenti quae de Antichristo agunt aut agere putantur. In qua via sternitur ad christianorum concordiam. Amsterdam, 1641.

—— De imperio summarum potestatum circa sacra. Paris, 1647.

Grotius, Hugo. De jure belli ac pacis. Tr. J. B. Scott. Oxford, 1925.

Guichard, Louis Anastase. Histoire du socinianisme. Paris, 1723. This work was written about a quarter of a century earlier and has been attributed to Bernhard l'Ami (Lamy).

Hamilton, Alexander. The Federalist. Everyman edition. New York, 1929.

Hobbes, Thomas. Behemoth. In Vol. VI of The English Works of Thomas Hobbes, ed. Sir William Molesworth. London, 1841.

—— Dialogue between a Philosopher and a Student of the Common Laws of England. In Vol. VI of The English Works, ed. Molesworth.

—— Philosophical Elements of a True Citizen (De cive). In Vol. II of The English Works, ed. Molesworth.

Hooker, Richard. Of the Laws of Ecclesiastical Polity. London, 1907.

Hotman, Francis. Brutum fulmen papae Sixti V adversus Henricum sereniss. Regem Navarrae et illustriss. Henricum Borbonium una cum protestatione multiplicis nullitatis. Leyden, 1586.

—— De jure regni galliae libri tres. Basel, 1585.

—— De jure successionis regiae in regno Francorum leges aliquot ex probatis auctoribus collectae, studio et opera F.H. obiter de jure regis Navarrae. n.p., 1588.

Huet, Gédéon. Apologie pour l'apologiste des tolérants. Deventer, 1690.

—— Apologie pour les vrais tolérants où l'on fait voir avec la dernière évidence et d'une manière à convaincre les plus préoccupez la pureté de leurs intentions et la vérité de leur dogme. Pour opposer aux fausses idées que M.J. en a voulu donner dans quelques uns de ses écrits; mais particulièrement dans son Tableau du socinianisme. Deventer, 1690.

—— Autre Lettre écrite de Suisse en Hollande pour répondre à la seconde partie de l'ouvrage du prétendu Nouveau Converti touchant les réflexions qu'il a fait sur ce qu'il appelle les guerres civiles des Protestants & la présente invasion de l'Angleterre. Dordrecht, 1690.

—— Lettre d'un des amis de M. Bayle aux amis de M. Jurieu. 1691.

—— Lettre écrite de Suisse en Hollande pour suppléer au défaut de la réponse que l'on avoit promis de donner à un certain ouvrage que Mons. Pellisson a publié sous le nom d'un Nouveau Converti touchant les récriminations qui y sont faites aux réformés des violences que les catholiques employent pour le conversion de ceux qu'ils appellent hérétiques. Dordrecht, 1690.

Huet, Pierre Daniel. Demonstratio evangelica. Paris, 1679.

Huisseau, Isaac d'. La Réunion du christianisme; ou, La Manière de rejoindre les chrétiens en une seule confession de foi. Saumur, 1670.

Jaquelot, Isaac. A Messieurs les pasteurs et les conducteurs des Eglises wallonnes assemblées en synode à Naerden. The Hague, 1691.

—— Avis sur Le Tableau du socinianisme. n.p., 1690. Wrongly attributed to Jurieu.

—— Lettre à Messieurs les prélats de l'Eglise gallicane. The Hague, 1700. Wrongly attributed to Jurieu.

Johnson, Samuel. Julian the Apostate with a Comparison of Popery and Paganism. London, 1682.

La Combe de Vrigny. Défense du parlement d'Angleterre dans la cause de Jacques II. Où il est traité de la puissance des rois & du droit des peuples, par les anciens conciles & par les sentimens des sages & des savans, particulièrement de l'Eglise romaine; & enfin par des raisons tireés du droit de la nature & des gens; auxquelles on fait voir que l'écriture sainte s'accorde parfaitement, bien loin d'y être contraire. Rotterdam, 1692.

La Monnoye, Bernard de. Histoire de Bayle et ses ouvrages. Amsterdam, 1716.

Larrey, Isaac de. Réponse à L'Avis aux réfugiés. Rotterdam, 1709.

Le Bret, Cardin. De la souveraineté du roy. Paris, 1632.

Le Clerc, Jean. Bibliothèque choisie, pour servir de suite à La Bibliothèque universelle. Amsterdam, 1703–1713.

—— Bibliothèque universelle et historique. Amsterdam, 1686–1702.

—— Lettre à M. Jurieu sur la manière dont il traite Episcopius dans son Tableau du socinianisme. 1690.

Lelong, Jacques. Bibliothèque historique de la France. Paris, 1768–78. This work was continued by M. Fevret de Fontette.

Le Noble, Eustache. Le Couronnement de Guillemet et de Guillemette avec le sermon du grand docteur Burnet, troisième dialogue entre Pasquier et Marforio sur les affaires du temps. London, 1689.

—— Le Festin de Guillemot, quatrième dialogue de Pasquin et de Marforio. London, 1689.

Leti, Gregorio. Teatro britannico. London, 1683.

Levassor, Michel. Histoire générale de l'Europe sous le règne de Louis XIII. Amsterdam, 1700–1711.

—— Lettres d'un gentil'homme françois sur l'établissement d'une capitation générale en France. Liége, 1695.

Locke, John. Of Civil Government: Two Treatises. Everyman edition. London, 1924.

——Works. 11th ed., London, 1812.

Louandre, Charles. Oeuvres politiques de Benjamin Constant. Paris, 1874.

Maimbourg, Louis. Histoire du calvinisme. Paris, 1682.

Maistre, Joseph de. Oeuvres complètes. Lyon, 1884.

Masius, Hector Gottfried. Interesse principum circa religionem evangelicam. 1688.

Ménage, Gilles. Menagiana. Paris, 1694.

Merlat, Elie. Traité sur les pouvoirs absolus des souverains, pour servir d'instruction, de consolation, et d'apologie aux Eglises Réformées de France qui sont affligées, Cologne, 1685.

Mill, John Stuart. On Liberty. Everyman Edition. London, 1931.

Milton, John. Pro populo anglicano defensio contra Claudii Anonymi, alias Salmasii, defensionem regiam. London, 1651.

Naudé, Gabriel. Science des princes; ou, Considérations politiques sur les coups d'état. Paris, 1752.

Nicole, Pierre. De l'unité de l'Eglise; ou, Réfutation du nouveau système de M. Jurieu. Paris, 1687.

—— Préjugez légitimes contre le calvinisme. Paris, 1671.

—— Les prétendus réformés convaincus de schisme. Paris, 1684.

Nizet, G. Réponse sommaire au livre intitulé Avis important aux réfugiés. Mastricht, 1690.

Novi de Caveirac, Jean. Apologie de Louis XIV et de son conseil sur la révocation l'édit de Nantes pour servir de Réponse à La Lettre d'un patriote sur la tolérance civile des Protestants de France. n.p., 1758.

Paets, H. V. H. V. P.(aets) ad B(ayle) de nuperis Angliae motibus epistola in qua de diversum a publica religione circa divina sentientium disseritur tolerantia. Rotterdam, 1685.

Paine, Thomas. Rights of Man (1791). In The Writings of Thomas Paine ed. M. D. Conway. New York, 1894.

Pajon, Claude. Examen du livre qui porte pour titre Préjugez légitmes contre le calvinisme. Charenton, 1675.

Papin, Issaac. Essais de théologie sur la providence et sur la grâce où l'on tache de délivrer M. Jurieu de toutes les difficultés accablantes qu'il rencontre dans son système. Rotterdam, 1687.

—— La Foy réduite à ses véritables principes, et réduite à ses justes bornes. Rotterdam, 1687.

—— La Tolérance des protestants et l'autorité de l'Eglise; ou, Réponse au livre de M. Jurieu qui porte pour titre Lettre pastorale aux fidèles de Paris et de Blois, etc. Avec une lettre à M. Jurieu sur ce qu'il y a de personnel dans ce libelle. Paris, 1692.

Pareus, David. In divinam ad Romanos S. Pauli . . . Epistolam Commentarius. Geneva, 1613.

Paulian, Pierre. Critique des Lettres pastorales de M. Jurieu. Lyon, 1689.

Pellisson-Fontanier, Paul. Les Chimères de M. Jurieu, réponse générale à ses Lettres pastorales de la seconde année contre le livre des Réflexions. Examen abrégé de ses prophéties, sa clarté prophétique et l'origine de cette clarté. Paris, 1689.

—— Réflexions sur les différends en matière de religion avec les preuves de la tradition ecclésiastique. Paris, 1686.

Perron, Jacques Davy, Cardinal du. Harangue faicte de la part de la chambre ecclésiastique en celle du tier-estat sur l'article du serment. Paris, 1615.

Philipot, Jacques. Les Justes Bornes de la tolérance avec la défense des mystères du christianisme. Amsterdam, 1691.

Proudhon, Pierre Joseph. General Idea of the Revolution in the Nineteenth Century. London, 1923.

Ramsay, Andrew M. Essay philosophique sur le gouvernement civil, où l'on traite de la necessité, de l'origine, des droits, des bornes, et des différentes formes de la souveraineté selon les principes de feu M. Francois de Salignac de La Motthe Fénelon. London, 1721.

Rocoles, Jean-Baptiste de. L'Histoire véritable du calvinisme; ou, Mémoires historiques touchant la réformation opposés à L'Histoire du calvinisme de M. Maimbourg. Amsterdam, 1683.

Rou, Jean. Remarques sur L'Histoire du calvinisme de M. Maimbourg. The Hague, 1682.

Rousseau, Jean Jacques. "Lettre à M. Le Marquis de Mirabeau." In C. E. Vaughan, *The Political Writings of Jean Jacques Rousseau*. Cambridge, 1915.

—— Oeuvres. Paris, 1821.

—— The Social Contract. Everyman edition. London, 1932.

Rutherford, Samuel. Lex, Rex: the Law and the Prince, n.p., 1644.

Saint-Blancard, Gaultier de. L'Histoire apologétique; ou, Défense des libertés des églises réformés de France. Amsterdam, 1688.

Sainte-Marthe, Denis de. Entretiens touchant l'entreprise du Prince d'Orange sur l'angleterre, où l'on prouve que cette action fait porter aux protestants les caractères de l'antichristianisme que M. Jurieu a reproché à l'Eglise romaine. Paris, 1689.

—— Réponse aux Plaintes des protestants touchant la prétendue persécution de France. Où l'on expose le sentiment de Calvin & tous les plus célèbres ministres, sur les peines dues aux hérétiques. Paris, 1688.

Saumaise, Claude (Salmasius). Ad Joann. Miltonem responsio. London, 1660.

—— Defensio regia pro Carolo I ad serenissimum Magnae Britanniae regem Carolum II filium natu majorem, heredem, et successorem legitimum, sumptibus regiis. n.p., 1649.

Saurin, Elie. Défense de la véritable doctrine de l'Eglise sur le principe de la foy contre le livre de M. Jurieu intitulé Défense . . . Utrecht, 1697.

—— Examen de la théologie de M. Jurieu où l'on traite de plusieurs points très importants de la religion chrétienne comme du principe de la foi, de l'idée de l'Eglise, de la justification, de l'efficace du batème, de la polygamie, de l'amour du prochain, etc., où l'on fait voir que la doctrine de M. Jurieu sur ces articles est non seulement contraire à celle des Eglises réformées, mais aussi d'une très dangereuse conséquence. The Hague, 1694.

Saurin, Elie. Justification de la doctrine du Saurin Pasteur de l'Eglise wallonne d'Utrecht contre deux libelles de M. Jurieu l'un intitulé Idée des sentiments de M. Saurin etc., et l'autre La Religion du latitudinaire. Utrecht, 1697.

—— Réflexions sur les droits de la conscience où l'on fait voir la différence entre les droits de la conscience éclairée et ceux de la conscience errante, on réfute le commentaire philosophique et le livre intitulé Droits des deux souverains et on marque les justes bornes de la tolérance civile en matière de religion. Utrecht, 1697.

—— Réflexions sur un libelle intitulé Information pour nosseigneurs les états & instruction sur ce qui s'est passé au synode de Ziericzée pour les églises qui doivent composer le synode de Breda. Utrecht, 1692.

Scultetus, Daniel Severinus. Animadversiones ad nuperum scriptum de Petri Jurieu, unionem ecclesiae lutheranae et reformatae concernens. Hamburg, 1687.

—— Epicrisis ad articulos argentoratenses nuperos unionem ecclesiae evangelicae & Romano-Catholicae concernentes. Frankfort, 1686.

Selden, John. Table Talk. London, 1927.

Simon, Richard. Histoire critique du vieux testament. Paris, 1678.

—— Lettre de quelques nouveaux convertis de France à M. Jurieu sur ses Lettres pastorales. Frankfort, 1687.

—— Lettres choisies. Amsterdam, 1730.

Soulier, Pierre. Histoire des édits de pacification et des moyens que les P.R. ont employé pour les obtenir contenant ce qui s'est passé de plus remarquable depuis la naissance du calvinisme jusqu'à présent. Paris, 1682.

—— Histoire du calvinisme contenant sa naissance, son progrès, sa décadence, & sa fin en France. Paris, 1686.

Tocqueville, Alexis de. De la démocratie en Amerique. Paris, 1864.

Tronchin du Breuil, Jean. Lettres sur les matières du temps. Amsterdam, 1688–1690.

Varillas, Antoine. Histoire de Charles IX. Paris, 1683.

—— Histoire de Francois I. Paris, 1685.

Voltaire, Francois M. Oeuvres complètes de Voltaire. 1785–1789.

ANNOYMOUS WORKS

Avis sincère de M. Jurieu . . . par lequel il fait voir que les plus savants et les plus éclairés docteurs de cette Eglise ont toujours eu l'esprit républicain et des sentiments opposés à la puissance absolue des souverains et monarques. Tiré de son livre qu'il intitule Examen d'un libelle pour combler de honte & de confusion le Sr. Becman & ses adhérents qui osent nier ce que Mons. Masius en avoit avancé avec vérité dans ces écrits, par un de ses amis. n.p., 1691.

Le Cinquième Empire. . . . Ouvrage très curieux dans lequel on explique diverses prophéties de l'écriture qui jusques ici ont été mal entendues. On y fait voir aussi la décadence des empires & le temps que Babylone sera détruite. The Hague, 1689. This little book has been erroneously attributed to Jurieu.

A Collection of State Tracts Published on the Occasion of the Late Revolution in 1688 and during the Reign of King William. London, 1705–1707.

Conformité de la conduite de l'Eglise de France pour ramener les protestants avec celle de l'Eglise d'Afrique pour ramener les donatistes à l'Eglise catholique. Paris, 1685.

Défense du Sr. Samuel Chappuzeau contre une satire intitulée L'Esprit de Mr. Arnaud. n.d., n.p.

De justa reipublicae Christianae in reges impios et haereticos auctoritate, justissimaque catholicorum ad Henricum Navarraeum et quemcumque hereticum ex regno Galliae repellendum confoederatione. Paris, 1590.

De l'adoration de l'eucharistie pour répondre aux faux raisonnements de MM. de la religion prétendue réformée dans leur Préservatif contre le changement de religion. Toulouse, 1683.

L'Europe esclave si l'Angleterre ne rompt ses fers. n.p., 1685.

Le Jésuite démasqué; ou, Entretien entre le très saint Père la Chaise, Confesseur de sa majesté très-Chrétienne, le très chaste Père Peters, confesseur de sa majesté britannique & le très pieux Père Tachart, ambassadeur de sa majesté siammoise, dans lequel on découvre les principaux moyens dont ces revérends pères prétendent se servir pour la conversion des hérétiques d'Angleterre & des idolatres de Siam avec une petite pasquinade contre les plus célèbres écrivains de l'Eglise gallicane. n.p., 1688.

Julien l'apostat; ou, Abrégé de sa vie . . . avec une comparison du papisme et du paganisme . . . et une autre idée générale du papisme avec un petit traité de l'antichrist. n.p., 1688. Translated from English. Cf. La Peste du genre humain ou la vie de Julien L'Apostat, mise en parallèle avec celle de Louis XIV, 1696; listed under Jurieu's writings.

Latitudinarius orthodoxus: in particulari de christianae religionis mysteriis, sancta trinitate Christi incarnatione corporis resurrectione caena Domini accesserunt vindiciae libertatis christianae ecclesiae anglianae et Arthuri Bury S. T. P. contra ineptias et calumnias Petri Jurieu. London, 1697.

A Letter of Several French Ministers Fled into Germany upon the Account of the Persecution in France: to Such of Their Brethren in England As Approved the King's Declaration Touching Liberty of Conscience. London, 1688.

Lettre à Monsieur Bl. . . . sur l'action extraordinaire d'un prêtre de l'Eglise romaine qui a embrassé la religion protestante. n.p., 1689.

Lettre d'un intolérant à un théologien intolérant aussi. n.p., 1690. Erroneously attributed to Jurieu.

Lettre d'un mylord absent de la convention à l'un de ses amis. n.p., 1689.

Lettre du R. P. Peters, Jésuite, premier aumonier du roi d'Angleterre écrite du R. P. La Chaise, confesseur du roi très-chrétien, touchant les affaires présentes d'Angleterre. n.p., 1688.

Lettre sur Les Avis sincères aux prélats de France. n.p., 1698.

Lettre sur l'état présent d'Angleterre & l'indépendance des rois. Amsterdam, 1685.

Manifeste des habitans des Cevennes sur leur prise d'armes. n.p., 1703.

Présages de la décadence des empires où sont melées plusieurs observations curieuses touchant la religion & les affaires du temps. Mecklenburg, 1688. Erroneously attributed to Jurieu.

The Proceedings of the Present Parliament Justified by the Opinion of the Most Judicious and Learned Hugo Grotius. Vol. III of *A Collection of State Tracts Published on the Occasion of the Late Revolution in 1688 and during the Reign of King William.* London, 1705–1707.

Réponse du R. P. La Chaise confesseur du roi très-chretien à la lettre du R. P. Peters, jésuite & premier aumonier du roi d'Angleterre sur la conduite qu'il doit tenir auprès de sa majesté pour la conversion de ses sujets protestants. n.p., 1688.

Le Réveille-Matin des françois et de leurs voisins. Edinburgh, 1574.

Les Sept Sages de France à leur roi Louis XIV sur les moyens de paix. Rotterdam, 1692.

Traité de la raison humaine, traduit de l'anglois. n.d., n.p.

Traité de l'autorité royale. Paris, 1691.

Le Triomphe de la liberté; ou, L'Irrévocabilité du test et autres lois fondamentales des états prouvés par le droit divin, par le droit naturel, par le droit de la nation & par la mort tragique de Charles Stuward Père du Roi Régnant. London, 1688.

La Tyrannie des préjugés; ou, Réflexions sur le fragment d'une lettre de Mlle Marie Du Moulin. Avec plusieurs éclaircissements, en forme d'épitres sur la puissance ecclésiastique et l'excommunication. Pour servir de réponse à M. Jurieu. London, 1678.

Vindiciae contra tyrannos. Amsterdam, 1610.

SECONDARY SOURCES

Acton, John E., Lord. "The Protestant Theory of Persecution." In *The History of Freedom and Other Essays.* London, 1922.

Adler, M. J., and Walter Farrell. "The Theory of Democracy." *The Thomist,* III (1941), 397–449, 588–652; IV (1942), 121–181, 286–354, 446–522, 692–761; VII (1944), 80–131.

Ainslie, J. L. The Doctrines of Ministerial Order in the Reformed Churches. Edinburgh, 1940.

Allen, John W. A History of Political Thought in the Sixteenth Century. New York, 1928.

Allier, Raoul. Anthologie protestante française XVIe et XVIIe siècles. Paris, 1918.

—— "L'Edit de Nantes et les débuts de la tolérance," *Revue Bleue Politique et Littéraire,* XCVIII, 4th ser., 675–681.

Armstrong, E. "The Political Theory of the Huguenots." *English Historical Review,* IV (1889), 13–40.

Arnal, J. "De l'influence des réfugiés français aux Pays-Bas." *Bulletin de la Commission des églises wallonnes* (Leyden), XXIX, 4th ser., No. 2, 1–21.

Ascoli, Georges. "Bayle et L'Avis aux Réfugiés." *Revue d'histoire littéraire de la France,* XX (1913), 517–545.

—— La Grande Bretagne devant l'opinion française au dix-septième siècle. Paris, 1930.

—— Relations intellectuels entre la France et l'Angleterre au XVIIe siècle. Paris, 1927.

Atger, Frederic. Essai sur l'histoire des doctrines du contrat social. Nîmes, 1906.

Bainton, Roland H. "The Appeal to Reason and the American Revolution." *The Constitution Reconsidered,* ed. Conyers Read. New York, 1938.

—— "The Parable of the Tares as the Proof Text for Religious Liberty to the End of the Sixteenth Century." *Church History,* I (June, 1932), 67–89.

—— "Sebastian Castellio and the Toleration Controversy of the Sixteenth Century." In *Persecution and Liberty; Essays in Honor of George Lincoln Burr.* New York, 1931.

—— "Servet et les Libertins de Genève." *Bulletin de la Société de l'Histoire du Protestantisme français,* LXXXVI–LXXXVII (July–September, 1938), 261–269.

—— "The Struggle for Religious Liberty," *Church History,* X (June, 1941), 95–124.

—— Ed. Concerning heretics; whether they are to be persecuted and how they are to be treated; a collection of the opinions of learned men, both ancient and modern; an anonymous work attributed to Sebastian Castellio, now first done into English, together with excerpts from other works of Sebastian Castellio and David Joris on religious liberty. New York, 1935.

Baird, Henry M. The Huguenots and the Revocation of the Edict of Nantes. New York, 1895.

Barbier, Antoine A. Dictionnaire des ouvrages anonymes et pseudonymes composés, traduits ou publiés en français et en latin. Paris, 1822–1827.

Barker, Ernest. "A Huguenot Theory of Politics: the Vindiciae contra Tyrannos." *Proceedings of the Huguenot Society of London,* XIV (1930), 39 ff.

Barnes, Annie. Jean Le Clerc et la République des Lettres. Paris, 1938.

Baron, Hans. "Calvinistic Republicanism and Its Historical Roots." *Church History,* VIII (March, 1939), 30–42.

Bastide, Charles. Anglais et Français du XVIIe siècle. Paris, 1912.

—— "Bayle, est-il l'auteur de l'Avis aux réfugiés?" *Bulletin de la Société de l'Histoire du Protestantisme français,* LVI (1907), 544–558.

—— John Locke: ses théories politiques et leur influence en Angleterre. Paris, 1907.

—— "Locke et les huguenots." *Bulletin de la Société de l'Histoire du Protestantisme français,* LXII (1913), 60 ff.

Bates, M. Searle. Religious Liberty. New York, 1945.

Batiffol, Louis. "Les idées de la Révolution sous Louis XIV." *Revue de Paris,* XXVIII, Part II (1854), 97–120.

Batten, J. Minton. John Dury. Chicago, 1944.

—— "Political Factors in Movements toward Christian Unity in Seventeenth Century Europe." *Church History,* XLII (September, 1943), 163–176.

Baumer, Franklin Le Van. "The Church of England and the Common Corps of Christendom." *The Journal of Modern History,* XVI (1944), 21 ff.

Beard, Charles. The Reformation of the Sixteenth Century in Its Relation to Modern Thought and Knowledge. London, 1883.

Blocaille, E. Etude sur François Hotman. Dijon, 1902.

Bonnet, Jules. "Les Lettres Pastorales de Pierre Jurieu." *Bulletin de la Société de l'Histoire du Protestantisme français,* XXXIV (1885), 404 ff.

—— "Sébastien Castellion; ou, La tolérance au XVIe siècle." *Bulletin de la Société de l'Histoire du Protestantisme français,* XVI (1867), 465 ff; XVII (1868), 529 ff.

Bonet-Maury, Gaston. Histoire de la liberté de conscience en France. Paris, 1900.

—— "Le Protestantisme français et la république aux XVIe et XVIIe siècles." *Bulletin de la Société de l'Histoire du Protestantisme français,* LIII (May-June, 1904), 234 ff.

Borgeaud, C. The Rise of Modern Democracy in Old and New England. London, 1894.

Bost, Charles. "Bibliographie des oeuvres de Jurieu." *Bulletin de la Société de l'Histoire du Protestantisme français.* LXXXIV (1935), 512 ff.

—— Les Prédicants Protestants des Cévennes et du Bas-Languedoc 1694–1700. Paris, 1912.

—— "Les Protestants français contre Louis XIV." *Revue Chrétienne,* LXXI (1923).

Bouchard, M. De l'humanisme à l'encyclopédie; essai sur l'évolution des esprits dans la bourgeoisie bourguignonne sous les règnes de Louis XIV et de Louis XV. Paris, 1929.

Bouchez, Ferdinand. Le Mouvement libéral en France au XVIIe siècle (1610–1700). Lille, 1908.

Boulenger, Jacques. The Seventeenth Century. London, 1920.

Bourelly, Elie. Jean Claude et la défense de la réformation. Montauban, 1887.

Bourgeois, Emile, and Louis André. Les Sources de l'Histoire de France XVIIe siècle 1610–1715. Paris, 1913–1935.

Bourne, H. R. Fox. The Life of John Locke. London, 1876.

Brémond, Henri. Histoire littéraire du sentiment religieux en France depuis la fin des guerres de religion jusqu'à nos jours. Paris, 1925.

Brunetière, Ferdinand. Etudes critiques sur l'histoire de la littérature française. Paris, 1894. Vol. IV.

Bryce, James. "The Law of Nature." In Vol. II of *Studies in History and Jurisprudence.* New York, 1901.

Buisson, Ferdinand. Sébastien Castellion; sa vie et son oeuvre (1515–1563); étude sur les origines du protestantisme libéral français. Paris, 1892.

Bury, J. B. A History of Freedom of Thought. London, 1920.

Camut, E. La Tolérance protestante. Paris, 1904.

Cardauns, Ludwig. Die Lehre vom Widerstandsrecht des Volks gegen die rechtmassige Obrigkeit im Luthertum und im Calvinismus des 16 Jahrhunderts. Bonn, 1903.

Cartier, A., "Les Idées politiques de Théodore de Bèze d'après Le Traité du droit des magistrats sur leurs sujets." *Bulletin de la Société d'Histoire et d'Archaeologie de Genève* (1900).

Charavay, E. Lettres autographes. Paris, 1887.

Chenevière, Marc-Edouard. La Pensée politique de Calvin. Geneva, 1937.

Church, William F. Constitutional Thought in Sixteenth Century France. Cambridge, Mass., 1941.

Clark, G. N. The Seventeenth Century. Oxford, 1929.

Cohen, Gustave. Ecrivains français en Hollande dans la première moitié du XVIIe siècle. Paris, 1920.

—— "Sur Grotius, Sorbière, les libertins et les sociniens dans la première moitié du dix-septième siècle." *Bulletin de la Société d'Histoire Moderne* (April, 1933).

Constantinescu-Bagdat, Elsie. Bayle (1647–1706). Paris, 1928.

Courtines, Leo Pierre. Bayle's Relations with England and the English. New York, 1938.

Creighton, Mandell. Persecution and Tolerance. London, 1906.

Crouslé, L. Bossuet et le protestantisme. Paris, 1901.

Dargaud, Jean Marie. Histoire de la liberté religieuse en France et de ses fondateurs. Paris, 1859.

Das, G. "Pierre Jurieu als middelpunt van een spionnagedienst 1689–1713." *Tijdschrift voor Geschiednis,* XLI (1926), 372 ff.

Daum, Hilde. Pierre Jurieu und seine Auseinandersetzung mit Antoine Arnauld im Streit um die Rechtfertigungs- und Gnadenlehre. Marburg, 1937.

Dedieu, Joseph. Montesquieu et la tradition politique anglaise en France. Paris, 1909.

—— Le Role politique des protestants français (1689–1715). Paris, 1920.

Delvolvé, Jean. Religion, critique et philosophie positive chez Pierre Bayle. Paris, 1906.

Denis, Jacques. Bayle et Jurieu. Caen, 1886.

—— "Essai sur la littérature morale et politique du XVIIe siècle." *Mémoires de l'Academie impériale des sciences, arts et belles-lettres de Caen* (1891), 3.

—— Le XVIIIe siècle dans le XVIIe siècle. Caen, 1896.

Douarche, Aristides. De tyrannicidio apud scriptores decimi sexti seculi. Paris, 1888.

Douen, O. Les Premiers Pasteurs du désert 1685–1700. Paris, 1879.

Doumerque, Emile. Jean Calvin. Les hommes et les choses de son temps. Lausanne, 1917.

—— Les origines historiques de La Déclaration des droits de l'homme et du citoyen. Paris, 1905.

Dowden, Edward. Puritan and Anglican. New York, 1901.

Dubois, Lucien. Bayle et la tolérance. Paris, 1902.

Durand, R. "Louis XIV et Jacques II à la veille de la Révolution de 1688." *Revue d'histoire moderne et contemporaine,* X (March and April, 1908), 28–44, 111–126, 162–204.

Egger, E. Etudes d'histoire et de morale sur le meutre politique. Torino, 1866.

Elkan, Albert. Die Publizistik der Bartholomäusnacht und Mornays "Vindiciae contra Tyrannos." Heidelberg, 1905.

Evans, John Y. "Erastianism." In Vol. V of the *Encyclopaedia of Religion and Ethics,* ed. James Hastings. New York, 1912.

Faguet, Emile. Dix-septième siècle: études littéraires. Paris, 1898.

—— Seizième siècle: études littéraires. Paris, 1894.

Fanfani, Amintore. Catholicism, Protestantism, and Capitalism. New York, 1935.

Faurey, Joseph. L'Edit de Nantes et la question de la tolérance. Paris, 1929.

—— La Monarchie française et le protestantisme français. Paris, 1923.

Fawker, A. "Persecution," in *Encyclopedia of Religion and Ethics,* ed. James Hastings. Vol. IX, New York, 1917.

Ferguson, W. K. "The Place of Jansenism in French History." *Journal of Religion,* VII (1927), 16–42.

Figgis, John N. The Divine Right of Kings. Cambridge, 1914.

—— Studies of Political Thought from Gerson to Grotius 1414–1625. Cambridge, 1931.

Flynn, J. S. The Influence of Puritanism on the Political and Religious Thought of the English. London, 1920.

Fonbrune-Berbinau, P. "Deux lettres inédites 'de Pierre Jurieu, 1697." *Bulletin de la Société de l'Histoire du Protestantisme français,* LIV (November–December, 1905), 552 ff.

Foster, Herbert D. "International Calvinism through Locke and the Revolution of 1688." *The American Historical Review,* XXXII (1926–27), 475–499.

—— "Liberal Calvinism: the Remonstrants at the Synod of the Dort." *Harvard Theological Review,* XVI (1923), 1–37.

—— "The Political Theories of Calvinists before the Puritan Exodus to America." *The American Historical Review,* XXI (1915–1916), 481–503.

Franck, Adolphe. Réformateurs et publicistes de l'Europe, dix-septième siècle. Paris, 1881.

Fréville, Henri. "Richard Simon et les protestants d'après sa correspondance." *Revue d'histoire moderne,* VI (1931), 30–55.

Frosterus, G. Les Insurgés protestants sous Louis XIV. Paris, 1868.

Gachet d'Artigny, Antoine. "Caractère de P. Bayle avec des réflexions sur ses amours avec Mad. Jurieu et de son dessein de se faire Catholique." *Mémoires nouveaux d'histoire, de critique et de littérature,* I, 287 ff., 466 ff.

Gagnebin, F. H. "Les Pasteurs de France réfugiés en Hollande après la révocation de l'Edit de Nantes." *Bulletin de la commission de l'histoire des églises wallonnes* (1884).

Galland, A. Les pasteurs français Amyraut, Bochart etc. et la royauté de droit divin de l'Edit de Nantes à la révocation 1629–1685. Paris, 1929. Also published in *Bulletin de la Société de l'Histoire du Protestantisme français,* 1928.

—— Quid S. Bochartus de jure regum anno 1650 disseruerit. Alençon, 1897.

Garnier, A., Agrippa d'Aubigné et le parti protestant. Paris, 1928.

Garrison, W. E. Intolerance. New York, 1934.

Gerig, J. L. and G. L. Van Roosbroeck. "Bayle Persecuted: an Unpublished Letter about Jurieu." *The Romanic Review,* XXIII (1932), 20 ff.

Gierke, Otto von. The Development of Political Theory. Ed. Bernard Freyd, New York, 1939.

Gierke, Otto von. Natural Law and the Theory of Society 1500 to 1800. Ed. Ernest Barker. Cambridge, 1934.

Gooch, G. P. English Democratic Ideas in the Seventeenth Century. Cambridge, 1927.

Gough, John. The Social Contract. Oxford, 1936.

Grant, A. J. The Huguenots. London, 1934.

—— "The Problem of Religious Toleration in XVIth Century France." *Proceedings of the Huguenot Society of London,* XIII (1923–1929), 154–172.

Griselle, Eugène. "Louis XIV et Jurieu d'après une Lettre Inédite de ce Dernier (4 Avril 1689)." *Bulletin de la Société de l'Histoire du Protestantisme français,* LV (1906), 147–167.

Grondin, Max. Les Doctrines politiques de Locke et les origines de La Déclaration des droits de l'homme de 1789. Bordeaux, 1920.

Grotz, A. Jurieu et la révocation de l'Edit de Nantes. Nîmes, 1902.

Guerard, A. The Life and Death of an Ideal: France in the Classical Age. New York, 1928.

Gurvitch, G. L'Idée du droit social. Paris, 1932.

—— "Natural Law." In Vol. XI of the *Encyclopaedia of the Social Sciences.* New York, 1933.

Haag, Eugène and Emile Haag. La France protestante. Paris, 1846–1859.

Hallam, Henry. Introduction to the Literature of Europe in the Fifteenth, Sixteenth, and Seventeenth Centuries. London, 1873.

Haller, William. *The Rise of Puritanism.* New York, 1938.

Harnack, Adolph. History of Dogma. Oxford, 1899.

Hatin, E. Les Gazettes de Hollande et la presse clandestine aux XVIIᵉ et XVIIIᵉ siècles. Paris, 1865.

Hazard, Paul. La Crise de la conscience Européenne (1680–1715). Paris, 1935.

Heinberg, John G. "Theories of Majority Rule." *American Political Science Review,* XXVI (1932), 452–469.

Hering, C. W., Geschichte der kirchliches Unionsversuche seit der Reformation bis auf unsere Zeit. Leipzig, 1836–1838.

Hitier, M. J. "La Doctrine de l'absolutisme." *Annales de l'Université de Grenoble,* XV (1903), 37 ff., 417 ff.

Hoe, Yung Chi. The Origin of Parliamentary Sovereignty or Mixed Monarchy. Shanghai, 1935.

Holborn, H. "Protestantismus und politische Ideengeschichte." *Historische Zeitschrift,* CXLIV (1931), 15–30.

Holzle, Erwin. "Naturrecht, Staatsrecht und Historisches Recht im Zeitalter der englischen und amerikanischer Revolution." *Vierteljahresschrift für Sozial- und Wirtschaftesgeschichte,* XXIV (1931), 452–465.

Honigsheim, Paul. Die Staats- und Sozial-Lehren der französischen Jansen-isten im 17 Jahrhundert. Heidelberg, 1914.

—— "Le Gallicanisme précurseur du XVIIIᵉ siècle." *Archives de philosophie de droit et de sociologie juridique* (1935).

Hudson, Winthrop S. "Democratic Freedom and Religious Faith in the Reformed Tradition." *Church History,* XV (September, 1946), 177–194.

—— John Ponet (1516?–1556) Advocate of Limited Monarchy. Chicago, 1942.

Hyma, Albert. Christianity and Politics: a History of the Principles and Struggles of Church and State. New York, 1938.

Jaulmes, Charles. Essai sur Le Préservatif contre le changement de religion de Pierre Jurieu. Montauban, 1888.

Jellinek, George. The Declaration of the Rights of Man and of Citizens. New York, 1907.

Jones, R. A. "Fénelon." In *The Social and Political Ideas of Some Great French Thinkers of the Age of Reason,* ed. F. J. C. Hearnshaw. London, 1930.

Jones, Rufus M. Spiritual Reformers in the 16th and 17th Centuries. London, 1914.

Jordan, W. K. The Development of Religious Toleration in England. Cambridge, Mass., 1932–1940.

Kaeppler-Vielzeuf, E. "Bibliographie chronologique des oeuvres de Pierre Jurieu (1637–1713)." *Bulletin de la Société de l'Histoire du Protestantisme français,* LXXXIV (July–September, 1935), 391–440.

—— "La Controverse Jurieu–De la Conseillère (1690)." *Bulletin de la Société de l'Histoire du Protestantisme français,* LXXXVI–LXXXVII (April–June, 1937), 146–152.

—— "Le droit de résistance à la tyrannie d'après Jurieu." *Revue d'Histoire et de Philosophie religieuses,* XVII (May–June, 1937), 201–246.

Kaltenborn, Karl, Baron von. Die Vorläufer des Hugo Grotius auf dem Gebiete des ius naturae et gentium sowie der Politik im Reformationszeitalter. Leipzig, 1848.

Kan, J. B. "Bayle et Jurieu." *Bulletin de la commission pour l'histoire des églises wallonnes,* IV (1890), 139–202.

Kendall, Willmoore. John Locke and the Majority Rule. Urbana, Ill., 1941.

Kleyser, Friedrich. Der Flugschriftenkampf gegen Ludwig XIV zur Zeit des pfälzischen Krieges. Berlin, 1935.

Knappen, Marshall M. Tudor Puritanism. Chicago, 1939.

Krop, F. J. "De ontwickkeling van de politieke denkbeelden der fransche protestanten an der Herroeping van het Edikt van Nantes." *Stemmen des Tijds,* XI (1922).

Labitte, Ch. De la démocratie chez les prédicateurs de la ligue. Paris, 1841.

Lachenmann, Eugen. "Eglises du réfuge." *Realencyklopädie für protes-tantische Theologie und Kirche* (Leipzig, 1896–1909), XVI, 536 ff.

La Cour-Gayet, Georges. L'Education politique de Louis XIV. Paris, 1898.

—— "Les Traductions françaises de Hobbes sous le règne de Louis XIV" *Archiv für Geschichte der Philosophie*, XII (1889), 202–207.

Lagarde, Georges de. Recherches sur l'esprit politique de la réforme. Paris, 1926.

Lang, A. Die Reformation und das Naturrecht. Gütersloh, 1909.

—— "The Reformation and Natural Law," tr. J. G. Machen. *Princeton Theological Review*. VII (1909), 177–218.

Lanson, Gustave. "Ecrivains français en Hollande pendant la deuxième moitié du XVIIᵉ siècle." *Revue des Deux-Mondes*, LXV (1921), 555–583.

—— "L'Eveil de la conscience sociale et les premières idées de réformes po-litiques (1690–1790)." *Revue du Mois* (April, 1910).

—— "Origines et premières manifestations de l'esprit philosophique dans la littérature française de 1675 à 1748." *Revue des cours et conferences* (1907–1910).

—— "Questions diverses sur l'histoire de l'esprit philosophique en France avant 1750." *Revue d'histoire littéraire de la France,* XIX (1912), 1–29, 293–317.

—— "La transformation des idées morales et la naissance des morales ration-nelles de 1689 à 1715." *Revue du Mois* (January, 1910).

Laski, Harold J. A Defense of Liberty against Tyrants by Junius Brutus. New York, 1927.

—— The Rise of European Liberalism. London, 1936.

—— "The Rise of Liberalism." In Vol. I of the *Encyclopedia of the Social Sciences.* New York, 1930.

—— Studies in the Problem of Sovereignty. New Haven, 1917.

Lavisse, Ernest. Histoire de France. Paris, 1905–1908. Vols. VII and VIII.

Lavisse, Ernest and A. Rambaud. Histoire générale du IVᵉ siècle à nos Jours. Vol. VI: Louis XIV 1643–1715. Paris, 1895.

Lecky, W. E. H. History of the Rise and Influence of the Spirit of Rationalism in Europe. London, 1910.

Le Cornu, Frank. Origine des églises réformées wallonnes des Pay-Bas: étude historique. Utrecht, 1938.

Lee, R. W. The Social Compact. Oxford, 1902.

Lemaire, André. Les Lois fondamentales de la monarchie française d'après les théoriciens de l'ancien régime. Paris, 1907.

Lemonnier, Chanoine P. "Espionage et Contre-espionage à Rochefort en 1696 (Lettres de Pierre Jurieu et de Pontchartrain)," *Bulletin de la Société des Archives historiques,* XLI (1924–1925), 1–20.

Lenient, Charles. La Satire en France, littérature militante au XVI siècle. Paris, 1886.

Léon, Paul L. "L'Évolution de l'idée de la souveraineté avant Rousseau." *Archives de philosophie du droit et de sociologie juridique* (1937).

—— "L'Idée de la volonté générale chez J. J. Rousseau et ses antécédents historiques." *Archives de philosophie du droit et de sociologie juridique* (1936).

Littlejohn, J. M. The Political Theory of the Schoolmen and Grotius. New York, 1896.

Loofs, Friedrich. Grundlinien der Kirchengeschichte in der Form von Dispositionen für seine Vorlesungen. Halle, 1901.

Lossen, Max. Die Lehre vom Tyrannenmord in der Christlichen Zeit. München, 1894.

Lureau, H. Les Doctrines démocratiques chez les écrivains protestants français de la seconde moitié de XVIᵉ siècle Bordeaux, 1900.

Lureau, Roger. Les Doctrines politiques de Jurieu. Bordeaux, 1904.

Lyon, T. The Theory of Religious Liberty in England 1603–1639. Cambridge, 1937.

McGiffert, Arthur C. Protestant Thought before Kant. New York, 1911.

McIlwain, C. H. Constitutionalism, Ancient and Modern. Ithaca, 1940.

—— Constitutionalism and the Changing World. Cambridge, 1939.

—— The Political Works of James I. Cambridge, 1918.

McNeill, John T. "The Church in Post Reformation Reformed Theology." *The Journal of Religion*, XXIII–XXIV (1944), 96–107.

—— "The Church in Sixteenth Century Reformed Theology." *The Journal of Religion*, XXII (1942), 251–269.

—— "The Doctrine of the Ministry in Reformed Theology." *Church History*, XII (1943), 77–97.

—— "Natural Law in the Teaching of the Reformers." *The Journal of Religion*, XXVI (1946), 168–182.

—— "Natural Law in the Thought of Luther." *Church History*, X (1941), 211–227.

—— Unititive Protestantism. New York, 1930.

Mackinnon, James. A History of Modern Liberty. London, 1907.

Mailhet, E. A. Jacques Basnage, théologien, controversiste, diplomate, et historien. Geneva, 1880.

Martin, Kingsley. French Liberal Thought in the Eighteenth Century. Boston, 1936.

Matagrin, Amédée. Histoire de la tolérance religieuse. Paris, 1905.

Méaly, F. M. Les Publicistes de la réforme sous Francois II et Charles IX. Paris, 1903.

Mégnin, C. E. Pierre Jurieu: notice sur sa vie et ses écrits. Strasbourg, 1854.

Mercier, Charles. "Le Calvinisme politique aux Pays-Bas." *Revue d'histoire ecclésiastique*, XXIX (1933), 25–73.

—— "L'Esprit de Calvin et la démocratie." Revue d'histoire ecclésiastique, XXX (1934), 5–53.

—— "Les théories politiques des calvinistes en France du cours des guerres de religion." *Bulletin de la Société de l'Histoire du Protestantisme français*, LXXXIII (1934), 225–260, 381–415.

Mesnard, Pierre. L'Essor de la philosophie politique au XVIe siècle. Paris, 1936.

Meyer, A. O. "Charles I and Rome." *American Historical Review*, XIX (1913–1914), 13–26.

Miller, Minnie M. "Science and Philosophy as Precursors of the English Influence in France: a Study of the Choix des Anciens Journaux." *Proceedings of the Modern Language Association*, XLV (Sept., 1930), 856–896.

Miller, Perry, and Thomas Johnson. The Puritans. New York, 1938.

Mirandolle, R. N. L. "A propos d'une lettre de Pierre Jurieu." *Bulletin de la commission pour l'histoire des églises wallonnes*, VII (1899), 237–270.

—— "Pierre Jurieu: de twisten in de Waalsche Kerk op het eind der 17e eeuw." *Nederlandsch Archief voor Kerkgeschiedenis*, VII (1910), 304–324.

Morize, André. "Thomas Hobbes et Samuel Sorbière: notes sur l'introduction de Hobbes en France." *Revue germanique*, IV (1908), 195–204.

Moussiegt, P. Hotman et Duplessis-Mornay: les théories politiques des réformés au XVIe siècle. Cahors, 1899.

Mueller, Gustav E. "Calvin's Institutes of the Christian Religion as an Illustration of Christian Thinking." *Journal of the History of Ideas*, IV (1943), 287–300.

Murray, R. H. Political Consequences of the Reformation. Boston, 1926.

Nelson, E. W. "The Theory of Persecution." In *Persecution and Liberty: Essays in Honor of George Lincoln Burr*. New York, 1931.

Niebuhr, Reinhold. The Nature and Destiny of Man. New York, 1941–1943.

Nobbs, Douglas. Theocracy and Toleration: a Study of the Disputes in Dutch Calvinism from 1600 to 1650. Cambridge, 1938.

Nodier, Ch. Mélanges tirés d'une petite bibliothèque; ou, Variétés littéraires et philosophiques. Paris, 1829.

Nourrisson, J. F., La Politique de Bossuet. Paris, 1867.

Nys, E. Les Théories politiques et le droit international en France jusqu'au dix-huitième siecle. Paris, 1899.

Ogg, David. Europe in the Seventeenth Century. London, 1925.

—— Louis XIV. London, 1933.

Orton, William A. The Liberal Tradition. New Haven, 1945.

Osgood, H. L. "Political Ideas of the Puritans." Political Science Quarterly, VI (1891), 1–28, 201–231.

Osterloh, Richard. Fénelon und die Anfänge der literarischen Opposition gegen das politische System Ludwigs XIV. Göttingen, 1913.

Passerin d'Entrèves, Allessandro. The Medieval Contribution to Political Thought. Oxford, 1939.

Patry, Raoul. Philippe Duplessis-Mornay, un huguenot homme d'état (1549–1623). Paris, 1933.

Pauck, Wilhelm. "Calvin's Institutes of the Christian Religion." Church History, XV (March, 1946), 17–27.

Paulus, Nikolaus. Protestantismus und Toleranz im 16 Jahrhundert. Freiburg, 1911.

Pearson, A. F. S. Church and State. Cambridge, 1928.

Perry, Ralph Barton. Puritanism and Democracy. New York, 1944.

Peyrat, Napoléon. Histoire des pasteurs du désert. Paris, 1842.

Pic, P. Les Idées politiques de Jurieu et les grands principes de 89. Montauban, 1907.

Picard, A. Théodore de Bèze: ses idées sur le droit d'insurrection et son rôle pendant les premières guerres de religion. Cahors, 1906.

Pickman, Edward M. "The Collapse of the Scholastic Hierarchy in Seventeenth Century France." Proceedings of the Massachusetts Historical Society, LXIV (1931), 212–249.

Platzhoff, Walter. Die Theorie von der Mordbefugnis der Obrigkeit im XVI Jahrhundert. Berlin, 1906.

Plum, Harry G. Restoration Puritanism. Chapel Hill, N.C., 1943.

Pollock, Sir Frederick. "The History of the Law of Nature," in Essays in the Law. London, 1922.

—— "Theory of Persecution," in Essays in Jurisprudence and Ethics. London, 1882. Chapter VI.

Poole, R. L. A History of the Huguenots of the Dispersion at the Recall of the Edict of Nantes. London, 1880.

Poujol, D. F. Histoire et influence des églises wallonnes dans les Pays-Bas. Paris, 1902.

Pradier-Fodéré, P. L. S. Essai sur Grotius et son temps. Paris, 1865.

Prévité-Orton, E. W. "Marsilius of Padua." Proceedings of the British Academy, XXI (1935), 137–183.

Prost, J. La Philosophie à l'Académie protestante de Saumur (1606–1685). Montauban, 1887.

Puaux, Frank. Les Défenseurs de la souveraineté du peuple sous le règne de Louis XIV. Paris, 1917.

—— "Essai sur les négociations des réfugiés pour obtenir le rétablissement de la religion réformée au traité de Ryswick." *Bulletin de la Société de l'Histoire du Protestantisme français,* XVI–XVII (1867), 257–305.

Puaux, Frank. "L'Evolution des théories du protestantisme français pendant le règne de Louis XIV." *Bulletin de la Société de l'Histoire du Protestantisme français,* LXII (1913), 386 ff., 481 ff.; (1914), 115 ff.

—— "Le Manifeste des habitans des Cévennes sur leur prise d'armes." *Bulletin de la Société de l'Histoire du Protestantisme français,* LXI (July–August, 1912), 338 ff.

—— "La Politique de Jurieu et la politique de Bossuet." *Revue Chrétienne,* XI (1900), 291 ff., 350 ff.

—— Les Précurseurs français de la tolérance au XVIIe siècle. Paris, 1881.

—— "Quid de Suprema Populi Potestate Jurieu Censuerit." *Faculté de théologie protestante de Paris,* Thèses, III (1880).

—— "Un dessein des pasteurs exilés en Hollande après la révocation de l'Edit de Nantes." *Bulletin de la Société de l'Histoire du Protestantisme français,* LXI (1912), 425–434.

Puaux, Frank and Louis A. Sabatier. Etudes sur la Révocation de l'Edit de Nantes. Paris, 1886.

Randall, John H., Jr. The Making of the Modern Mind. Boston, 1940.

Read, Charles. "Les Démarches des réfugiés huguenots auprès des négociateurs de la paix de Ryswick pour leur rétablissement en France, 1697." *Bulletin de la Société de l'Histoire du Protestantisme français,* XL (1891), 169 ff.

—— "Les Réfugiés huguenots, lors du traité de Ryswick." *Bulletin de la Société de l'Histoire du Protestantisme français,* XL (1891), 384 ff.

—— "Vauban, Fénelon et le duc de Chevreuse sur la Tolérance et le Rappel des Protestants." *Bulletin de la Société de l'Histoire du Protestantisme français,* XXXIX (1890), 113–128.

Rébelliau, Alfred. Bossuet: historien du protestantisme. Paris, 1909.

Reesink, H. J. L'Angleterre et la littérature anglaise dans les trois plus anciens périodiques français de Hollande de 1684 à 1709. Paris, 1931.

Reynolds, Beatrice. Proponents of Limited Monarchy in Sixteenth Century France: Francis Hotman and Jean Bodin. New York, 1931.

Richard, Gaston. "La Critique de l'hypothèse du contrat social avant Jean Jacques Rousseau." *Archives de philosophie du droit et de sociologie juridique* (1937).

Riemann, Gotthold. Der Verfasser der "Soupirs de la France esclave qui aspire après la liberté" (1689–1690): ein Beitrag zur Geschichte der politischen Idéen in der Zeit Ludwigs XIV. Berlin, 1938.

Ritchie, D. G. "Contributions to the History of the Social Contract Theory." *Political Science Quarterly,* VI (1891), 664 ff.

—— Natural Rights. London, 1916.

Robertson, John M. A Short History of Free Thought. London, 1936.

Robinson, Howard. Bayle the Skeptic. New York, 1931.

Robinson, James H. "The French Declaration of the Rights of Man of 1789." *Political Science Quarterly,* XIV (1899), 653–662.

Rollier, Théophile. "La Tolérance." *Revue chrétienne,* XXVIII (1881), 348–359.

Rommen, Heinrich A. The State in Catholic Thought. St. Louis, Mo., 1945.

Rossel, Virgile. Histoire de la littérature français hors de France. Paris, 1897.

Rouquette, J. "Les Fugitifs (1685–1715)." In Vol. III of *Etudes sur la révocation de l'Edit de Nantes en Languedoc.* Paris, 1908.

Ruffini, Francesco. Religious Liberty. Tr. J. P. Heyes. London, 1912.

Ruggiero, Guido de. The History of European Liberalism. Tr. R. G. Collingwood. London, 1927.

Rutgers, V. H. "Le Calvinisme et l'état chrétien." *Bulletin de la Société de l'Histoire du Protestantisme français,* LXXXIV (April–June, 1935), 151 ff.

Saigen. "Jurieu et Pajon." *Revue de théologie de Strasbourg,* XIV, 335 ff.

St. Cyres, Viscount. "The Gallican Church." In Vol. V of *The Cambridge Modern History.* New York, 1908.

Sainte-Beuve, Charles A. Port-Royal. Paris, 1860.

Saint-Leger, A. de, and Philippe Sagnac. La Prépondérance français: Louis XIV (1661–1715). Paris, 1935.

Salmond, J. W. "The Law of Nature." *Law Quarterly Review,* XI (1895), 121 ff.

Sayous, A. Etudes littéraires sur les écrivains français de la réformation. Paris, 1854.

—— Histoire de la littérature française à l'étranger depuis le commencement du XVIIe siècle. Paris, 1853.

Scherger, George L. The Evolution of Modern Liberty. New York, 1904.

Schneider, Herbert W. The Puritan Mind. New York, 1930.

Schoell, Th. "Le Protestantisme de Bayle, à propos de deux livres récents." *Bulletin de la Société de l'Histoire du protestantisme français,* LVII (1908), 359–375.

Seaton, Alexander A. The Theory of Toleration under the Later Stuarts. Cambridge, 1911.

Sée, Henri. Les Idées politiques en France au XVIIe siècle. Paris, 1923.

Seippel, Paul. "Un précurseur de la Démocratie." *Bulletin de la Société de l'Histoire du Protestantisme français,* LXV–LXVI (1916–1917), 164–168.

Serrurier, Cornelia. Pierre Bayle en Hollande: étude historique et critique. Apeldoorn, 1912.

Slosser, G. J. Christian Unity, Its History and Challenge. New York, 1929.

Smith, H. F. Russell. The Theory of Religious Liberty in the Reigns of Charles II and James II. Cambridge, 1911.

Strohl, H. "Le Droit de résistance à la tyrannie d'après les conceptions protestantes." *Revue d'histoire et de philosophie religieuses,* X (1930), 126 ff.

Struman, R. "La Perpétuité de la foi dans la controverse Bossuet-Jurieu, 1686–1691." *Revue d'histoire ecclésiastique,* XXXVII (1941), Nos. 1–4.

Sturzo, Don Luigi. Church and State. Tr. Barbara Carter. New York, 1939.

Sykes, N. "Bossuet." In *The Social and Political Ideas of Some Great French Thinkers of the Age of Reason,* ed. F. J. C. Hearnshaw. London, 1930.

Tabaraud, M. T. De la réunion des communions chrétiennes. Paris, 1808.

Tawney, Richard Henry. Religion and the Rise of Capitalism. London, 1926.

Temple, W. Christianity and the State. London, 1928.

Texte, Joseph. J. J. Rousseau et les origines du cosmopolitanisme littéraire. Paris, 1895.

Thamin, Raymond. "Les Idées morales au XVIIe siècle." *Revue des cours et conférences* (January 2, 1896).

Tilley, A. The Decline of the Age of Louis XIV; or, French Literature, 1687–1715. Cambridge, 1929.

Tréca, George. Les Doctrines et les réformes de droit public en réaction contre l'absolutisme de Louis XIV dans l'entourage du duc de Bourgogne. Paris, 1909.

Treumann, Rudolf. Die Monarchomachen: Eine Darstellung der revolutionären Staatslehren des XVI Jahrhunderts (1573–1599). Leipzig, 1895.

Troeltsch, Ernst. The Social Teachings of the Christian Churches. Tr. Olive Wyon. New York, 1931.

Tulloch, John. Leaders of the Reformation: Luther, Calvin, Latimer, Knox, the Representative Men of Germany, France, England and Scotland. Boston, 1859.

Ulbach, Louis. La Hollande et la liberté de penser aux XVIIe et XVIIIe siècles. Paris, 1884.

Van Goens, F. C. J. "La Tolérance selon Bayle." *Revue de théologie et de philosophie,* XXII (1889), 113 ff. and 462 ff.

Van Malssen, P. J. W. Louis XIV d'après les pamphlets répondus en Hollande. Amsterdam, 1938.

Van Oordt, C. Pierre Jurieu: historien apologiste de la réformation. Geneva, 1879.

Van Schelven, "La Notion politique de la tolérance religieuse." *Revue Historique,* CLXXI (March, 1933), 299–314.

Vermeersch, Arthur. Tolerance. London, 1913.

Viénot, John. Histoire de la réforme française des origines à l'édit de Nantes. Paris, 1926–1934.

—— Histoire de la réforme française de l'édit de Nantes à sa révocation. Paris, 1926.

Wach, Joachim. Sociology of Religion. Chicago, 1944.

Warfield, B. B. Calvin and Calvinism. London, 1931.

Weber, Max. The Protestant Ethic and the Spirit of Capitalism. Tr. Talcott Parsons. London, 1930.

Weill, Georges. Les Théories sur le pouvoir royal en France pendant les guerres de religion. Paris, 1892.

Westin, Gunnar. Negotiations about Church Unity, 1628–1634. Uppsala, 1932.

Whitney, Edward A. "Erastianism and Divine Right." *Huntington Library Quarterly*, II (1938–39), 373–398.

Wilbur, Earl M. A History of Unitarianism. Cambridge, 1945.

Wolzendorff, Kurt. Staatsrecht und Naturrecht in der Lehre vom Widerstandsrecht des Volkes gegen rechtswidrige Ausübung der Staatsgewalt; zugleich ein Beitrag zur Entwicklungs Geschichte des modernen Staatsgedankens. Breslau, 1916.

Zweig, Stefan. The Right to Heresy: Castellio against Calvin. New York, 1936.

Index